Hammers

Dedication

This book is dedicated to the fighting men of 69 Squadron past, present and future

Hammers

Israel's Long-Range Heavy Bomber Arm: The Story of 69 Squadron

Shlomo Aloni & Zvi Avidror

Schiffer Military History
Atglen, PA

Acknowledgments

The authors wish to express gratitude to Hammers air crews and ground crews, and to friends and colleagues who contributed their personal materials, memories, and photos for the production of this volume.

Special thanks to Eliezer Adar, Yoram Agmon, Uri Bacal, Shlomo Bar-Lev, Abraham Baruch, Dror Ben-David, Avihu Ben-Nun, Herzle Bodinger, Yehuda Borovik, David Brisk, Jules Cuburnek, David de Mayo, Leslie David Easterman, Nahum Efrat, Yoav Efrati, Amiram Eliasaf, Achikar Eyal, Ron Feldman, Sam Feldman, Yitzhak Gat, Abraham Goldreich, Ran Goren, GPO, Uri Gil, Joshua Gilutz, Meir (Guri) Gur, Rami Harpaz, John Harris, Artur Hecht, Shlomo Isovich, David Ivry, Shabtai Katz, Paul Keidar, Andreas Klein, Avishai Knaan, Yaron Kranz, Shmuel Laron (aka Stefan Falc), Gideon Magen, IDFA, IDFS, Israel Mei-Tal, Eran Mor, Reuben Narunsky, Nathan Navot, Micha Netser, Yosi Offer, Amos Peleg, Moshe Pinto, Israel Primor, Zeev Raz, Asher Roth, Yoram Rubinstein, Meir Ruff, Nathan Segall, Aviem Sella, Guy (Shelly) Shalev, Menachem Sharon, Gideon Shenhav, Dani Shpitzer, Tommy Silberring, Smoky Simon, Harel, Yosi Toister, Eli Tovel, Raanan Weiss, Daniel Wittmann, Arie Jacobi, Yosi Yaari, Gidon Yahalom, Ran Yahalom, and Ofer Zidon. Regrettably several of the aforementioned (Ran Yahalom and Ofer Zidon) have passed away prior to completion of this demanding research and writing project.

All photos originated from the collections of the aforementioned; in many cases the same photo originated from several collections. To save space, as well as to avoid confusion, the formal military style presentation of [rank] [name] was rejected in favor of the less formal [name] only.

Thanks also to to Israeli Censorship, which reviewed and approved this title for publication.

This book is not an official history of Israeli Air Force 69 Squadron; it is merely a humble tribute to a Hammering heritage.

Book Design by Ian Robertson.

Library of Congress Control Number: 2010933362

Printed in China.
ISBN: 978-0-7643-3655-3

We are interested in hearing from authors with book ideas on related topics.

Published by Schiffer Publishing Ltd.
4880 Lower Valley Road
Atglen, PA 19310
Phone: (610) 593-1777
FAX: (610) 593-2002
E-mail: Info@schifferbooks.com.
Visit our web site at: www.schifferbooks.com
Please write for a free catalog.
This book may be purchased from the publisher.
Please include $5.00 postage.
Try your bookstore first.

In Europe, Schiffer books are distributed by:
Bushwood Books
6 Marksbury Avenue
Kew Gardens
Surrey TW9 4JF, England
Phone: 44 (0) 20 8392-8585
FAX: 44 (0) 20 8392-9876
E-mail: Info@bushwoodbooks.co.uk.
Visit our website at: www.bushwoodbooks.co.uk

Contents

Foreword

by Avihu Ben-Nun

69 Squadron is a very unusual unit by many yardsticks: by the variety of the aircraft it flew, by the aircrew who served in it, and by the dedicated ground crews who kept the planes flying. In each of its three periods of commission there was always something special.

The legendary B-17 – the Flying Fortress legacy of the Second World War – was flown by overseas volunteers from all over the globe. They spoke different languages; they came from different cultures and from a variety of flying disciplines.

The "acquisition" in 1948 of the B-17 and their flight to Israel around half the globe is the stuff Hollywood hits are made of. All this without proper navigation instruments and risking life and limb is by all yardsticks an extraordinary achievement.

After the decommissioning of the Squadron at the end of the Suez War in 1956, the Veterans of the squadron were instrumental in creating a link between the air crews who served in her, in all the periods of her commission. They established a Veterans Club unique in the IAF, who created a living link between the 69ers in the Squadron's lifetime to this very day.

The second era in the Squadron history, with the introduction of the F-4 Phantom, is replete with action and operational sorties. The introduction of the American F-4 – IAF name Kurnass (Sledgehammer) – was simultaneous with the reactivation of 69 Squadron as a fighting unit and a meaningful upgrade in operational capabilities over French made aircraft. Training air and ground crews and introduction of a new "trade" to the IAF – Navigator – meant team work on all levels. The challenge of reactivating the Squadron with the absorption of the Phantom took place while the newly recreated Squadron was deeply involved daily in the War of Attrition, with creditable results. Despite losses of aircraft and air crews, including air crews that ejected and became Prisoners of War, the Squadron kept up its morale in an admirable manner.

69 is leading again, flying the spearhead of the IAF, the F-15I Thunder. This third era, from 1998 until today, is remarkable by the Squadron's ability to carry out challenging missions by day and night, at long range in all weather with results second to none; remarkable achievements that enable the IAF to meet future threats.

During all this time the Squadron kept in close touch with its remarkable history through the members of the Veterans Club.

This work encompasses the history of the Squadron through its three main ages, while the Squadron is still very much active to add future chapters to this work.

I enjoyed reading about the memorable past of the Squadron, including stories and tales of which I was not aware until delving into the pages of this special documentation.

My thanks to all who took part in bringing this remarkable story to print.

Major General (retired) Avihu Ben Nun
69 Squadron Commander, 1969 to 1972
IAF Commander, 1987 to 1992

Foreword by Avihu Ben-Nun

1

B-17 Flying Fortress
1948-1949: Flying for Revival of the Israeli Fortress

Heavy bombers and strategic operations were seemingly out of context to the type of warfare that Palestine witnessed after the November 29, 1947, UN Resolution 181 that called for the partition of Palestine into two states, an Arab state and a Jewish state. Yet Egypt was the first of the warring nations to launch a strategic air campaign, bombing Israel's temporary capital Tel Aviv from May 15, 1948, a day after the Jewish state announced independence. Only two months later Israel responded to the Egyptian challenge when one of three Boeing B-17 Flying Fortress bombers raided Cairo.

Bill Katz (standing third from left) with his crew in England during World War II. Katz accumulated 1,900 flying hours in USAAF service (including 350 flying hours on 25 missions), mostly in the B-17, but also in the B-29. The professional background of most of the would be Israeli B-17 aircrew was pretty much similar. They were seasoned USAAF veterans that volunteered to secure the survival of Israel.

Jules Cuburnek (fifth from left) was trained as a USAAF navigator-bombardier and flew 25 missions with the 332nd Bomb Squadron of the 94th Bomb Group as a B-17 navigator from October 1943 until March 8, 1944; the target of his final mission was Berlin. The crew was photographed on March 8, 1944, in front of B-17 *Idiot's Delight*, which reportedly set a European Theater of Operations record of 50 missions with no abortions.

Acquisition

The Jewish community in Palestine launched in early 1948 a worldwide effort to purchase warplanes in the face of a UN arms embargo. Great hopes were placed on the large USA market of World War II surplus equipment, but not a single combat aircraft acquired in the USA was in country by May 14, 1948, to defend the fledgling state of Israel from Arab League invasion. Deliveries of 25 Avia S-199[1] fighters purchased from Czechoslovakia were initiated later in May 1948, so in line with the visionary Remez-Shamir plan for Israeli air power,[2] the logical next step would have been acquisition of bombers.

Failure of Israeli acquisition agents in the USA to deliver combat aircraft for the defense of Israel during the critical days after Prime Minister David Ben-Gurion announced independence on May 14, 1948, prompted a new approach. Instead of purchasing war surplus equipment that would have taken months to prepare for shipment and actually smuggle to Israel, Al Schwimmer[3] arranged acquisition of four legally registered, commercially modified, airworthy bombers that could fly on their own power all the way from the USA to Israel.

Two B-17 bombers were purchased from Donald H Roberts of Tulsa, Oklahoma, and two B-17 bombers were acquired from Charles T Winters of San Juan, Puerto Rico. Roberts delivered B-17 NL5014N[4] to Abraham G Levin of Levin and Co. of Hollywood, California, at Van Nuys, California, on June 5, 1948. Ownership was traded for 20,000 US dollars that Schwimmer's associate, Leo Gardner, paid to Roberts. Four days later the B-17's ownership was changed to "Ervin L Johnson" of Miami, Florida. The same day – June 9, 1948 – "Johnson" also purchased – from Charwin Sales Co. of Miami, Florida – B-17s NL1098M and NL5024N, which Winters' defunct airline previously operated to haul cargo around the Caribbean.

The scene was thus set for three B-17 bombers to embark upon an epic 10,600 kilometer flight of at least 38 hours duration over the Atlantic Ocean and across the Iron Curtain.

From Florida

Planned route for the B-17s was Miami to San Juan (1,700 kilometers, planned flying six hours); San Juan to Santa Maria, Azores (4,400 kilometers, planned flying 16 hours); and Azores to Zatec, Czechoslovakia (4,500 kilometers, planned flying 16 hours). The three ferry pilots applied for U.S. Customs clearance on June 11, 1948, for a flight from Miami to San Juan that required only routine clearance, as the planes were supposedly proceeding

Sam Feldman (sitting third from left) underwent combat crew training in the B-24 at Pueblo, Colorado, prior to assignment to the USAAF 8th Air Force in England during December 1944, where he converted to the B-17 and flew 23 missions until the end of war in Europe.

to American territory, Puerto Rico. The pilots were RGWM (NL5014N), Naron H Lee (NL5024N), and Harold Rothstein (NL1098M). Total number of airmen onboard the three B-17s was 21. The two ex-Charwin B-17s departed Miami on June 12, 1948, while NL5014N followed the next day.[5] Dave Goldberg recalled:

> "I had flown B-24s with the 15th Air Force in Italy during the war. While making cargo runs out of Miami in the spring of 1948, I was contacted by phone and asked if I'd be interested in earning $1000 to ferry an airplane to Europe. I said, sure.
>
> That was supposed to be one of the Constellations at Millville, New Jersey,[6] but they got impounded or something by the FBI, so I was sent back to Miami and asked if I'd take a B-17 over. I was to be working for Charlie Winters. I would fly one Fort, Smokey Lee another, and Harold Rothstein the third.
>
> A few days before we were to depart I was asked if I'd fly as co-pilot instead of pilot, since they now had found a colonel who was supposed to have had a great deal of B-17 time, and, also, his name would look better on the documents. The money was the same, so I agreed.
>
> Our flight from Miami to San Juan, Puerto Rico, was uneventful. Besides the colonel and myself we had picked up a navigator and about ten young men classified as 'cargo handlers.'
>
> The colonel got roaring drunk at San Juan and stayed that way up to departure time. The next morning we managed to pour him into the plane, and the navigator and I flew it out. From San Juan we were heading to the Azores Islands. That would take 21 hours, and we had 24 hours of fuel on board.
>
> When we were about 10 hours out the colonel was coming around and offered to relieve me so I could get some rest. I had just fallen asleep in the back when I was awakened with a great deal of excitement and told that Cohen, the navigator, had fallen through a glassed-over section in the floor of the nose that had been put there for aerial photography. The guy was barely hanging on, and was slowly being sucked out by the slipstream.
>
> I ran back to the cockpit to get the aircraft slowed down. Col. B--- had gone to pieces and was shaking like a leaf. I slowed the plane down and put it on auto-pilot and went down to help pull the navigator back in. We succeeded, but he was absolutely useless after that, and we now had to find the Azores without him.
>
> By a stroke of luck we were able to pick up the airway radio beacon from Santa Maria after 20 hours of flying – but the weather had turned bad and the ceiling was low. The island is covered with mountains, and Col. B--- then announced that an instrument approach would be too risky, so he was going to ditch the plane off the coast.
>
> I said that was crazy, and that I would make the approach. He refused to get out of the left-hand seat. It was time for some drastic action. I grabbed a fire extinguisher and told him I'd crush his skull if he didn't get out of the f----ing seat. He left, we landed safely . . . and I completed the rest of the flight to Czechoslovakia alone in the cockpit!'"[7]

Mystery Shrouds Miami-Palestine Fortress Mission

Fatal Flight May Involve Soldiers For Holy Land; U. S. Investigating

By CHARLES FERNANDEZ
Herald Staff Writer

Mystery clouds the Flying Fortress mission of 21 airmen from Miami to Palestine—a mission that met partial disaster when one of the three Forts apparently crashed in the Atlantic.

The mission was still pretty much as hush-hush Thursday as it was last Friday when the three B-17s took off from Miami's 20th Street airport, but unconfirmed reports hinted at a Miami springboard for soldiers of fortune for Palestine's embattled Jews.

Considering the supposedly hush-hush nature of the B-17 smuggling operation, U.S. press reports were amazingly accurate, as authorities leaked information to avoid a flood of aircraft flying from the USA to Israel, while people involved in the operation also shared their knowledge with journalists.

Scandal

The three B-17s were planned to fly from Santa Maria, Azores, to Zatec, Czechoslovakia, but flight plans were forwarded for a flight to Ajaccio, Corsica. IAF cargo aircraft flying an air bridge from Tel Nof, Israel, to Zatec, Czechoslovakia, regularly transited via Ajaccio, Corsica, so arrangements were made for Ajaccio to confirm that the B-17s landed safely at Corsica, rather than actually disappearing across the Iron Curtain.

Apparently the cover story held for almost two days, as the first two B-17s landed at Zatec on the evening of June 14, 1948, while USA press reports exploded the affair from June 16, 1948, after Lisbon, Portugal, reported missing aircraft on June 15, 1948. The USA press reported that two B-17s made it to Corsica and took off immediately after refueling, presumably to "Palestine." According to contemporary press reports, the third B-17 radioed soon after take-off from the Azores that an engine was on fire, and what was believed to be its wreckage was sighted later in the ocean. The journalists concluded that the former bombers were bound to "Palestine," and also reported that airmen on board the aircraft included World War II veterans signed up to ferry the

The trio of B-17 demilitarized bombers at Zatec, Czechoslovakia, prior to the fitting of makeshift military equipment and painting in a temporary camouflage scheme.

aircraft to the new state of Israel for tempting payment; $1,000 a month plus $300 to cover expenses.

The Fourth B-17

Public exposure of the B-17s' epic flight had devastating impact upon the Israeli military acquisition network in the USA. The FBI, already tailing Schwimmer's organization, tightened security, and no more combat aircraft were flown to Israel from the USA, though smaller fighting machines were smuggled and shipped to Israel, including P-51 Mustang fighters. While the first flight of Israeli purchased would-be combat aircraft from the USA involved three B-17s, the final flight also involved a Flying Fortress, but was less successful. Again, Al Schwimmer made arrangements and a crew was prepared to fly the Flying Fortress from the USA with Irwin "Swifty" Schindler in command. Al Schwimmer recalled:

> "We bought one in Ekron, Ohio, from an ex-USAAF guy. He double crossed us because he sold it to us, got the money, and then reported it to the authorities. They had a guy watching it on the side of the military and there was a sign on it SEIZED BY THE US GOVERNMENT, but this guy happened to be a friend of a friend. He was a young mechanic paid to stay there and watch the airplane. We arranged with him that we would come there and take the airplane out. The airplane was fully fueled before it was seized, so we did not have to worry about fueling it.

B-17 44-85764 NL7712M was the airplane that Gardner and Schwimmer ferried from Ekron, Ohio, to Westchester, New York, on the evening of July 10, 1948. Schindler then attempted a flight to Israel but was delayed at Halifax, Canada, and stopped at the Azores.

Flight Engineer Al Schwimmer (left) with pilot Leo Gardner (right) ferried the unfortunate fourth B-17 from Ohio to New York prior to the attempted ferry flight to Israel that routed via Canada to the Azores. This photo was taken in November 1949 when Schwimmer and Gardner – as well as Air Transport Command navigator Steve Schwartz (center) – departed Israel back to the USA. Schwimmer returned to Israel to found Bedek Aviation, which in due course transformed into Israel Aircraft Industries, and was Chief Executive Officer from 1953 until 1977.

There was a party on the military side of the airfield for a reserve unit that night, and we drove up a taxi cab to the military side of the airport in Ekron. The guard there, a U.S. soldier, said 'are you going to the party?' and we said 'yes,' so he said to the taxi cab 'go in.' We went in, and this young guy was waiting for us there; the airplane was all ready. Neither Leo Gardner nor I had ever flown in a B-17. We got in the cockpit, Leo in the left side, me on the right side. What to do? But we figured it out, and we got the engines started, and this kid was helping us outside; he directed us out to the runway. We turned the radio on, but all we heard was the tower saying 'Who are you? Who are you? Identify yourself!,' and we were taxiing to the runway. Then we heard him say to another airplane, 'Go around because there is someone approaching the runway!,' and we took off at night in an airplane we had never been in before. We made a mistake after take-off; instead of bringing the gear up we opened the bomb bay doors. I didn't know what to push. I finally found a switch, I pushed it, and the doors closed.

We followed the airways and flew to New York. Schindler was waiting there with a crew, but he had never flown a B-17, nor was he a co-pilot on the B-17, but he had to go up with Leo and have one flight around the airport there just to familiarize himself. Swifty Schindler insisted upon making a familiarity flight just around the airport for half an hour or so; he insisted upon being checked-out by Leo, who never flew a B-17 before that night! He delayed for five or six hours and then took off to the Azores. That delay finished us off, because the authorities notified the

JULY 13 1948

Flying Fort Held In Canada

Said To Be On Way to Israel

HALIFAX, Monday (UP). — A war surplus American Flying Fortress which made an emergency landing here was grounded by airport officials today pending an inquiry into the legality of its projected trans-Atlantic flight — believed to be to Israel. The officials said the aircraft would not be allowed to take off until its status had been cleared up.

Captain Chandler, the pilot of the four-engined plane, which was said to be carrying a cargo of spare aircraft parts, said the plane encountered heavy weather and was running short of petrol when he decided to land at Dartmouth airfield. Members of the crew denied a report that Barney Ross, former welter-weight boxing champion and the "one-man hero of Guadalcanal" was aboard.

The bomber left the U.S. yesterday without filing a flight plan with the Civil Aeronautics Administration. Airport officials said that if the plane was destined for the Israel Air Force it was breaking the U.S. ban on the shipment of arms to the Middle East.

The crew members told the authorities conflicting stories about the plane's destination. One said it was to fly to Richmond, Virginia. Another said its destination was the west coast of the U.S. as a freight carrier, while a third said the plane was to fly to the Azores.

After R.C.A.F. officials and Customs Officers had begun a routine investigation, the crew told Air Force officials that they had decided to return to New York. Canadian officials, however, later refused to release the plane.

The men aboard the Flying Fortress were identified as Captain R. J. Chandler, S. Reedman, Victor Carl, M. Croft, G. Brown, Fred Fink, Albert Schayer, H. Travis, and an unidentified flight engineer.

JULY 19 1948

Impounded Plane Heads for Europe

HALIFAX, Sunday (UP). — The U.S. B. 17 Flying Fortress impounded at Halifax, Canada, last week, landed in the Azores today, despite a low petrol supply and strict orders to return to the U.S.

The Air-Sea Rescue Centre of the Royal Canadian Air Force at Halifax reported that the converted bomber landed at the Azores shortly after 9 a.m. this morning. The plane, which made a forced landing at Halifax last Sunday amid reports that it was being ferried to Israel, made the 1,500 mile flight to the Azores in less than 12 hours.

When it took off from Halifax last night in bright moonlight the plane apparently headed out to sea towards Europe immediately, although the nine members of the crew had filed a flight plan that would have taken them to Boston.

The plane had been given only enough petrol to take it to New York, with little to spare. However, R.C.A.F. authorities said that by economizing and cutting off one engine at a time, the plane could have made the trip easily.

They say also that it is impossible to gauge correctly the amount carried in the auxiliary tanks of a B.17. The aircraft, according to its crew, is owned by "Overseas Air Training," a private organization.

US INVESTIGATES MISSING B.17

WASHINGTON, Monday (PTA). — The State Department has ordered the U.S. Consul at Ponta del Grada, in the Azores, Mr. Clifton Wharton, to investigate the landing of a B.17 Flying Fortress allegedly en route for Palestine.

The State Department press officer, Mr. Lincoln White, told reporters that he did not know if the nine members of the plane's crew carried U.S. passports. Even if they did, he said, the passports could be made valid only for return to the U.S.

He said the Canadian authorities were conducting an investigation to see how the plane, officially thought to be fuelled sufficiently only to reach New York, got enough petrol to fly all the way to the Azores.

Asked if the Department had determined through investigation whether the plane was actually bound for Palestine, Mr. White replied that he did not know. Department officials, however, are known to be very sceptical that the stated purpose of "navigation training cruise" was the real one. Officially, however, they will only comment that it is a matter for legal experts to decide.

Asked if the Department was involved in any investigation of the origin of the plane, the press officer said that investigations were in the hands of "domestic" agencies, such as the Department of Justice.

JULY 20 1948

Two views reportedly taken in Zatec, Czechoslovakia, of NL5014N, a former commercial air photography ship that was the best equipped aircraft among the trio of demilitarized bombers. As such NL5014N became Hammer Number 1, the Hammers' lead ship, and was the only bomber to be fully camouflaged prior to departure from Czechoslovakia to Israel.

Azores, and when they landed there they were waiting for them. The favoritism that we had arranged in the Azores did not hold out once the FBI got on the trail—they got in touch with the Portuguese authorities and they stopped the aircraft."

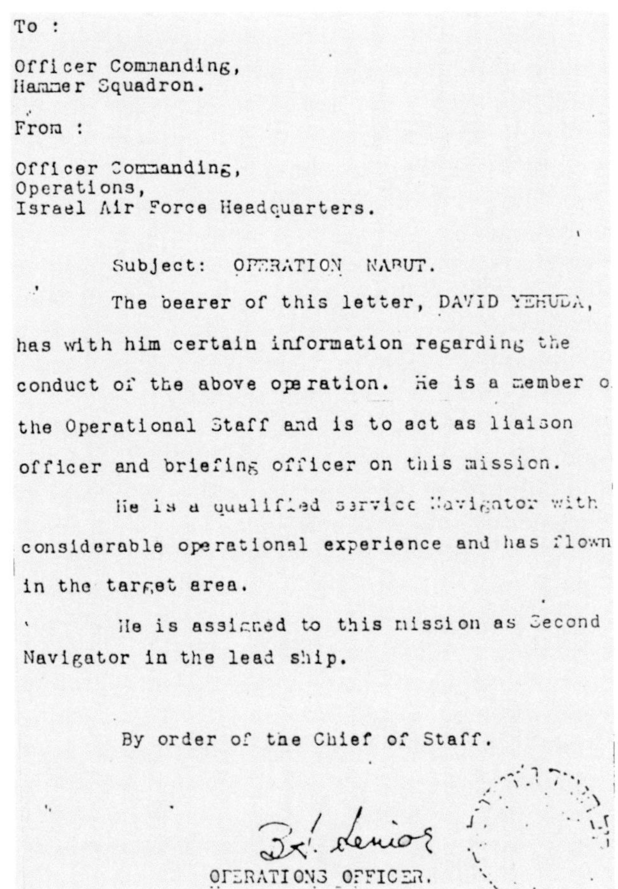

To :

Officer Commanding,
Hammer Squadron.

From :

Officer Commanding,
Operations,
Israel Air Force Headquarters.

Subject: OPERATION NAPUT.

The bearer of this letter, DAVID YEHUDA, has with him certain information regarding the conduct of the above operation. He is a member of the Operational Staff and is to act as liaison officer and briefing officer on this mission.

He is a qualified service Navigator with considerable operational experience and has flown in the target area.

He is assigned to this mission as Second Navigator in the lead ship.

By order of the Chief of Staff.

OPERATIONS OFFICER.

The letter that IAF Director of Operations David Judah conveyed to "Hammer Squadron" Commander Ray Kurtz at the end of his journey from Israel to Czechoslovakia on July 9, 1948.

Schindler was originally planned to fly to the Azores via St John, Canada, but diverted to Halifax, Canada, due to bad weather. The unexpected arrival of the B-17 prompted a Canadian enquiry until the airplane was released on July 17, 1948, after Schindler filed a flight plan back to the USA; departure from Halifax was at 20:10. However, the B-17 flew to the Azores, where it landed the next morning. Instead of immediate refuel and departure the crew opted for a rest, giving ample time for the USA to approach the Portuguese authorities, and Israel's fourth B-17 was seized and stopped at the Azores.

Commander Kurtz

Many of the airmen who ferried the B-17s from the USA to Czechoslovakia returned to their homes, as they were hired to ferry commercial aircraft, not flying bombers in combat. The somewhat unexpected arrival of the first Israeli purchased, "real" combat aircraft smuggled out of the USA puzzled the IAF command. UN Truce was in effect, and the arrival of large aircraft such as the B-17s would have been a blunt violation of the UN embargo. The B-17s were commercial aircraft and had to be militarized, and this could have been better achieved in Czechoslovakia. IAF Head of Staff Aharon Remez therefore ordered on June 19, 1948, to prepare the trio for combat, but to avoid ferrying the B-17s to Israel until advised otherwise.

The seemingly lazy effort to militarize the B-17s at Zatec was closely watched by IAF Air Transport Command airmen who maintained the air bridge between Czechoslovakia and Israel. Most of the Air Transport Command airmen were World War II veterans; many of them flew bombers during World War II, and several had significant combat experience on the B-17. Ray Kurtz was among the latter, reportedly having flown 31 B-17 bombing missions over Europe during World War II. Obviously preparations ran into difficulties, as air bridge operations were prioritized while essential parts were still missing (including original bomb shackles, original bomb sights, oxygen systems, and defensive weapons). With Kurtz in command the militarization process got underway

Czechoslovak note signed on both sides by Hammers airmen prior to departure from Zatec at 10:14 on the morning of July 15, 1948.

Norman Moonitz's crew number 2 at Zatec, Czechoslovakia, in front of the Hammer that became 693 and later 1603, prior to take-off on July 15, 1948. Standing from left to right: second pilot Herman "Dusty" Miller, radio operator/gunner Ray Bloch, first pilot Moontiz, radio operator/waist gunner Joe Ber, navigator/bombardier Al Dobrowitz, and gunner Allan Schlaff. Kneeling from left to right: waist gunner Harold Duboff, IAF Operations officer navigator David Judah, gunner Bernd Sigmar (aka Sigmar Dinn), nose gunner George Meyerson, and flight engineer Bill Baltman.

and air crews – mostly Air Transport Command airmen – were assembled to operate the B-17s.

Truncheon

Egyptian aircraft bombed the Israeli temporary capital Tel Aviv from May 15, 1948 – a day after the new state announced independence. Israel's first bombing of an Arab capital was in the early morning hours of June 1, 1948, when three light planes raided Amman, Jordan. IAF impact on the conduct of war was far from satisfactory. There were too few fighters to challenge Egyptian air superiority, so the assortment of makeshift bombers had to operate under the cover of darkness.

The watershed for IAF offensive operations finally came on the evening of July 15, 1948, when the three B-17s flew their first bombing missions during the bitter conflict. Operation Truncheon listed IAF missions in support of an Israeli offensive that was launched on July 9, 1948, as the UN Truce ended. Truncheon called for the B-17 trio to bomb Cairo on the evening of D-Day (July 9, 1948) and Baghdad, Iraq, on the morning of Day 3. IAF Deputy Director of Operations Smoky Simon[8] proposed to bomb Cairo with all three bombers during the ferry flight from Czechoslovakia to Israel. Yet the bombers were ill equipped, the crews were concerned about being intercepted by RAF night-fighters based in the Suez Canal Zone, and the IAF top brass feared of losing all three bombers on their first mission, so the plan was changed. Only the lead B-17 – equipped with oxygen systems and proper sight – would bomb Cairo. The other two B-17s were assigned to bomb El Arish air base in Sinai, with Gaza as an alternative target.

IAF Director of Operations David Judah[9] flew to Zatec to convey Truncheon orders, as well as to accompany the B-17s' mission. Apparently Judah and Kurtz disagreed regarding tactics and timetables. U.S. World War II bomb crews were accustomed to high altitude daytime operations. British Commonwealth bombers mainly flew medium altitude nighttime missions. Though bombing Cairo was planned to be flown under cover of darkness, Kurtz opted for high altitude bombing despite Judah's preference for medium altitude approach. While Kurtz figured that the B-17s were ready to depart on the morning of July 9, 1948, Judah thought the opposite and delayed the operation.

Arab aircraft repeatedly bombed Israeli targets, as the IAF mostly failed to achieve air superiority and to properly support the IDF. Not only the IDF felt disappointment with IAF's actual productivity, but the Israeli population also suffered from IAF helplessness. A deadly Arab bombing was recorded on July 13, 1948, when Egyptian bombers raided Tel Aviv; contemporary press reports indicated 17 dead and 39 wounded. Ready or not, it was time for the B-17s to take-off.

IAF Deputy Commander Heyman Shamir flew from Israel to Czechoslovakia on July 14, 1948, to speed up B-17 preparations at Zatec, and the three bombers took off the next morning. Then bombardier of the Number 3 B-17, Jules Cuburnek, recalled:

> "There was a lot of disagreement between Ray Kurtz and Bill Katz. Bill Katz was an experienced B-17 pilot, probably more experienced than Ray … so they made a

compromise: Bill would be the first pilot, but Ray would be the commander, so it was done that way. Bill sat in the pilot`s seat and Ray was in the co-pilot`s seat, but he was the commander of the B-17s."

The bombers flew south to the Adriatic Sea and then along the coasts of Yugoslavia, Albania, and Greece. Over Crete the lead bomber set course to Cairo, with the other two B-17s headed to Sinai. As often has been the case, the supposedly dangerous mission turned out to be pretty much uneventful, while the milk run operation got into troubles. Katz and Kurtz bombed Cairo unchallenged.[10] Debriefed service persons reported:

> "Three Forts in formation departed from Zebra[11] at approximately 10:14 hours on 15 July 1948. While flying over ALBANIA anti-aircraft was thrown at the flight, but no damage was sustained by the aircraft or personnel. South of CRETE, one aircraft set course for the Egyptian coast and approached CAIRO on a 097 course and flew in to target on the Fayid Beacon. Time over target, which was the ABDIN PALACE and the Government Buildings: 21:40 hours. Visibility was excellent and identification of area was easy. Route in was past the ENGLISH BRIDGE over the Nile and over target. Aiming point used by lead ship were the flashing green and red lights atop structure in MIDAN, SULIMAN PASHA. Entire city was lit up before, during, and after bombing. ABDIN PALACE was encircled by a ring of lights which also were not extinguished. No ack ack or enemy interception was encountered at all. At M. MATRUH Airfield many Spitfires were observed on the ground. Twelve searchlights from the north of CAIRO attempted to catch the aircraft but were unsuccessful. The total bomb load of 2.5 tons[12] fell in the vicinity of the ABDIN PALACE and nearby Government Buildings. Possible resultant fires were seen in the bombing area. This mission was completed successfully despite the fact that the aircraft was insufficiently equipped to perform this type of attack."

Reportedly only a single B-17 was fully repainted at Czechoslovakia in the camouflage scheme prior to the take-off for Operation Truncheon on July 15, 1948; the other two bombers were only partially camouflaged prior to departure. The photographed B-17 is "692" flown by Al Raisin's crew number 3 with co-pilot Harry Schwartz, navigator Hans Weissbrod, bombardier Jules Cuburnek, flight engineer William Lichtman, Erwin Aronson as "armorer, chucker, gunner," Abe Berger as waist gunner, Maurice Poll as waist gunner, and gunners Elliot Rosenberg and Otto Steinberg.

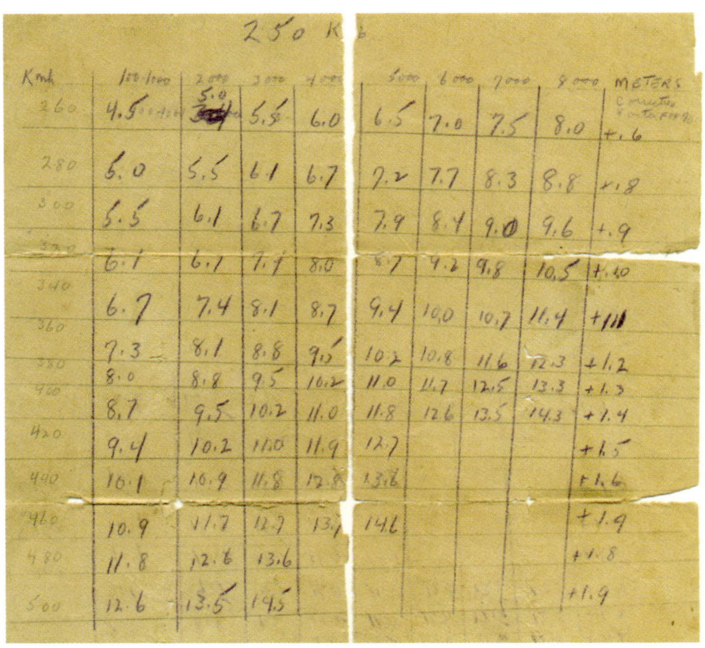

250 Kg

Kmh	100-1000	2000	3000	4000	5000	6000	7000	8000	METERS
260	4.5	5.0	5.5	6.0	6.5	7.0	7.5	8.0	+.6
280	6.0	5.5	6.1	6.7	7.2	7.7	8.3	8.8	+.8
300	5.5	6.1	6.7	7.3	7.9	8.4	9.0	9.6	+.9
320	6.1	6.1	7.1	8.0	8.7	9.2	9.8	10.5	+1.0
340	6.7	7.4	8.1	8.7	9.4	10.0	10.7	11.4	+1.1
360	7.3	8.1	8.8	9.5	10.2	10.8	11.6	12.3	+1.2
380	8.0	8.8	9.5	10.2	11.0	11.7	12.5	13.3	+1.3
400	8.7	9.5	10.2	11.0	11.8	12.6	13.5	14.3	+1.4
420	9.4	10.2	11.0	11.9	12.7				+1.5
440	10.1	10.9	11.8	12.8	13.6				+1.6
460	10.9	11.7	12.7	13.7	14.6				+1.9
480	11.8	12.6	13.6						+1.8
500	12.6	13.5	14.5						+1.9

Bomb table prepared in Czechoslovakia. Two bombers were planned to bomb El Arish, but leader Norman Moonitz decided to bomb Gaza while the pair actually bombed Rafah. The trio of Hammers eventually bombed El Arish on the morning of July 16, 1948.

The other B-17s did run into difficulties. They failed to properly aim at El Arish, so they headed to Gaza when they noted a "big place lit-up." The Number 3 B-17 – flown by Al Raisin, with Cuburnek as bombardier[13] – bombed first, with the Number 2 B-17 following. They actually bombed Rafah and then overflew Gaza, which was heavily defended. The mostly American airmen were accustomed to World War II anti-aircraft artillery fire, but searchlights were a surprise—they only flew daytime missions in their USAAF days. Having somehow escaped the searchlights they headed to the Air Transport Command base at Tel Nof, with which they were well accustomed and where they were joined by the lead B-17, which landed at 22:45 on the evening of July 15, 1948.

Mission 2: El Arish

The three bombers took off at 06:30 on the morning of July 16, 1948, to bomb El Arish air base, which was missed the previous night. They flew over the coastline at an altitude of 13,000 feet and circled 360 degrees over El Arish town until the airfield

Hammers' lead ship – later 691 and then 1601 – in a pen at Ramat David. At the time 69 Squadron did not exist yet and the B-17s were subordinated to Air Transport Command as the "Hammer Program."

was located. Setting course towards the air base, the B-17s flew a first dummy bombing run roughly north to south, turned right 260 degrees, and returned for the real bombing run flying roughly west to east. IAF staff officer Dan Tolkowsky accompanied the lead bomber as assistant navigator and reported two C-47s and 20 Spitfires down at El Arish, as well as "Slight – only at the end of actual bombing – ack ack of 40 mm." The tail gunner of the lead aircraft reported that bombs of the first aircraft "straddled the air field, second aircraft had also good results, and third aircraft overshot just a bit."

The raid on the main Egyptian forward air base was considered successful, but was a fine example of inaccurate reporting. Prime Minister Ben-Gurion was notified that the three bombers dropped 7,500 kg of bombs, yet the lead aircraft only bombed with 1,270 kg bombs.

Ramat David

Tel Nof was not considered a safe place for the three bombers. Egyptian aircraft attacked the Air Transport Command center of activity again and again after resumption of hostilities on July 9, 1948. Air Transport Command aircraft maintaining the air bridge between Czechoslovakia and Israel usually arrived at Tel Nof during the evening and departed before dawn. While Air Transport Command's nocturnal operations could tolerate daytime Egyptian attacks, the basing of bombers planned to operate during broad daylight at an air base that was regularly attacked was obviously to be avoided.

For this reason the B-17s did not return to Tel Nof after the mission to El Arish. The lead B-17 flew to Even Yehuda air strip, where it landed at 07:45, while the other two B-17s flew farther north to Ramat David air base. The plan was to disperse the bombers in the event of an Egyptian reprisal bombing that actually materialized, but mostly targeted Tel Aviv, as the Israeli city was heavily bombed from July 16, 1948.

The concept of splitting the three bombers between two bases was short lived, and all three bombers were united at Ramat David, at the time the IAF air base furthest away from the Egyptian front.

Ray Kurtz flew in the lead ship on the July 17, 1948, morning mission to Mishmar HaYarden, which still had two D/F loop antenna on top of the fuselage; later on the forward D/F loop antenna was removed. At the time debriefing a B-17 mission was a tiring process, as initially all airmen were asked for opinions and lessons! The debrief report of the first mission to Mishmar HaYarden on the morning of July 17, 1948, was no exception. Al Raisin (pilot of the Number 3 ship) reported "No flak, no fighters. Did 6 bomb runs, all bombs got away. Could not see where they were falling because I was watching formation. Nothing happened along route. Plane OK. We need Oil. 100 kilo bombs went out OK." His co-pilot, Schwartz, remarked "Cannot add anything further. Have a twitching hand from flying in formation." While the navigator elaborated "There was nothing on the way out. No flak. On the first run one bomb hit west of the Police Station, north of the Bridge. Second run was a dummy run. East of the target area is covered with dust. Gunner saw the bomb explode in target area (NE of the settlement). The Third run on the Customs house – missed completely. Fourth run – did not see bombs explode. There was lots of transport on the road to the Bridge. West of the Customs House there is a grove with lots of transport. The target is very small for us. We took off at 07:47. Time over target 08:05. Time off target 09:05. Landed 09:22."

Missions 3 and 4: Mishmar HaYarden

From inception the IAF struggled in between air superiority and air support. IAF's plan for the first fighter operation was a classic air superiority mission, an air base attack against El Arish. Yet the reality of late May 1948 forced the IAF to scrap the El Arish air superiority mission. Instead, the IAF's first fighter operation was an air support mission. Likewise, the IAF favored air superiority as the mission of the first in-country proper bomber operation, while the IDF requested air support over the Syrian bridgehead at Mishmar HaYarden, where fierce fighting was raging since July 9, 1948.

The B-17s' first mission in Israel was the air base attack to El Arish on July 16, 1948 – on the same day the Syrian forces attacked and Command North desperately called for air support over Mishmar HaYarden. Yet the most capable IAF offensive toll, the B-17s, was regrouping and reorganizing at Ramat David, less than 100 km away from the frontline. The B-17s did not fly any more missions on July 16, 1948. They bombed Mishmar HaYarden twice the next day – on the morning and in the afternoon of July 17, 1948 – leading Command North Commander Moshe Carmel to conclude that IAF air support always surprised the IDF, as it was not available when needed and available when not needed....

Mission 5: Majdal

Fifteen minutes before dawn on July 18, 1948, the B-17s departed Ramat David to bomb Majdal, a town across the Egyptian frontline. They returned to Ramat David after two hours and 15 minutes flying.

Mission 6: Damascus

On the morning of July 18, 1948, the trio split to bomb two targets: the Syrian capital Damascus and Majdal, behind the Egyptian frontline. Pilots Norman Moonitz and Dusty Miller with navigator Smoky Simon, bombardier David Judah, flight engineer Bill Baltman, and three air gunners – Ray Bloch, Bert Dinn,[14] and George Meyerson – flew the mission in B-17 Number 2; the first IAF daylight raid on an Arab capital. The lone B-17 flew over Damascus at 12,000 feet to drop eight 100 kg bombs, four 25 kg bombs, and 30 ten kg bombs, plus two cases of bottles!

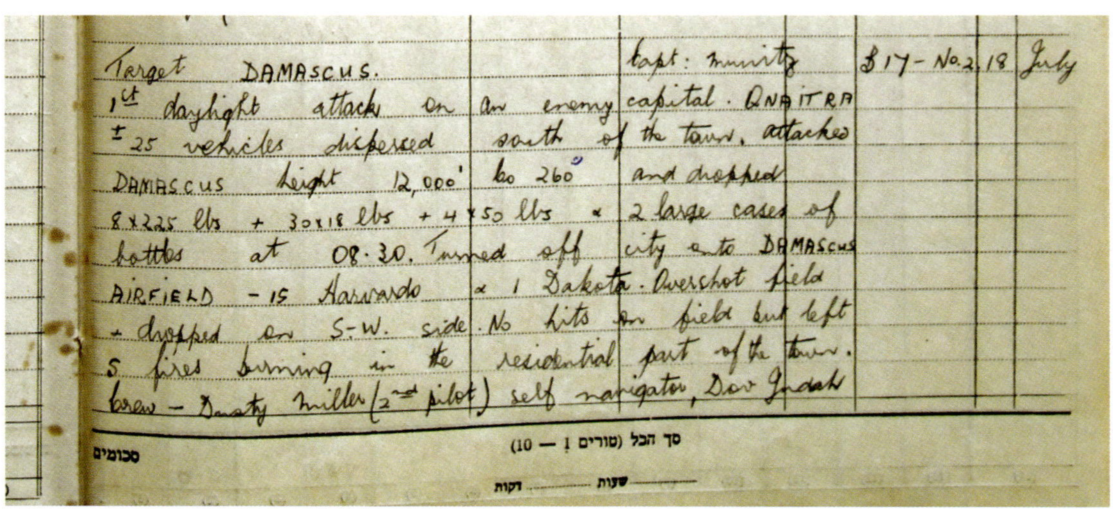
Target DAMASCUS. Capt: Moonitz B17 - No.2 18 July
1st daylight attack on an enemy capital. QNAITRA
± 25 vehicles dispersed south of the town, attacked
DAMASCUS height 12,000' ho 260° and dropped
8 x 225 lbs + 30 x 18 lbs + 4 x 50 lbs & 2 large cases of
bottles at 08.30. Turned off city onto DAMASCUS
AIRFIELD – 15 Harvards & 1 Dakota. Overshot field
& dropped on S-W. side. No hits on field but left
5 fires burning in the residential part of the town.
Crew – Dusty Miller (2nd pilot) self navigator, Dov Judah
סך הכל (טורים 1 — 10)
סכומים
שעות ...... דקות

Smoky Simon's logbook entry reporting the July 18, 1948, raid on Damascus.

The B-17 that became 692 and later 1602 being refueled at Ramat David; of note is the BESA machine gun that protrudes from the right hand nose section gun position. The two B-17 wing ships arrived from Czechoslovakia with five BESA machine guns each (two in the nose, two waist guns, and one tail gun), while the lead ship had three heavier 14 mm BESA machine guns.

The B-17 crew noted a C-47 and 15 Harvards at Damascus' Elmaza airfield and left behind several fires; later reports indicated 20 killed and 80 wounded at Damascus.

Mission 7: Mishmar HaYarden and Majdal

At noon on the final day of the Ten Days Fighting the B-17s flew a unique double mission to bomb a target on the Syrian front up north, and then another target across the Egyptian frontline down south. Ray Kurtz was leading the trio of bombers that first bombed Mishmar HaYarden. B-17 Number 2 – with Norman Moonitz as pilot and Smoky Simon as navigator – dropped 16 25 kg bombs "by hand" over the Syrian bridgehead, and Simon reported that the air raid "knocked out 2 tanks and Jewish forces took Hill 4233."

Flying south towards the Egyptian frontline, the B-17s rendezvoused over Hertzeliya with two 101 Squadron S-199 fighters (pilots Ruch and Freeman that took off at 14:20 to 14:23). Over Tel Aviv the formation set course to Faluja, and hence to Majdal, which was bombed from 9,500 feet with 12 100 kg bombs dropped from B-17 Number 2. Simon reported "Results were good and next day intercepted Egyptian army radio message to the effect that heavy casualties were inflicted and immediate reinforcements were requested. No ack-ack encountered."

Mission 8: Tul Karrem

Upon their return to Ramat David the B-17 crews were upset to see that the meal they had been promised prior to take-off was extremely poor, so Ray Kurtz organized transport to Haifa and about two thirds of the airmen joined him to look for a decent meal. The minority of men preferred sleep over eating and remained at Ramat David. Jules Cuburnek recalled:

Crude conditions at Ramat David – obvious as Hammers airmen and engineers attend Hammer number 1 ship – were not unique to the Hammers, but commonplace across all levels of IAF operations of the era. The July 18, 1948, Tul Karrem raid is a fine example of conflicting reports: Cuburnek's logbook indicates that he flew Hammer number 1 with Raisin, while Simon's logbooks also reports that he flew with Raisin to Tul Karrem but in Hammer number 3.

"IAF Deputy Director of Operations Smoky Simon flew up from Tel Aviv. He woke me and asked about Ray and Bill. I told him they rightfully had gone to Haifa for a decent meal. Smoky explained that another Truce would take place at 19:00. He wanted 69 Squadron to bomb Tul Karrem before the Truce took effect. The senior pilot at the base was Al Raisin. I woke him up and somehow we assembled two makeshift crews. The planes were ready to go when IAF Commander Aharon Remez and his deputy, Heyman Shamir, arrived from Tel Aviv. They told us not to carry out the mission because the Truce would take place before we could bomb. We argued that we had enough time. I told Heyman that I was the navigator for the mission, and that we would complete the mission in time. Heyman and Aharon looked at each other and Heyman yelled 'Promise?' 'Promise' I answered. 'Go' he shouted, and off we went. We bombed Tul Karrem minutes before the Truce and returned to base. As we were on our approach we saw smoke on the runway and the tower flashed a red warning light. We pulled up and circled. We decided that enemy aircraft were bombing the airfield, so we cleared the area and headed to the sea. We flew over the sea for about twenty minutes and returned to base. We got the green light and landed. Kurtz met us when we landed. He wanted to know why we didn't shoot down the Arab aircraft that bombed Ramat David!

The Arab aircraft that bombed Ramat David were possibly Iraqi Ansons in a raid that was most likely a reprisal to the Israeli bombing of Damascus earlier that day.

Hammers Impact

More than any other type of aircraft, the B-17 introduced the IAF into the realm of modern air warfare. The B-17s began operations during the Ten Day Fighting that lasted from July 9 to 18, 1948. During the first six days of fighting the IAF flew 78 bombing sorties and dropped 7,790 kg of bombs for an average of only 100 kg per sortie. During the final four days the IAF flew 45 bombing sorties and dropped 33,430 kg of bombs to achieve an average of 743 kg per sortie.

The Hammers used bombs of both German and U.S. origin; the former were referred to in kilograms and the latter in pounds. This often resulted in inaccurate reports, mostly when the American cultured Hammers reported in pounds and Israeli staff officers accustomed to kilograms artificially "upped" the reported bomb load as briefing and summaries were piped up the command chain.

Such was the B-17's impact, but the logistics surrounding the operation of heavy bombers was also demanding. The Hammers lifted more bombs and a heavier total bomb load than all other types of makeshift bombers that the IAF operated before and after the arrival of the Flying Fortresses. The B-17s also operated at a higher tempo, and normally flew two sorties per fighting day to double the burden on the logistics rear that had to support their operations. In sharp contrast to all other types of IAF aircraft – fighter, transport, and light planes – the B-17s – regardless of being a large size four-engined complex aircraft with scarce spares availability and improvised support systems – were still surprisingly serviceable.

Mission 9: Policeman

The second UN Truce ended the Ten Days Fighting on the evening of July 18, 1948. Hostilities between Arabs and Jews did not

Ray Kurtz flew B-17 692 in the lead of the Operation Policeman bombing mission with Smoky Simon as navigator and Jules Cuburnek as bombardier. The mission debrief report stated "B-17 No 2 had 10 hang ups. Went out to sea after replacing fuse jettisoned 2 over the sea. Then proceeded to target Jaba dropped 4 100 kgs which just overshot the target. Did another run over Ein Ghazal and dropped 4 100 kgs in target area."

B-17 693, most likely flying over Small Triangle on July 20, 1948. Clearly both 692 and 693, which arrived from Czechoslovakia partially camouflaged and partially in metal finish, had been camouflaged by then.

cease, however, and regardless of the Truce the IDF launched a major offensive that targeted three Arab villages south of Haifa: En Razal, Igzim, and Jaba. These villages – colloquially known to the Israelis at the time as Small Triangle – blocked the road to Haifa. Effectively the Small Triangle was an enclave surrounded by Israeli territory, thus prompting the disguise of the military attack as merely an internal policing affair; the appropriate attack code name was Operation Policeman.

Massive air support included the Hammers, which departed Ramat David at 18:40 in the late afternoon hours of July 20, 1948, along with a Douglas DC-5 makeshift bomber. The 4-ship formation flew six bombing runs (three over En Razal, one over Jaba, and two over Igzim), facing no opposition over the villages, but encountering IDF anti-aircraft artillery fire over Haifa on their way back to Ramat David. Smoky Simon wrote in his logbook:

> "During Truce period Arab irregulars had cut the Haifa-Tel Aviv road. 3 B-17s. Load 12 225 lbs. We had 11 hang ups. S/C (set course) out to sea and tried jettisoning. Jettisoned 2 at sea then returned and bombed the targets. Results – army tried to capture these places but failed."

As Simon mentioned, the follow up IDF attack failed to dislodge the villagers from their land, but for whatever reason – air power protagonists would undoubtedly claim that air bombardment made the difference – the villagers evacuated the Small Triangle; sneaking at night through IDF lines towards Wadi Ara, which was still in Arab hands.

Commander Katz

Initial cadre of the B-17 outfit was almost entirely drawn from Air Transport Command resources, and the whole operation was an element of Air Transport Command operations. Reorganization was launched once the Ten Days Fighting was over, and the Hammers Program was separated from Air Transport Command as an independent squadron based at Ramat David with Bill Katz in command, while Ray Kurtz remained a senior Air Transport Command officer. The earliest document to mention "69 Squadron" to be unearthed thus far is dated August 8, 1948.

Friction between Ramat David Air Base Commander Joshua Gilutz and the B-17 airmen surfaced at the end of July 1948 as operational activity slowed down. The B-17 airmen focused on "flying and fighting" – as well as having an inclination for having a good time – while the Ramat David Air Base Commander emphasized discipline and manners. Ramat David Chief Technical Officer Maurice "Ray" Commanday wrote in 1993:

> "'Do you think you can do things THE RAF WAY?' That question was posed by the Station Commander in his resplendent starched tropical white uniform. Startled by what was clearly a gross irrelevancy, I managed to convey the idea that I had spent three and a half years in

Jules Cuburnek, Norman Moonitz, and Ray Kurtz relax in Haifa; Kurtz and Moonitz remained Air Transport Command service persons when 69 Squadron was separated from the IAF air lift organization.

OFFICE DIRECTOR OPERATIONS ATC

JULY 21, 1948.

HAMMER PROGRAM

OK N. 5014N OKLAHOMA
OK N. 5024N OKLAHOMA
OK N. 1698N OKLAHOMA
GR N. 9912N AZORES (INT)

PILOTS	L	RADIO	L	NAVIGATORS	L	ARMAMENT	
Moonitz	Bristol	Bloch	Roger	Cabernic	Roger	Albrecht	Rog
Kurtz	24P	Goldstein	Roger	Gross	Roger	Paris	Yard
Raisin	Roger			Nachman	Roger		
Katz	Roger			Dobrowitz	22P		
Miller	Roger						
Schwartz	Roger						

IAF Air Transport Command reported the status of the "HAMMER PROGRAM" on July 21, 1948, as at the time 69 Squadron did not exist. Selection of "69" is reportedly attributed to Kurtz and Moonitz being New York Fire Department firemen with Engine 69 prior to their volunteering to support Israel's cause. Sexual connotations of "69" appear to have only surfaced at a later date when 1601 was painted with the title SOIXANTE NEUF on the right-hand side of its nose section and the Hammers adopted the slogan "69 IS MORE THAN A NUMBER" (also sometimes referred to as "69 ON THE LINE," but "69 IS MORE THAN A NUMBER" is the exact translation of the Hebrew slogan, with "NUMBER" having a double meaning: the number 69 and the Hebrew slang of sexual act).

Israel Prime Minister David Ben-Gurion in the cockpit of Hammer number 1 during his visit to Ramat David on August 10, 1948.

The recently appointed Ramat David Air Base Commander Dov Ben-Zvi points at the Hammers' lead ship air photography modification as IAF Commander Aharon Remez stands to the left of Prime Minister David Ben-Gurion.

the ETO, mostly in Britain. Yes, I could probably even manage to brew a proper cup of tea!

That was my invitation to serve as Chief Technical Officer at Ramat David Air Base in the summer of 1948. The new state of Israel was engaged in desperate warfare with its five Arab neighbors. Its air force was, then, a heterogeneous collection of aircraft and personnel struggling to organize itself into some semblance of effectiveness. I had wandered onto the scene as part of a plan to obtain and ship maintenance equipment which, I felt, would be overlooked in the hasty planning. Circumstances, however, changed all that, and I found myself in the middle of a conflict between a commanding officer and a group of raunchy volunteers from the U.S. newly arrived with the country's most potent military equipment... three mostly disarmed B-17s.

Part of the conflict related to the maintenance arrangements for these aircraft, which failed to provide anybody with previous B-17 or any other American aircraft experience. When I came upon the scene I was seen as a solution to at least that aspect of the problem. The balance of the problem derived from the fact that the CO failed to understand that his World War II experience as an RAF officer was not totally applicable to the situation, and he tried, desperately, to organize the station according to RAF disciplinary tradition.

The American B-17 crews, led by veteran World War II 8th Air Force pilots, saw themselves as specialist saviors and entitled to the best the country had to offer, including unlimited leave to booze up in Haifa with transportation permanently assigned. Furthermore, their quarters were entirely unsuited to aeronautical heroes and the food... Indescribable in polite English!

The CO, on the other hand, was scandalized by the lack of military discipline, and the harder he tried to apply it the more outrageous was the behavior pattern of our B-17 heroes. It grew worse, until it became common practice for them to steal whatever military or civilian vehicle was available for their private purposes."

IAF Commander Aharon Remez (left) leans out of Hammer number 1's left hand waist gun position during Prime Minister David Ben-Gurion's visit to Ramat David on August 10, 1948.

The clash ended on August 1, 1948, when Ramat David Air Base Deputy Commander Dov Ben-Zvi (aka Baron Wiseberg, a former British Fleet Air Arm fighter pilot) was named the new Ramat David Air Base Commander. Ten days later Ben-Zvi hosted Prime Minister David Ben-Gurion during a visit to Ramat David. All four elements – Ramat David Air Base officers, 69 Squadron airmen, friction over discipline and Ben-Gurion – combined on August 17, 1948, to set the scene for Bill Katz's departure from the command post.

Air Transport Command organized a festive inauguration of Tel Nof, with Prime Minister Ben-Gurion as guest of honor. The highlight of the celebration was an assault demonstration, so the transport aircraft deployed north to Ramat David, from where they were planned to take-off to the inauguration's assault demo. Up north Bill Katz was already preparing for a 3-ship training flight "to check bombsight coordination between new bombardier and pilot" when he learnt of the festival down at Tel Nof, so he asked Ramat David Air Base Deputy Commander Claude Duval if he might fly over Tel Nof, but "was given to understand – No – but not definite."

Bill Katz led the B-17 trio on a fly over Tel Nof during the inauguration ceremony. Prime Minister Ben-Gurion was surely impressed, as he wrote in his diary "in the afternoon I went to Tel Nof, where the airfield was inaugurated. I inspected a spectacular array of fighters and bombers, Flying Fortresses and airborne army that battled the 'enemy.' An air force is growing." But IAF Operations officers were less impressed, and ordered an investigation to understand how the B-17s appeared over Tel Nof to capture the imagination of the Prime Minister. In fact, Ben-Gurion only specifically mentioned "Flying Fortresses," while referring in general to all other aircraft types!

Staff officer Coleman Goldstein investigated the incident at Ramat David and submitted the following information "in reference to future Operations of Hammer Squadron":

> "– Security – No good. Living in Haifa – with obvious results. Mattresses required (26) to move to base.
> – Morale very low. Suggest that intelligence briefing of pilots and other key crewmen be given daily to keep them informed of military situation."

The result of this affair was that, officially, the command of the Squadron was passed to Al Raisin on August 18, 1948.[15]

Truce Training

Operations were not flown beyond Operation Policeman on July 20, 1948, and training flights were scarce. An exciting moment was recorded on September 7, 1949, as Smoky Simon noted in his logbook:

> "Comm flight to RD to attend bombing trials by B-17 dropping 44 gal drum Napalm incendiaries. On 3rd bomb detonator exploded almost 200' below a/c – no damage."

The B-17 trio in close formation. Interestingly, IAF official history of the Israeli War for Independence description of the incident over Tel Nof on August 17, 1948, states "first to arrive were the Flying Fortresses, that bombed 'enemy positions' and turned away…," but the incident's investigator, Coleman Goldstein, reported on August 20, 1948, about the 69 Squadron fly over Tel Nof "No bombs on plane. Checked out new pilot and wireless operator. Planes were not effectively armed."

Hammers airmen. Standing left to right: Irving Soltan, Al Raisin, Jules Cuburnek, Manny Feldman, and Bill Lichtman. Front from left to right: Abe Berger, Len Kaplan, Jack Goldstein, Irving Aronson, and David Hill. IAF Navigation Department announced Manny Feldman as 69 Squadron Lead Navigator on September 8, 1948.

No one really knew if fighting would ever resume, so foreign volunteers who came to Israel looking for action were at a crossroads. Hammers airmen returned to Air Transport Command, which continued operational flying; others got tired of the inactivity and returned home. However, someone somewhere did think that hostilities would resume, as can be easily understood from a document that Bill Katz (signing as "acting CO 69th Sq") prepared on September 12, 1948:

"I am in receipt of memorandum requesting my opinion on the number of sorties to be required for an operational tour of this squadron.

In view of the limited number of trained personnel and inadequacy of reserves it is my opinion that no set of sorties be set. Crewmen should fly until otherwise recommended for rest leave by doctor or squadron commander, after which he shall return to operations unless declared unfit for combat duty.'

The break in operations also gave the IAF an opportunity to better equip the austere bombers. A memo from IAF Operations Bomber Command Officer Smoky Simon to IAF Director of Maintenance dated September 21, 1948, discussed two issues: "we must request that these ships be fitted immediately with twin .30 guns instead of the present guns; as these aircraft may have to proceed on long distance operations their armament is vitally important because of the impossibility of fighter cover," and "we are this day sending a signal to the CTO and Wing Armament Officer at Ramat David to commence immediately with the increase of bomb stations on No. 2 Ship i.e. the ship without the bomb sight at present. Then No. 3 Ship will be done and No. 1 Ship to follow No. 3 Ship."

Most of the 69 Squadron airmen were volunteers who came to fight for Israel. Many of them did not even enlist in the IDF, and from their perspective they were foreign citizens free to return home. The Truce complicated matters, as there was no fighting but the war did not end. Most men were eager to stay until the end of war to secure the future of Israel. Yet they were away from their families for a long time; some of the first volunteers who later served with Air Transport Command departed the USA in

IAF Operations Bomber Command Officer Smoky Simon to IAF Director of Maintenance mentioned on September 21, 1948, a requirement for a twin 0.3 inch machine gun installation in the tail positions of the B-17s, and this requirement indeed materialized in due course as illustrated. These postwar images depict Air Gunners Course Number 1 graduate Johanan Hollander.

late 1947, and many had unfinished affairs and businesses to sort out. The logical compromise would have been a leave to visit home, sort out issues that had to be sorted, and return to Israel. Others wished to unite with their families in Israel. There were also concerns regarding temporary assignment of airmen to Air Transport Command. The logbook of navigator-bombardier Jules Cuburnek highlighted two issues: lack of activity and temporary assignment to Air Transport Command.[16] Finally, IAF Director of Operations David Judah wrote to the 69 Squadron Commander on October 8, 1948:

> "The following decisions are to be communicated to all men of 69 Squadron:
>
> – The Air Council has decided that there will be no overseas leave for IAF personnel. No further applications will be entertained by the Air Council until further notice.
>
> – There is no obligation upon the IAF to provide any facilities for residence of wives of IAF personnel who are not themselves members of the IAF. The welfare branch of the IAF will, however, make available such facilities within its own discretion as may be possible.
>
> – The pilots, Navigator, and Wireless Operator of any one crew may be ordered to detach service with ATC for periods of seven days within the coming month.
>
> – Of the remaining crews, one crew may be allowed to go on 48 hours leave, but each crew member must give an address to the OC Squadron where he may be contacted and recalled to duty if required.
>
> The remaining crews are to remain on the Station on such standby as may be in force from time to time."

Mission 10: Majdal

Almost three months of Truce and relative inactivity ended on October 15, 1948, when Israel launched an offensive to break the deadlock on the Egyptian front. Operation Yoav lasted from October 15 to 22, 1948, and was aimed at the lift of the Egyptian siege on the Negev Desert.

69 Squadron's first mission during the renewed round of hostilities was bombing of Majdal, an Arab town just across the frontline. The trio of bombers departed Ramat David at 17:19 (Al Raisin in 691), 17:20 (Bill Katz in 693), and 17:21 (Sam Feldman in 692). Bomb load was 12 100 kg bombs; two 250 kg bombs and 22 100 kg bombs; and two 500 kg and ten 100 kg bombs respectively. Raisin had no co-pilot and flew with Smoky Simon from IAF Operations, Manny Feldman (navigator), Jules Cuburnek (bombardier), Bill Lichtman (flight engineer), Jack Goldstein (radio operator), and air gunners Irving Aronson, Abe Berger, and Irving Soltan. Katz flew with pilot Pinchas Ben-Porat, navigator Tucker, bombardier Hans Weissbrod, radio operator Joe Ber, and air gunners Sam Camerman, Ira Kahn, George Meyerson, Roy Nash, and Daniel Spicehandler. Feldman's crew was McConville, Fink, Duboff, Axelrod, Griver, Merovitz, Gershalter, Lazarus, Poll, and Michel. Smoky Simon wrote in his logbook:

> "Ran up on target … but bombardier picked up El JURA in his sight, turned onto target and dropped a perfect pattern. What a pity! Arab POWs on interrogation report 400 killed on the raid. Bombing height 11,000 ft. Co 160 degrees. TOT 1804-06. Heavy accurate 88 mm flack bursting very close."

Reportedly a photograph taken during a 69 Squadron mission to Majdal. Air photographers accompanied Hammers missions right from the very beginning; the photographer that flew the October 15, 1948, mission to Majdal was David Griver. Air photographers compiled a post mission report to correlate between negative frames and actual scenes; negatives disappeared over time but many reports still exist.

Mission 11: Gaza

Bill Katz departed Ramat David at 23:13 on the evening of October 15, 1948, in B-17 693, along with almost exactly the same crew that accompanied him on his first Operation Yoav mission; radio operator Harry Dinkin joined in for the evening mission. Armed with 13 45 kg bombs, the lone bomber – mutual defense against hostile interceptors was not needed during nighttime operations – approached Gaza, but did not bomb its designated target. Bomb doors were opened during the run to Gaza, yet all bombs were dropped over the Mediterranean Sea. Bill Katz summed up his brief report: "bombardier error."

Mission 12: Majdal

Sam Feldman took off in B-17 692 at 23:15 on the evening of October 15, 1948, to bomb Majdal. Feldman's crew was John McConville (second pilot), Manny Feldman (navigator), Basil Michel (bombardier), Harold Duboff (radio operator), and air gunners Raphael Blumen, Dave Fink, Eddie Gershalter, Joseph Lazarus, Harry Merovitz, and Maurice Poll. Loaded with 12 100 kg bombs, the B-17 arrived over a completely blacked out target at 00:28 on October 16, 1948. Weather was fair to good, and visibility was hazy as six Egyptian searchlights tracked the sky all around the lone bomber. No anti-aircraft artillery was noticed; bombs were dropped from 11,000 feet, and the Hammers spent only half a minute over the target area. The mission's "Report of Flight Order No. ___" document survived, but regrettably it was written in absolutely unreadable hand writing!

Mission 13: El Arish

Al Raisin flew B-17 691 during the third Hammers nighttime operation on the night of October 15/16, 1948. The crew was pilot Isidore Noach, navigator Smoky Simon, bombardier Jules Cuburnek (written as THE GREAT JULES in the debrief!), radio operator Jack Goldstein, flight engineer Bill Lichtman,[17] and air gunners Irving Aronson, Abe Berger, David Hill, and Irving Soltan. Loaded with 12 100 kg bombs, they departed Ramat David at 23:25 and cruised to the target at 8,000 feet. Time over Target was 00:20, but they bombed at 00:53. Again, the mission's "Report of Flight Order No. ___" document is unreadable, and only Smoky Simon's logbook remains to shed more light on this flight:

> "Track right over the field without being able to do a bombing run. Had to do 4 runs and then attacked. Over target 00:20 to 00:54. Height 8,000 ft. 40 mm ack-ack not accurate. 6 searchlights. Also dropped 24 2 kg butterfly bombs. 2 fires left burning. Landed 01:50."

Bill Katz flew B-17 693 to El Arish on the morning of October 16, 1948. The IAF officially assigned H-1 to H-3 (H for Haftzatza, Hebrew for Bombing) as B-17 serials, but the Hammers referred to the bombers as 691 to 693 and affectionately called them Lofty 1 to Lofty 3.

Mission 14: El Arish

Maintaining pressure on El Arish – the principle Egyptian forward air base – was vital to disrupt Egyptian offensive air operations that were so destructive to IDF troops and IAF prestige during the Ten Days Fighting. Al Raisin (flying 691) departed Ramat David at 08:09, two minutes after Bill Katz took off in 693 and three minutes before Sam Feldman departed in 692.

Raisin's crew was pilot Noach, navigator Feldman, bombardier Cuburnek, radio operator Goldstein, flight engineer Lichtman, and air gunners Aronson, Berger, Hill, and Soltan. Katz's co-pilot was Ben-Porat, Tucker was navigator, Weissbrod bombardier, Dinkin radio operator, and air gunners were Camerman, Kahn, Meyerson, Nash, and Spicehandler. Feldman flew with pilot McConville, navigator Simon, bombardier Michel, radio operator Duboff, and air gunners Blumen, Fink, Gershalter, Lazarus, Merovitz, and Poll. B-17s 691 and 693 were armed with 12 45 kg bombs each, while 692 lifted 13 45 kg bombs.

The trio of bombers rendezvoused with two 101 Squadron Spitfires (Mann, who took off at 08:35, and McElroy, who took off at 08:40) that escorted the bombers – cruising at 11,000 feet – down to El Arish. Raisin's 691 was over El Arish from 09:29 until 09:31 and Katz followed from 09:31 until 09:33, while Feldman, who flew over El Arish from 09:30 until 09;31, had to return from 09:46 until 09:47. Smoky Simon wrote in his logbook:

> "On first run no bombs dropped by us due to circuit failure. We did a 2nd run. Fairly heavy ack-ack. No bombs dropped again. Fighters remained with us. We picked the other 2 B-17s out at sea. Very good bombing on runways, disposals, and tented area."

Mission 15: Faluja

IDF's main offensive effort was launched on the morning of October 16, 1948, at the Iraq El Manshiya sector. If successful the attack would have lifted the Egyptian siege on the Negev Desert, but the IDF action failed, and around 14:30 the Israeli troops were ordered to retreat. Roughly half an hour later the B-17 trio departed Ramat David to bomb nearby Faluja.

B-17 691 took off at 14:55 with Raisin, Noach, Feldman, Cuburnek, Goldstein, Lichtman, Aronson, Berger, Hill, and Soltan; offensive load was two 500 kg bombs and ten 70 kg bombs. B-17 693 followed at 14:59 with Katz, Ben-Porat, Tucker, Weissbrod, Ber, Dinkin, Camerman, Kahn, Meyerson, Nash, and Spicehandler;

The Hammers first bombed Faluja on October 16, 1948, and again on October 17 and 18, 1948. Hammers then bombed Faluja from November 5 to 17 - when the desert town was the "capital" of a besieged Egyptian brigade's enclave – and in late December 1948.

offensive load was 13 70 kg bombs. B-17 692 departed Ramat David at 15:00 with Feldman, McConville, Simon, Michel, Duboff, Blumen, Fink, Gershaw, Jackson, Lazarus, and Merovitz; offensive load was 12 45 kg bombs.

Fighter escort included a single 101 Squadron Spitfire (pilot Antin took off at 15:30), and the formation arrived over Faluja at 15:54. Bombing from 10,000 feet, reports regarding local anti-aircraft artillery fire varied. Raisin reported "6 Bursts (40 mm?) almost 11,000. Accurate, if aimed at Spit, above them. If at formation 7-800 yds to rear and 1,000 ft high," while Katz reported "negligible 40 and 20 mm," and Feldman "flack was seen bursting near Spit." Smoky Simon wrote in his logbook:

> "40 mm ack-ack not accurate. Beautiful bombing pattern. Load included 500 kg bombs. Tim Michel (bombardier) had 4 overshoots – late release."

Mission 16: Majdal

Al Raisin (in 691 with Noach, Cuburnek, Feldman, Goldstein, Lichtman, Schwarzbach, Berger, Aronson, Soltan, and Hill) and Sam Feldman (in 692 with McConville, Michel, Jackson, Duboff, Fink, Gershalter, Lazarus, Gershaw, Merovitz, and Blumen) departed Ramat David at 06:30 on the morning of October 17, 1948, with Bill Katz (in 693 with Ben-Porat, Weissbrod, Tucker, Ber, Kahn, Spicehandler, Meyerson, Camerman, Dinkin, and Nash) following at 06:40. Load was four 100 kg and eight 45 kg bombs on 691; eight 100 kg and ten 45 kg bombs on 692; and seven 100 kg and ten 45 kg bombs on 693. Fighter escort included two 101 Squadron S-199s (pilots Syd Cohen and Giddy Lichtman took off at 06:55).

Torched mission log! The Hammers' missions were engraved in fire; this photo was taken when the October 17, 1948, mission to Majdal was thus honored.

Sam Feldman (standing first from left) flew two missions on October 17, 1948, the day this photograph was presumably taken. In the first mission Feldman flew with McConville, Tim Michel (sitting in front with bag), Jackson, Hal Duboff (standing third from left), Fink, Gershalter, Joe Lazarus (kneeling first from left), Gershaw, Merovitz, and Blumen. In the second mission Feldman flew with Noach, Michel, Harris, Duboff, Fink, Blumen, Gershaw, Lazarus, Kaplan, Jackson, and air photographer David Griver.

First over Majdal was Raisin at 07:16, followed by Feldman at 07:19 and Katz at 07:25; all three bombed from 12,000 feet in the face of accurate Egyptian anti-aircraft artillery fire that reportedly included radar guided 88 mm guns.

Mission 17: Faluja

Hammers' second mission on Operation Yoav's Day 3 was again to Faluja. Al Raisin departed Ramat David at 16:06 in B-17 691 with McConville, Feldman, Cuburnek, Goldstein, Lichtman, Aronson, Soltan, Berger, and Hill; 691 lifted 12 45 kg bombs. Feldman and Katz followed at 16:08. Feldman was in 692 with Noach, Michel, John Harris on his first 69 Squadron mission, Duboff, Fink, Blumen, Gershaw, Lazarus, Kaplan, Jackson, and air photographer David Griver, who presumably shot several historical frames at Ramat David the same day. Katz flew 693 with Ben-Porat, Weissbrod, Tucker, Ber, Spicehandler, Meyerson, Kahn, Nash, Dinkin, and Camerman. The former was loaded with seven 100 kg and nine 45 kg bombs, while the latter lifted eight 100 kg and eight 45 kg bombs. Newcomer John Harris – who was a World War II RAF Mosquito navigator, a postwar Imperial Airways/BOAC flying boat navigator, and who would soon become Hammers' Lead Navigator – suffered terribly from the cold due to inadequate equipment:

> "I flew up from Sde Dov that day in a Rapide, went directly to the airplane, and flew a mission in a civilian suit which I had made in Karachi shortly before. The mission was to bomb the Faluja road, and it was Sam's second mission of the day."

Fighter escort was a pair of Spitfires (pilots Cohen and Senior took off at 16:35), and the trio was over target from 16:57 until 16:58 (Raisin), 16:57 to 16:59 (Katz), and 16:58 (Feldman). Bombing from 11,000 ft, the Hammers reported good weather, negligible anti-aircraft artillery fire, and accurate attack. Raisin's report stated "Bombs fell in exact area as ordered in briefing."

Mission 18: Majdal

69 Squadron stepped up operations on Operation Yoav Day 4 when three missions were flown; the first was a morning raid on Majdal. The three B-17s departed Ramat David at 06:31 (Raisin in 691 with McConville, Feldman, Cuburnek, Goldstein, Lichtman, Berger, Hill, Soltan, Aronson, and Kaplan), 06:32 (Feldman in 692 with Noach, Michel, Harris, Fink, Duboff, Blumen, Gershaw, Gershalter, Jackson, and Lazarus), and 06:32 (Katz in 693 with Ben-Porat, Tucker, Weissbrod, Ber, Spicehandler, Meyerson, Kahn, Camerman, Nash, Dinkin, and Griver). B-17 691 lifted two 250 kg plus ten 70 kg bombs, while 692 and 693 flew with identical loads of two 250 kg and 14 70 kg bombs each.

A lone Spitfire (Rudy Augarten took off at 06:40) was tasked to escort the B-17s, which arrived over Majdal from 07:21 and bombed from 13,500 feet against "fairly accurate 88 mm" anti-aircraft artillery fire. A novelty introduced in the debrief form of this mission was captions to attached photos of the raid. Typical captions were "stationary vehicles," "bomb line fall," and "ack ack positions."

Egyptian anti-aircraft artillery fire damaged Hammer 692 during the October 18, 1948, mission to Majdal. Yet the bomber that returned to Ramat David at 1614 was quickly repaired and departed for its next mission at 05:38 on the morning of October 19, 1948.

Mission 19: Majdal

The Flying Fortress returned to Majdal to bomb a former British fort, the local police station. Raisin departed Ramat David at 14:25 in 691 with McConville, Feldman, Cuburnek, Goldstein, Aronson, Lichtman, Hill, Kaplan, Soltan, and Berger. Katz followed at 14:26 with Ben-Porat, Tucker, Weissbrod, Meyerson, Kahn, Ber, Spicehandler, Nash, Camerman, Dinkin, and air photographer Jacobson. Feldman took off 692 at 14:28 with Noach, Harris, Michel, and nine more airmen, names unreadable. The respective loads were: two 250 kg and ten 70 kg bombs; 17 70 kg bombs; and two 250 kg and 14 70 kg bombs.

Two S-199 fighters (Weizman took off at 14:50 and Antin followed at 14:55) were tasked to escort the B-17s and reported, "Escorted bombers over target, observed smoke and dust rising from center of Majdal town. After the bombing one of the bombers left the formation and disappeared. Escorted the remaining 2 bombers to about 7 miles off the coast of Tel Aviv. They then circled around for about 20 minutes, and then both fighters left them because of lack of fuel." Raisin and Katz reported time over target from 15:09 and 15:10 respectively, but Feldman's time over target was 15:41. Raisin bombed from 13,500 feet and reported regarding enemy anti-aircraft activity "several bursts on level 50-100 yds off," while Katz, who bombed from 13,000 feet, added "nine bursts of 88 on level well between #3 + #1,2 ships." Sam Feldman reported "heavy and accurate flack over target. Hits on (1) Port wing trailing edge near fuselage … (2) Port tail … (3) Inside tail wheel well …," and concluded his debrief report with the bold statement that 692 was unserviceable due to "radio burnt out, wiring of bomb release system … bomb bay door damaged."

Mission 20: Faluja

With 692 unserviceable only two B-17s participated in the Hammers' third mission on October 18, 1948, but tactically this fact hardly mattered, as the bombers flew a nighttime mission to attack one after the other, rather than the usual daytime formation bombing pattern. Al Raisin flew "his" 691 with McConville, Feldman, Cuburnek, Goldstein, Lichtman, Aronson, Berger, Hill, Soltan, and Kaplan. They departed Ramat David at 18:27 with a bomb load of six 70 kg and five 45 kg bombs. There was no opposition over Faluja, which 691 bombed from 19:12 while flying at 10,000 feet.

Bill Katz departed Ramat David at 19:02 in "his" 693 with Ben-Porat, Tucker, Weissbrod, Ber, Meyerson, Spicehandler, Kahn, Camerman, Nash, and Dinkin. Their load was eight 100 kg and eight 70 kg bombs. Just like the preceding Hammer, B-17 693 did not encounter any anti-aircraft artillery fire over Faluja. Bombing was accomplished from 19:35 while flying at 10,500 feet.

Thus, the two Hammers crews unleashed a total of 27 bombs weighing 2,005 kg, but quite surprisingly the IAF official history of the Israeli War for Independence claims that the two bombers dropped eight tons of bombs!

Mission 21: El Arish

B-17 692 was serviceable again on the morning of October 19, 1948, when the Forts revisited El Arish. Sam Feldman was the first to take-off at 05:38 (in 692 with Noach, Michel, Harris, Soltan, Duboff, Fink, Gershalter, Jackson, and Lazarus); the bomber lifted 16 45 kg bombs. Next to take-off at 05;40 was Bill Katz (in 693 with Ben-Porat, Weissbrod, Tucker, Ber, Kahn, Meyerson, Dinkin, Camerman, Spicehandler, and Nash) with similar bomb load to 692. Al Raisin then took off at 05:45 in 691 with McConville, Cuburnek, Berger, Goldstein, Aronson, Lichtman, Hill, Kaplan, and Gershaw; their load was 22 45 kg bombs. Exactly an hour later the Hammers' escorts – two 101 Squadron S-199 fighters flown by Syd Cohen and Giddy Lichtman – departed Hertzeliya, too late to protect the bombers over El Arish.

Raisin and Feldman appeared over El Arish air base at 06:42 and bombed from 12,500 feet. Katz followed at 06:47, also bombing from 12,500 feet and reporting "heavy but inaccurate fire over target – 40s + 88s." Again the IAF official history of the Israeli War for Independence claims that the bombers dropped 5,200 kg of bombs, whereas the total weight of 54 45 kg bombs was 2,430 kg. The discrepancy is between the 69 Squadron's "Report of Flight Order No. ___" documents and an IAF Intelligence report from October 20, 1948, stating the trio's bomb load was "16x100 kg; 20x100 kg; 16x100 kg." The IAF Intelligence report also indicated that four aircraft were noted at El Arish (Raisin reported "direct hits on 2 a/c"), while anti-aircraft artillery was "light and accurate."

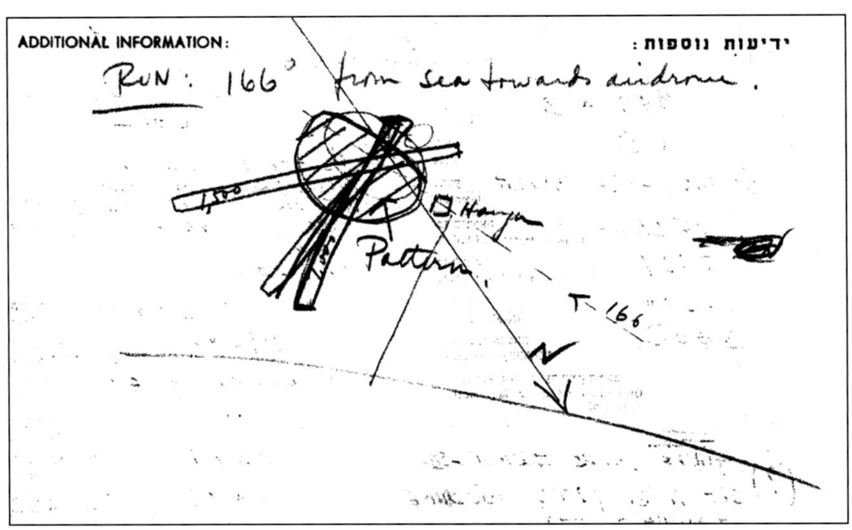

Adding to the debrief form, a sketch for clearer presentation of bombing was introduced during Operation Yoav; the first known sketch is believed to be this scribble of the October 19, 1948, El Arish bombing pattern from Bill Katz's debrief form. Obviously the clarity and quality of sketches depended upon the artistic talent of painters, but even this department improved along the war's time line.

Crude conditions at Ramat David are apparent from this image of Hammers handling 691 without unified military outfit, with no proper tools but with a lot of dedication and improvisation.

Mission 22: Gaza

Two pilots flew their first 69 Squadron mission, and one pilot progressed from the right hand seat to the left hand aircraft commander position during the Hammers' second mission on Operation Yoav Day 5. Al Raisin departed Ramat David in 691 at 12:59 with pilot Jack Ratushniak, Feldman, Cuburnek, Goldstein, Lichtman, Aronson, Berger, and Gershaw; bomb load was 20 45 kg bombs. B-17s 692 (Sam Feldman with Noach, Michel, IAF Operations navigator Morris Segal, Duboff, Fink, Soltan, Lazarus, Jackson, Nash, 103 Squadron pilot Paul Orringer, and air photographer Griver) and 693 (John McConville on his first mission as B-17 commander, with pilot Trig Maseng, Tucker, Hill, Ber, Schwarzbach, and five more airmen with unreadable names) followed a minute later loaded with 16 70 kg bombs each. The 101 Squadron S-199 fighter escort (pilots Syd Cohen and Sid Antin) took off from Hertzeliya at 13:30.

Raisin and McConville were over the Gaza railway station at 13:53 with Feldman following at 13:55, all bombing from 12,500 feet. Bombing was reported as accurate, as was the Egyptian anti-aircraft artillery fire, though none of the bombers suffered damage. Again, the IAF Intelligence report varied from the 69 Squadron's "Report of Flight Order No. ___" documents with a statement of "20x100 kg; 16x70 kg; 16x70 kg" for total bomb load of 4,240 kg. Apparently there was misunderstanding over 100 lb (45 kg) bombs as stated in the 69 Squadron's "Report of Flight Order No. ___" documents and 100 kg bombs as IAF Intelligence reported.

Mission 23: Holikat Hill 138

Close air support was definitely not an ordinary mission for a heavy bomber. Yet IAF combat aircraft inventory only included a pair of serviceable 103 Squadron Beaufighters that departed Ramat David at 16:55 and 16:58 to raid the Egyptian fort at Iraq El Suidan. No other IAF real attack aircraft were available other than the B-17s, so Al Raisin took off in 691 (loaded with 21 45 kg bombs) at 17:07 (with Ratushniak, Feldman, Cuburnek, Berger, Lichtman, Gershaw, Hill, Aronson, and Goldstein) to bomb Hill 138, near Holikat.[18] Fighter escort was provided by two 101 Squadron Spitfires (pilots Weizman and Doyle).

The bomber was over Hill 138 at 17:35 flying at 5,000 feet, and bombed with only 15 45 kg bombs that exploded along a trail from the foot of the hill up to almost the top. Anti-aircraft artillery was reported "approx 40 puffs 40 + 20 mm, accurately trailing," while fighter pilot Doyle concluded "bombing good, flak accurate for height."

Apparently all three B-17s were ordered to fly the mission, so an epilogue to this episode was a letter that Ramat David Air Base Commander Dov Ben-Zvi signed on October 20, 1948:

> "On October 19th the Fortresses landed at 14:33, 14:35, and 14:36. Were parked in revetments in the presence of Heyman Shechtman[19] by 14:50. Bombing up orders No. 26, 27, and 28, times of origin 14:20, 14:22, and 14:25 were passed to Engineering by David Ben Or by 14:30. Tractor was sent to Bomb Dump immediately to collect American bombs as required by Bombing up order. Armament section at that time was (missing number) men strong and (missing number) helpers, of which (missing number) were with the bomb tractor and trailer. Mr Giladi asked the Station Adjutant for help in men, which help turned up promptly by 15:40. Therefore it was not until 15:40 that work really got under way on bombing-up. A/c No. 1 was ready on time at 16:30 and took off. No. 3 was finished by 16:45, and when going out to take off had its tail wheel burst. No. 2 was finished by 16:50, when it was too late to take-off.
>
> "The sheer physical facts of limited capacity on one tractor and one trailer for bombs, one jeep, and one lorry (which was a civilian lorry hijacked from Haifa and too high to load bombs on to) were mainly responsible for the Section's inability to cope with the work laid on it.
>
> "The solution suggested and agreed to last night between the CO, the HQ Armament Officer, and the Station Armament Officer (Acting), together with Ronnie Cohen of HQ Ops, can only be implemented when Air Force Headquarters lets the Station have the fundamental equipment and manpower it has been demanding constantly over the period that the present CO has been in command."

Supporting operations of three B-17 bombers in a country under UN embargo, without any prior experience in flying heavy bombers, was a challenge. Compared to most IAF assets the B-17s were complicated and demanding. Yet despite all hurdles the B-17s flew and generated remarkable serviceability by the then IAF standards. The heavy bombers may have been late on the afternoon of October 19, 1948, but this was the exception. Overall the Hammers were a decisive force in the success of Operation Yoav. Ramat David Chief Technical Officer Maurice "Ray" Commanday wrote in 1993:

"I somehow had to try and make sense out of the problems associated with keeping aircraft glued together without a source of spare parts, with few qualified technicians, and with no maintenance records for any of the miscellaneous second hand equipment to which we had fallen heir. Added to that state of affairs was the fact that I did not share a common language with the majority of the personnel I was expected to lead. Happily my immediate subordinate, Sam Glickman, admitted to seven fluent tongues (including English) and could make himself understood in several more.

RD, as it was popularly called, was intended to be the 'bomber base.' Organized after the fighter base and the air transport base were in operation, we acquired most of the leftovers in personnel as well as equipment... The three B-17s, with little accumulated flying time... a few Besa 7.9 mm infantry machine guns were mounted where the mighty 0.50 calibre turrets had been; a German bombsight was installed in the nose of one of them; some makeshift bomb shackles were mounted and off to war they went. They were defended mostly by their reputation. I am not aware that they were ever attacked by an enemy fighter!

The B-17s were a special case. Aware that every pilot knew that their formation of three aircraft brought 23 0.50 caliber guns to bear on a fighter attacking from any angle, I felt especially concerned that they be serviceable to fly as a group of three at all times. There were no spares. We did have a few R-1820 engines all encased in shipping containers. There were no spare engine mounts and no spare accessories, so making up 'quick change' engine assemblies was out of the question. Hence, I worried about one of the three coming back with a feathered prop. It could mean a good week of engine change effort with totally inexperienced men and very limited equipment.

Since the war consisted of a series of truces and fractured truces there were periods of little or no flying interspersed with brief periods of intense activity. During that period (Operation Yoav) we had two B-17 maintenance crises.

One day two of the 17s returned from operations well before the third, which we 'sweated out' in the traditional manner. I expressed concern that there be no feathered prop and, lo and behold, number one was seen to be feathered! Jumping into our jeep we headed for its revetment, partly to effect a kind of engineer's prayer and to support poor Sam Glickman, whose consternation was at an all-time high. I said that I has seen pilots feather props for insufficient reasons... a bit of oil on a nacelle... Then, arriving at the revetment we saw the ground crew already getting ready to remove the cowl from the number one, whose nacelle had a nice film of oil reaching back from the trailing edge of the cowling. By this time I had said, 'It could be a simple thing, maybe a small piece of shrapnel struck a... (and here I prayed a wishful thought) a rockerbox cover (please God!). And so it was! We were back in service fifteen minutes later with a rockerbox cover borrowed from a spare engine.

A few days later I was presented with two tail wheel tires. One looked like shredded wheat but was still inflated. The second was worn well down to the cord. Number so and so B-17 had just blown its tail wheel tire on landing, and what was presented comprised our spare tail wheels. B-17s did not operate in the Middle East during World War II. There were some aeronautical bits and pieces around, but no tail wheel tires, or even tires, that would fit a B-17 tail wheel. What to do? I suggested that the better tire would make one more take off and the other could be used to taxi the plane to its revetment when the first one blew on landing (which it did). The shredded wheat managed to last long enough to park the plane and it, too, gave up the ghost at that point, as anticipated.

Meanwhile, I ascertained that the transport guys, operating C-46s, had plenty of tail wheels and tires and got them to deliver one. Naturally, the bearing race of the C-46 was much too small to fit the B-17, so we had to devise a plan of desperate action. Our little base machine shop was headed by David Kushnir who, in civil life, was a machinist from Haifa. I provided him with the C-46 wheel, a tireless B-17 wheel, a jeep, a driver, and Sten gun with orders to collar someone in Haifa with a lathe and material with which he was to make a wheel that would accept the outer B-17 bearing races and the C-46 tire. He was not to stop for anything or anybody until he returned with the wheel from Haifa, some twenty miles away. Money was no object, but the Sten gun, if necessary, could be.

Next day, Operation Yoav continued apace and the B-17s took off. On landing the tire blew. Ten minutes later Kushnir puffed into sight with the heaviest solid steel tail wheel ever flown and we were back in business!"

Mission 24: El Arish

The Hammers returned to El Arish on the morning of October 20, 1948, with two 101 Squadron Spitfires as escorts (pilots Antin and Wilson took off at 06:55). This was also the first Operation Yoav mission that Al Raisin did not lead, and the first that John Harris flew as 69 Squadron lead navigator. Bill Katz took off first in 693 at 06:23 with Ben-Porat, Weissbrod, Harris, Gershalter, Ber, Kahn, Meyerson, and Camerman; the bomber lifted 19 45 kg bombs. Next to take-off was Sam Feldman in 692 with Noach, Michel, Segal, Duboff, Fink, Soltan, Jackson, Nash, Lazarus, and Griver; the load was 22 45 kg bombs. Third and final, at 06:40, was John McConville in "Raisin's" 691 with Maseng, Tucker, Dinkin, Blumen, Schwarzbach, and two airmen with unreadable names; load was similar to 692.

Katz and McConville were over El Arish at 07:22 with Feldman following at 07:23, and all bombed from 14,000 feet. Katz reported Egyptian anti-aircraft artillery as "not very heavy," Feldman "moderate," and McConville "heavy, very inaccurate." The IAF still suffered from inaccurate reporting, as IAF Intelligence Report

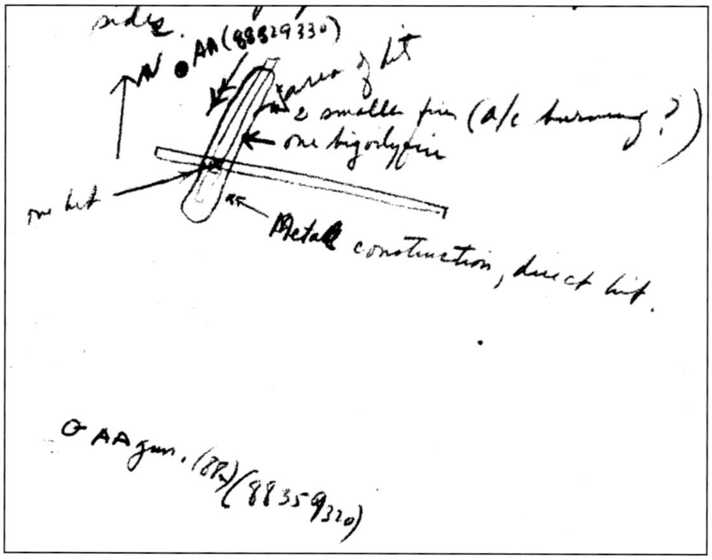

Sam Feldman produced the neatest debrief forms as, naturally, these documents mirrored personal characters. This sketch was added to Sam Feldman's debrief report from the October 20, 1948, mission to El Arish.

7 dated October 21, 1948, stated that bomb load was "22x100 kg; 22x100 kg; 19x100 kg" for a total of 6,300 kg, instead of the actual 2,835 kg.

Mission 25: Rafah

The target of the Hammers' second mission on Operation Yoav Day 6 was Rafah. Al Raisin departed Ramat David in 691 with Ratushniak, Cuburnek, Feldman, Lichtman, Goldstein, Dinkin, Berger, Gershaw, Aronson, and Griver at 13:26. Bill Katz followed two minutes later in 692 with Ben-Porat, Weissbrod, Harris, Spicehandler, Ber, Kahn, Meyerson, Camerman, and an unnamed "photographer." Bomb load was 24 and 20 45 kg bombs respectively. The planned fighter escort (pilots Syd Cohen and Giddy Lichtman) took off from Hertzeliya at 14:05, but the bombers and fighters did not rendezvous.

Raisin arrived over Rafah at 14:36 and Katz followed at 14:38; both bombed from 13,500 feet. Anti-aircraft artillery was reportedly light and exploded well below the aircraft. The 69 Squadron's "Report of Flight Order No. ___" documents are mostly unreadable, but the target is clearly stated as Rafah for both bombers. Yet IAF Intelligence Report Number 7 dated October 21, 1948, states that the first B-17 bombed Rafah (with "24x100 kg" bombs), but that the second bombed Gaza (with "20x100 kg" bombs)!

Mission 26: Beer Sheba and Gaza

IDF success prompted stepped up operations, and the B-17s again flew nighttime missions on the evening of October 20, 1948. Al Raisin flew the first evening mission with Ratushniak, Cuburnek, Feldman, Lichtman, Goldstein, Berger, Gershaw, and Aronson. B-17 691 took off at 19:45 with a load of 24 70 kg bombs. Arriving over Beer Sheba at 20:33, the bomber loitered over the first target for 20 minutes at 10,000 feet in the face of "very slight 20 mm" anti-aircraft artillery fire but did not bomb. No proper aiming could be achieved, as Beer Sheba was only visible when the B-17 was directly above the town. Diverting to Gaza, the Hammer flew two runs at 12,000 feet from 21:21 and bombed during the second run; the crew reported "no ack ack, 3 searchlights" and aimed at the searchlights, but these were switched off before bombing.

Mission 27: Gaza

The second 69 Squadron nighttime mission on the evening of October 20, 1948, departed Ramat David at 21:10. Sam Feldman flew 692 with Noach, Michel, Tucker, Duboff, Meyerson, Soltan, Fink, Jackson, Lazarus, and Nash. Load was 18 70 kg bombs, and the B-17 was over Gaza from 22:00, flying at 12,500 feet. Anti-aircraft artillery defending Gaza was reported as "4 Bofors and 6 searchlights." IAF Intelligence Report Number 7 dated October 21, 1948, stated that the city's north was bombed, and the load was "18x17 kg" bombs....

Mission 28: Majdal

Operation Yoav's final full day of fighting was October 21, 1948, during which the Hammers flew two missions; the first was to Majdal. Again flying as a 3-ship formation, the Flying Fortresses departed Ramat David at 06:05 (693 and 691) and at 06:06 with a load of 26, 24, and 29 45 kg bombs respectively. Bill Katz commanded 693 and was leading the mission, along with Ben-Porat, Weissbrod, Harris, Ber, Kahn, Spicehandler, Meyerson, and Camerman. John McConville flew 691 with Maseng, Tucker, Dinkin, Aronson, "Swartzman" (presumably Schwarzbach), Kaplan, Hill, and Bloom (most likely Blumen, but possibly 103 Squadron radio operator David Bloom). Sam Feldman trailed in 692 with Noach, Michel, Bressloff, Duboff, Fink, Soltan, Jackson, Lazarus, Nash, and Griver.

Apparently there was no fighter escort for that mission. Two 101 Squadron Spitfires that took off at 06:55 and 0700 engaged Egyptian fighters, yet the Flying Fortresses maintained their flawless record of not encountering enemy fighters. The lead Hammer was over Majdal from 06:50 until 07:00 and flew two runs; the wingmen were over Majdal from 07:00 until 07:01, and all three flew at 14,000 feet. Sam Feldman reported that Egyptian anti-aircraft artillery was "heavy very accurate 88 mm fire," and indeed B-17 693 was damaged, as Katz reported "Hit... Not much on first circuit, but on second run the anti-aircraft was very intense and accurate." As usual there is a discrepancy between

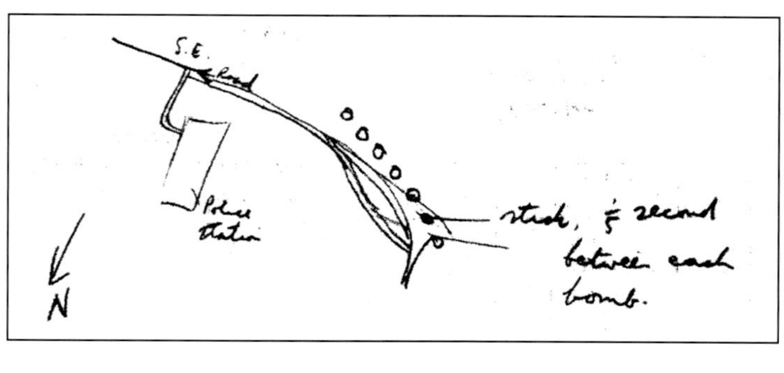

A sketch of the October 21, 1948, mission to Majdal from McConville's debrief report.

South African radio operator Milton Bottger in his "office"; Bottger first flew a Hammers mission on October 21, 1948, but officially joined 69 Squadron only after the Israeli War for Independence had ended.

the 69 Squadron's "Report of Flight Order No. ___" documents (reporting 79 45 kg bombs for a total load of 3,555 kg) and the IAF Intelligence/ IAF official history of the Israeli War for Independence, claiming that 7,500 kg of bombs were dropped over Majdal on the morning of October 21, 1948.

Mission 29: Majdal

Damaged 693 did not fly the second 69 Squadron mission on Operation Yoav Day 7; the target was again Majdal. Al Raisin departed Ramat David at 13:39 in 691 with Ratushniak, Feldman, Cuburnek, Goldstein, Lichtman, Berger, Gershaw, Aronson, and Griver. John McConville followed a minute later, flying 692 with Maseng, Tucker, Bressloff, Dinkin, Soltan, Schwarzbach, Kaplan, Hill, Blumen, and Milton Bottger (former 103 Squadron radio operator – who "Hebrewed" his name to "Butch Ben-Yok" – on his first recorded 69 Squadron mission). The bombers lifted 24 45 kg bombs (691), plus 11 100 kg and 17 70 kg bombs (692). This time fighter escort was flown by two 101 Squadron S-199s; pilots Weizman and Antin took off at 14:05 and 14:10 respectively.

Egyptian anti-aircraft artillery fire over Majdal was still reported heavy and accurate; the two bombers were over the Arab town from 14:51 until 14:53, flying three runs at 14,000 feet. Apparently the crews were warned of enemy aircraft, as McConville remarked in the "Enemy Activity A/C" section of the debrief report "none seen but some expected!!!!" As a result of this expectation, and 692's malfunctioning Number 4 engine, the bombers separated, with 692 landing at 15:23 and 691 following at 15:37. McConville reported "Holding 2,400 RPM on 3 engines (No 4 – only 20 in) (turbocharger). Fuel consumed too rapidly, so proceeded to base directly when #1 ship headed to sea to avoid reported A/C."

Mission 30: Gaza

The 21st and final 69 Squadron bombing mission during the eight day long Operation Yoav was flown on the morning of the offensive's Day 8 when two B-17s raided Gaza. Al Raisin flew 691 that departed Ramat David at 10:32 with Noach, Cuburnek, Feldman, Goldstein, Kaplan, Lichtman, Aronson, Berger, and Gershaw. Sam Feldman followed at 10:33 in 692 with Ratushniak, 103 Squadron navigator Denis Gochen, Michel, Soltan, Duboff, Fink, Lazarus, Jackson, "Jorgen" (possibly Jorgen Christienson, an air gunner from Denmark), and Nash. Load was 24 45 kg bombs (691), plus 18 70 kg and 11 45 kg bombs (692); fighter escort was provided in the shape of two 101 Squadron S-199s (pilots Augarten and Lichtman took off from Hertzeliya at 11:00).

The bombers were over Gaza from 11:26 until 11:28, and Raisin reported that Egyptian anti-aircraft artillery over the city was "very little, approx 6 bursts 88 mm inaccurate," and Feldman added "approx 30 blasts inaccurate 88 mm." Cruising at 13,000 feet, the pair bombed the area of the Gaza railway station, with 691 reporting "bombs fell parallel to and west of station" and 692 "bombs dropped in target area on west side south of railway tracks."

American volunteer, USAAF veteran, and Hammers aircraft commander Sam Feldman first flew a mission with native Israeli, RAF World War II pilot, and Hammers pilot Jack Ratushniak on the October 22, 1948, mission to Gaza. Feldman and Ratushniak flew together a total of 15 bombing missions from October 22, 1948, until January 4, 1949.

69 Squadron toured Tarshicha after Operation Hiram; this image presents the extent of damage that Israeli bombings inflicted upon Palestinian villages.

Yoav

A UN negotiated cease fire ended Operation Yoav at 15:00 on October 22, 1948. Israel's objective to lift the Egyptian siege on the Negev Desert was only achieved on the morning of October 20, 1948, when Holikat was captured after fierce fighting.

The Hammers were instrumental in the support of the IDF offensive. IAF Intelligence reported that 69 Squadron flew 47 sorties and dropped 52,060 kg of bombs during Operation Yoav from October 15 to 22, 1948. Obviously IAF Intelligence reports were not absolutely accurate, and there was distinct difficulty differentiating between kilograms and pounds, as on many occasions 69 Squadron airmen stated pounds, but IAF Intelligence reported kilograms. Nevertheless, the IAF Intelligence report (assuming similar levels of inaccurate reporting for all involved) clearly indicated that the Hammers trio flew 16% of IAF sorties, yet dropped 35% of the total bomb load.

Summarizing available 69 Squadron's "Report of Flight Order No. ___" documents for the duration of Operation Yoav yields that the B-17s flew 46 bombing sorties. Principle targets for the B-17s were Majdal (17 sorties), El Arish (10 sorties), Faluja (8 sorties), Gaza (7 sorties), and Rafah (2 sorties), with a single sortie each flown to bomb Hill 138 at Holikat and Beer Sheba (but actually bombing Gaza). The trio of bombers lifted 820 bombs weighing 50,845 kg, including 491 45 kg bombs, 225 70 kg bombs, 90 100 kg bombs, 12 250 kg bombs, and two 500 kg bombs. Daytime missions were flown as a trio (ten missions) or in pairs (four missions) to maximize self defense firepower, with fighters escorting a dozen of these missions. Eight nighttime missions were flown in singles.

Mission 31: Tarshicha

None of Egypt's Arab allies attacked Israel during Operation Yoav; none except Fawzi El Qawuqji, commander of the semi-regular Arab Liberation Army, which was deployed in the Upper Galilee, with headquarters at Tarshicha. Eventually the Arab Liberation Army attack was launched too late (on October 22, 1948), achieved little, and offered Israel an opportunity to "counterattack." IDF Operation Hiram D-Day and H-Hour were October 28, 1948, at 19:30, and Israel's objectives were to topple the Arab Liberation Army and to liberate Upper Galilee. A massive IAF bombardment effort was planned to soften the enemy prior to H-Hour and to support the IDF afterwards. The IAF heavy bombers were tasked to bomb the highest value target, the Arab Liberation Army headquarters town of Tarshicha.

Al Raisin flew 691 in the lead of the mission, taking off from Ramat David at 17:00 with Noach, Simon, Cuburnek, Feldman, Lichtman, Goldstein, Aronson, Berger, Gershaw, and Hill. Bill Katz and Sam Feldman followed two minutes later in 693 and 691 respectively. Katz's crew was Ben-Porat, Weissbrod, Harris, Ber, Kahn, Meyerson, Seymour Bressloff, Camerman, and Spicehandler. Feldman's crew was Ratushniak, Boris Bressloff, Michel, Fink, Duboff, Lazarus, Jackson, Nash, Soltan, and Griver. Each Hammer was loaded with 14 100 kg bombs.

The trio flew west to the Mediterranean Sea and then headed northeast and southwest to the target. Sadly the hand written 69 Squadron's "Report of Flight Order No. ___" documents are almost unreadable, but lead navigator Smoky Simon wrote in his logbook:

> "Target – Tarshiha – Feldman and I slipped badly on navigation and we bombed the neighbouring village of Suhamata... (no excuses claimed, but the navigational features at the (bombed) target resembled those of the real target ie the village itself, the road, hills, and wadi."

John Harris recalled:

> "There was a campaign in the Galilee and we had to bomb Tarshicha. Our friends from headquarters came, Dan Tolkowsky came, and Smoky Simon came; they flew

Hammers gathered around an old Arab waving a white flag to signal surrender during their tour of Tarshicha.

Al Raisin (third from left), Bill Lichtman (fourth from left), and Joe Ber (sixth from left) among a group of IDF troops during the Hammers' tour of Tarshicha.

69 Squadron Commander Al Raisin peering into an Arab house at Tarshicha with drawn pistol.

the lead airplane as guests and we got to the back. I saw them go straight over Tarshicha and bomb a small village. As we went up to the target with Bill Hans Weissbrod was behind me. I said to Bill 'they are bombing the wrong target!' (Bill took a deep breath from the cigar he used to smoke while flying and answered) 'So what?'

Our bombs did not drop thank God, they were hung up, so we flew back to Tarshicha and had them dropped one at a time, the armorer with an axe banging over each one."

Probably for this reason Katz landed 32 minutes after Raisin. In fact, while Katz reported route in as "No 1 and No 2," the third B-17 flew back to the Mediterranean Sea and returned to Ramat David from the west via Haifa, while the first two Hammers flew east from the "target" and returned to Ramat David overland flying southwest.

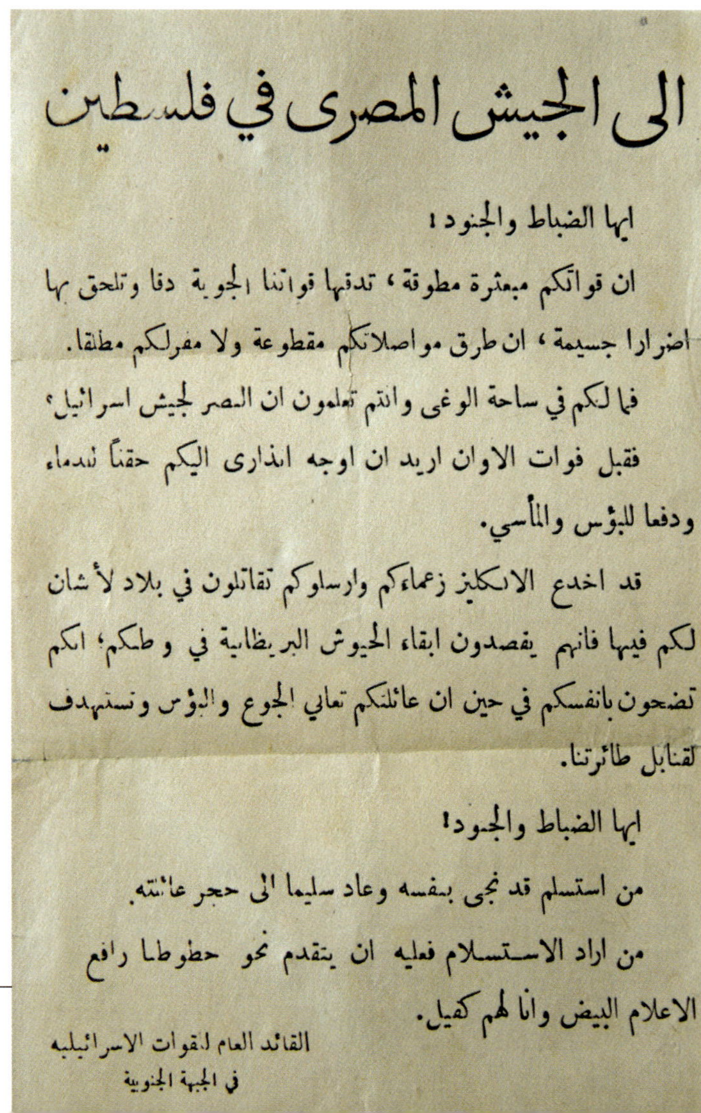

الى الجيش المصرى في فلسطين

ايها الضباط والجنود !

ان قواتكم مبعثرة مطوقة ، تدقها قواتنا الجوية دقا وتلحق بها
اضرارا جسيمة ، ان طرق مواصلاتكم مقطوعة ولا مفر لكم مطلقا.
فما لكم في ساحة الوغى وانتم تعلمون ان النصر لجيش اسرائيل؟
فقبل فوات الاوان اريد ان اوجه انذارى اليكم حقناً للدماء
ودفعا للبؤس والمآسي.

قد اخدع الانكليز زعماءكم وارسلوكم تقاتلون في بلاد لا شان
لكم فيها فانهم يقصدون ابقاء الجيوش البريطانية في وطنكم؛ انكم
تضحون بانفسكم في حين ان عائلتكم تعاني الجوع والبؤس وتستهدف
لقنابل طائرتنا.

ايها الضباط والجنود!

من استسلم قد نجى بنفسه وعاد سليما الى حجر عائلته.

من اراد الاستسلام فعليه ان يتقدم نحو خطوطنا رافع
الاعلام البيض وانا لهم كفيل.

القائد العام للقوات الاسرائيليه
في الجبهة الجنوبية

Leaflet that the Hammers used to drop was addressed to "officers and soldiers of the Egyptian army in Palestine," calling them to surrender as "Your forces are scattered and surrounded, bombed by our air force that inflict heavy losses, your transport has been cut off and there is no sanctuary for you. Why fight if you already know that Israel has won? Before it will be too late, you are warned to avoid bloodshed, disaster, and tragedy. England cheated your leaders, who sent you to fight in a foreign country while the English army is firmly based in your homeland. You sacrifice your soles while your families suffer from hunger and you are the target of the bombs our aircraft drop. Officers and soldiers! Who will surrender will save his soul and will reunite with his family. To surrender advance towards our lines with a white flag and I guarantee that surrenders will not be harmed." Signed "Israel Command South Supreme Commander."

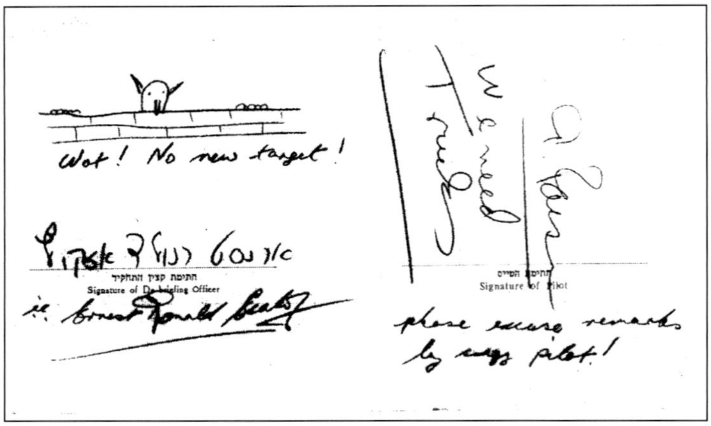

Wartime sense of humor. 69 Squadron Commander Al Raisin signed the November 6, 1948, debrief with a remark "We need Truce," then "please excuse remarks by crazy pilot!" was added.

IAF official history of the Israeli War for Independence maintains that the B-17s returned to bomb Tarshicha on the morning of October 29, 1948. No 69 Squadron's "Report of Flight Order No. ___" documents and/or logbook entries covering such a mission were not traced.[20]

Faluja Pocket

The Truce from October 22, 1948, was eventually shorter and rather more operationally eventful for the Hammers than the Truce that lasted from July 19, 1948, until October 15, 1948. Therefore, service person issues that surfaced during the First Truce were not repeated during the Second Truce.

After the successful Operation Hiram that expelled Fawzi El Qawuqji's Arab Liberation Army from the Upper Galilee the IDF again turned south. As a result of Operation Yoav an Egyptian brigade deployed around the town of Faluja was under IDF siege. Israel viewed the "Faluja Pocket" as an internal "policing" issue, so attacks against the besieged Egyptians continued regardless of Truce and despite Israeli protest against similar Egyptian action when the Israeli Negev Desert was under Egyptian blockade prior to Operation Yoav. The IAF was ordered to bomb the Faluja Pocket around the clock in the hope that the Egyptians' will to fight would crack and may lead to an eventual surrender. IAF divided time slots for bombing operations over the Faluja Pocket with the Hammers mostly bombing during the afternoon.

Mission 32: Faluja

The first Hammers mission over the Faluja Pocket was accomplished during the afternoon hours of November 5, 1948. Bill Katz was in command of the lead 691 that departed Ramat David at 16:03 with co-pilot Ben-Porat, navigator Harris, Weissbrod as bombardier, radio operator Ber, Meyerson as armorer, Spicehandler as flight engineer, and air gunners Camerman, Bressloff, and Kahn. Load on board 691 was 20 45 kg and four 70 kg bombs. John McConville followed in 693 at 16:04 with co-pilot Maseng, navigator Tucker, bombardier Weinstein, radio operator Dinkin, and air gunners Christienson, Robinson, Bottger, and Kaplan; their load was 20 45 kg and eight 70 kg bombs. Third and final to take-off – at 16:06 – was Sam Feldman in 692 with co-pilot Noach, Michel as bombardier, Bressloff as navigator, radio operator Duboff, and air gunners Fink, Lazarus, Soltan, Jackson, and Nash. Load for 692 was 23 45 kg and six 70 kg bombs.

The trio flew from Ramat David to Tantura, over the Mediterranean Sea, and inland to Tel Nof, from where course was set to Faluja. McConville was over target from 16:38 until 16:39, Katz from 16:39 until 16:40, and Feldman at 16:40. Bombing was done from 8,000 feet against active Egyptian anti-aircraft artillery fire; McConville reported "1 20 mm, 2 bursts at 3,000 feet," Katz "6 bursts of 88 (?) (possibly 40) at 6,000 feet," and Feldman "black puffs at formation height… 17 puffs seen." The Hammers returned to Ramat David via Ishdud, over the Mediterranean Sea and inland over Hadera; 691 landed at 17:25, 692 at 17:28, and 693 at 17:30.

Mission 33: Faluja

Two Hammers returned to Faluja on November 6, 1948, with all four Flying Fortress commanders flying the B-17s. Al Raisin, with Sam Feldman as co-pilot, took off in 691 at 15:57 with Cuburnek, Tucker, Duboff, Lichtman, Fink, Gershaw, Hill, and Berger; their load was 16 70 kg and eight 45 kg bombs. Bill Katz and John McConville as co-pilot departed Ramat David in 693 at 15:58 with Weissbrod, Harris, Ber, Spicehandler as flight engineer, Kahn as armorer, and air gunners Meyerson, Bressloff, and Camerman; load was 20 70 kg and eight 45 kg bombs.

Route to target was "base-sea-Ishdud-Faluja," with 691 flying over target at 16:32, while 693 flew two bombing runs at 16:31 to 16:32 and 16:39 to 16:40. There was absolutely no anti-aircraft artillery fire; Raisin reported "NIL" and Katz elaborated "Not a Puff!!" Bombing from 10,000 feet, Katz reported:

> "1st Run: 153 degrees – 4xUS100lb + 19xD70. Cluster at point E9N5 road and 200 ft S of wadi. Rest of stick along east side of N5 road. Our bomb in center of town W of road.
>
> 2nd Run: 153 degrees – 4xUS100lb 1xD70 salvo dropped in center of town 200 feet W of N/S road.
> Fire seen in Iraq (El) Suidan."

Route back home was "target-Majdal-sea-Hadera-base," where 691 landed at 17:10, followed by 693 a minute later.

Mission 34: Faluja

Again involving a pair of B-17s, the next Hammers raid on Faluja was on November 9, 1948. Apparently the bombers attacked one after the other, rather than in formation, while for the first time fighter escort was provided by two P-51s that took off from Hertzeliya at 15:40 and 15:45, escorted the bombers, and landed at Hatzor, 101 Squadron's new base.

Sam Feldman flew 693, which took off at 15:09 with Ratushniak, Michel, Bressloff, Duboff, Fink, Soltan, Lazarus, Nash, and Jackson, plus a load of 20 70 kg and eight 45 kg bombs. Al Raisin followed at 15:33 in 691 with Noach, Cuburnek, Feldman, Lichtman, Goldstein, Aronson, Berger, Meyerson, Hill,

The Hammers could fly a straight line from Ramat David to Faluja, but mostly flew west to the Mediterranean Sea, then south along the coast, until turning inland again towards targets over the Egyptian front. Flying over the coastline was avoided, as such a flight pattern would have brought the Hammers into direct confrontation with Israeli anti-aircraft artillery gunners defending Tel Aviv and Haifa; the latter engaged B-17s twice during early Hammers operations in July 1948.

and Gershaw; their load was 16 70 kg and eight 45 kg bombs. B-17 693's route in was "base-sea-Herzeliya-sea-Nabi Rubin-target" (over Hertzeliya, most likely to rendezvous with escort), while 691 flew "sea-Nebi Rubin-target"; the former cruised at 4,000 feet and bombed (at 16:01 to 16:03) from 10,000 feet, while the latter cruised and bombed (at 16:15 to 16:16) from 9,000 feet. Egyptian anti-aircraft artillery opened fire at 693 but did not engage the following 691; fighter escort remained at 4,000 feet and did not accompany 693 back home, so Raisin remarked "some A/C low over target." Sam Feldman reported:

> "Escort pulled off after leaving target towards another A/C heading S (ours???). Smoke from Karatiya. Bomb run 180 degrees long stick along W side of NS road. First two bombs in wadi – rest of stick down to bend in road at S end of town. Most bombs in target area (SW corner of town)."

Charles William Wadman first appeared in a 69 Squadron's "Report of Flight Order No. ___" document on November 15, 1948, when he flew in 1603. Bill Wadman, age 18, joined the Royal Canadian Air Force in 1941; trained at Number 2 Wireless School, Calgary, and at Number 10 Bombing and Gunnery School, Mountain View, Wadman was posted to Number 424 Squadron and flew coastal patrol from Scotland until grounded for slight medical problems and returned to Canada, where he served at Number 22 Elementary Flying School, Air Traffic Control; he flew 351 hours in RCAF service. Recruited to the IAF on June 28, 1948, but delayed in Europe until September, Wadman was posted to 69 Squadron during the first week of November and flew as armorer and air gunner until 1951 to accumulate 471 flying hours in the B-17. Wadman returned to Canada but remained in touch with fellow Hammers, and planned to participate in the defunct 1998 Flight of the Septuagenarians. Charles William Wadman passed away on November 29, 1999.

Feldman's route back to Ramat David was "target-sea-Hadera-base," landing at 16:39; Raisin followed the same route and landed at 16:46.

Mission 35: Faluja

Still referring to the Hammers as B-17 #1 and B-17 #3 in the 69 Squadron's "Report of Flight Order No. ___" documents for the November 15, 1948, mission, the B-17s had been allocated new serial numbers by then, with 691 becoming 1601, 692 transformed into 1602, and 693 was assigned 1603.[21] Both bombers departed Ramat David at 15:57. Bill Katz flew 1601 with Ben-Porat, Harris, Weissbrod, Spicehandler, Ber, Meyerson, Kahn, Bressloff, and Camerman. Flying his first 69 Squadron mission as commander was Issy Noach in 1603, with Sam Feldman as co-pilot, Tucker, Weinstein, Lichtman, Dinkin, Duboff, Treisman, Soltan, Kaplan, Christienson, and Wadman—a larger than normal crew of 13 airmen, including two radio operators, two armorers, and four air gunners. Respective loads were 15 70 kg plus eight 45 kg bombs and 20 70 kg plus eight 45 kg bombs.

Katz reported cruising at 5,000 feet along the route "base-sea-Jura-target," while Noach reported 4,500 feet along "base-sea-Majdal-target." The lead B-17 flew two bombing runs (altitude 5,000 feet) at 16:35 and 16:40, with the wingman bombing at 16:52 also from 5,000 feet. No Egyptian anti-aircraft artillery activity was noted over the target. Bill Katz reported:

> "Fires in Beit Affa and Iraq (El) Suidan. 2 Runs: track 104 degrees. 1st run 6 bombs off (2 delayed) 2 within edge of town; 2 S of center of town; 2 just beyond SE corner of built up area. 2nd run: after hang up on first run tried second run, hung again – jettisoned 17 bombs..."

The wingman B-17 experienced similar difficulties, as Issy Noach reported:

> "Run 100 degrees. 5 hang ups (later jettisoned at sea). Stick run. Main cluster (short stick) in center of town. 3-4 bombs in eastern section of town just across

the wadi. 1 bomb at eastern edge of town. East part of town – just outside built up area appeared to have troop or MT dispersal – unable to identify."

Return to base was accomplished along the Hammers' regular route, with 1601 landing at 17:17 and 1603 following at 17:37.

Mission 36: Faluja
A break from routine was achieved during the Hammers' next mission to Faluja on November 16, 1948. Again flown by a pair of B-17s, the usual afternoon time over target was changed for an early morning visit. The four pilots who flew the previous afternoon mission were on board the two Flying Fortresses the next morning. Katz and Ben-Porat flew 1601 with Harris, Weissbrod, Spicehandler, Ber, Kahn, Meyerson, Bressloff, and Camerman. Noach and Feldman's crew in 1603 was Lazarus, Lichtman, Duboff, Bressloff, Michel, Jackson, Soltan, Nash, Fink, and one airman with an unreadable name. Both bombers took off at 06:01 with a load of 22 70 kg and 28 70 kg bombs respectively.

Flying the usual route from Ramat David to Faluja, the pair bombed from 6,000 feet, with the lead ship flying two bombing runs (at 06:48 and at 06:56), while the trailing ship flew a single bombing run at 06:47. Again there was enemy anti-aircraft artillery fire over Faluja, but the bombers did not report any aircraft activity either, though a pair of 101 Squadron P-51s (pilots Doyle and Peake) was tasked and flew an escort mission with take-off at 06:15. The lead B-17 flew two runs after suffering ten hung up bombs during the first run; all 12 remaining bombs were jettisoned during the second run. Issy Noach reported:

"All bombs away in one stick running in line across southern center of town. First bomb of stick fell short half kilometer west of outskirts. Normal bomb explosions. Last bomb (south eastern edge) caused heavy abnormally dark cloud on explosion."

Improvised bomb load device. Bombing malfunctions were especially frustrating for Hammers airmen geared to attack enemy positions but forced to dump bombs into the Mediterranean Sea.

All three bomb runs were flown from west to east (1601 flew 100 degrees both runs and 1603 flew 104 degrees), so Bill Katz ended his report with a remark to the attention of the Director of Operations, "Bombardier suggest TOT 45 mins after sunrise. Bomb run necessary have calls for going into sun – so suggest waiting till sun is high."

Mission 37: Faluja
The two Hammers returned to harass Faluja on the afternoon of November 16, 1948. Issy Noach in 1603 departed first at 15:40, followed a minute later by his leader, Bill Katz, in 1601; the pair of escorting Spitfires took off at 16:05. Katz flew with Maseng, Harris, Weissbrod, Spicehandler, Kahn, Meyerson, Camerman, Duboff, and Bressloff; the load was 22 70 kg bombs. Noach's crew was Sam Feldman, Tucker as navigator, and Ramat David Air Base Commander Dov Ben-Zvi as "co-nav," Weinstein, Michel, Dinkin, Lichtman, Treisman, Christienson, Wadman, Kaplan, and Robinson; the load was 28 70 kg bombs.

Flying their usual outflank route over the Mediterranean Sea, the bombers were over target from 16:34 until 16:36 and bombed from 6,000 feet. Enemy anti-aircraft fire was reported "nil." Bill Katz reported:

"8 explosions were seen at 12611147 after leaving target, still burning till air/c out of vision. Color of explosion: red. Presumed petrol dump."

Mission 38: Faluja
The November 17, 1948, morning mission to Faluja again involved a pair of Hammers. Bill Katz in 691 departed Ramat David at 05:15 and Issy Noach in 692 followed at 05:17. Katz flew with Maseng, Harris, Weissbrod, Spicehandler, Kahn, Dinkin, Meyerson, Seymour Bressloff, and Kaplan. Noach's crew was Sam Feldman, Boris Bressloff, Michel, Lichtman, Duboff, Soltan, Lazarus, Nash, and Jackson. The innovation in this "routine" mission to Faluja was the bomb load; the leader lifted 42 50 kg fragmentation bombs and the wingman flew with 46 50 kg fragmentation bombs.

The new bomb load posed difficulties for the lead bomber, which did not attack Faluja as planned. Bill Katz reported:

"Bombs were dropped off TA[22]..., at 05:48-05:50, bombs were dropped safe, but 5 seen to explode. The bombs moved out of position in bomb bay, also were loose, making it unsafe to drop armed. Bombardier[23] claims that through incompetent loading crew and a/c were unnecessarily endangered. At present base has no arm officer, bombardier refuses to fly with frag bombs until methods of safety are applied. Safety precautions include delay fuse, making bombs safe till clear of a/c."

Arriving over Faluja alone – no fighter escort – at 05:58, Noach and Feldman bombed from 5,500 feet as planned. Noach

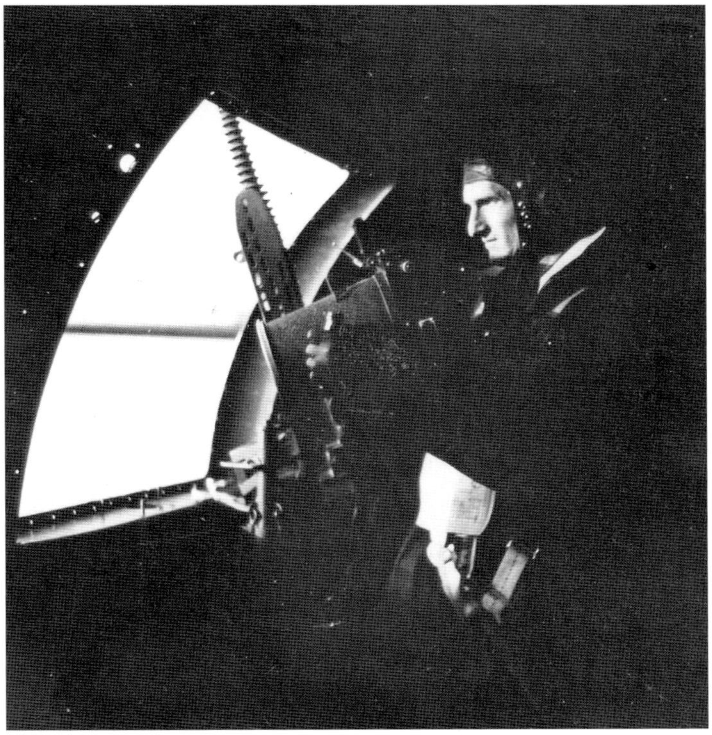

Airman holding a camera in the waist gunner position of a B-17 armed with BESA machine gun.

also reported troubles with bombs, as well as conveying a message from bombardier Tim Michel, "Bombardier refuses to fly in the ship until Plexiglas is cleaned!!!!!!"

Mission 39: Iraq El Manshiya

Perhaps to restore faith of the crew that jettisoned bombs the previous day, Hammer 691 departed Ramat David at 05:30 on the morning of November 18, 1948, to bomb Iraq El Manshiya, an Arab town within the confinement of the Faluja Pocket, midway between Faluja and Hebron. The crew was Katz, Maseng, Harris, Weissbrod, Spicehandler, Ber, Kahn, Meyerson, Bressloff, and Lowenberg; all except Ber and Lowenberg flew the previous day's "dumping bombs" mission. The load was 42 45 kg armor piercing bombs ("6 bombs per station on internal 7 stations").

Flying the usual route via the Mediterranean Sea, the Hammer arrived over Iraq El Manshiya at 06:13 and bombed from 7,000 feet. Bombs fell "southern side of town," with four overshoots noticed, including two bombs that fell safe and did not explode due to "lack of arming wires."

Air Gunners' Refreshment

Hammers' cadre of airmen was a mixed bag of volunteers, mostly Jewish, mostly World War II veterans, and mostly former U.S. and Commonwealth service persons. Volunteers stated their qualifications and these were verified, if possible, during an interview. Obviously even a truly qualified World War II veteran was hardly expected to be up to the standard of his past glory days by 1948. They were all rusty – at least initially – while in some cases the IAF HQ questioned the sincerity of stated qualifications. However, volunteering was a supreme virtue during the Israeli War for Independence. In a nation struggling for survival, dealing harshly with volunteers risking their lives about the supposed accuracy of their stated qualifications was obviously petty. Yet along the war's time line and as Israel, IDF, and IAF institutions became more and more established, the questions of qualifications and competence were raised.

As early as November 21, 1948, the IAF HQ Aircrew Pool asked for a list of 69 Squadron pilots and a record of their flight experience. The Hammers' reply from November 29, 1948, listed seven pilots:

- Albert Raisin – total flying hours 1,800, including 1,200 hours B-17 (1,000 as first pilot), 50 hours B-24 (25 as first pilot), and 50 hours B-29 (25 as first pilot).
- William Katz – total flying hours 2,000, including 1,500 hours B-17 (1,300 as first pilot).
- Pinchas Ben-Porat – total flying hours 800, including 35 hours B-17.

Air Gunner Joe Lazarus

- Samuel Feldman – total flying hours 1,100, including 400 hours B-17, 400 hours B-24, and six hours B-25.
- Jack Ratushniak – total flying hours 1,300, including 25 hours B-17, 140 hours B-24, 170 hours B-26, 100 hours Baltimore, 300 hours Beaufighter, 80 hours Warwick, and 100 hours Wellington.
- Isidore Noach.

A unique Hammers qualification was air gunners. There were air gunners from Britain, Canada, Denmark, Israel, South Africa, and the USA. 69 Squadron Gunnery Officer George Meyerson reported:

> "It became apparent to me soon after my arrival in this country that men were being classified as A/Gs who were not entitled to this claim. Moreover, the men who were qualified A/Gs had long forgotten the practical and theoretical knowledge which they once possessed.
>
> At first I took no action to rectify these matters, firstly because I felt I had not the authority to query another man's word as to his Gunnery status in other Air Forces, and secondly it appeared to me that any man who was prepared to give his life for this cause deserved to have at least his word respected.
>
> But by early December 1948, 69 Squadron Commander Al Raisin was compelled to hand over the air gunners' qualification issue to George Meyerson, and the latter (aided by former RAF instructor Jack Gershaw and 69 Squadron Armament Officer Irving Aronson) prepared an initial examination paper that 'was welcomed by some members of the Squadron and deplored by others, but the result of the examination, practical and theoretical, showed immediately that a Refresher Course for the whole squadron was essential.'"

All leaves were cancelled, and the air gunners' Refresher Course got underway. Subjects covered were: Browning 0.303 and 0.3 (inch) and BESA; Deflection – Zone system of Sighting and Allowances; Rules of Aiming; Curve Pursuit Attacks; Range estimation; Group Classification; Key Ranges; Bullet Group; Bullet Pattern; Bullet Trail; Gravity Drop; Harmonization; General Sighting; Evasive Action for the Squadron; Coordination of the crews; and General Information required for Air Crew. Two subjects not covered due to lack of facilities were Aircraft Recognition and Air Gunnery Practice. George Meyerson reported on January 10, 1949:

> "At the conclusion of these lectures I set a final examination paper, of a higher standard, and judged the practice section of the Browning, BESA, and the theory paper with more strictness.
>
> I was satisfied with the results, except in a few cases, who had individually created their own reasons for not giving me their fullest cooperation. In making my final decision in regard to these few individuals I took into account my experience with gunners and treated them fairly and with understanding.
>
> Until now, all the decisions I took which presented their difficulties at the time have been rewarded, due to the fact that those men who made my task a difficult one came round to seeing my point of view, and thus a more efficient standard than had previously existed has been built up."

Winter Offensive

Israel launched the final major offensive of the Israeli War for Independence on December 22, 1948. The objective of Operation Horev (Mt Sinai) was to defeat the Egyptian expeditionary force; the IDF plan covered a diversion attack northeast of the Gaza Strip and a main effort offensive in Sinai, south of the Gaza Strip, that was planned to cut off the Egyptian expeditionary force. Detailed planning of air support was prepared for the first two days of the offensive. 69 Squadron was tasked to bomb El Arish air base in

69 Squadron Commander Al Raisin flew in the lead of the opening Operation Horev air support mission in B-17 1603, which was at the time still referred to as "693." The target of the Hammer's first mission during Operation Horev was El Arish air base in northeast Sinai, the hub of Egyptian air activity over the front.

northeast Sinai during the afternoon of Day 1, the morning of Day 2, and the afternoon of Day 2. Air support from Day 3 onwards was to be planned in line with the offensive's actual progress.

Mission 40: El Arish

The Hammers launched the IAF air support effort for Operation Horev when 1603 (still reported as "693") departed Ramat David at 14:50 with Raisin, Noach, Harris, Cuburnek, Goldstein, Lichtman, Aronson, Meyerson, Duboff, Gershaw, and air photographer Jaffe; the load was two 250 kg bombs and 30 100 lb bombs. Eight minutes later 1602 took off with Sam Feldman, Ratushniak, Jacobs, Michel, Soltan, Fink, Lowenberg, Lazarus, Nash, and Jackson; their load was 30 100 lb bombs.

The bombers flew their usual outflank route to the Egyptians over the Mediterranean Sea. Fighter escort was provided by two Spitfires (pilots Weizman and Wilson) that took off from Hatzor at 15:20. The Hammers cruised at and bombed from 15,000 feet and 16,000 feet respectively, one after the other; the leader was over El Arish from 16:04 to 16:06, and the wingman from 16:06 to 16:07. The lead bomber reported that Egyptian anti-aircraft artillery was heavy but inaccurate; the wingman reported "1 Dakota seen on field west of intersection of runways (color light brown)." Lead bombardier Cuburnek reported "The 500 lb bombs struck south of intersection of runways. The string of 100 lb hit across runways and edge of encampment north of intersection towards center." Feldman opened his report with "stick fell bang on target" and ended with a framed capital letters statement:

> "Crew COMPLAINS INSUFFICIENT WARM CLOTHING. ADEQUATE GLOVES SOCKS & BOOTS MUST BE OBTAINED. Crew'S FINGERS SOREIY AFFECTED. SILK & CHAMOIS GLOVES NEEDED."

Mission 41: Khan Yunes

Bad winter weather grounded IAF air support operations on Day 2 of the offensive, and the two Hammers missions to El Arish were not flown as planned. Operation Horev air support missions resumed on the morning of Day 3; two Hammers departed Ramat David at 09:30 and 09:31 to bomb Khan Yunes. Bill Katz flew the lead B-17 with Ben-Porat, Boris Bressloff, Weissbrod, Ber, Max Cohen, Jacobson, Swiel, Spicehandler, and Kahn. John McConville flew wingman with Maseng, Weinstein, Seftel, Robinson, Liponetzky, Wadman, J Cohen, Swartzberg, and Jaffe. The load was 15 "100-50" and 20 "A50.15" bombs; 16 100 lb and 16 fragmentation bombs respectively. Two Spitfires (pilots Doyle and Feldman) that took off at 10:05 flew fighter escort.

The bombers flew via the Mediterranean Sea at 13,000 feet and were over Khan Yunes from 10:38; heavy but inaccurate anti-aircraft fire coming from Rafah was noted. Clouds disrupted bombing, with wingman bombing and leader returning for a second run over Khan Yunes but suffering 30 bombs hung up. The lead ship therefore tried to jettison bombs over Gaza but none dropped, so the armorer released two bombs "by hand" and the rest were jettisoned over sea.

B-17 1601 at Ramat David with bombs attached to the external bomb racks and 33 or 35 mission markings painted on the nose. Hammer Number 1 most likely flew its 35th mission during the early stages of Operation Horev in December 1948.

Confusingly, both Debriefing Report documents for the December 24, 1948, mission to Khan Yunes stated that 1602 was the bomber flown by Katz as well as by McConville. However, a weak pen may have changed "1602" to "1603" in McConville's Debriefing Report, so it is highly likely that 1602 was the bomber that had to jettison bombs over the Mediterranean Sea. In this image 1602 was photographed over the Mediterranean Sea with open bomb bay doors.

Mission 42: Gaza

Two Hammers returned to the Gaza Strip on the afternoon of December 24, 1948, to harass the center of Egyptian administration and command, as well as in line with the ongoing effort to divert Egyptian attention from the IDF's main effort. The bombers flew and bombed one after the other with no fighter escort. Sam Feldman departed Ramat David at 15:22 with Ratushniak, Jacobs, Michel, Fink, Lowenberg, Soltan, Lazarus, Jackson, Nash, and air photographer Yale Joffe; the load was 28 D70 bombs. Al Raisin followed at 15:45 with Noach, Harris, Cuburnek, Goldstein, Aronson, Duboff, Meyerson, Gershaw, and Lichtman; their load was 14 D70 bombs.

The first B-17 was over Gaza from 16:04 until 16:05. Bombing from 15,500 feet, the crew reported inaccurate anti-aircraft fire, cloudy sky, and bad visibility. Raisin's B-17 1601 was over Gaza from 16:21 until 16:23 and bombed from 13,000 feet. Weather was reported as "good," and visibility over target was reported "good," while enemy anti-aircraft artillery was "accurate" and "appeared to follow us, looking like radar controlled." Raisin summed up "Raid was a success."

Mission 43: El Arish

The Hammers again flew as a trio on the December 25, 1948, morning mission to El Arish. Al Raisin departed Ramat David in 1601 at 10:11 with pilot Shiftman, navigator Harris, bombardier Cuburnek, engineer Lichtman, radio operator Goldstein, armorer Aronson, and gunners Meyerson, Gershaw, and Duboff; load was 26 D70 bombs. John McConville followed a minute later in 1603 with pilot Noach, navigator Seftel, bombardier Weinstein, flight engineer Max Cohen, radio operator Swartzberg, armorer Kahn, and gunners Robinson, Cohen, and Liponetzky; load was 25 D70 bombs. Third and final to take off was Sam Feldman in 1602, which departed Ramat David at 10:20 with pilot Ratushniak, navigator Jacobs, bombardier Michel, engineer Fink, radio man Lowenberg, armorer Soltan, and gunners Nash, Jacobson, and Lazarus; load was 26 D70 bombs. A Spitfire (pilot Syd Cohen) and a P-51 (pilot Boris Senior) that took off at 10:35 were tasked to escort the bombers.

John McConville and crew in 1602 – photographed in flight - aborted their attack on Rafah during the afternoon of December 25, 1948, and jettisoned the bomb load to sea after reporting enemy aircraft, while intercepted radio chatter in English may point out that these were British fighters on a visual reconnaissance mission over the front.

The trio was over El Arish from 11:25 to 11:28 and bombed from 15,500 feet. Anti-aircraft artillery was "fairly accurate," and Feldman reported "kite has 1 hole near right waist ¾" in diameter." Raisin's debrief concluded "All bombs went. Bombs fell in a East-West direction bang across intersection of runways. Bomb hitting both runways and intersection of runways. Perfect bombing."

Mission 44: Rafah

Second mission on December 25, 1948, was again flown in 3-ship formation. Al Raisin departed Ramat David in 1601 at 16:00 with Shiftman, Harris, Cuburnek, Lichtman, Goldstein, Aronson,

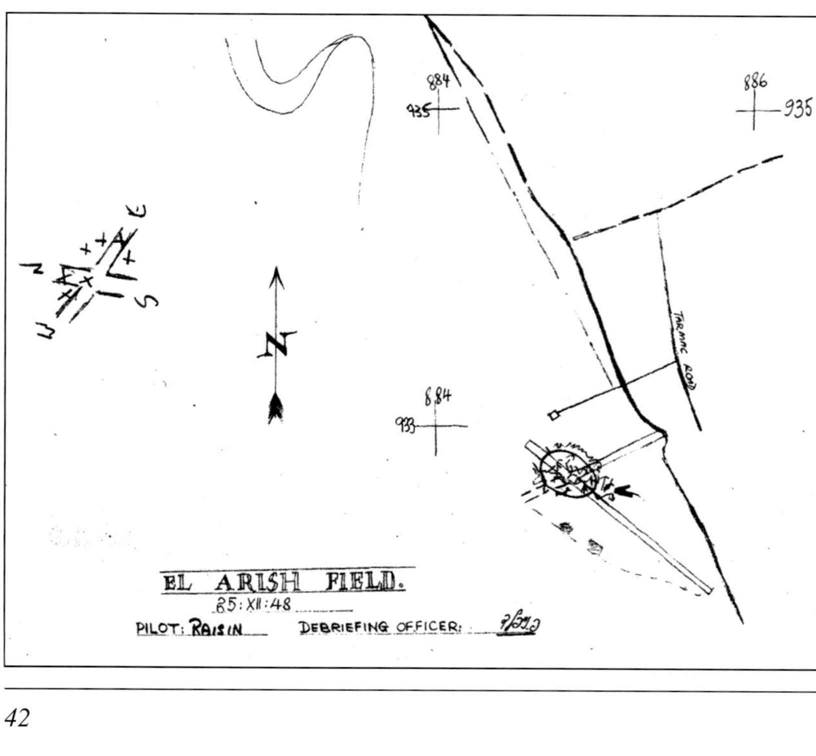

Al Raisin's debrief drawing of the "perfect bombing" of El Arish air base on December 25, 1948.

Hans Weissbrod in the bombardier station of a Hammers B-17; RAF service person from 1940 until 1946, the German born navigator-bombardier saw action with SAAF 34 Squadron, which flew Wellington bombers from Italy. Weissbrod was one of the few "native Israelis" to serve as Hammer airmen right from the very first mission on July 15, 1948, until the Hammers' final Israeli War for Independence mission on January 7, 1949, for a personal total of 42 missions. Weissbrod was lead bombardier on the December 26, 1948, morning mission to El Arish; a mission that generated concerns, as though bombing El Arish was a waste of effort since the Egyptians had redeployed their aircraft elsewhere in Sinai.

Meyerson, Duboff, Gershaw, and air photographer Joffe; load was 30 100 lb bombs. A minute later John McConville took off in 16:02 with Noach, Seftel, Weinstein, Cohen, Soltan, Swartzberg, Liponetzky, Robinson, and Cohen; load was 30 100 lb bombs. Bill Katz followed at 16:02 in 1603 with Ben-Porat, Bressloff, Weissbrod, Kahn, Spicehandler, Jackson, Swiel, Ber, and IAF staff officer Dan Tolkowsky as observer; load was 27 100 lb bombs.

The Hammers flew a single bomb run at 14,500 feet (except for Katz, who flew at 14,000 feet) from 16:54 to 16:55. Egyptian anti-aircraft artillery was described as heavy, accurate, thick, and plenty. Bombing of 1601 and 1603 was reportedly successful, but 1602 broke off the attack and jettisoned bombs over the Mediterranean Sea (northwest of Tel Aviv) after the tail gunner saw "2 a/c west of Gaza over sea" and the waist gunner saw "1 a/c at same place." McConville reported "Fighters made pass so plane took evasive action out to sea." None of the other airmen on board 1601 and 1603 saw enemy aircraft, while not a single Israeli fighter was airborne at the time of the Hammers raid, but the crew of 1603 reported hearing radio chatter – in English – "Jack 1 calling Jack 2" and "Hearing you 1 by 1."[24]

The crews, however, devoted most of the space in the debriefing reports to criticize blackout over Israel. Raisin remarked "Blackout (Israel) poor," while Harris added "KFAR YEHOSHUA is presumed to be celebrating Xmas with Chanuka lights. This Kibbutz[25] is ½ mile from west end of 270 runway.[26]" Cuburnek was not less colorful in his statement "Tel Aviv and Haifa lit up like the Mardi Gras."

Mission 45: El Arish

The morning mission on December 26, 1948, returned the Hammers to El Arish. Bill Katz, in 1603, departed Ramat David at 06:27 with Ben-Porat, Bressloff, Weissbrod, Kahn, Ber, Spicehandler, Swiel, and Jacobson; load was 36 100 lb "frags." Sam Feldman followed in 1602 at 06:30 with Ratushniak, Jacobs, Michel, Lowenberg, Fink, Soltan, Nash, Jackson, Lazarus, and Joffe; load was "30 fragmentation (A50-15)" bombs. Fighter escort was again a mixed pair of a Spitfire (Cohen) and P-51 (Weizman) that took off at 06:49 and 06:39 respectively.

Time over target was from 07:41, and bombing altitude was 15,000 feet. Anti-aircraft artillery over El Arish was reportedly heavy but inaccurate. Feldman's crew stated in the debriefing report "Crew observed no enemy aircraft on field or revetments. Field appears deserted but for AA." The debriefing officer added at the bottom of the Katz's crew debrief report form, "It is my opinion that, keeping in mind recent debriefings, the field is used as a decoy for our bombs."

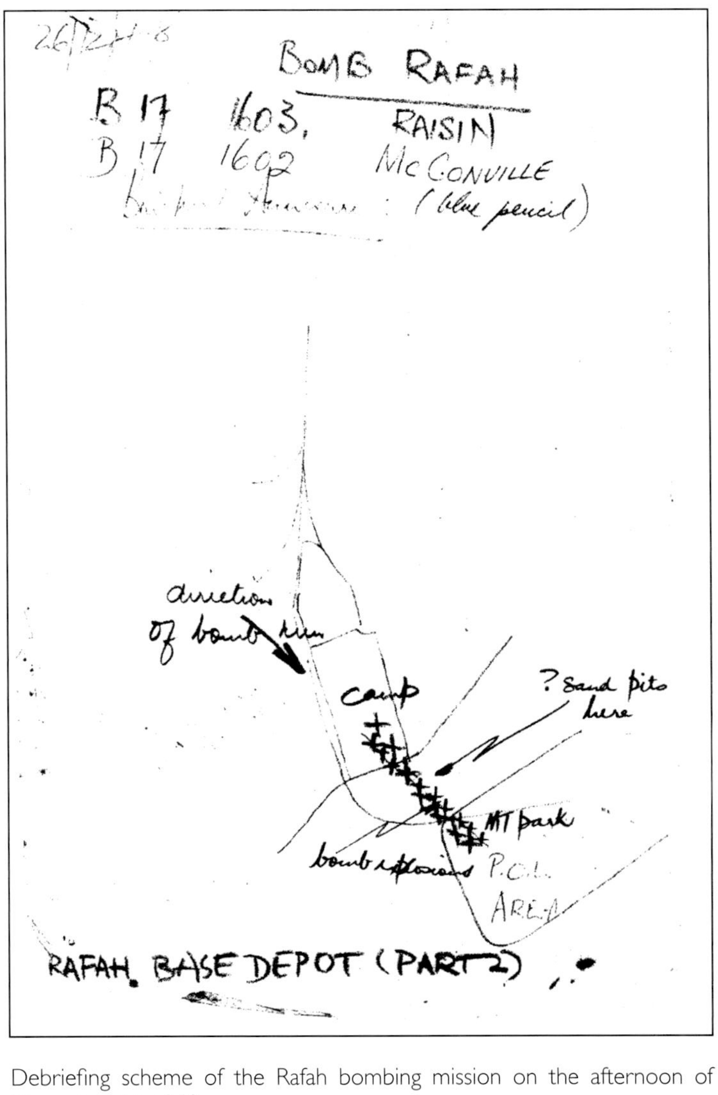

Debriefing scheme of the Rafah bombing mission on the afternoon of December 26, 1948.

Mission 46: Rafah

The afternoon mission on December 26, 1948, completed a repeat of the December 25, 1948, missions, as on both days the Hammers raided El Arish in the morning and bombed Rafah during the afternoon. Al Raisin departed Ramat David in 1603 at 15:25 with Ratushniak, Harris, Cuburnek, Lichtman, Duboff, Aronson, Kaplan, Meyerson, Gershaw, and Joffe; load was 29 D70 bombs. John McConville followed a minute later in 1602 with Noach, Seftel, Weinstein, Christienson, Swartzberg, Kahn, Max Cohen, Robinson, J Cohen, Liponetzky, and Lazarus; their load was 28 70 kg bombs.

Flying without escort along the coastline, the two Hammers bombed from 16:16 flying at 16,000 feet. Nothing exceptional was reported regarding Egyptian anti-aircraft artillery, but the wingman reported "unidentified a/c (fighter type)" over "same place (Gaza) where planes seen yesterday." Bombing was not considered a success. Lead bombardier Cuburnek reported "All bombs considerably overshot," while wingman navigator Seftel added "Raid not a great success. Missed given target. Believe that some damage done to some dumps." The briefings' punch line this time was the product of wingman armorer Christienson, "4 wires broken on dropping bombs. Rotten wires."

Mission 47: Faluja

Awful desert winter weather continued to disrupt IAF offensive operations, and the Hammers only returned to bomb at noon on December 28, 1948, after an operational break of more than 40 hours. Weather was still not good, but a critical situation prompted a raid on the Faluja pocket. Earlier on December 28, 1948, the IDF launched Operation Elimination, an offensive against the Egyptian brigade under blockade in the Faluja Pocket. The IDF offensive was a disaster. Decisive Egyptian counterattack divided the IDF attackers, and the latter were soon in full retreat; the IDF suffered 91 dead and five prisoners of war in one of the worst offensive battle failures in its entire history. Looking for assets to harass Faluja, the IDF turned to the IAF, which ordered the three B-17s to attack. Al Raisin, in 1601, departed Ramat David at 12:11 with Ben-Porat, Harris, Cuburnek, Lichtman, Goldstein, Aronson, Meyerson, Gershaw, Duboff, and Kaplan; their load was 38 50 kg bombs. Second to take-off, one minute later, was Issy Noach in 1603 with Maseng, Weissbrod, Bressloff, Kahn, Spicehandler, Ber, Swiel, and Jacobson; load was 34 50 kg bombs. Sam Feldman took off at 12:14 in 1602 with Ratushniak, Jacobs, Michel, Fink, Lowenberg, Soltan, Nash, Jackson, and Lazarus; load on board 1602 was 34 "anti-personnel" bombs. Fighter escort was a mixed pair of a P-51 (pilot Goodlin took off at 12:35) and a Spitfire (pilot Seymour Feldman took off at 12:45).

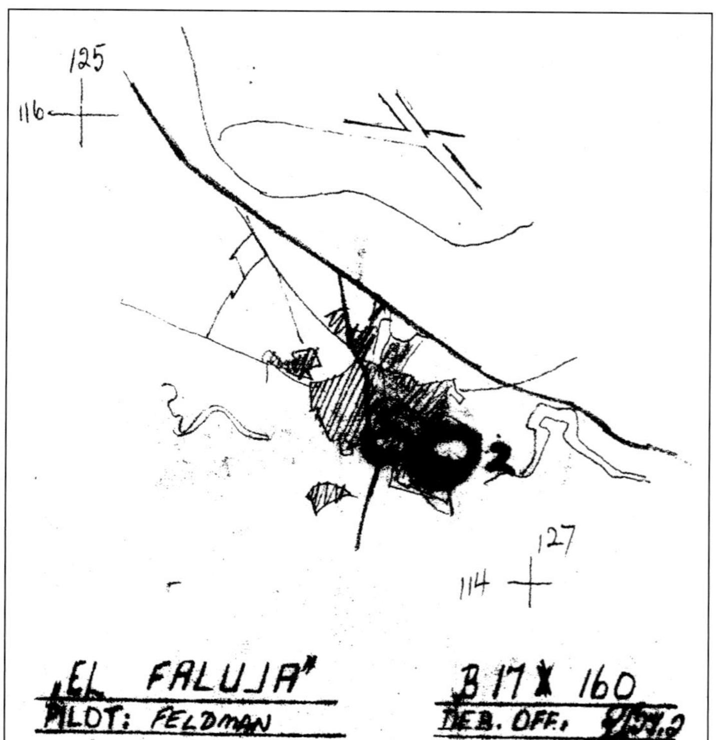

Sam Feldman's crew added this scheme to their debrief report, showing hits during the first bombing run over Faluja on the noon mission of December 28, 1948 (smaller circle numbered "1" at the south section of town) and second run hits (larger circle numbered "2" over the southeast section of town). Faluja airfield has been loosely sketched across the road to the north of town.

The trio flew two bombing runs from 12:55 until 13:10. Clouds disrupted bombing and observation as the B-17s cruised at 10,000 feet. The lead ship dropped six bombs during the first run; two more bombs "lying loose in bomb bay were jettisoned off Nebi Yunes into the sea." Noach's crew dropped four bombs during the first run and Feldman's added ten bombs. There was no opposition—no enemy aircraft and no anti-aircraft artillery. All remaining bombs were dropped during the second run, and the raid was considered mostly uneventful yet successful.

Mission 48: Faluja

IDF feared that the successful Egyptian counterattack in the Faluja Pocket would be followed by a breakthrough attempt, and thus triggered acceleration of aerial bombardment of the Egyptian brigade under siege. Two Hammers flew a relatively low altitude, unescorted afternoon mission to Faluja. Issy Noach, in 1603, departed Ramat David at 16:32 with Sam Feldman, Bressloff, Weissbrod, Ber, Spicehandler, Kahn, Swiel, and Jacobson; load was 37 "A50.15" bombs. John McConville followed two minutes later in 1602 with Spink, Seftel, Weinstein, Max Cohen, Christienson, Swartzberg, Robinson, Liponetzky, Kaplan, J Cohen, and air photographer Joffe; load was 38 "A50/15" bombs.

The B-17s flew their usual route to the front over the Mediterranean Sea, but cruised lower than usual at 4,000 feet. Egyptian anti-aircraft artillery over Faluja was relatively light. The first bomber was over target from 17:03 until 17:04, the second from 17:15 until 17:16. The former bombed from 4,500 feet and the latter from 4,000 feet. The crew of 1603 reported four hang ups and nine duds; as it was too dark for a second run the four hang ups were jettisoned over the sea on the way back to Ramat David. The debrief report of 1603 was concluded "Crew complains very bad blackout at KFAR JOSHUA. Correction: NO BLACKOUT."

Technical reliability also affected 1602, as the crew reported "Bombs overshot slightly due to some failure in electrical release

Hammer 1602 flew two missions to Faluja on December 28, 1948. Sam Feldman piloted 1602 on both missions, in the first with copilot Jack Ratushniak and in the second as copilot to Issy Noach.

Air gunner Wilfred Jackson flew 25 missions in 69 Squadron service, many of these with fellow gunners Joe Lazarus and Stanley Nash. Jackson was wounded over Rafah on December 29, 1948, when Egyptian anti-aircraft artillery damaged B-17 1602. This view captured Wilfred Jackson (sitting on stairway), Joe Lazarus (in white shirt), and Tim Michel (with binoculars) in the Hammers' austere living quarters.

circuit. 18 bombs fell safe due to f… poor arming wires. This is a standard complaint!!!"

Mission 49: Rafah

The trio of bombers returned to Rafah on the December 29, 1948, morning mission. Al Raisin departed Ramat David in 1601 at 07:30 with Ben-Porat, Harris, Cuburnek, Lichtman, Goldstein, Aronson, Meyerson, Duboff, and Gershaw; load was two 250 kg and 22 50 kg bombs. Also taking off at 07:30 was Sam Feldman in 1602 with Ratushniak, Jacobs, Michel, Lowenberg, Soltan, Fink, Lazarus, Nash, and Jackson; their load was two 250 kg and 28 50 kg bombs. Departing 13 minutes later was John McConville in 1603 with Spink, Seftel, Weinstein, Max Cohen, Christienson, Swartzberg, Robinson, Kaplan, Liponetzky, and air photographer Kapusa; load was two 250 kg and 22 50 kg bombs. A P-51 that took off at 07:45 (pilot Dangott) and a Spitfire (pilot Goodling) that followed at 07:50 were the fighter escort.

The Hammers bombed from 15,500 feet in the face of heavy accurate Egyptian anti-aircraft fire. Raisin bombed Rafah camp, while Feldman first flew a dummy run over Khan Yunes before flying a bomb run over Rafah. Only half the bombs on board 1602 were dropped, as the crew reported "whole side of bomb bay hung up." The half that dropped overshot Rafah and the Egyptian anti-aircraft artillery damaged 1602; waist gunner Jackson was wounded. Hammer 1603 was also damaged (a small hole in the tail), while four of the bombs fell safe.

Mission 50: El Arish

The Hammers' 50th mission[27] during the Israeli War for Independence was the December 29, 1948, afternoon bombing of El Arish. Despite anti-aircraft artillery damage suffered by two of the bombers during the same day's morning mission all three Hammers were airborne again that afternoon. El Arish was the principle Egyptian war zone air base from May 1948, and Egyptian fighters were indeed active over the frontline during Operation Horev. By then, however, El Arish was no longer the center of Egyptian air operations over the front, as already speculated in the debrief of the Hammers' December 26, 1948, mission to El Arish. Nevertheless, the IAF continued to hammer El Arish.

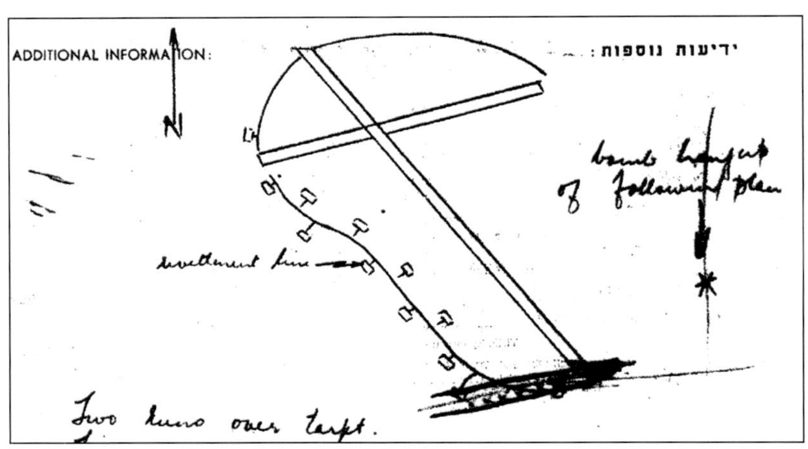

The Hammers bombed El Arish on December 29, 1948, despite bad weather thanks to superb navigation of lead navigator John Harris. The bombing pattern scheme, from Raisin crew debrief, reveals hits along the southern part of the air base. The dot next to the bombing pattern is marked "bomb hang up of following plane," but Feldman reported "no hang ups" and Noach stated "6 overshoots." Feldman's tail gunner Joe Lazarus reported "no kites in revetments."

Al Raisin departed Ramat David in 1601 at 15:10 with Ben-Porat, Harris, Cuburnek, Lichtman, Aronson, Goldstein, Gershaw, Joe Cohen, and Duboff; load was 30 "100 U.S. (M30)" bombs. George Meyerson also appeared on the list of Raisin's crew as well as in the list of 1602 crew; it is likely that he actually flew in the latter B-17, replacing Wilfred Jackson, who was injured during the morning mission. Sam Feldman, in 1602, also took off at 15:10 with co-pilot Ratushniak, navigator Jacobs, bombardier Michel, radio operator Lowenberg, armorer Soltan, flight engineer Fink, waist gunner Nash, waist gunner Meyerson, tail gunner Lazarus, and air photographer Jaffe; load was 26 100 lb demolition bombs. Third to take-off, at 15:16, was Issy Noach in 1603, with Maseng, Bressloff, Weissbrod, Ber, Kahn, Majzels, Spicehandler, Swiel, and Jacobson; their load was 26 "A50/50" and four "A50/15" bombs. Two Spitfires that took off at 15:25 (pilots Syd Cohen and Wilson) escorted the B-17s.

The lead bomber was over target from 16:12 until 16:35, with the two wingmen joining at 16:35. Raisin's crew description of anti-aircraft artillery was "few bursts, medium and heavy, very inaccurate." Cloudy weather was the problem, and the leader flew two bombing runs: during the first the "whole area completely covered, no bombs dropped," but then the trio returned at 15,000 feet for a live bombing run. The crew of 1603 stated "Target found due to SUPERB navigation by lead nav" John Harris.

Crude Hammers living conditions are apparent in this view; standing from left to right: Trig Maseng and Coleman Goldstein; sitting from left to right: Maurice Kellman, Harry Dinkin, and Moshe Citrinbaum, who later changed his name to Moshe Hadari and was 69 Squadron Chief Technical Officer in 1950.

Mission 51: El Arish → Faluja

Poor weather continued to hamper full scale unrestricted IAF air operations. Perhaps previous reports that El Arish was no longer the hub of Egyptian frontline air activity sunk in, as the target of the Hammers' December 31, 1948, mission was El Arish in general, but more specifically the local marshalling yards and not the northeast Sinai air base. Al Raisin, in 1601, departed Ramat David at 11:30 with pilot Coleman Goldstein, navigator Harris, bombardier Cuburnek, engineer Lichtman, radio operator Goldstein, armorer Aronson, and gunners Meyerson, Duboff, Gershaw, and Hill; load was 16 100 kg bombs. Issy Noach followed two minutes later in 1603 with Maseng, Bressloff, Weissbrod, Ber, Kahn, Majzels, Spicehandler, Swiel, and Jacobson; load was 24 "A100-50" bombs. A minute afterwards John McConville departed in 1602 with Spink, Seftel, Weinstein, Max Cohen, Swartzberg, Christienson, J Cohen, Robinson, Kaplan, and Liponetzky; their load was also 16

B-17 1602 returned to Ramat David with bombs on December 31, 1948, after flying to El Arish and attempting to bomb Faluja. Bomb hang ups were common during Hammers missions, but B-17 airmen mostly managed to jettison the objector weapons prior to return to base.

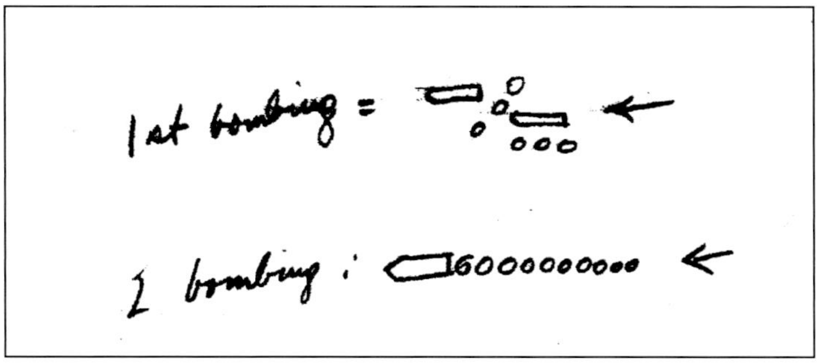

A scheme of the two bombing runs that B-17 1602 made against Egyptian warships on the morning of January 1, 1949, indicates several near misses. The naval observers remarked "Cooperation of B17 crew excellent."

100 kg bombs. Fighter escort took off at 1154 in the shape of two Spitfires flown by Goodlin and Dangott.

El Arish was completely covered with cloud layer from 6,000 feet to 7,000 feet, and the Hammers could not bomb. Rafah was the alternative target, but it was also covered with clouds. Raisin's crew complained "no adequate code system exists to ask for alternate target." Marginally better weather over Faluja enabled the B-17s to bomb, but the bombs of 1602 did not drop. McConville reported "at Faluja had 100% hang up. Electrical circuit – cause. Bombs brought back to base, unable to jettison. Suggest weather flight made by single-engined A/C ½ hr before take-off."

Mission 52: Mediterranean Sea

Having celebrated New Year's on the night of December 31, 1948, to January 1, 1949, the Hammers were put on standby for a maritime search and attack mission at 04:00 on the morning of January 1, 1949, as Egyptian ships shelled Tel Aviv. Crew No. 1 was scheduled to take off at 06:00, but 1603 was not ready and the crew had to switch to 1602, whose reported time of departure was 07:50. Al Raisin was in command, with pilot Coleman Goldstein, navigator Harris, bombardier Cuburnek, flight engineer Lichtman, radio operator Jack Goldstein, armorer Kahn, and gunners Meyerson, Duboff, Lazarus, and Hill, plus two navy observers to identify ships as well as to code/decode naval messages. Load was 16 100 kg bombs.

Nine flying minutes from Hertzeliya on the briefed course the Hammers saw two ships that opened fire at the bomber. Raisin climbed from 3,000 to 10,000 feet as the naval observers tried to contact the Israeli Navy; they were positive that the ships were not Israeli, but were undecided as to the actual type of ship. Simultaneously the crew tried to notify AHQ at Tel Aviv but to no avail. AHQ was to wire bombing orders, so the B-17 circled the ships, which changed heading and sailed west to the open sea. Meanwhile three more ships were spotted; the naval observers explained that these were Israeli Navy ships approaching to intercept the enemy. The Hammers crew tried to contact the Israeli ships in order to coordinate the attack but again without success; AHQ did not respond either.

The naval observers reported that the Egyptian ships were "1 corvette or minesweeper, 1 merchant ship (armed) of considerable speed and good gunnery." As the two naval forces engaged each other the B-17 flew four bombing runs at 10,000 feet. Bombs were dropped on two of the runs, and although these did not seem to cause any damage, Raisin reported:

> "Thus the enemy fire was directed into two areas, greatly reducing his maximum concentration of fire power... As we finished our last bomb run and dropped our last bombs at an altitude of 12,000 ft the enemy disengaged from the battle and headed, like a shot out of hell, toward Port Said. Still without instruction from Tel Aviv we continued to follow and attempted by false passes to divert his attempt. After 3 hours and 15 minutes over the target and frantic radioing for instructions and assistance, constantly reporting back the exact enemy position, we finally received word to return to base."

Apparently this mission surfaced in Hammers' memories from many previous ill conceived operations. So much that 69 Squadron Commander Al Raisin – usually not a man of words and mostly responsible for stenograph reports, if any at all – prepared an exceptionally long and detailed report of that mission on January 3, 1949. Raisin summed up his report with six major deficiencies from which lessons had to be drawn:

> "It seems to the Crew that there were many glaring errors in judgement by the planners of this operation.
>
> 1st. There should have been no reason why the H.Q. that we were contacting should not have had the Naval Code that we were using.

The Hammers Crew Number 1 flew B-17 1602 on the maritime search and attack mission on January 1, 1949. 69 Squadron Lead Navigator John Harris recalled: "Just about new years day we had a party, and we got a message that we had to fly to intercept the ships and bomb them from medium altitude. We tried and Jules the bombardier got very close. Then our fighters thought we were an Egyptian airplane so they came right behind us but they didn't shoot."

2nd. Though one Mustang[28] did arrive and stayed there for a maximum of 2 minutes and then vanished, it was a pity that no support should have arrived to continue the attack upon the enemy. We kept calling for Helen (P-51) and for Mickey (Spits.) and for Ginger (B-17), but none arrived. The Beaufighter would have been a tremendous help, especially with us above and the Navy on the sea diverting the attention of the enemy.

3rd. This is the second time that we have called for bombing instructions (once previously for Faluja) that a complete lack of coordination has resulted.

4th. Though the Bombardier considers that the A 100-50 is an excellent G.P. Bomb, a much heavier bomb, such as the A-250-50 or the 500 Kilo bomb, should have been used on this operation, and one of the near misses would surely have caused considerable damage.

5th. It is pitiful that whenever we have attempted to contact our fighters and our Navy as briefed we cannot do this for the apparent reason that our briefed frequencies are not guarded by them.

6th. Our Radio Operator challenged the message that we received about returning to base. He was told to stand by. Then he received a message in Q.Code from Headquarters stating that they could not understand his message. A challenge from us to Headquarters should bring out an immediate response. Our Radio Operator then had to resend his challenge message, and at the end of this message he added clearly the word CHALLENGE. Then, after another 5 minutes delay, our challenge was answered by the correct code and we proceeded back to base."

Sam Feldman (center) was photographed at Ramat David on January 1, 1949, as he greeted the new year in good spirit with South African 103 Squadron radio operators Phil Kemp (left) and Milton Bottger (right); the latter called himself in Israel "Butch Ben-Yok" and was a Hammers airman postwar. Feldman flew in the lead of the Hammers the next day and succeeded Al Raisin as 69 Squadron Commander later that month.

Mission 53: El Arish

Sam Feldman flew his first mission as Hammers leader on the morning of January 2, 1949; the target was El Arish marshalling yards. Feldman, who until then mostly piloted 1602, flew the Hammers lead ship 1601, which departed Ramat David at 08:50 with Ratushniak, Jacobs, Weissbrod, Fink, Soltan, Lowenberg, Lazarus, Gershaw, and Nash. John McConville followed five minutes later in 1602 with Spink, Seftel, Weinstein, Max Cohen, Swartzberg, Christienson, Kaplan, Robinson, Liponetzky, J Cohen, and air photographer Joffe. Two more minutes followed until 1603 took off with Noach, Maseng, Bressloff, Michel, Swiel, Majzels, Wadman, Spicehandler, and Jacobson. Each of the bombers lifted 16 100 kg bombs. Their fighter escort was a pair of Spitfires (Wilson and Goodlin) that took off at 09:20.

The Hammers were over target from 10:00 until 10:01 (1601 and 1602) and from 10:01 until 10:02 (1603), flying at 13,500 feet. Anti-aircraft fire was reportedly active but inaccurate, yet so was the bombing. Sam Feldman reported "Missed target, hit sea. Drop started 100 yds from coast, did not reach land at all."

Mission 54: El Arish

After the January 2, 1949, morning mission to El Arish marshalling yards failed, as bombs missed the target and fell into sea, the three Hammers returned to the El Arish marshalling yards that same afternoon to finish off their mission. Issy Noach departed Ramat David in 1603 at 14:55 with Maseng, Jacobs, Michel, Majzels, Swiel, Kahn, Spicehandler, and Jacobson. Mission leader Sam Feldman followed two minutes later in 1601 with Ratushniak, Bressloff, Weissbrod, Soltan, Lowenberg, Fink, Lazarus, Nash, and Wadman. Also taking off at 14:57 was John McConville in 1602 with Spink, Seftel, Weinstein, Christienson, Max Cohen, J

B-17 1601 was not only "Hammer # 1," but was also lead ship on most of the 69 Squadron missions during the Israeli War for Independence. For this reason probably Sam Feldman, who previously flew most of his missions in 692/1602, switched to 1601 when flying as Hammers leader on January 2, 1949. The lead bomber arrived in country with two Direction Finding loop antennas in streamlined casings right behind a sword antenna that towered above the cockpit, but after arrival the forward DF antenna was removed.

B-17 1601 (nearest camera) and 1602 (farther away from camera) flew together on the January 3, 1949, morning mission to Rafah; Al Raisin and Sam Feldman were in command of 1601 and 1602 respectively. This image was taken postwar when 1601 was adorned with the Hammers' badge on the nose section, where mission markings were previously painted. The sexual connotation of "69" was boldly addressed with the title SOIXANTE NEUF painted below the badge.

Cohen, Robinson, Kaplan, Liponetzky, and air photographer Leslie Kapusa. The load of all three bombers was 16 100 kg bombs. Escort was again planned to be two Spitfires (McElroy and Sinclair), that indeed took off at 15:26, but did not rendezvous with the bombers; the Hammers still pressed on with their mission.

The trio flew one bombing run from 16:05. Bombing from 12,500 feet, the Hammers improved their accuracy. The trail of bombs fell roughly sixty degrees to the railway line, with some of the bombs falling on the railway line. Tail gunner of the lead ship reported "saw fire started in housing and installations like petrol fire lot of black thick smoke." Issy Noach concluded his report with a gladdening observation "El Arish A/F seemed completely deserted."

Mission 55: Rafah

69 Squadron Commander Al Raisin was again at the helm on the January 3, 1949, morning mission to Rafah. Raisin departed Ramat David in the lead ship (1601) at 09:00 with Ben-Porat, Harris, Cuburnek, Lichtman, Goldstein, Aronson, Meyerson, Duboff, Gershaw, and Gershenson. Sam Feldman returned to fly "his" 1602 and took off at 09:01 with Ratushniak, Bressloff, Weissbrod, Fink, Soltan, Lowenberg, Lazarus, Nash, and Wadman, plus an unnamed air photographer. Both bombers lifted a similar load of 16 100 kg bombs each; their fighter escort was two Spitfires that took off at 09:23 flown by Red Finkel and Seymour Feldman.

The pair flew two bombing runs over Rafah railway station; the first, from 09:52 until 09:56 at 15,500 feet, and the second from 10:03 until 10:07 at 16,500 feet. Weather was good; anti-aircraft artillery was heavy and accurate. During the first bombing run the lead bomber dropped six bombs and the wingman dropped eight bombs. Feldman's crew reported "a building was hit and blew up with great impact, and then black smoke came high up. By the blast presumed to be ammo dump."

The second bomb run aimed at the marshalling yards, but was less successful. Raisin's crew reported "overshoot due to bomb aimer... Bombs overshot marshalling yard. Burst started at north edge of yards and landed amongst four buildings and in tented area. Arming wires are of insufficient strength and improperly rigged." The second B-17 also reported missing the marshalling yards, as well as "Crew recommends hitting target again as well as Khan Yunes. Both places packed with 'goods!'"

Mission 56: Rafah

Feldman's crew recommendation after the morning mission may well have been considered, and the Hammers returned to Rafah on the afternoon of January 3, 1949. Again flying in pair, the leader was Al Raisin, who departed Ramat David in 1601 at 15:00 with

The B-17s were escorted on most of the daytime bombings over the Egyptian front but were never intercepted by Egyptian fighters. 101 Squadron's Spitfires "17" (then piloted by Jack Cohen) and "18" (piloted by Syd Cohen) escorted two B-17s to bomb Rafah on January 3, 1949. This image of the two aforementioned Spitfires flying with Hammer 1602 was most likely taken on April 25, 1949, during fighter affiliation training.

Coleman Goldstein, Harris, Cuburnek, Lichtman, Jack Goldstein, Aronson, Meyerson, Duboff, Gershaw, and Gershenson. Wingman Issy Noach also took off at 15:00 with Maseng, Jacobs, Michel, Kellman, Swiel, Kahn, Spicehandler, Jacobson, and Hill. Load was the by then standard 16 100 kg bombs per bomber, and fighter escort was the usual pair of Spitfires, Syd Cohen and Jack Cohen having taken off at 15:35 and 15:27 respectively.

Raisin was over Rafah from 15:58 until 16:02, and Noach followed from 16:00 to 16:03; weather was hazy, as both aimed at Rafah barracks and bombed from 16,500 feet in the face of inaccurate Egyptian anti-aircraft artillery of medium and heavy caliber. Lead bombardier reported to the debriefing officer:

> "This was a typical 'Cuburnek maneuver.' There was much haze over the target – after 2 mins search, with capable support from the navigator (Harris) we identified the target. I dropped 1 side of bomb bay. Noticing that I was a fraction of an inch left off center of target, I gave the pilot a fast 1 degree right and then dropped the rest of the load. This split second decision made the difference between a good hit and an excellent one – which it was. Nearly all the bombs hit various buildings in target area."

All bombs were released during the single bombing run and "fell in target area," according to lead crew, or "Bull on target area" as reported by the wingman crew. Three single engine aircraft heading south were observed west of Gaza at 1609 and the fighter escort went to intercept them. Raisin's crew also remarked "Crew reports one of the escorting fighters did not have its nose painted red (Mustang).[29] It would be advisable to use uniform nose colour for our fighters to avoid misunderstandings."

Mission 57: Gaza

69 Squadron's final raid on Gaza during the Israeli War for Independence was recorded during the morning hours of January 4, 1949, when a pair of Hammers bombed this Arab city. Sam

Hammers at Ramat David, from left to right: Israeli Hans Weissbrod, British Johnny Harris, American Lem Kaplan, Danish Jorgen Christienson, Paul, South African Zan Swartzberg, and American Max Cohen.

Reportedly a photo of the Rafah bombing mission on January 4, 1949; a total of about 24 bomb explosions can be counted in this image.

Feldman was leading the mission in 1601, which took off at 09:13 along with Ratushniak, Bressloff, Weissbrod, Soltan, Dinkin, Fink, Nash, Lazarus, Wadman, and air photographer Kapusa; load was 40 50 kg bombs. John McConville followed a minute later in 1603 with Spink, Weinstein, Seftel, Max Cohen, Christienson, Swartzberg, Gershenson, Robinson, Kaplan, J Cohen, and Liponetzky; load was 32 50 kg bombs.

The pair flew a single bombing run at 12,000 feet from 09:56 until 09:57; weather was good, and the enemy's anti-aircraft artillery fire was "wide and inaccurate." Israeli superiority was by then so distinct that fighter escort – a pair of Spitfires – separated from the unchallenged bombers to fly combat air patrol over northeast Sinai.

Mission 58: Rafah

The afternoon mission on January 4, 1949, was flown to Rafah. Sam Feldman departed Ramat David in the lead 1601 at 15:25 with Ratushniak, Bressloff, Weissbrod, Dinkin, Soltan, Fink, Nash, Lazarus, and Jackson. John McConville followed at 15:26 in 1602 with Spink, Seftel, Weinstein, Max Cohen, Christienson, Swartzberg, Gershenson, Robinson, Kaplan, and J Cohen.[30] Leader's load was 39 "A50/15" bombs, while the wingman lifted 40 50 kg fragmentation bombs. Another Feldman – 101 Squadron's fighter pilot Seymour Feldman – was in the lead of the escorting Spitfires that took off at 15:45. However, only a single Feldman arrived over Rafah, since the bombers and fighters did not rendezvous. As usual, the B-17 crews pressed ahead with their mission regardless of the lack of escort.

The two Hammers flew a single bombing run at 16,000 feet from 16:19 to 16:20. Egyptian anti-aircraft artillery fire over Rafah was reported as "heavy, including 88 mm guns. Accurate." Flying the bomb run from south to north (heading 340 degrees), six of 1601's bombs fell late, of which two fell on land and four fell

Hammers' lead ship 1601 was adorned postwar with 33 mission markings on both the left and right hand sides of the nose section, though the arrangement of these markings varied from side to side. In any case, the number of recorded missions that B-17 1601 flew during the Israeli War for Independence is 46, and was surely more than 50, as the July 1948 missions were not properly recorded.

in the sea. The crews were assigned three targets; McConville's crew reported "Stick fell in the W part of target No 3 and along to target No 1. Flak bursts above plane and there were medium bursts below. When well at sea they still tried to fire on the planes from Gaza. Target No 2 was entirely missed due to faulty approach. Crew not very happy about the result."

Mission 59: El Arish

El Arish air base was no longer the center of Egyptian air power over the front. IAF failure to pinpoint the exact whereabouts of the Egyptian aerial expeditionary force to Sinai, as well as IDF offensive success, shifted Hammers' attention to Egyptian rear logistics infrastructure. Special emphasis was placed on the railway line to the Gaza Strip, and the January 5, 1949, morning mission targeted the El Arish marshalling yards. For the first time since November 18, 1948, a Hammer flew a lone overland bombing mission. Al Raisin departed Ramat David in 1601 at 08:46 with Coleman Goldstein, Harris, Cuburnek, Aronson, Jack Goldstein, Lichtman, Meyerson, Duboff, Gershaw, and Gershenson; load was ten 250 kg bombs.

Planned fighter escort was a pair of Spitfires that took off at 09:02, but one had to abort the mission due to engine trouble, so Schroeder orbited until Sinclair took off at 09:17. This commendable effort to commit two fighters to the mission as planned was all in vain, as the Spitfires did not rendezvous with the Flying Fortress, which pressed ahead alone towards El Arish. Weather was clear as the Hammer flew over El Arish at 14,500 feet from 09:47 until 09:53. Egyptian anti-aircraft artillery fire damaged the lone bomber as the crew reported "88's accurate, little hole made in the tail." Bombing was not a success, as navigator John Harris remarked "bombs fell southeast of target area," while bombardier Jules Cuburnek added "bombs fell 100-200 yds east of target, hitting buildings."

B-17 1603 as photographed right through the 0.5 inch Browning sight of a fellow Hammer.

Mission 60: Rafah

Afternoon mission of January 5, 1949, returned the Hammers to Rafah's "targets 2 & 3," which they missed the previous day. Al Raisin departed Ramat David in 1601 at 15:06 with Ben-Porat, Harris, Cuburnek, Lichtman, Goldstein, Aronson, Meyerson, Gershaw, Duboff, and Gershenson. Issy Noach took to the air a minute earlier in 1603 with Maseng, Jacobs, Michel, Majzels, Swiel, Kahn, Spicehandler, Jacobson, Hill, and air photographer Jaffe. Both bombers lifted ten "A250/50" bombs, but 1601 was also loaded with two "A100/50" bombs. Their fighter escort was again a pair of Spitfires that took off at 15:22.

Good weather welcomed the bombers over Rafah from 15:55 to 15:59 (leader), and from 15:57 to 15:57 (wingman) at 15,500 feet (both). Raisin's and Noach's crews reported the Egyptian anti-aircraft artillery fire as "less than expected" and "not up to Rafah standards" respectively. Jules Cuburnek reported "Buildings hit to the right side of target No 2... 3 distinct columns of smoke were seen spreading, these columns could be seen from over TA,"[31] and the debrief officer summed up his report "Raid considered a success!!!"

Mission 61: Rafah

The Hammers pressed ahead with their offensive against Rafah on the morning of January 6, 1949, when a lone B-17 flew the bombing mission. Al Raisin departed Ramat David in 1601 at 07:55 with Ben-Porat, Harris, Cuburnek, Lichtman, Goldstein, Aronson, Meyerson, Gershaw, Duboff, and Gershenson; load was 16 "A100/50" bombs. Fighter escort – two Spitfires – also took off at 07:55 and escorted the bomber up to Gaza.

The Hammer was over Rafah from 08:33 until 08:36; weather was generally clear, but sand haze was reported over target. Bombing from 16,000 feet against inaccurate anti-aircraft artillery, the crew flew a single run and aimed at a schoolhouse that IAF official history reported was "used for headquarters." Navigator John Harris reported "Bombs fell alongside schoolhouse," while bombardier Jules Cuburnek added "around the schoolhouse

Perhaps sarcastically, bombardier Jules Cuburnek suggested to AHQ – in the January 6, 1949, mission debrief - that the correct size for a Hammers' target was the Yarkon Hotel in Tel Aviv, where AHQ was based!

building A/A positions were spotted. 88s probably. Brown haze obstructed view on the ground. Railway line may have been hit below schoolhouse."

The crew was quite critical after this mission. Raisin remarked "cannot communicate with fighters, ships, or base; can something be done about contact? It is suggested that targets to be attacked be chosen well in advance of the proposed take-off time and not in the last moment – insufficient information as to this target. The briefing folder says area contains well but nothing else is mentioned." Cuburnek summed up the report "had no target photo, almost impossible to identify aiming point, however, with excellent cooperation from the navigator identified it. The target covered too big an area. Next time give us a suitable area about the size of 100 nails piece or the Yarkon Hotel."[32]

Mission 62: Rafah

Rafah was also the target of the final Hammers bombing mission during the Israeli War for Independence. Sam Feldman departed Ramat David in the lead ship (1601) at 07:07 with Ben-Porat, Bressloff, Weissbrod, Fink, Dinkin, Soltan, Lazarus, Nash, and

Rafah was the target that B-17 1603 bombed on its first and last Israeli War for Independence missions on July 15, 1948, and January 7, 1949, respectively!

Jackson. John McConville preceded two minutes earlier in 1603 with Ratushniak, Seftel, Weinstein, Kahn, Swartzberg, Wadman, Kaplan, Robinson, Liponetzky, and J Cohen. Both aircraft were loaded with 16 100 kg bombs and fighter escort was the usual pair of Spitfires.

Good weather but heavy accurate anti-aircraft artillery fire welcomed the Hammers over Rafah; Feldman was over target from 07:55 to 07:56, and McConville followed from 08:04 until 08:05. Both flew a single run – leader heading 330 and wingman heading 320 – and bombed from 15,000 feet. The designated target was missed, but the raid was still rated successful, as "the area is full of troops and tents, some damage must have been caused although original target is left undamaged."

After mostly evading Egyptian anti-aircraft artillery fire throughout the Israeli War for Independence, both Hammers were hit during this last mission. B-17 1601's damage was described as "ship hit in the left wing and underneath," while McConville stated about 1603 "owing to flak hit on the tail, ship unserviceable."

TABLE 1 – 69 Squadron Airmen During Israel War for Independence

QUALIFICATION	NAME	ORIGIN	Missions	NOTES
Pilot	Ben-Porat Pinchas	Israel	22	69 Squadron postwar count
Pilot	Brodigan Charles	Canada	-	
Pilot	Feldman Sam	USA	36	69 Squadron postwar count
Pilot	Goldstein Coleman	USA	4	69 Squadron postwar count
Pilot	Katz Bill	USA	35	69 Squadron postwar count
Pilot	Kurtz Ray	USA	7	Estimate due to lack of documentation
Pilot	Maseng Trig	USA	20	69 Squadron postwar count
Pilot	McConville John	USA	35	69 Squadron postwar count
Pilot	Miller 'Dusty'	USA	7	Estimate due to lack of documentation
Pilot	Moonitz Norman	USA	7	Estimate due to lack of documentation
Pilot	Noach Isidore	South Africa	36	69 Squadron postwar count
Pilot	Raisin Al	USA	43	69 Squadron postwar count
Pilot	Ratushniak Jack	Israel	22	69 Squadron postwar count
Pilot	Schwartz Harry	USA	7	Estimate due to lack of documentation
Pilot	Segal Maurice	South Africa	-	
Pilot	Yankner Morris	USA	-	
Navigator	Beckwith Morris	Canada	-	
Navigator	Falc Stefan (Laron)	Poland	-	
Navigator	Feldman Manny	South Africa	17	Count from available documentation
Navigator	Harris John	UK	30	69 Squadron postwar count
Navigator	Jacobs John	UK	11	69 Squadron postwar count
Navigator	Nachman Harvey	USA	7	Estimate due to lack of documentation
Navigator	Seftel Sydney	South Africa	11	69 Squadron postwar count
Navigator	Simon Smoky	South Africa	9	Logbook count
Navigator	Tucker Samuel	South Africa	18	Count from available documentation
Bombardier	Bressloff Boris	UK	20	69 Squadron postwar count
Bombardier	Cuburnek Jules	USA	43	69 Squadron postwar count
Bombardier	Garbovitsky Morely	Canada	-	
Bombardier	Michel Tim	South Africa	33	69 Squadron postwar count
Bombardier	Weinstein Jerry	USA	15	69 Squadron postwar count
Bombardier	Weissbrod Hans	Israel	42	69 Squadron postwar count
Radio Operator	Ber Joseph	South Africa	37	69 Squadron postwar count
Radio Operator	Bloch Raymond	UK	7	Estimate due to lack of documentation
Radio Operator	Bottger Milton (Butch Ben-Yok)	South Africa	2	103 Squadron airman
Radio Operator	Dinkin Harry	Canada	22	69 Squadron postwar count
Radio Operator	Duboff Harold	USA	42	69 Squadron postwar count
Radio Operator	Goldstein Jack	Canada	43	69 Squadron postwar count
Radio Operator	Lowenberg Ralph	USA	12	69 Squadron postwar count
Radio Operator	Swartzberg Zan	South Africa	13	69 Squadron postwar count
Radio Operator	Vons Mendy	South Africa	-	
Flight Engineer	Baltman Bill	Canada	7	Estimate due to lack of documentation
Flight Engineer	Cohen Max	USA	11	Count from available documentation
Flight Engineer	Kellman Mori	USA	5	69 Squadron postwar count

QUALIFICATION	NAME	ORIGIN	Missions	NOTES
Flight Engineer	Lichtman Bill	USA	47	69 Squadron postwar count
Flight Engineer	Majzels Leo	USA	5	69 Squadron postwar count
Armorer	Aronson Irving	USA	43	69 Squadron postwar count
Armorer	Christienson Jorgen	Denmark	12	69 Squadron postwar count
Armorer	Kahn Ira	USA	41	69 Squadron postwar count
Armorer	Soltan Irving	USA	38	69 Squadron postwar count
Armorer	Swiel Cyril	South Africa	11	69 Squadron postwar count
Armorer	Wadman Bill	Canada	10	69 Squadron postwar count
Air Gunner	Axelrod Abraham	South Africa	8	Estimate due to lack of documentation
Air Gunner	Berger Abe	South Africa	26	Estimate due to lack of documentation
Air Gunner	Blumen Raphael	Israel	9	Count from available documentation
Air Gunner	Bressloff Seymour	UK	8	Count from available documentation
Air Gunner	Camerman Sam	Canada	18	Count from available documentation
Air Gunner	Cohen J	Canada	13	69 Squadron postwar count
Air Gunner	Fink David	USA	32	69 Squadron postwar count
Air Gunner	Gershalter Edward	USA	7	Count from available documentation
Air Gunner	Gershaw Jack	UK	30	69 Squadron postwar count
Air Gunner	Gershenson Harry	UK	7	69 Squadron postwar count
Air Gunner	Hill David	UK	20	69 Squadron postwar count
Air Gunner	Hiller Ivan	UK	-	
Air Gunner	Jackson Wilfred	UK	25	69 Squadron postwar count
Air Gunner	Jacobson Ken	South Africa	11	69 Squadron postwar count
Air Gunner	Kaplan Lem	USA	24	69 Squadron postwar count
Air Gunner	Lazarus Joe	South Africa	35	69 Squadron postwar count
Air Gunner	Leibowitz Joe	South Africa	-	
Air Gunner	Liponetzky Jack	USA	12	69 Squadron postwar count
Air Gunner	Merovitz Harry	Canada	5	Count from available documentation
Air Gunner	Meyerson George	South Africa	48	69 Squadron postwar count
Air Gunner	Nash Stanley	South Africa	35	69 Squadron postwar count
Air Gunner	Poll Maurice	USA	10	Estimate due to lack of documentation
Air Gunner	Robinson Joshua	UK	15	69 Squadron postwar count
Air Gunner	Schwarzbach Marshall	USA	5	Count from available documentation
Air Gunner	Spicehandler Daniel	USA	48	69 Squadron postwar count
Air Gunner	Steinberg Otto	Canada	7	Estimate due to lack of documentation
Air Gunner	Treisman Ray	South Africa	2	Count from available documentation
Air Photographer	Griver David	USA	9	Count from available documentation
Air Photographer	Joffe Yale	Canada	6	Count from available documentation
Air Photographer	Kapusa Leslie	UK	3	Count from available documentation
Air Photographer	Paris Marvin	USA	1	Count from available documentation

Notes:

[1] The Avia S-199 was a Czechoslovak manufactured Messerschmitt Me 109.

[2] Ex-RAF pilot Aharon Remez and former USAAF navigator Heyman Shamir outlined in late 1947 a plan for Israeli air power; in due course Remez would be IAF Commander with Shamir as his deputy.

[3] A World War II USAAF flight engineer, Schwimmer envisioned a Jewish airline that would airlift Holocaust refugees from Europe to Israel. During the second half of 1947 Schwimmer recruited airmen and purchased surplus transport aircraft; this eventually transformed into the IAF Air Transport Command, which airlifted arms and weapons from Czechoslovakia to Israel, as well as being in charge of the B-17 project's first days.

[4] Universal Aviation of Tulsa utilized NL5014N (USAF 44-83811) for aerial photography to chart Midwestern and Southeastern USA under U.S. Army contract.

[5] The popular story has been that the three B-17s were planned to depart Miami together on midnight of June 12, 1948, for a night flight to San Juan. Two B-17s took off as planned, but the third suffered a flat tire, so the two circled Miami for a long time until ordered to proceed, with the third B-17 departing Miami on the morning of June 13, 1948, to join the two other B-17s at San Juan. However, the flight was flown separately all the way from Miami to Zatec (actually the pair landed at Ajaccio while the single did not, thus setting the search and rescue alarm bells), and there is no concrete evidence to support the tire burst story.

[6] As indicated, Schwimmer initially purchased surplus transport aircraft – a C-46 Commando and C-69 Constellation – for his planned airline.

[7] "The Queen's Last Battle: The Story Of Israel's Three Bomber, B-17 Air Force!" by Mike Minnich, *Wings Magazine* Volume 11 No. 1 p20-23 and p49, February 1981; reproduced with permission from *Wings Magazine* Editor Mike Machat. The drama on board B-17 NL5014N en route from San Juan to Santa Maria has also been recalled by flight engineer William Lichtman. Obviously the recollections of Goldberg and Lichtman differ in details.

[8] Formerly South African Air Force navigator.

[9] Formerly South African Air Force navigator.

[10] Positively known airmen aboard the Cairo bomber were IAF Deputy Commander Heyman Shamir, navigator Harvey Nachman, bombardier Jack Gross, and air photographer Marvin Paris.

[11] Zebra was IAF code name for Zatec, Czechoslovakia.

[12] Conflicting reports cover the bomb load of the Cairo raid. Prime Minister David Ben-Gurion reported to the Israeli Government of July 16, 1948, that the bomber dropped eight 250 kg and eight 76 kg bombs, but in their combined debriefing report lead navigator Harvey Nachman and lead bombardier Jack Gross reported eight 500 lb and four 70 kg bombs. In a separate debriefing report IAF Deputy Commander Heyman Shamir stated "10x500 lbs, 6x250 lbs. 4x70."

[13] Raisin's crew was pilot Schwartz, flight engineer Lichtman, navigator Weissbrod, bombardier Cuburnek, and gunners Aronson, Berger, Poll, Rosenberg, and Steinberg.

[14] Bert Dinn is not included as such in the official IAF list of airmen serving during the War for Independence that Eddy Kaplansky compiled in 1993, but the character was most likely South African volunteer Bernd/Bert/Burt Sigmar Dinn.

[15] Al Raisin "Raison" is an exact quotation. Anyway, Bill Katz signed a 69 Squadron document on September 12, 1948, as "acting CO 69th Sq."

[16] Cuburnek flew only eight "practice mission" sorties after July 20, 1948, and until September 19, 1948; he then flew four Air Transport Command sorties from September 30, 1948, until October 5, 1948, with no flying at all until October 15, 1948, when fighting resumed.

[17] Lichtman was the only flight engineer assigned to 69 Squadron at the time, so he usually flew in the lead ship during daytime operations or with the squadron commander's crew on nighttime missions.

[18] Again the IAF Intelligence Report Number 6 dated October 20, 1948, is in discrepancy with the 69 Squadron's "Report of Flight Order No. ___" document. The IAF Intelligence Report stated that two Beaufighters took off at 1707 to bomb Hill 138. The IAF official history of the Israeli War for Independence follows the IAF Intelligence report and ignores the 69 Squadron's "Report of Flight Order No. ___" document.

[19] IAF Deputy Commander Heyman Shamir.

[20] 69 Squadron's reports of the Tarshicha raid are all dated October 28, 1948, and so are known logbook entries. However, 101 Squadron's debrief reports – and logbook entries – indicate a B-17 escort mission to Tarshicha on October 29, 1948: Spitfire pilot Boris Senior took off at 12:55, with Jack Doyle, also in a Spitfire, following five minutes late.

[21] The IAF serial system that was introduced in November 1948 assigned a four digit number to each aircraft, with the first two digits denoting type (1600 for the B-17) and the final two digits identifying every single aircraft of the type block. Since there were only three B-17s these became 1601 to 1603. First mention in the Ramat David daily reports of these new serial numbers appeared on November 14, 1948.

[22] Tel Aviv.

[23] Hans Weissbrod.

[24] Hinting that these aircraft were RAF fighters monitoring the Israeli offensive, the presence of British airmen over the war zone eventually culminated in air combats between IAF and RAF fighters on January 7, 1949.

[25] Kfar Yehushua was, and still is, a village (moshav in Hebrew) and not a commune (kibbutz in Hebrew).

[26] At Ramat David.

[27] The count is provisional for this study pending more information about the early July 1948 missions; especially enveloped in fog are the July 18, 1948, operations.

[28] 101 Squadron pilot Rudy Augarten departed Hatzor in a P-51 2301 at 10:05 and returned to his base at 12:17.

[29] As indicated, both escorts were Spitfires according to 101 Squadron's records.

[30] Ben-Porat, Wadman, and Liponetzky may also flown that mission on board 1602, but it is rather difficult to ascertain this from the available poor copy of the surviving debrief report.

[31] Tel Aviv.

[32] The Yarkon Hotel in Tel Aviv was IAF AHQ during the Israeli War for Independence; Cuburnek's reference to the Yarkon Hotel in this context is undoubtedly an ambiguous cynical arrow aimed at the AHQ officers.

2

B-17 Flying Fortress
1949-1954: First Migration from North to South

Sam Feldman succeeded Al Raisin as 69 Squadron Commander sometime between January 10 and 17, 1949, and commanded the squadron until Trig Maseng was assigned as 69 Squadron Acting Commander on July 25, 1949. During this time frame the Hammers' top priorities were preparations for possible resumption of hostilities, realignment with IAF staff standards, and training Israeli airmen.

Ranks

The IAF introduced ranks from the summer of 1948. Postwar, issues of seniority and status – mostly set aside during hostilities – grew in importance. Prompted by IAF HQ initiatives, 69 Squadron Commander Sam Feldman issued on January 17, 1949, a proposition for the ranks structure of the Hammers. Feldman proposed Major to Squadron Commander, Captain to Adjutant, Lead Navigator, and Lead Bombardier, and to aircraft commanders: 1st Lieutenant to Lead Air Gunner, Assistant Lead Air Gunner, Lead Radio Operator, Lead Armament Officer, Lead Flight Engineer, and pilots. Additionally, the rank of 1st Lieutenant was proposed for navigators and bombardiers who flew more than 20 missions during the Israeli War for Independence. The rank of 2nd Lieutenant was proposed for navigators and bombardiers who flew less than 20 missions, as well as for radio operators, armament officers, flight engineers, and air gunners who flew more than 20 missions. All radio operators, armament officers, flight engineers, and air gunners who flew less than 20 missions were recommended for warrant officer.

Urging the IAF HQ to streamline ranks structure and solve status issues as soon as possible, Feldman mentioned an embarrassing incident:

> "We want to draw your attention to the fact that Soltan ... and Kahn ... were appointed 1st Lieutenants on the 1st January 1949, reference your letter 75/10 dated 31st December 1948. These men were appointed WO reference your letter 82/213 dated 11th January 1949."

IAF Director of Operations David Judah mostly approved Feldman's proposal, and a Commissioning Board visited Ramat David on February 12, 1949, to interview men recommended for commission based on seniority, number of missions flown, and duty. Though ranks were issued mostly in line with Sam Feldman's proposition, these were not IDF ranks. The IAF introduced a separate set of RAF style ranks.[1] Notwithstanding the style of ranks, the actual introduction of ranks involved emotions and ill feelings that continued to occupy the attention of 69 Squadron Commander Sam Feldman throughout the first half of 1949.

Above (Radio Operator Rafi Goldman) and opposite (Air Gunner Zvi Avidror): BESA machine guns still equipped the waist positions of the three B-17s by January 10, 1949, but were superseded by Browning 0.5inch as illustrated.

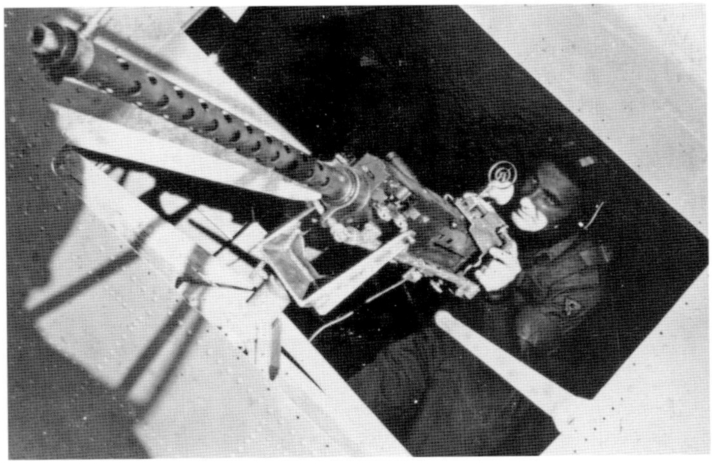

IAF Director of Operations David Judah wrote to Director of Maintenance & Engineering on January 24, 1949: "On B.17s 2 and 3 it is strongly recommended that a manual Mickey Mouse be installed. With the additional wing bomb racks the process of dropping bombs by pressing all the necessary switches is lengthy and definitely detracts from bombing efficiency and accuracy. Squadron members believe that this installation could be effected quite easily, and we agree that there is a very pressing need for same. The Mickey Mouse will be required to have 32 points."

Operation Rain

Hostilities did not formally end yet, but nevertheless Israel was initiating a slow and painful process of return to normal "peacetime" life. Only 17 days after the B-17s flew their final Israeli War for Independence bombing mission, the Israeli Ministry of Agriculture issued a memorandum that would eventually lead to the Hammers' first humanitarian mission. The Ministry of Agriculture, in cooperation with the Ministry of Transport Meteorology Service, requested IAF Commander Aharon Remez to join forces in the exploration of artificial rain making. The "operational requirement" was for an aircraft equipped with cloud seeding gear to be scrambled in line with favorable weather forecasts, climb above the top of clouds stretching up to 21,000 to 24,000 feet, and seed the clouds with CO_2 to produce rain. Learning from Canadian experience, the required aircraft was expected to be fully equipped for instruments flying, along with an oxygen system and de-icing system.

The IAF launched a feasibility study, and 505 Squadron Commander responded on January 31, 1949, "505 Squadron has been tracking clouds and rains for some time. We are in contact with the Meteorology Service and fully capable regarding this issue. I am convinced that the project is feasible and that the IAF should participate." Therefore, IAF Deputy Commander Heyman Shamir issued on February 3, 1949, a positive answer to the Ministry of Agriculture request. By then the 1948/1949 winter season was almost over, but nevertheless Operation Rain was launched as summarized in an IAF Operations meeting on April 10, 1949:

> "The object of the operation is to produce rain as attempted in a number of other countries. Here the northern fringe of the Negev is a suitable area for experiments, and one where additional rain would be useful. We know yet little about the suitability of the Negev itself. The first thing is to acquire the technique of rain making, the second thing is to find out whether it is useful. There were three flights so far: a dummy flight and two real experiments. In the first flight we did not know what was accomplished. The second experiment was more successful, despite the failure of communication. The Piper happened to be in position and gave an excellent report. Meteorologists appreciate that the cloud may have given rain on its own, especially further inland over the hills. It would be too much of a coincidence that the cloud began to grow and give rain soon after seeding."

Air Gunners' Course Number 1

Having secured the survival of Israel, the majority of volunteers felt that their job was done and the time was right to return home. Many Israelis shared this opinion, but from a different point of view that highlighted the transformation of the mostly English speaking IAF into a Hebrew speaking, Israeli cultured organization. IAF Training was already busy qualifying Israeli airmen to take over from repatriating volunteers, but the trade of air gunner was unique to 69 Squadron, so on February 7, 1949, IAF Director of Operations David Judah requested from IAF Training to "take appropriate measures to make sure that all candidates for Air Gunners' Course will be at Ramat David when needed. Commanding Officer for this course is Pilot Officer George Meyerson from Ramat David."

69 Squadron Commander Sam Feldman proposed on March 26, 1949, a standard bomb load configuration of 18 225kg bombs plus two 110kg bombs, including eight 225kg bombs loaded on to the external bomb racks. B-17 1603 was tested with eight external 225kg bombs on February 15, 1949, and 1601 was tested on March 24, 1949. Feldman concluded that bombs "fell away beautifully with a very nice trajectory" and "racks worked excellently," but also added "it must be borne in mind that with external bombs the aircraft is just a trifle sluggish in climbing with normal power." The external bomb racks are clearly visible in this view of 1601.

Air Gunners' Course Number 1 students fell into three groups: air cadets from IAF Flying School at St Jean who were posted to Ramat David along with their Air Cadets Officer Zvi Freier (Avidror) as Air Gunners' Course Adjutant, as well as student, translator, and liaison officer; air cadets who graduated primary training in South Africa and were awaiting advanced training in Israel; plus a few individuals from various IAF units.[2] The course started on February 28, 1949, but did not report directly to 69 Squadron. Issues of status and ranks continued to draw attention; George Meyerson asked for classification of his status on March 15, 1949:

> "To the best of my knowledge I personally come under the command of the Directorate of Operations. The course is presumably under Air Directorate Training. The original arrangements made to make this present course possible were carried out between the Director of Operations and staff and myself. I assumed from those conversations that I fall under the command of the first addresses. For that reason I have kept the Directorate of Operations informed of my progress... I will therefore be realized that I am 'in the middle.' Who is my Chief? Who is doing anything to clarify this fact? My obligation to the directorate of Operations? Now my obligation to the Air Directorate Training? Nothing has been done to give me the rank befitting my occupation? My instructors have not been given ranks! I completed a tour of Operations (48) with 69 Squadron as Gunnery Leader from July to January. I was recommended for 1st Lieutenant when filling that post – I was made a 2nd Lieutenant. Since being withdrawn by HQ from 69 Squadron my post has been filled in 69 Squadron by Jack Gershaw and Joseph Lazarus as 2nd l/c (these two men are my present co-instructors.) Out of fairness and by the correct procedure, would not it be correct for me to be designated accordingly, and lastly, placed in my position, would not the reader feel that I had been unjustifiably neglected?"

To which query IAF Director of Operations David Judah replied on March 24, 1949:

> "In regard to the various questions posed I set out hereunder the answers immediately available:
>
> 1. For the duration of the Course you will be responsible to the Director of Training as of this date.
>
> 2. The facts are clarified by the answer to 1.
>
> 3. Your obligation to the Directorate of Operations as of the Course flows through your obligation to the Directorate of Training.
>
> 4. Your obligation to the Director of Training will be more fully defined by that Officer.
>
> 5. You have been given the rank of Flying Officer by the AOC.
>
> 6. Your instructors have been given rank by the AOC."

Four Crews

Operations ended on January 7, 1949; training flights were scarce; engineering was busy maintaining the trio of Hammers and the additional purchase of B-17s was planned but not likely, so service person issues focused attention during the immediate postwar era. Still most airmen were foreign volunteers, English was the common language, and World War II heritage influenced thinking, including a bias towards regular crews. 69 Squadron Commander Sam Feldman divided the 35 Hammers airmen into four crews on February 22, 1949:

Crew 1: pilot Feldman, co-pilot Ilowite, navigator Harris, bombardier Weissbrod, engineer Kellman, radio Ber, armorer Swiel, waist gunner Gershenson, waist gunner Cohen, and tail gunner Lazarus.
Crew 2: pilot Maseng, co-pilot Ben-Porat, navigator Jacobs, bombardier Bressloff, engineer Spicehandler, radio Dinkin, armorer Wadman, waist gunner Nash, waist gunner Robinson, and tail gunner Gershaw.
Crew 3: pilot McConville, co-pilot Ratushniak, navigator Falc, bombardier Weinstein, engineer Majzels, radio Lowenberg, armorer Christensen, waist gunner Jackson, waist gunner Liponetzky, and tail gunner Jacobson.

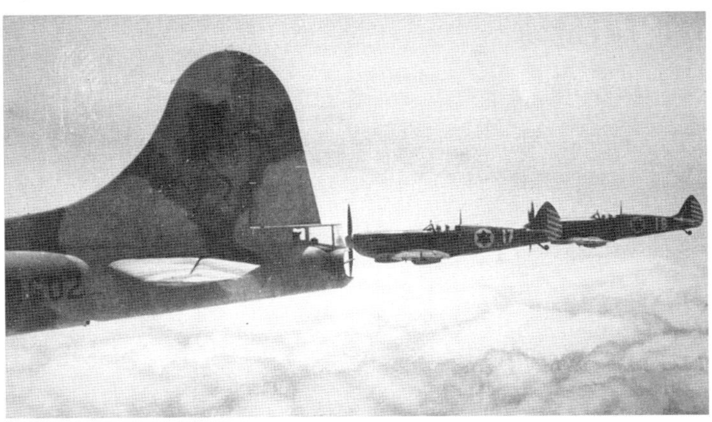

101 Squadron pilots Jack Doyle in Spitfire Call Sign 17 and Seymour Feldman in Spitfire Call Sign 18 flew from Hatzor to Ramat David on April 25, 1949, from where they flew a "bomber affiliation" training sortie prior to a ferry flight back to their base.

On stage during Air Gunners Course Number 1 graduation at Ramat David on May 12, 1949, from left to right: Air Gunners Course Commander George Meyerson, IAF Commander Aharon Remez, IAF Deputy Commander Heyman Shamir, 69 Squadron Commander Sam Feldman, Ramat David Commander Arnie Ilowite, and IAF Director of Operations David Judah.

Crew 4: pilot Goldstein, co-pilot Nemer, bombardier Gorbovitzky, engineer Zytrynbaum, and radio Swartzberg.

Obviously to maintain four crews the Hammers needed more airmen. By March 7, 1949 – when the Hammers' cadre of airmen was down to 33 – 69 Squadron Commander Sam Feldman requested posting of two pilots, a navigator, a flight engineer, an armorer, and five air gunners. Feldman stressed that "The Squadron strength, allowing for replacements because of illness and men on leave, should be approximately 43 men." And if the requested personnel would augment the then existing cadre, then the squadron "should be able to operate on the basis of four crews with no difficulty whatsoever."

Air Gunners' Graduation

Following a "muddy" start at the austere Ramat David during the winter, Air Gunners' Course Number 1 got underway as weather and conditions improved towards the spring and early summer. Determined instructors, enthusiastic students, and a comprehensive syllabus defeated all hurdles, and on May 10, 1949, IAF Training issued the list of 12 graduates: Johanan Hollander, Rafi Goldman, Zvi Freier (Avidror), Moshe Pinto, Johanan Jacobson, Uri Galin, Reuben Narunsky, Gerald Kaplan, Nathan Friedman, Sokkie Kramer, Amior Manson, and Pinchas Heisler. All graduates, except Hollander, were to be posted to 69 Squadron.

The highlight of Air Gunners' Course Number 1 was obviously the wings parade at Ramat David on May 12, 1949, in the presence of IAF Commander Aharon Remez, IAF Deputy Commander Heyman Shamir, IAF Director of Operations David Judah, Ramat David Commander Bill Katz, and 69 Squadron Commander Sam Feldman. B-17 1603 was at the background of the impressive parade while 1602 and 1601 staged a low level fly over; the lowest widely recorded flight of a B-17 over Israeli soil. Leading the fly over was Jack Ratushniak with co-pilot Maurice Segal, who had just joined the squadron (Segal was first included in the 69 Squadron's monthly flying hours report for April 1949 but did not fly that month.) Maurice Segal recalled:

> "I joined 69 Squadron in January 1949, and although it soon became clear that the war was (temporarily) over, I was persuaded to stay on. But all dangers were not passed. Jack Ratushniak invited me to be his co-pilot on a fly over (nearly a fly under) on the 1st Air Gunners' Wing Parade at Ramat David IAF Base, and I must admit that it frightened me more than any war experience in Italy. Ratushniak flew the B-17 Fortress in a wide circle with the four propellers literally cutting the grass. Then, on his long run up in line with the runway he pushed the

Air Gunners Course Number 1 on graduation parade at Ramat David with course commander George Meyerson in front, and instructors Joe Lazarus (left) and Jack Gershaw (right) in the middle with the dozen newly qualified air gunners in the back.

The Hammers arrive for the low altitude post ceremony fly over with the lead B-17 (1602) appreciably lower than the wing B-17 (1601).

Surprised IAF officers turn back and duck as the pair of bombers sneak over their shoulders. IAF Director of Training Dan Tolkowsky is second from right.

stick forward until I judged the propellers were less than a meter above the ground. At the same time Aaron Remez, Hayman Shamir, Bill Katz, Sam Feldman, and Shlomo Landau, and everybody else on the base at Ramat David were flinging themselves on to the tarmac, drums were rolling on the ground, gravel started hitting the bystanders, and I was amazed that nobody died of a heart attack."

Eyewitnesses described the incident as "good damn low flying," but with IAF top brass officers ducking as a roaring four-engined bomber shaved earth right behind their backs, Jack Ratushniak was indeed court martialed. The court reported:

"the defendant flew low at an altitude of 2-3 meters, thus endangering the lives of crew and of people on the ground. Though court is convinced that orders and instructions at Ramat David were not clear enough and precise as should have been, the defendant – an experienced pilot with 1,500 flying hours – should have known that his act was careless and irresponsible regarding valuable IDF material, and could have resulted in a disaster. The court can not accept the defendant's statement that all pilots, without exceptions, sometimes act out of line. Additionally the court can not justify the claim that if a pilot flew routine flying for a long while in line with orders and instructions, then he may at a certain moment spontaneously deviate from normal practice and fly the airplane as he wishes. IDF officers should act in a calculated manner under all circumstances and remember the difficulties to purchase and bring to the country military equipment, and especially aircraft such as the B-17, that are worthless."

The court took into consideration that the low flying was accomplished successfully, the positive character testimony given by Ramat David Flying Officer Arnold Ilowite, and the fact that Ratushniak was grounded for six weeks after the incident to ease sentence to reprimand; a sentence that IAF Commander Aharon Remez approved on August 4, 1949.

Bombing Tests

69 Squadron Commander Sam Feldman reported two "experimental bombing" flights over the Mediterranean Sea in 1602 on May 16, 1949. The morning flight tested four types of bombs released from various stations. The bomb load was three 450 kg bombs, three 225 kg bombs, three 110 kg bombs, and three 45 kg bombs. The heavier bombs were carried internally, while four of the lighter bombs were attached to the external bomb racks. Sam Feldman reported:

Certainly an impressive display of low flying as the two B-17s drop lower over the IAF top officers.

Looking at the Hammers flying away, from left to right: IAF Deputy Commander Heyman Shamir, 69 Squadron Commander Sam Feldman, IAF Commander Aharon Remez, and Ramat David Commander Bill Katz.

The "Mickey Mouse" bomber 1602 photographed in flight via the sight of a waist gunner. B-17 1602, which was grounded until the spring of 1949, flew two "experimental bombing" flights on May 16, 1949.

> "The bombs carried on the wing racks were released from the bombardier's selector panel with no stoppages. Internal bombs were carried on stations 4, 7, 10, and 12 on both sides. When left 4 and 7 were selected bombs dropped off the stations 4 and 7 left and right. All other stations did not work off the selector panel and the bombs had to be released manually."

The afternoon test flight lifted eight "British 100 kilo depth charges," including four loaded to the external bomb racks. The four inside the bomb bay were loaded to the station that functioned in the morning flight. This time none of the depth charges could be released from the bombardier's panel and all were released manually. Seven fell away over the target area; the first did not explode, but the following six exploded successfully. One depth charge attached to an external bomb rack could not be jettisoned manually so 1602 headed back to base; the rationale was that the depth charge posed no danger, as it was activated by a hydrostatic pressure detonator. En route to Ramat David the depth charge suddenly fell into the water. Sam Feldman concluded:

> "The bombing circuit in aircraft 1602 was tested and was 100% satisfactory before the bombs were loaded into the aircraft; however, the bomb shackles used were not proper shackles for such bombs. It is strongly recommended that we get a complete briefing well in advance for any subsequent bombing experiments, as we were given very little time to ascertain that the aircraft was completely suited for this type of work."

Moving Out

Ramat David was the Hammers' home base since July 1948. The B-17s flew the lion's share of their Israeli War for Independence missions from Ramat David until January 1949, when fire officially ceased. At first the January 1949 cease fire was treated in similar fashion to the June and July 1948 cease fires that only signaled a break in hostilities, rather than an end to the war. Yet by the spring of 1949 Egypt, Jordan, Lebanon, and Syria signed with Israel a set of cease fire agreements that effectively ended the Israeli War for Independence. If IAF mostly prepared for resumption of hostilities following the January 7, 1949, cease fire, then the spring agreements changed perspective, and towards the summer of 1949 Israel, the IDF, and the IAF began to evaluate trimming and restructure as the nation and its armed forces shifted from wartime mobilization to a peacetime posture.

Left hand side view and right hand side view in the air and on the ground of 1602; the "Mickey Mouse" bomber's tail art that adorned Hammer Number 2 during the spring and summer of 1949.

101 Squadron ground crew Shabtai Katz photographed Hammers 1602 (left) and 1603 (right), still at Ramat David after arrival of the single-engine fighters on May 30, 1949.

The IAF cutting edge of one fighter squadron, one bomber squadron, two transport squadrons, and one light transport squadron could not have been scaled down – except for the amalgamation of the two transport squadrons – but the number of active major air bases was cut from three to two and deployment was changed. IAF Commander Aharon Remez issued on May 10, 1949, a preliminary order covering the first phase of reorganization for peacetime:

> "Relocation of bomber wings (69 Squadron and 103 Squadron) from Ramat David to Ekron.[3] Relocation of fighter wing (101 Squadron) from Qastina[4] to Ramat David. Change of Qastina's status from air base to auxiliary field to Ekron. Phase A will be completed by June 15, 1949."

The actual relocation order was issued on May 26, 1949. 69 Squadron was ordered to move from Ramat David to Tel Nof until 00:01 on June 2, 1949. Accordingly a new 69 Squadron reactivation order was issued on June 2, 1949, stating that the Hammers were reactivated on June 1, 1949, based at Tel Nof.

First Days at Tel Nof

Ranks and personnel issues continued to keep a busy correspondence. Apparently most Israeli War for Independence air gunners were commissioned postwar in light of their wartime missions, so the 69 Squadron standard reflected this status with 16 commissioned air gunners, yet the graduates of Air Gunnery Course Number 1 were not commissioned. Considerable red tape covered that issue. The induction of so many gunners was also a problem; four of them (Narunsky, Friedman, Kaplan, and Kramer) graduated a South Africa Zionist Federation flying course, and 69 Squadron Commander Sam Feldman strongly recommended on June 12, 1949, that they complete their training as pilots. Despite the more than adequate number of air gunners, the old aim of four

A crew in front of 1602, standing from left to right: Jacobs, Robinson, Liponetzky, Jacobson, Ratushniak, and Falc. In front from left to right: Marmelstein, Heissler, Kramer, and Swartzberg. Director of Operations Boris El-Dor (Senior) forwarded to IAF Deputy Commander on August 1, 1949, a document "Efficient Flying in the Force," in which he stated "Further to our agreement to decrease as much as possible flights that are of no value to the air force, I request your decision re Marmelstein now assigned to 69 Squadron. He is training on B-17 aircraft. This pilot notified me that he will stay here during the winter. His future plans are unknown. In light of the fact that every flying hour in B-17 aircraft costs us more than 150 Israeli Pounds, I request your decision." IAF Acting Deputy Commander Nathan Cohen replied on August 3, 1949, "With the agreement of IAF Commander I hereby instruct that no pilots are to be trained on B-17 aircraft unless they will obligate for long term service."

crews was not achieved. The Hammers roster on June 25, 1949, was:

Crew 1: pilot Sam Feldman, co-pilot Phil Marmelstein, navigator John Harris, bombardier Boris Bressloff, radio operator Harry Dinkin, flight engineer M Kellman, armorer Cyril Swiel, and air gunners Jack Gershaw, W Jackson, and H Gershenson.
Crew 2: pilot Roscoe Nemer, co-pilot Maurice Segal, navigator J Jacobs, bombardier Jerry Weinstein, radio operator R Lowenberg, no flight engineer, armorer C Wadman, and air gunners Joe Lazarus, J Liponetzky, and S Nash.
Crew 3: pilot Jack Ratushniak, co-pilot Hugo Alperstein (Agmon), navigator Stefan Falc (Laron), no bombardier, radio operator Z Swartzberg, no flight engineer, armorer J Christensen, and air gunners K Jacobson, I Robinson, and Nathan Friedman.

Ten air gunners were spare: J Smith, J Siegel, Pinchas Heisler, Gerald Kaplan, Amior Manson, Uri Galin, M Pinto, Sokkie Kramer, Zvi Freier (Avidror), and Reuben Narunsky.

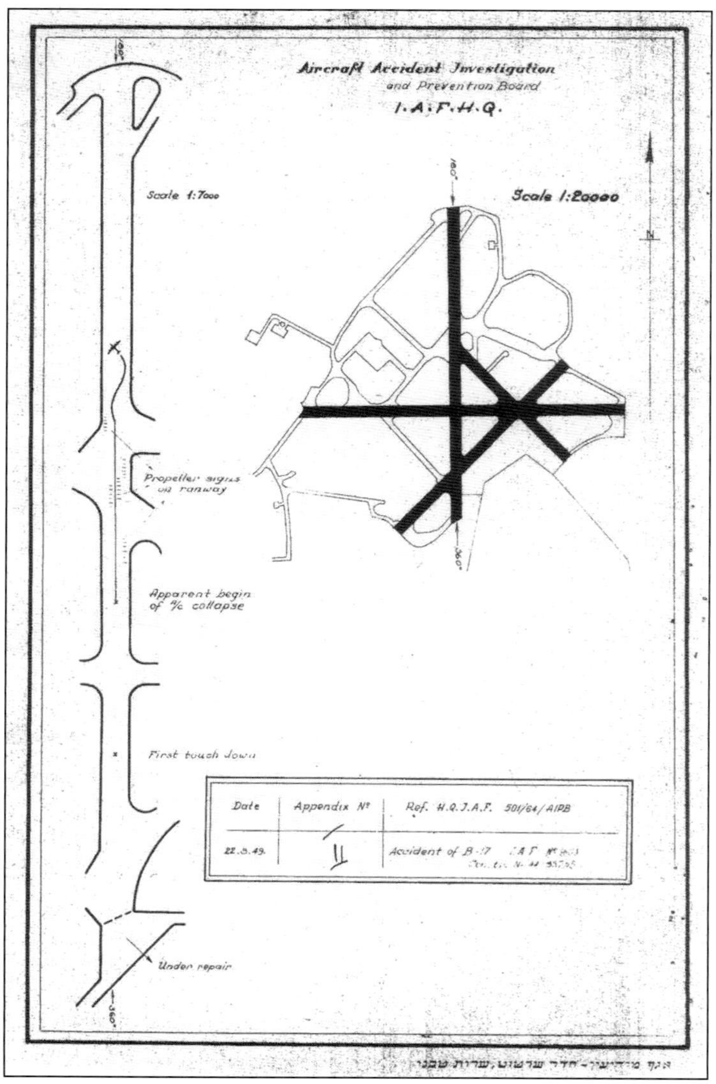

A scheme of 1603's accident upon landing at Tel Nof on August 22, 1949.

The first major operation flown from Tel Nof was actually IDF Day on July 17, 1949, when the IAF's planned contribution was a mixed formation of 12 Spitfires (flying at 700 feet), three B-17s (cruising at 1,500 feet), and three C-47s (closing at 1,100 feet). The unique formation was instructed to rendezvous over Bat Yam, fly from south to north, and again from west to east over Ben Ami Camp, and then fly over Tel Aviv. Apparently not all went according to plan, as Smoky Simon (who flew in 1601, along with Sam Feldman, Hugo Aplerstein (Agmon), and John Harris, among others) noted in his logbook:

> "Army Day fly past. Flew in lead B-17 in formation of 3. Take off 16:30… Rendezvous Bat Yam with 6 Spits at 17:40. Our ht 1,500' theirs 1,200'. Contact with mobile radio armored car at parade ground and with fighters. 3 runs over parade ground at Ben Ami Camp. Beautiful formation by Jack Ratushniak and Rocky Nemer. Hugo led."

This fly-past was also the last major 69 Squadron operation that the Hammers flew with Sam Feldman in command. Trig Maseng was 69 Squadron Acting Commander from July 25, 1949.

Landing Accident

B-17 1603 was at the focus of an incident and an accident during August 1949. The incident surfaced on the morning of August 16, 1949, when Hammers engineers noticed that 1603's switches were ON. An internal enquiry revealed that the crew chief checked and verified that switches were OFF the previous day at 17:00. 69 Squadron Technical Officer reported to 69 Squadron Commander "The damage is discharged batteries and a few lamps – very difficult to obtain – were unnecessarily on throughout the night. The conclusion is that there is a danger, as unskilled people enter the cockpit and touch various switches."

The accident occurred on August 22, 1949. Trainee pilot Hugo Alperstein (Agmon) in the left hand seat and instructor pilot Jack Ratushniak in the right hand seat returned to land at Tel Nof after a three hour flight. Ratushniak ordered Alperstein (Agmon) to prepare for "go around," as he wanted trainee pilot Phil Marmelstein to practice landing as well. However, the Accident Inquiry Board concluded that "After the aircraft began to roll on its wheels captain Ratushniak moved the flaps switch to lift flaps, and apparently at the same time activated inadvertently the landing gear up switch." The landing gear began to detract and the bomber sunk onto the runway.

A list of airmen on board 1603 during the accident was compiled by Wing 4 Acting Commander Sam Boshes: Joseph Citron, Harry Gershenson, Gideon Cohen, John Jacobs, Kenneth Jacobson, Laurence Kellman, Sokkie Kramer, Jack Liponetzky, Robert Lowenberg, Philip Marmelstein, Amior Manson, and Gabriel Piqel (Makosh). The Accident Inquiry Board report also listed Belzer, Orkin, Rapoport, and Schneider. None of the airmen was injured, but damage to 1603 was extensive.

B-17 1603 rests on its damaged belly at Tel Nof after the landing accident on August 22, 1949. A lengthy repair followed, and available documentation indicates that 1603 returned to normal squadron flying service in October 1950.

B-17 1603 was equipped with a nose turret during the lengthy repair after the belly landing on August 22, 1949, and prior to return to service in late 1950. Dorsal and belly turrets were added during 1951.

Limited Flying, Sinking Morale

69 Squadron Commander reported on August 26, 1948, that aircraft serviceability was "One plane for approximately ten working days out of a thirty day period." Low serviceability was attributed to 1601 being in 50 hours inspection and 1602 attending 500 hours inspection, as well as "only 7% of qualified maintenance personnel that are needed are on squadron strength," shortage of spares, lack of equipment, and inadequate transport. The major accident of 1603 exacerbated the already annoying situation.

The same day Director of Operations Bomber Operations officer Hanns Weissbrod addressed the sorry state of the Hammers:

> "In view of the fact that a very limited amount of hours are being flown by 103 and 69 Squadrons, especially the latter due to the low serviceability, it is suggested to bring an immediate programme into force in order to lift the morale of the crews, which is now sinking low.
>
> The following suggestions will mainly concern 69 Squadron. The Squadron should be set up immediately into three crews, with spare members of the Squadron being attached to these crews, so that an air crew member of the Squadron should not be without a particular crew.

B-17 1602 lost the Mickey Mouse decoration during 500 hours inspection in the summer of 1949 and was honored with a thorough "photo op" in October 1949, as illustrated.

One crew should start immediately to work on the crashed aircraft 1603 for a period of seven days under the supervision of the Squadron Technical Officer, the captain of the crew being in charge of his crew. This will enable the men to learn a little about the aircraft and ground technical knowledge. Besides this it would help the Technical Department, which is suffering from an acute shortage of manpower.

The second crew should start training on emergency procedure. By this it is suggested that practical dinghy training in the swimming pool be done, jumping with flying clothing from the diving board, launching a kite with the aerial of the Gibson Girl, practical dinghy drill in the aircraft, parachute jumping drill from the hangar of the Parachutists which is stationed at your base, etc., first aid, survival procedure in desert areas and in the sea, and how and when to economise water and emergency rations, etc.

The third crew should go on tours to learn more about the country, or arrangements could be made to send them for a week to Akaba, or to one of the Fronts, or to the Navy in order to make them familiar with the difficulties and conditions of the other services. One system would be to send one of the crews to the Navy to go with them to sea for a few days so that Navigators can learn about sea navigation, and Wireless Operators and other crew members about their equivalent trades. In return the wing could receive visits from the Navy and take them up on a trip, if possible, to make them air minded, showing them the Squadron life and spirit, maintenance, and workshops on the base. These aspects have been discussed with the Navy and agreement has been reached.

Pilots, Navigators, and Bombardiers should be given a chance to fly with other Squadrons in order to keep their standard up. Navigators and Bombardiers should start immediately in the construction of a DR Trainer. They should try to build and construct this themselves with the assistance of the corresponding sections of the Field. OC Wing 4 should endeavour to give all the assistance possible by providing space and material.

This Directorate will approach the AOC to provide No. 4 Wing with a three ton truck in order to enable the crews to do trips around the country.

It was suggested by the OC 69 Squadron to have a clay pigeon shooting range set up. This Directorate has taken up the matter and will inform you as soon as anything develops.

It is also suggested that Pilots of both Squadrons do a tour of two to four weeks with 100 Squadron or their various detachments. This would give them a chance to do some flying and learn the geography of the country."

Posed image of a crew "pre-flight" 1602 during the autumn of 1949, with pilot Jack Ratushniak checking the propeller blade on the inner left hand engine.

Training Program

Obviously the August 26, 1949, proposal was merely an emergency program to fight poor serviceability and sinking morale. A routine training program had to be devised to form a link between reality and expected levels of proficiency. Directorate of Operations therefore submitted on September 22, 1949, a baseline routine squadron training program for all Wing 4 squadrons, including 69 Squadron. Surely the Hammers' plan was the most complex and demanding due to the high number of air crew trades.

A minimum flying hours was set per each trade to preserve operational qualifications in light of poor serviceability. Should serviceability allow, 69 Squadron Commander was urged to increase flying hours on top of the minimum. Pilots were to practice general flying, instruments, formation, bombing, emergency procedures, and night flying during seven hours. Navigators' minimum was two hours (night and day cross country), bombardiers four hours (day and night exercises plus cross country), radio operators five hours (normal flying duties, radio compass bearings, aural null and loop range), flight engineers five hours (routine flying, emergency procedures, and field transfer), and air gunners five hours (fighter affiliation, air to air firing, air to ground firing, and general flying).

All airmen were to attend a basic set of classes and lectures covering physical training, rifle and revolver shooting, clay pigeon shooting, aircraft recognition, instruction in films, tactics, dinghy and parachute drill, intelligence, escape and emergency drill, morse and aldis lamp, meteorology, armaments, medical and first aid, and organization and administration of the aircraft. Additionally, pilots were to attend lectures about engine assembly, navigation, engine handling, airframe, theory of flight, fighter affiliation, theory of bombing, and link trainer. Navigators were to hone navigation, radar, radio aids, and synthetic bomb trainer, as well as "30 Astro shots day and night." Bombardiers were to learn the theory of bombing, bombs, and bomb gear and panel gear, as well as exercising on synthetic bomb trainer. Radio operator classes included D/F loop, sense aerial, and methods of calibration. Flight engineers and air gunners were grouped to learn aircraft recognition, armaments, turret drill, and theory of gunnery.

69 Squadron Commander Trig Maseng flew B-17 1601 in the lead of a unique formation on IAF Day ("second anniversary"), November 3, 1949; leading five C-46s with three C-47s flying alongside. Maseng's crew included co-pilot Maurice Segal, navigators John Harris and Smoky Simon, navigator/bombardier Gabriel Piqel (Makosh), and wireless operator/air gunner Robert Lowenberg. The fly-past route was "EKRON-MAJDAL-BEERSHEBA-RAMLE-LYDDA-HADERA-HAIFA-NAHARIYA-TARSHIHA-SAFAD-TIBERIAS-AFULA-ATLIT-NATHANYA-TEL AVIV" at 1,500 feet. Smoky Simon wrote in his logbook "Formations converged over Tel Aviv – 12 Spits, 1 B-17 leading 5 C-46s and 3 C-47s, 8 Harvards, 3 Consuls, 1 Rapide leading 1 Nord and 1 Bonanza, while a Stearman was doing aerobatics over the sea. Good formation flying generally. The public was impressed."

Rain Again

Well in advance of winter, the Ministry of Agriculture notified the IAF on August 19, 1949, that rain making experiments were planned to renew during the winter of 1949/1950. The agriculturists were pleased with IAF cooperation during the initial tests of winter 1948/1949 and were asking for similar support: a seeding aircraft that would fly at 15,000 to 18,000 feet with a load of 500 kg, plus a team of six to eight and an observation aircraft to fly underneath the cloud and report the results of seeding. Accordingly, IAF Acting Director of Operations Robert Butler instructed on October 2, 1949, to equip B-17 1602 with a sprayer and to prepare for 15 to 18 cloud seeding flights during a time frame of four months. Maurice Segal, who flew an early season flight (he was transferred from the squadron by January 1950), recalled:

> "We picked up two scientists from Mikveh Yisrael who brought with them an old bathtub containing silver iodide and maybe some salt. The idea was that we were going to fly above clouds and seed the clouds with silver iodide. Les Easterman was going to fly a Harvard below the cloud and radio us as to whether there was any precipitation. We brought the scientists to Ekron and found that there was a problem. The clouds were strato-cumulous with the top surface about 14,000 feet above the ground. There was only one Fortress serviceable and no oxygen bottles were available. We were forbidden to fly above 10,000 feet without oxygen, and I refused to fly. For more than an hour I was adamant. An appeal was made to headquarters and they ordered us to go ahead; to fly above the clouds for a maximum of twenty minutes at a time and to breathe deeply.
>
> We took off and flew above the clouds with the scientists seeding the clouds soberly at first, and after a few minutes happily. This was because deprivation of oxygen acts like drinking too much alcohol. We stayed above the clouds for more than twenty minutes and suddenly Les Easterman, who was flying under the clouds, reported that precipitation had commenced. There was cheering and congratulations. We could make rain whenever we needed to. Had there been a bottle of whiskey aboard it would have been speedily consumed, although drinking while flying was strictly forbidden, but hell, we were already breaking all the rules.
>
> When we landed we sobered up. No whiskey and no euphoria. We learned that it was raining everywhere, from Metullah to the Negev."

B-17 1602 served as the background for this impressive display of Wing 4 rescue teams to honor IAF Day on November 3, 1949. Wing 4 Commander Bill Katz leads the assembly with 103 Squadron Commander Sam Boshes and 69 Squadron Commander Trig Maseng to his left and right, respectively. Hammer 1602 was the platform of Operation Rain experiments during the winter of 1949/1950 and was equipped with AN/APS-3 radar for this purpose.

To improve further upon previous experiments it was decided to equip 1602 with AN/APS-3 radar, a modification that required elimination of the bomb aimer's position and the subject of a specific request for authorization on November 7, 1949. Rain making flights during the winter season of 1949/1950 continued at least until March 29, 1950, when the new 69 Squadron Commander, Jacob Ben-Haim, flew 1602 with Nahum Efrat – who was assigned to 69 Squadron in January 1950 – as co-pilot.

Hammers in front of 1602 during the summer of 1950, from left to right: Manson, Bauer, Marx, Heisler, Efrat, Wadman, Ben-Haim, Ber, Pinto, Bottger, Schneider, and Hollander.

Illustrating the low intensity of 69 Squadron flying at the time is the fact that the abovementioned flight was only one of two flights that Nahum Efrat flew in March 1950; the two flights' total was three hours and ten minutes flying. Previously the same month Jacob Ben-Haim became – from March 1, 1950 – the first Israeli to command the Hammers.

Ill-Equipped Bombers

Almost two years after their arrival the B-17s were still pretty much improvised bombers. 69 Squadron Commander Jacob Ben-Haim addressed on June 4, 1950, the poor state of the bombers' armament, communication, and navigation equipment. The only defensive weapons of the two active bombers were two 0.5" machine guns in the waist positions and two 0.3" machine guns in the tail position; Ben-Haim stressed that the optimum defensive fit would be eight 0.5" machine guns. The communication sets were reportedly old and suffered from shaky installation. Navigation gear was missing key instruments, such as astrodome, drift sight, and radio compass, in the navigator's compartment.

Loading the piano into the bomb bay of 1603 for the return trip to Ramat David on October 24, 1950. B-17 1603 was the first Hammer to be armed with a turret; a nose turret was installed during the lengthy repair that followed the belly landing on August 22, 1949, and was completed a short while prior to the piano incident.

The IAF Chief engineer responded later in June 1950 that a nose turret had already been fitted to 1603 that was undergoing repairs at Wing 22 as the first step to improve the defensive weapon fit of the bombers. While steps were taken to improve upon the technical operational status of the B-17s, the Hammers' cadre was depleted progressively to the point that four crews was a bygone fantasy.[5] Airmen cadre on June 30, 1950, was two pilots (Jacob Ben-Haim and Nahum Efrat), three navigators (Shmuel Falc (Laron), Karl Marx (!), and Moshe Bauer), three radio operators (Joseph Ber, Louis Mazarow, and Milton Bottger), a flight engineer (Moshe Zitrinbaum (Hadari)), an armorer (Bill Wadman), and four air gunners (Moshe Pinto, Amior Manson, Johanan Hollander, and Pinchas Heisler).

Flying Piano

Exercise North-Center-South lasted from October 16 to 20, 1950, and confronted the 69 Squadron airmen with their old time rivals, the fighter pilots of 101 Squadron. The Hammers deployed to Ramat David and returned to Tel Nof on October 21, 1950, with a piano on board 1602. Not a simple piano though, but 101 Squadron's beloved piano.

Once the steal was discovered the fighter pilots issued an ultimatum. To avoid hostilities between Ramat David and Tel Nof fighter pilots and bomber crews, AHQ instructed 69 Squadron to return the piano to its rightful owners. The Hammers toyed with the idea to bomb Ramat David with the piano, but temper was not lost, and 1603 departed Tel Nof on October 24, 1950, bound to Ramat David with a single piano on board.

Operation Blacky

An Israeli War for Independence appendix resulted in the return of an IAF B-17 to Europe. Two Israeli Spitfires made emergency landings in Greece during September 1948 while on delivery ferry flight from Czechoslovakia to Israel; both were seized and interned, but in 1950 one was handed back to Israel after protracted diplomatic negotiation. IAF Operations issued in June 1950 an order to cover Operation Blacky, with a B-17 planned to fly from Israel to Greece – with a Spitfire pilot, technical team, and essential spare parts on board – and return in formation with the Spitfire. Operations named Maseng, Ben-Haim, Efrat, Falc (Laron), Bottger (Ben-Yok), Zitrinbaum (Harari), and Avni as the B-17 crew.

With ten men on board (including 101 Squadron Commander Meir Ruff as Spitfire pilot, two engineers, and a signals officer) the B-17 (1602 according to IAF reports, or 1603 according to Nahum Efrat's logbook) flew a four hour 40 minute flight from Tel Nof to Athens on November 1, 1949.

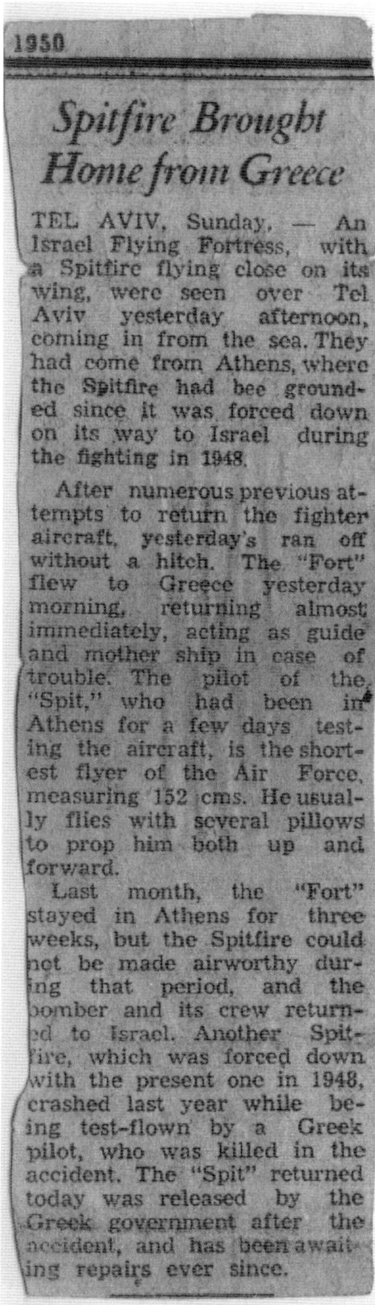

1950

Spitfire Brought Home from Greece

TEL AVIV, Sunday. — An Israel Flying Fortress, with a Spitfire flying close on its wing, were seen over Tel Aviv yesterday afternoon, coming in from the sea. They had come from Athens, where the Spitfire had bee grounded since it was forced down on its way to Israel during the fighting in 1948.

After numerous previous attempts to return the fighter aircraft, yesterday's ran off without a hitch. The "Fort" flew to Greece yesterday morning, returning almost immediately, acting as guide and mother ship in case of trouble. The pilot of the "Spit," who had been in Athens for a few days testing the aircraft, is the shortest flyer of the Air Force, measuring 152 cms. He usually flies with several pillows to prop him both up and forward.

Last month, the "Fort" stayed in Athens for three weeks, but the Spitfire could not be made airworthy during that period, and the bomber and its crew returned to Israel. Another Spitfire, which was forced down with the present one in 1948, crashed last year while being test-flown by a Greek pilot, who was killed in the accident. The "Spit" returned today was released by the Greek government after the accident, and has been awaiting repairs ever since.

A Jerusalem Post newspaper clip reporting Operation Blacky.

The Operation Blacky team at the Israeli Embassy in Athens, Greece. Standing from left: Falc, engineer Bazar, technical officer Hadari, Efrat, and Ben-Haim. Front from left: Bottger, Spitfire pilot Meir Ruff, engineer Giladi, and communications technician Avni.

Apparently the Spitfire was not ready for the ferry flight, so IAF HQ ordered the return of the B-17, with an actual four hour flight from Athens to Tel Nof accomplished on November 18, 1950. Finally the Spitfire was ready and the B-17 – again 1602 according to IAF reports, or 1603 according to Nahum Efrat's logbook, only this time with Trig Maseng as pilot – flew from Tel Nof to Athens on December 9, 1950, and returned to Israel the same day via an unplanned refueling stop at Rhodes, to where the Spitfire pilot diverted. Initially the B-17 circled overhead waiting for the Spitfire to refuel and take-off, but the locals claimed that the Spitfire's fuel payment bills were not valid, so Ruff asked the B-17 to land. Maseng performed a superb short landing, the issue was sorted out, and the strange pair of a large bomber and a small fighter continued the flight to Israel.

Bombardiers' Course

69 Squadron Commander Jacob Ben-Haim was on leave from December 5, 1950, until March 12, 1951, so Pinchas Ben-Porat was 69 Squadron Acting Commander. Hammers' cadre somewhat improved, but on December 31, 1950, only 17 airmen were listed as regular 69 Squadron service persons, including six pilots (Jacob Ben-Haim, Pinchas Ben-Porat, Nahum Efrat, Trig Maseng, Robert Kosta, and Naftali Blau), four navigators (Stefan Falc (Laron),

IAF Armament notified 69 Squadron on December 11, 1950, that Wing 22 was ready to install lower and upper turrets in 1603, which was already equipped with a nose turret. Assembly was predicted to last seven to 14 days, but 69 Squadron Acting Commander Pinchas Ben Porat replied on December 17, 1950, that due to low availability and serviceability the Hammers' 1603 would only be handed over to Wing 22 after the return of 1601.

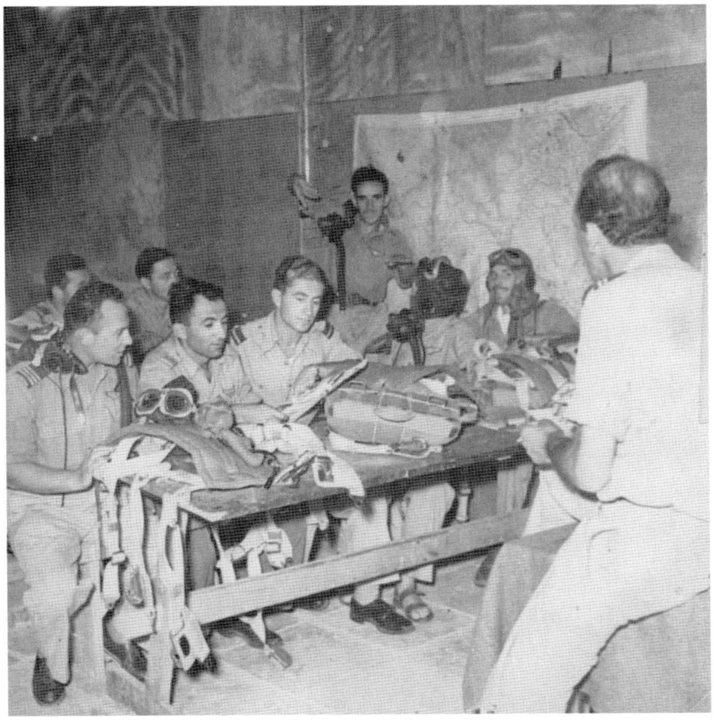

Hammers briefing with pilot Robert Kosta (right) facing the crew. Pilots sitting in the front row from left to right are Nahum Efrat and Pinchas Ben-Porat.

Moshe Bauer, Abraham Goldreich, and Milosh Yalinek (Yaeli)), one navigator/bombardier (Karl Marx), two radio operators (Joseph Ber and Milton Bottger (Butch Ben-Yok)), one flight engineer (Moshe Harari), and only three air gunners (Bill Wadman, Bernard Rosenberg, and Haim Goldberg). The air gunner shortage was considered acute, as many of the demobilized gunners were not assigned to Flight 762 for 69 Squadron reserve service.

Shortage of bombardiers was the first to be addressed, as the Hammers organized a Bombardiers' Course with all four navigators as students. The Bombardiers' Course was scheduled to graduate on March 13, 1951. Since the age of jet fighters was beginning to dawn across Israel's borders, B-17 night bombing skills had to be honed during the final phase of the Bombardiers' Course. 69 Squadron Operations Officer Nahum Efrat issued on March 4, 1951, a briefing covering the first night in a series of nocturnal bombing training that was launched on the evening of March 5, 1951. Participating airmen were four pilots (Ben-Porat, Ben-Haim, Efrat, and Kosta), radio operator Bottger, lead bombardier Karl Marx, four bombardiers (Falc (Laron), Bauer, Yalinek (Yaeli), and Goldreich), and armorer Bill Wadman. Two bombing sorties were to be flown on the first night, with 1601 lifting 32 bombs on the first sortie (planned take off at 18:30 and planned landing at 21:00) and 40 bombs during the second (planned take off at 23:00 and planned landing at 01:30). The range team (call sign SHARK) was to use lights to signal the B-17 (call sign CORAL): green for bomb, white for wait, and red for stop.

Night bombing training sorties continued on the evenings of March 6, 8, 13, and 20, 1951; all flown in 1601.

Service Person Issues

Nahum Efrat was 69 Squadron Acting Commander from March 26, 1951. As usual, the new commander's major concern was personnel. The number of regular airmen was down to seven by May 2, 1951: one pilot, four navigators/bombardiers,[6] one radio operator, and one air gunner. Training bombing flights were stopped as a half-truck was not made available to the range party, while co-pilot qualification training of two new pilots was planned.[7] Efrat stressed that training each trade separately was a waste of scarce resources and requested assignment of more airmen to "achieve a minimum of four trained crews," with every crew consisting of nine airmen (two pilots, navigator, radio operator, flight engineer, and four air gunners).

Technical staff fared no better, with 16 service persons lacking in qualifications and disturbed in their work by various rotational camp duties. The bright side was the aircraft, as all three were available and mostly serviceable, though still somewhat lacking

Poor but rare views showing a B-17 during a fly past (with a C-46!) equipped with nose turret only; 1603 was the first to be so equipped from October 1950, while 1601 followed and had its first nose turret firing test flight on April 12, 1951.

Flying School Air Gunners Course Number 1 air cadets at Tel Nof during air gunnery practice in July 1951. Standing from left to right Lazar Heskia; Reuben Narunsky, navigator; and Nahum Efrat, wireless operator. Front from left to right: Jacob Yatom, Alfonso Hadad, Gideon Shenhav, Artur Hecht, and Shaul Kilion. 69 Squadron Acting Commander Nahum Efrat flew seven "gunners training" sorties from July 22 to 26, 1951, all in 1601; three with co-pilot Sher, two with co-pilot Louis, and two with co-pilot Narunsky.

in equipment, including 0.3" tail guns instead of the requested 0.5" guns. With all three B-17s available to the Hammers and serviceable, enough airmen were recruited to stage a 3-ship formation fly past during the Israeli Independence Day on May 10, 1951.

Second Air Gunners' Course Number 1

Not a single air gunner was listed in the Hammers' regular cadre of airmen for July 1, 1951. By then a second "Air Gunners' Course Number 1" was nearing completion at the IAF Flying School at Kfar Sirkin. 69 Squadron supported the course and flew eight air gunnery cadet training sorties (total flying time 10 hours 20 minutes) until July 29, 1951. Practice covered air to sea gunnery without and with target and air to air gunnery. The latter involved a Harvard target tug and included altitude and speed parity practice with the Harvard flying beside the B-17, as well as firing at a "moving" target accelerating hence and forth. Gideon Shenhav recalled:

> "The course was a mix of different people from different countries and cultures, and was mainly conducted in English; chief instructor was Joe Lazarus. Some of the cadets hardly understood English or even Hebrew, yet most cadets made it. During classes you could hear every now and then someone yelling "Amos Translate!," as Amos Yarden was the main real time translator, since he had mastered English. He grew up in Jordan and attended an English boarding school in Jerusalem."

IAF Flying School Air Gunners' Course Number 1 graduated at Kfar Sirkin on August 14, 1951. The 14 graduates were: Shlomo Bar-Lev, David de Mayo, Alfonso Hadad, Artur Hecht, Dave Helfman, Lazar Heskia, Shaul Kilion, Yeshayahu Lazarson, Eddie Levy, Israel Montilevsky (Mei-Tal), Emmanuel Nahir, Gideon Weiss (Shenhav), Amos Yarden, and Jacob Yatom. To qualify as operational airmen they attended a 69 Squadron Air Gunners' Operational Training Unit course during September and October 1951; Artur Hecht flew 16 hours 15 minutes during September and October 1951 in six sorties, though only one was defined as "gunnery training" (four were "navigation training" and one was "bombing training").

Wing 4 Hatzor

Expansion of the IAF fighter-bomber force motivated reactivation of Haztor as a new home for Wing 4 that, since 1949, was based at Tel Nof alongside the IAF air maintenance unit 22 Wing. In preparation to moving out, Wing 4 was transferred to a tent camp inside Tel Nof, a move that was also attributed to the infantry heritage of the new IAF Commander Haim Laskov. Reuben Narunsky recalled:

Flying School Air Gunners Course Number 1 air cadet Artur Hecht practice firing from the waist gun positions.

IAF Flying School Air Gunners Course Number 1 graduates. Standing from left to right: David de Mayo, Lazar Heskia, Amos Yarden, Eddie Levy, Shlomo Bar-Lev, and Alfonso Hadad. Sitting from left to right: David Helfman, Artur Hecht, Yeshayahu Lazarson, Gideon Shenhav, and Emmanuel Nahir. Kneeling from left to right: Jacob Yatom, Israel Montilevsky (May-Tal), and Shaul Kilion.

Hammer 1602 was the subject of 22 Wing routine maintenance (300 hours inspection) from October 1951 until March 1952. During maintenance the lower turret was fitted, the upper turret installation was strengthened, and the waist guns were equipped with ammunition boxes and stoppers. When handed back to 69 Squadron in metal finish (first of the three Hammers to dispense with camouflage scheme), the bomber was equipped with AN/APS-3 radar, Identification Friend or Foe interrogator, and Mark 14 bomb sight.

> "IAF Commander Laskov decided that the living conditions of the squadrons in the former RAF dormitories at Tel Nof were too good. Our conditions had to be the same as those of infantry soldiers, and so it was. We moved into tents."

The Hammers' move from Tel Nof to Hatzor was completed on October 29, 1951, with the ferry of the two serviceable bombers; 1602 was grounded for 22 Wing maintenance from October 1951 to March 1952. Nahum Efrat and Len Louis had to fly twice, ferrying 1603 in their first flight and 1601 in their second. Shortly after the

4 Wing parade at Tel Nof, with 69 Squadron's 1603 already equipped with the dorsal turret that was installed in March 1951.

Post 22 Wing maintenance; 69 Squadron Acting Commander Nahum Efrat with co-pilot Len Louis flew a test flight in 1602 on March 12, 1952, but engine fire erupted when Efrat, with co-pilot Shmuel Wedeles, prepared for flight on March 17, 1952. Damage was light and Efrat again flew 1602 on April 1, 1952.

move 69 Squadron Acting Commander Nahum Efrat forwarded an ambitious proposal for a new standard. The Hammers were to be equipped with the trio of B-17s plus one Piper and one Stearman, while airmen standard during "peacetime" would be four crews ("three flying and one resting") and six crews ("2 crews per aircraft") during wartime.

Achikar Los (Eyal)

Three navigators – Yehuda Katz, Achikar Los (Eyal), and Gideon Steinovic (Shani) – graduated Flying School Navigation Course Number 3 on February 15, 1952, and all were posted to Wing 4 at Hatzor. Achikar Eyal recalled:

> "My first flight in the B-17[8] was on April 1, 1952, and it was not a joke! The acceleration I felt when the pilot opened the throttles for the take-off only repeated in later years when I moved on to fly jet fighters.
>
> The squadron cadre was a collection of pilots, navigators, radio operators, gunners, and photographers; each group with a different code of behavior. For us, as newcomers from Flying School, the squadron opened new horizons with interesting people, less formality, more practical attitude, and the main thing was flying. The environment was still a mixture of the founding foreign volunteers' spirit and of the new generation of Israeli airmen that was forming IAF patterns: procedures, training plans, operational orders, and all the characteristics of regular army. As youngsters we tried to enjoy both worlds.
>
> 69 Squadron Commander Nahum Efrat was a quite pleasant man who did not demand too much from us. One of the pilots was Sokkie Kramer, a nice guy from South Africa with a wild sense of humor. Everyone knew that I was eager to fly, and often I nagged to be assigned to fly, especially for long range flights. One day when Nahum was away and Sokkie was acting commander I asked Sokkie if a flight was planned. He answered that a flight to Crete was indeed being prepared, and that if I would

IAF Engineering ordered on June 12, 1952, a test flight in 1602 to try the lower, upper turrets, and the improved waist gun installations; Nahum Efrat and Misha Kener flew "defensive weapons test" flight in 1602 on July 17, 1952. The AN/APS-3 radar was tested on September 7, 1952, but no conclusion regarding the planned tasking of air to sea rescue could be drawn from this flight.

69 Squadron deployed to Ramat David for an exercise during September 2 to 10, 1952, and again during October 12 to 16, 1952. The former deployment included 1602 and 1603, which flew training bombing missions. The latter deployment involved 1601 and 1602, which flew fighter affiliation and evasive maneuvers training sorties from Ramat David. Standing in front of the Hammers airmen (with 1603 as background) are 69 Squadron Commander Nahum Efrat (left) and his would-be successor, Misha Kener (right).

like to participate then I should prepare the navigation chart. In those days planning a navigation chart was a major task: drafting maps, calculating fuel, and preparing equipment. I recruited navigator Arnon Knoll as my assistant, and together we worked very hard to finish preparations on time. At the exact moment we entered the officers club, to where we were ordered to arrive with the finished navigation charts, I saw that all present barely succeeded in hiding their grins and smiles; the flight to Crete was nothing but a joke."

Catalina

The combat aircraft inventory of the smallest IAF frontline squadron was exactly doubled during the winter of 1952/1953, when three Consolidated PBY Catalina amphibian patrol aircraft joined the trio of bombers. IAF interest in the Catalina dated back to 1949, when IAF Acting Director of Operations Boris Senior related – in a September 7, 1949, letter to IAF Commander – to the report "Roles of Maritime Aircraft Squadron" that Robert Butler prepared and forwarded to IAF Commander on September 1, 1949. Senior endorsed the report and recommended that such a squadron would be activated. Paul Keidar[9] recalled:

"The idea was started when Shlomo Shamir was Israeli Navy Commander. The Navy asked me 'How can you guarantee supply to Eilat?' The runway at Eilat was very soft and the C-47s used to entrench in the sand, so I told the Navy that we would have a Catalina type of aircraft, then we would be able to guarantee the supply of Eilat. Shlomo Shamir then became IAF Commander so the idea was rolled forward."

If fact, three Catalina amphibians were purchased, and the first arrived in April 1952, but apparently the IAF did not know exactly what to do with the newcomers, which were initially under

22 Wing Chief Test Pilot Seymour Feldman ferried Catalina 3403 from Tel Nof to Hatzor on December 23, 1952. All three Catalinas accumulated few flying hours in Hammers service, but the most highly utilized was definitely 3401, which was captured in the background of this image and on which Nahum Efrat checked out Misha Kener and Reuben Narunsky during April and May 1953.

the care of Wing 22. IAF Commander Haim Laskov reported to IDF Chief of Staff on August 24, 1952:

> "If we will be allocated with the required budget to operate the aircraft, then I remind you of the agreement between Israeli Navy Commander Shamir and IAF Commander Remez that 120 service persons will be transferred from the Navy to the IAF.
>
> Without allocation of currency and manpower we will not be able to operate these aircraft, so in light of present conditions we recommend that the aircraft be sold and the income used for the purchase of spare parts for other aircraft in our possession that we must operate."

The opinion that IAF Commander Haim Laskov expressed was not accepted, so by October 12, 1952, IAF Chief of Staff Dan Tolkowsky instructed AHQ to produce a plan that would cover IAF operation of the Catalina. Tolkowsky ordered "Head of Air3[10] will propose the organization (squadron) to operate the aircraft during peacetime, and in cooperation with Head of Air5 will submit dates for completion of air crew training, as well as the integration of the Catalina within the IAF operational firepower plan." The plan was also to cover an estimated budget to cover spare parts and infrastructure. Accordingly Head of Air3 issued on December 2, 1952, a plan for pilots' Catalina Operational Training Unit course to prepare B-17, C-47, or C-46 qualified pilots to fly the Catalina in coast guard and naval cooperation missions.

The Catalina amphibians were delivered to 69 Squadron. Nahum Efrat – with Wing 22 Commander Geda Shochat as co-pilot – ferried Catalina 3402 from Tel Nof to Hatzor on December 15, 1952. The first 69 Squadron Catalina sortie was recorded on December 29, 1952, but utilization was low and mostly covered training of crews and testing of systems. The latter included an air gunnery test flight on February 3, 1953, with Nahum Efrat as pilot and Misha Kener as co-pilot. Another air gunnery test flight was flown on February 26, 1953, in 3401, again with Nahum Efrat as pilot, but this time with Reuben Narunsky as co-pilot and Artur Hecht as air gunner. Yossi Toister recalled:

> "I did a little bit of flying in the Catalina. The flight engineer sat inside the tower, on top of which the wing was attached. Communication between pilot and flight engineer was via a lights system. If the pilot wanted rich mixture then he had to switch ON the light of the rich mixture on the panel in between the two pilots. The flight engineer changed mixture and then set OFF the rich mixture light in his panel to signal the pilot that the order was fulfilled. There were two turrets on both sides and one at the nose. The nose turret could be opened, and a large eye catching placard was placed there NO FISHING WITH DYNAMITE! A very easy aircraft to fly, the Catalina easily landed on land and sea; we used to land on the Sea of Galilee. Once Sokkie Kramer could not lower the undercarriage so he belly landed the Catalina with no apparent damage. Eventually the IAF stopped flying the Catalina because only a single nose wheel was available."

The beginning of the end for the Hammers' flirt with the Catalina was signaled on June 21, 1953, when Wing 22 was ordered to store the three amphibians with one aircraft ready to fly at any given moment. Sporadic Catalina flights continued, and in due course the type would enjoy a brief IAF resurrection, but not as a 69 Squadron element; the revived Catalina service during 1955/1956 was a 103 Squadron affair.

Red Sea Search

Possessing high endurance capability and four engine safety margins, the IAF B-17s were utilized for over water long range missions. The AN/APS-3 equipped B-17 1602 flew air to sea rescue operational missions on November 25 to 27, 1952, when Israeli Navy boats went missing. Nahum Efrat flew all three sorties as pilot, while co-pilots were Abraham Portugali on the first sortie and Misha Kener during the second and third flights. The area covered over the Mediterranean Sea ranged from the coasts of Lebanon, Syria, and Turkey to Cyprus. Total flying time was 15 hours; the longest sortie lasted 6 hours 10 minutes.

An even higher endurance over water flight was flown on January 5, 1953. Yet after take-off, B-17 1602 – with Nahum Efrat as pilot and Reuben Narunsky as co-pilot – did not head to the Mediterranean Sea, but flew south to the Red Sea. Achikar Eyal recalled:

> "The task was to search for a ship that was reportedly sailing to Eilat, but radio contact with the ship was lost. At the time of our flight the ship was supposed to sail

Nahum Efrat and Misha Kener were at the controls of 1602 during yet another AN/APS-3 test flight on December 2, 1952, but Air3 ordered on December 29, 1952, to install a chin turret in 1602, effectively ending the first IAF iteration of radar installation on the B-17.

B-17 1602 after removal of the AN/APS-3 radar and installation of a chin turret.

Misha Kener (Keren) was 69 Squadron Commander from February 1953. Standing sixth from left, the Hammers' commander is mostly surrounded by ground crew in this group photo in front of 1601, which was taken during Kener's final day as 69 Commander on September 30, 1953. B-17 1601 was the last of the trio to adopt the full metal finish look sometime after January 21, 1953, and before April 20, 1953.

somewhere off Ghardaka, Egypt, so we were instructed to do a square search over that area until finding the ship or until running out of fuel. Two navigators were assigned to fly the long range mission; Milosh Yalinek was the senior navigator, so it was decided that I would navigate on the outbound leg while there was still daylight. We flew unescorted at low altitude without any navigational aids.

Apparently AHQ looked at a 1:5,000,000 scale map, on which the distance between the shores of the Red Sea may have appeared short. The distance was actually 150 to 180 miles, or 1 hour flight in a B-17. Many ships were sailing in the Read Sea, and we flew from one ship to another, but after only two sides of the first square we ran out of fuel. While flying back home darkness closed on us and we could not even see the Saudi coastline that we planned to follow. Yalinek took over, but I restlessly remained awake, looking out for familiar terrain features. After 10 flying hours we began climbing to fly over clouds and higher than mountains when suddenly we spotted lights through the clouds that we identified as our capital, Jerusalem."

The crew of 1602 flew 6 hours 10 minutes daytime and 3 hours 55 minutes nighttime in what was probably the longest IAF B-17 mission up until then. Incidentally, the ship was tracked down four days later when Achikar Eyal flew as navigator in a Mosquito fighter-bomber with pilot Dov Erlich.

Ceremonial Year

B-17 1603 suffered Category 2A damage during a taxi accident on January 19, 1953, so only two Hammers took part in the impressive Wing 4 command hand-over fly-past two days later. 69 Squadron Commander Nahum Efrat flew 1601 with co-pilot Emmanuel Giladi, while Reuben Narunsky flew 1602 with Misha Kener as co-pilot. The same day 121 Air Photography Technical Services Unit reported that all three B-17s were equipped with K-21 cameras.

Misha Kener was 69 Squadron Commander from February 1953, and the Hammers staged an impressive Israeli Independence Day 3-ship fly-past on April 20, 1953. B-17 1603 flew lead with Reuben Narunsky and Yossi Toister in 1601 and Nahum Efrat and Beni Yoskovic in 1602. Yossi Toister – who joined the Hammers in April 1953 along with fellow Flying School Class 9 graduate Gideon Levanon – recalled:

> "The B-17 flew easily; if you missed on landing and the aircraft jumped back in the air you could open the throttles and cling to the air like a Piper; a very powerful aircraft. Human engineering was not good; for example, the electrical switches of wheels and flaps were identical.

Pilots Sokkie Kramer (standing third from left) and Reuben Narunsky (standing fourth from left) with their crew in front of 1601 prior to Independence Day fly-past on April 20, 1953.

Pilots Nahum Efrat and Beni Yoskovic, fourth and second from left respectively, with their crew in front of 1602 prior to Independence Day fly-past on April 20, 1953.

Mass assembly of 69 Squadron service persons in front of 1603 prior to Independence Day fly-past on April 20, 1953.

The procedure was to retract flaps after landing. Once a pilot made an error and retracted the landing gear, and the airplane slid on its belly. The pilot could not be blamed because it was a case of lousy human engineering with two similar switches one beside the other. It had an early 'fly by wire' system, an automatic pilot with a formation stick that eased formation flying, but this system did not function in our aircraft.

Operating the B-17 was easy; there were almost no technical malfunctions and most systems were electrical. Maintaining electrical motors and electrical cables was simple enough; there were not leaks in an electrical system, and if there was a 'leak' – electrical short – the fuse jumped off. Our Technical Officer was a maintenance wizard, and he had an excellent team of engineers, so all three aircraft were always in flying condition.

We flew up to 30,000 feet, and we had electrically warmed suits that we plugged in to special sockets. These had a thermostat and were used until one airmen's bottom was barbecued; henceforth we wore boots and gloves and hats, but it was still very cold. You had to be careful not to touch metal with bare hands, as metal was so cold that hands could glue to the metal. The aircraft was not pressurized and we breathed oxygen. The air that we blew condensed and the water leaked onto our clothes – it was very uncomfortable.

The bomb bay could haul 16 bombs that did not release at once but in certain sequence, with the lower bombs dropping first. The upper gunner was behind the pilots and behind his position was a narrow – 30 cm wide – bridge over the bomb bay that linked the cockpit to the fuselage. It was not a pleasant sight to look from this bridge down when the bomb bay doors were open.

Nahum Efrat starts 1602 prior to Independence Day fly-past on April 20, 1953.

The Hammers' trio photographed from 1602 during the Independence Day fly-past on April 20, 1953, with 1603 leading and 1601 flying left wing.

We mostly flew single aircraft training sorties, but we also practiced bombing in formation. The lead navigator signaled when to drop the bombs; he had a Mark 9 bombsight and he was also the bombardier. During the bomb run the navigator steered the pilot '1 degree right,' '2 degrees left,' and the pilot had to maintain heading regardless of the enemy's anti-aircraft artillery fire. The bombsight was primitive, but we did area bombing and flew in formation of three aircraft because that was what we had."

In his report for April to June 1953 (issued on July 15, 1953), IAF Acting Commander Dan Tolkowsky stated "In 69 Squadron an increase in flying hours is noticeable. The Catalinas are grounded as usual." Reuben Narunsky was 69 Squadron Acting Commander in August 1953, while Misha Kener handed over command of the Hammers to Sokkie Kramer on September 30, 1953.

Inactivation

Hammers activity during the autumn of 1953 included deployment to Ramat David from October 5 to 18, 1953, as part of a major IAF exercise and participation in the Israeli Navy maneuvers from November 1 to 5, 1953. The three B-17s flew 60 sorties (100 hours 5 minutes) during the final three months of 1953, while Catalina flights during the same time frame totaled 1 sortie of 1 hour 20 minutes duration. Lack of B-17 tires grounded the Hammers towards the end of 1953, but by then the official inventory of 69 Squadron included nine aircraft: the three B-17s, the three Catalinas, and three Harvards.

At the time Wing 4's attention focused on the Mosquito fighter-bomber force, which grew into two squadrons during the second half of 1953. The small and not too busy 69 Squadron had to make way, so Air1 issued on March 11, 1954, a new Organization Order for 69 Squadron that effectively covered the inactivation of the Hammers. Air1 called for 69 Squadron to inactivate during the time frame from March 23, 1954, until April 1, 1954. All of the Hammers' assets – human and material – were to be handed over to 103 Squadron at Tel Nof. Wing 4 Commander and 103 Squadron Commander were instructed to report execution of the order not later than April 15, 1954. Thus ended the first Hammer incarnation of 69 Squadron.

Notes:

[1] Aluf Avir (Air Marshal), Rosh Lahak (Group Commander), Rosh Kanaf (Wing Commander), Rosh Tayeset (Squadron Commander), Pakad Teuffah (Flight Lieutenant), Pakad Tayiss (Flying Officer), and Pakad Avir (Pilot Officer).

[2] David Hill, who flew 20 69 Squadron missions during the Israeli War for Independence, was named as Air Gunners' Course Number 1 student, but did not start the course.

[3] The former RAF Aqir Station was initially known to the IAF as Ekron and then Tel Nof; the latter title is used throughout this work except for quotations.

[4] The former RAF Qastina Station became IAF Hatzor, a name that is used in this work except for quotations.

[5] IAF personnel status changed by then to include regular, Emergency Posting, and reserve airmen, so the regular cadre of all frontline squadrons depleted accordingly. Reserve Hammers were assigned to Flight 762, which was activated on March 20, 1950. During wartime regular, Emergency Posting, and reserve airmen were expected to enable the Hammers to fly the trio of bombers on operations.

[6] The 69 Squadron Bombardiers Course officially ended on May 20, 1951, with three graduates: Moshe Bauer, Abraham Goldreich, and Milosh Yalinek.

[7] Reuben Narunsky and Len Louis were indeed assigned to 69 Squadron before the end of May 1951. A graduate of Air Gunners' Course Number 1, Narunsky – in line with the warm recommendation of then 69 Squadron Commander Sam Feldman – returned to South Africa in September 1949 to properly finish his flying course and to return to IAF service as a pilot in September 1950.

[8] The flight was classed "radio compass calibration" in B-17 1602 and lasted two hours 15 minutes; Nahum Efrat was pilot and Gideon Buchman was navigator.

[9] Yosef Keidar (previously Paul Homsky) was a World War II RAF 205 Squadron pilot who flew Catalina and Sunderland flying boats from India. Homsky (Keidar) commanded 103 Squadron from November 1949 until February 1950, succeeded Bob Butler at IAF Operations from February 1950, and later became IAF Director of Operations.

[10] By then AHQ structure had changed. Air Division became Air Department and the Directorate of Operations became Operations Branch, the third branch of Air Department or Air3. In similar fashion Air1 was Planning Branch, Air2 was Weapon Systems Branch, Air4 was Intelligence Branch, and Air5 was Training Group.

3

B-17 Flying Fortress 1956-1957: The Suez War

Hammers' resurrection in the early summer of 1956 was a surprising renaissance for the veteran bombers. Originally planned to serve the IAF until 1956, growing diplomatic tension in the Middle East and escalating armed clashes along Israel's frontiers motivated the IDF to pull all available resources, including the B-17s. Yet from late 1955 – and mostly in line with the same abovementioned process of gearing to war – 103 Squadron was expanded and modernized. The former 69 Squadron assets had to make way for 103 Squadron's expansion and modernization. The Catalinas were retired, but the B-17s were still considered unique and indispensible for the time being.

Return to Ramat David

From 1948 until 1954 the Hammers were based at the three principle IAF air bases of that era. Starting at Ramat David in the north, 69 Squadron moved to midland Tel Nof during 1949 and to the southern Hatzor in 1951 before deactivation by 1954. The same three air bases changed significantly by the summer of 1956. Hatzor became the first IAF jet fighter wing; Tel Nof hosted the Flying School and transport force, while Ramat David was still a mixed wing of jet and piston fighters.

Ramat David was selected as the Hammers' renewed home base when the decision was made to resurrect 69 Squadron as the IAF's B-17 operator. Air1 issued an Organization Order covering the activation of 69 Squadron on April 19, 1956. The time frame specified for the activation was April 22 to May 3, 1956. In preparation to completion of activation of the "new" unit, Air5 issued on May 2, 1956, a directive to "train all operational squadrons and bring them to high operational standard by July 1, 1956" that already included 69 Squadron. The paragraph concerning 69 Squadron and 103 Squadron stated:

> "The reserves (pilots and navigators) of 69 Squadron and 103 Squadron will be called to reserve service

IAF's four digit "tail number" style was changed to final two digits from January 1954. 103 Squadron's B-17 03 was on display at Hatzor during IAF Day in July 1954.

A fading 69 Squadron badge still adorned this 103 Squadron Flying Fortress on March 3, 1955. This B-17 was photographed during a major IAF fire demonstration gathering at Hatzor; it was most likely 01, which former 69 Squadron Commander Misha Kener and current 103 Squadron Commander Nathan Navot ferried from Tel Nof to Hatzor on February 27, 1955.

> (time frame to be decided by squadron commander) in line with current level of professionalism, in order to bring them to the operational level dictated by Air3. The squadron commanders will make sure that as many reserves as possible will participate in Exercise Ballista 1. 69 Squadron's Emergency Posting airmen from Flying School 12 will be called for training every Thursday evening and during Fridays."

The next day – May 3, 1956 – Nahum Efrat was officially assigned as 69 Squadron Commander. Efrat flew his first B-17 flight as the new 69 Squadron Commander on May 8, 1956, when – together with Beni Yoskovic as co-pilot – he ferried B-17 1622[1] to Ramat David.

Operations and Training

Air3 assigned a mission to 69 Squadron even before the Hammers were established at Ramat David on May 8, 1956. Operation Cesar covered the ferry of Mystere jet fighters from France to Israel in line with an Air3 order dated May 1, 1956. 69 Squadron was tasked to allocate two B-17s for maritime search and rescue. One B-17 (radio call sign 4X-FAV) was to be in position at 35 degrees 00 minutes North, 28 degrees 00 minutes East at 13:00 GMT on D-Day and fly between this point and 35 degrees 00 minutes North, 30 degrees 00 minutes East. Another B-17 (radio call sign 4X-FAW) was to be stationed over 34 degrees 00 minutes North, 30 degrees 00 minutes East from 13:00 GMT on D-Day and patrolling from this point to 34 degrees 00 minutes North, 32 degrees 00 minutes East. The B-17s were to cooperate with Israeli Navy ships sailing in the Mediterranean Sea, and the latter were to control the B-17s if a search and rescue operation would be needed. Operation Cesar actually covered several ferry flights. 69 Squadron Commander Nahum Efrat flew two Operation Cesar missions, both with Beni Yoskovic as co-pilot and both in 1622; the first 5 hour 45 minute duration flight was on May 27, 1956, and the second 8 hour 20 minute flight was on June 15, 1956. 69 Squadron Acting Commander Beni Yoskovic reported on June 30, 1956, that total Operation Cesar flying time during May-June 1956 amounted to 20 hours 25 minutes.

The Hammers' reserve crews were planned to attend two fortnight training camps per year, covering studying during the first week and flying during the second week. The first such concentrated training period for all of 69 Squadron cadre (regulars, Emergency Postings, and reserves) was planned from June 10, 1956. The studying week ran as planned from Sunday to Thursday, June 10 to 14, 1956. As many airmen, especially reservists, were considered "rusty," the five days of studies mostly covered refreshment of B-17 handling and IAF procedures. General classes covered B-17 overview, IAF standard procedures, B-17 systems (fuel, oil, hydraulics, electricity, oxygen, and bombing), turrets, emergency procedures, intelligence overview, escape techniques, medical aid, aircraft recognition, and anti-aircraft artillery. Specific lectures were divided into trades: pilots (bombing and navigation), navigators (bombing and navigation), wireless operators (R/T), and air gunners (machine guns, turrets, and gunnery). Interestingly, navigators/bombardiers were tested in the dark to verify their blind acquaintance with the bombing switches panel.

The following flying week did not continue as planned due to technical malfunctions that grounded the B-17s. Only a single training sorties was flown, after which the reservists were discharged earlier than planned.

Squadron Status

Separation of the B-17s from 103 Squadron as an independent entity did not mean that IAF investment in the time expired warplanes had been increased. The IAF was allocating most of the available resources to the purchase of jet fighters and modernization of infrastructure. Reactivation of the Hammers was in line with overall restructuring to better suit the IAF against an immediate or near future threat. The report that 69 Squadron Acting Commander Beni Yoskovic forwarded to Wing 1 Commander on June 30, 1956, is therefore enlightening.

Yoskovic reported that during May-June 1956 the Hammers concentrated in settling down at their new home, as well as training the 69 Squadron reserves. The airmen cadre of the squadron was a regular nucleus of a single crew (two pilots, two navigators, one radio operator, and one air gunner), plus three crews of Emergency Postings and reserves (39 reserve airmen were assigned to the Hammers). The regular ground crew only covered 19 service persons, mostly unfamiliar with the B-17. Though 69 Squadron's

B-17 1623 equipped with AN/APS-4 radar for maritime patrol duties. Maritime patrol was a major Hammers qualification during their second stint as a B-17 unit. The B-17's over water long range multi-engine safety features were utilized during the summer of 1956. Following Operation Cesar in May and June 1956, Israel purchased additional Mystere jet fighters that were ferried to Israel in August 1956. Nahum Efrat and Beni Yoskovic flew two missions in 1622 to support the ferry of the Mysteres, the first on August 22, 1956 (10 hours 15 minutes duration, including 1 hour 45 minutes night flying), and the second on August 28, 1956 (8 hours 25 minutes daylight flying).

standard was circa 100 ground crews, only six reservists were assigned to augment the regular cadre of engineers.

The Hammers arrived at Ramat David on May 8, 1956, with two B-17s, but Nahum Efrat and Beni Yoskovic ferried 1623 to Air Maintenance Unit 22 at Tel Nof on June 19, 1956, so by the end of the month the Hammers only had 1622 and all three B-17s were reported grounded.[2] Despite all of these difficulties the Hammers flew 40 hours 15 minutes during May-June 1956 (including Operation Cesar missions).

Preparing for War

Invisible clouds of war loomed over the bright summer Middle East sky. Head of Air5, Sid Kentridge (Keni), issued on July 18, 1956, another detailed directive covering training from August to November 1956. The objective was to improve personal and unit level readiness for war; achievement of this objective would then be tested in major exercise, so the second phase of the plan would be implementation of lessons. Squadron commanders were instructed to forward to Air5 – not later than August 1, 1956 – detailed planning of their unit's training schedule and required logistic support. They were also ordered to preserve 20% of ammunition rations for the major exercise, while the Flying School was notified that all regular courses would stop by November 19, 1956, just prior to the exercise when all Flying School airmen with Emergency Posting would report to their units.

The constraints presented to 69 Squadron were Emergency Posting training scheduled for August 1 to 8, 1956; allocation of range facilities on 8 to 10 August, and allocation of range facilities for training of reserves on August 4 to 14, 1956. Training objectives for 69 Squadron were training crews in night flying at 700 to 1,000 feet altitude above ground level, navigating at the same altitude day and night, practice bombing of air bases and other targets from medium altitude, air to sea training, and instruments flying practice.

The Hammers (referred to in the document sometimes as Flight 69 and sometimes as 69 Squadron) were instructed to achieve a set of quantified goals:

- Low flying at night efficiently and safely.
- Instruments flying to white card rating.
- Contact navigation tolerance of 2 miles from planned route and 1% of ETA.[3]
- Computational navigation accuracy of 3% of air mileage per 1 minute of ETA.
- Astro navigation accuracy of 20 miles per fix from three readings.
- Bombing in level flight from medium altitude – accuracy of 200 meters from center of target.
- Efficient homing, aircraft to aircraft and aircraft to ship.
- Efficient operation of AN/APS-4 and SARAH during maritime search missions.

Ammunition allocation to "69 Flight" was 80 50 kg bombs, four 250 kg bombs, and four 550 kg bombs (all to be used in night bombing sorties), as well as 1,500 0.5 rounds (for air-to-air gunnery practice) and eight 4.5 inch flares. Standard allocation per sortie was eight 50 kg bombs. For training purposes four 250 kg bombs or four 550 kg bombs; 100 0.5 rounds; four 4.5 inch flares, but for training purposes the Hammers were instructed that every take-off would be with full load, the bomber landing with the subtraction between full load and training ration used on sortie thus adding the aspect of landing with semi-loaded aircraft to the crew's overall training experience.

Status Change

Despite the emergency situation and regardless of preparations to war, the Hammers' status was changed from regular unit to reserve squadron during September 1956. Difficulties involving the operation of a regular B-17 unit surfaced the previous month. Inactivity frustrated regular airmen, so Wing 1 Commander Gideon Elrom suggested on August 10, 1956, to assign 69 Squadron airmen on 103 Squadron overseas transport flights; the wing commander understatement was "69 Squadron's planned schedule allows the undertaking of additional missions and there is no doubt that these flights will contribute to airmen's professionalism." Five days later Wing 1 Commander Gideon Elrom complained in a letter to Head of Air5 that 69 Squadron was unable to train as planned due to Emergency Posting airmen not reporting to fly as they should. Elrom concluded "I think that the squadron does not have the right to exist without Emergency Posting, and if such difficulties of Emergency Posting training will persist in the future then there is no point to invest any effort." Deputy Head of Air5 Jacob Ben-Haim (himself a 69 Squadron Emergency Posting pilot) replied on August 23, 1956, "The Emergency Posting airmen did not report to training the previous months as they were confined to their routine duties. The issue was presented to Head of Air Department and to IAF Commander, the latter ordered on August 17, 1956, to release them for training purposes. Please designate a new schedule for the training of Emergency Posting air crews. It is advisable to notify as soon as possible of the training schedule to ensure release of crews."

Nevertheless, the decision to change the status of 69 Squadron from regular to reserve was made soon afterwards. Israel purchased more jet fighters, a new jet fighter unit was planned for activation at Ramat David during the autumn of 1956 (for which space had to be allocated at the northern air base), and drawdown of IAF piston engine combat types was accelerated. Head of Air2 Nathan Eldar ordered on September 10, 1956, to stop immediately development of any kind of weapon system for the B-17s, as these were being withdrawn from IAF's regular order of battle. Air1 ordered the change of status from September 21, 1956, in a new 69 Squadron Organization Order that was issued on September 16, 1956. Five days later the Material Department instructed to prepare an emergency logistic storage facility at Ramat David that would hold critical equipment and spare parts to enable 69 Squadron to operate for a month during an emergency. All other equipment and spare parts were to be delivered to Air Support Base 18.

Storage of the three B-17s was contracted to the Israeli Ministry of Defense owned Bedek Aviation[4] at Lod. Under the terms of the storage contract, Bedek had to hand over to the IAF an airworthy B-17 up to 48 hours after notified to do so. Eight years after Al Schwimmer arranged the purchase of the B-17s in the USA, the trio of Hammers was again under the care of Schwimmer as Chief Executive Officer of Bedek Aviation. Weeks later it was again a Schwimmer organization that was asked to prepare the B-17s to fight for the defense of Israel.

Mobilization

Head of Air2 Nathan Eldar included the three B-17s "stored at Bedek" in his October 3, 1956, IAF order of battle report, but apparently development of weapon systems for the Flying Fortresses did not end. IAF Electronics asked on October 9, 1956, that Air Maintenance Unit 22 would be instructed to install a B-17 AN/APS-4 radar prototype installation and to prepare the aircraft for test flights. Five days later IAF Electronics Officer Paltiel Maklef requested approval for actual B-17 AN/APS-4 test flights.

By then Israel was gearing to war with Egypt in cooperation with an Anglo-French coalition. Preparations for the Sinai Campaign were covered by the IDF Operation Kadesh[5] order, of which the first version was issued on October 5, 1956. The definite

Hammers crew gather for a group photo at Ramat David in front of 1621.

Operation Kadesh order was distributed on October 25, 1956. The same day IAF issued Order Avshalom that instructed air units to prepare for an intensive training for war period of ten days, to call to active duty all reservists, and to activate the three reserve squadrons, including 69 Squadron. Also on October 25, 1956, the IAF Adjutant Department reshuffled Emergency Posting air men; those assigned to the Hammers were Jacob Ben-Haim (IAF staff officer), Nahum Efrat, Beni Yoskovic, and Yashayahu Lazarson (all three from Flying School). The next day the IAF issued its own Order Kadesh that outlined three phases: Phase 1 was training to war, Phase 2 was mobilizing reserves, and Phase 3 was warfare. Effectively IAF preparations to war started on October 26, 1956, so the ten days training to war time frame defined in Avshalom was dramatically squeezed and eventually overlapped the reserves' mobilization phase.

The IAF part of the IDF Operation Kadesh plan for war was Operation Press, which was issued on October 28, 1956, and clearly defined the objectives, missions, and task assignment program of IAF units for the first 48 hours of war. 69 Squadron, however, was not included in Operation Press. The first B-17 to be ferried from Bedek Aviation at Lod to the Hammers emergency deployment at Ramat David was 1623, which arrived at Ramat David at 16:00 on October 27, 1956, after a ferry flight from Tel Nof. The second B-17 was 1622, which Nahum Efrat and Yossi Toister ferried from Lod to Ramat David on the evening of October 28, 1956, in a 35 minute nighttime flight. The Hammers reported that 1622 arrived at 20:00 on October 28, 1956, after the IAF Material Department authorized 50 flying hours beyond the schedule for the next 100 hours inspection. Despite Avshalom, the Hammers did not fly training sorties prior to D-Day, and on the eve of H-Hour the IAF order of battle included 69 Squadron with three B-17s and two crews ready for war.

From Avshalom to Press

In line with Order Avshalom, 69 Squadron was mobilized on October 26, 1956, when Emergency Posting airmen reported to the squadron and reserves were called. Of the 81 assigned reserve service persons, 45 reported on October 26, 1956, with 15 more reporting on October 27, 1956, and three reporting on October 28, 1956. Seven of the reporting reserves were released from duty due to various reasons. When manpower level stabilized, 69 Squadron Commander Jacob Ben-Haim organized two full air crews plus a third partial crew.

B-17 23 was lead ship on the first Hammers mission during the Sinai Campaign/Operation Kadesh.

Actual preparations to war included getting organized in the assigned facilities at Ramat David, acceptance from Bedek of the squadron's technical storehouse (received at 18:00 on October 28, 1956), and refreshment studies that covered flying procedures, maps and targets, aircraft recognition, air gunnery, operational equipment, and emergency procedures. Postwar 69 Squadron Commander Jacob Ben-Haim concluded "proficiency of each airman in his own trade and as air crew was inadequate due to lack of introductory training."

While lack of pilots and navigators precluded assembly of a third crew, the number of air gunners exceeded requirement for two crews, so 69 Squadron Commander Jacob Ben-Haim reportedly adopted the rule "last out, first in."[6] The official IAF list of 69 Squadron airmen in the Sinai Campaign/Operation Kadesh is obviously incomplete[7]:

- Pilots: Jacob Ben-Haim, Nahum Efrat, Reuben Narunsky,[8] Sokkie Kramer,[9] Yossi Toister, and Beni Yoskovic.
- Navigators/bombardiers: Karl Marx (Manor),[10] Peter Tausig (Tadmor), and Yosef Nahir.
- Air Gunners: Yeshayahu Lazarson, David de Mayo, Shaul Kilion,[11] Israel Montilevsky (May-Tal), Eddie Levy, and Amos Yarden.

Reporting airmen not included in the official IAF list of 69 Squadron airmen in the Sinai Campaign/Operation Kadesh and not assigned to the two full crews were air gunners Yitzhak Cohen, Zvi Freier (Avidror),[12] Adrian Penitz, Joshua Robinson, Netzer Saloki, and Jacob Yatom.

Mission 1: Rafah

IAF piston combat aircraft did not fly air support missions during Day 1 and Day 2 of the war except for a few P-51 special operations sorties. The Mosquito was the first to fly offensive operations over Sinai from October 31, 1956 (first take off at 03:20), followed by the P-51 (first take off at 07:45) and finally the B-17. Air3 issued at 16:45 on October 31, 1956, Operation Order J180[13] to bomb Rafah as air support to IDF Brigade 27 with time over target at 18:00.[14]

The squadron considered the time frame unrealistic. 69 Squadron Commander Jacob Ben-Haim reported:

> "It is our experience that the standard time frame for preparations and departure up to take-off is 1 hour 30 minutes to 2 hours if the aircraft were already armed. Learning target, details of defending anti-aircraft artillery, topography, and flight plan can take 1 hour 30 minutes to 2 hours. An additional 1 hour 30 minutes to 2 hours time frame is required for briefing, pre-flight preparations,

start up, and taxi. The total time frame can be halved if the squadron would receive routes to the target, in which case we can take off within 1 hour from acceptance of order."

Also delaying departure and complicating preparations was the fact that Air3 defined routes flying over "no fly" zones. This required a telephone conversation to clear up the issue. 69 Squadron Commander Jacob Ben-Haim remarked "conflicting instructions between operation order and standing order re forbidden flying zones are always a source for misunderstandings."

The two B-17s (Jacob Ben-Haim with Yossi Toister and crew in 1623; Nahum Efrat with Beni Yoskovic and crew in 1622) departed Ramat David at 02:00 on November 1, 1956, and arrived over Rafah at 03:00. The bombers initially flew over land, but could not identify their target due to darkness and haze; they were not in contact with the IDF Brigade 27 Air Liaison Officer mobile units throughout the mission. The Hammers returned for a second lower run flying at 3,500 feet from north to south, from the Mediterranean Sea inland to Sinai, which enabled the airmen better discrimination of land. Rafah was identified and navigators/bombardiers triggered the release of load, but not a single bomb fell away, as pilots had switched OFF the bombing master switch. At the last moment Central Control Unit 333 ordered the Hammers not to bomb due to inability to positively identify the whereabouts of the Brigade 27 troops. The B-17s suggested a third run, but Central Control Unit 333 did not grant permission and the bombs were jettisoned over the Mediterranean Sea at 04:45. IAF official summary of Sinai Campaign/Operation Kadesh operations reported that the two bombers returned to Ramat David, but at least 1622 laded at Tel Nof after 3 hours 55 minutes night flying and then flew to Ramat David in a 35 minute daylight ferry flight.

The fact that the pre-flight Ground Liaison Officer briefing regarding the exact location of Brigade 27 units and front line of troops was not given to the B-17 air crews, and that during the mission they were not in contact with the Brigade 27 Air Liaison Officer, obviously hampered the mission. 69 Squadron Commander Jacob Ben-Haim concluded:

> "We were only notified that our troops were very close to the targets, so we could only bomb if we had positive identification of the target. Darkness and haze over target made this positive identification very difficult, but if we had known that our troops were west of the fire line (we clearly saw the front line by tracking down the sources of light arms fire) we could have bombed using distance and time method. The fact that we were not in contact with the Air Liaison Officer mobile units prevented real time discussion of this issue."

Mission 2: Gaza

Rafah was overtaken on November 1, 1956, and IDF forces were tasked to advance on Gaza and El Arish. The same day Brigade 27 advanced from Rafah to El Arish, while the battle of Gaza was planned for November 2, 1956. To soften Gaza in preparation of the battle, the IAF launched air support missions over the Gaza sector from the afternoon hours of November 1, 1956. The Hammers joined the Gaza campaign during the night of November 1 to 2, 1956, when the pair of bombers departed Ramat David at 04:10.

Air3 Operation Order K13 to bomb El Arish was accepted by 69 Squadron at 02:25, but a phone call from Head of Air3 changed the Hammers' target to a point along the Sinai Mediterranean Sea coast road that the B-17s were instructed to bomb in order to disrupt retreat of Egyptian forces. This change of mission posed a problem

Bombs ready for loading on to 1623 at Ramat David during the Sinai Campaign.

to the squadron, as optimum armament for the new mission would have been semi armor penetration bombs with 0.3 to 0.7 seconds delay detonators, but these were not available at Ramat David, so the bombers were loaded with 250 kg general purpose bombs with 0.1 second delay fuses. Again the routes that Air3 specified were over forbidden flying zones, and again no Ground Liaison Officer defined front line of troops was conveyed to the squadron, except for notification that IDF troops were also on the Sinai coast road west of El Arish in pursuit of the retreating Egyptians. Moreover, it was up to the squadron to decide which spot to bomb along the road in line of available information regarding the positions of the warring sides.

In light of development of events, it was no wonder that the B-17s bombed Gaza. To assist the bombers an Israeli village was illuminated as Initial Point for the final run, and the plan was that the trailing bomber (Nahum Efrat with Beni Yoskovic and crew in 1622) would bomb five minutes after the lead bomber (Jacob Ben-Haim and crew in 1623). Low clouds, at an altitude of 3,500 feet, covered the sky along the route from Ramat David to Gaza and prevented visual contact between the bombers. This was obviously not critical if the plan would have been adhered to, but Central Control Unit 333 rushed the two crews to bomb Gaza as soon as possible. The pilots changed headings and speeded up in line with Central Control Unit 333 urgency, but this disrupted bombing. The two bombers were heading towards Gaza with an identical estimated time of bombing. To minimize the risk of collision the leader split the target into two sectors, with the trailing bomber targeting the northern outskirts of Gaza and the leading bomber focusing on the southern part of the city. As a result of the Central Control Unit 333 rushing the center of Gaza was not bombed as planned in a concentrated manner and bombs were scattered over the outskirts of the city.

Mission 3: Sharem El Sheikh

IDF Brigade 9 began to get closer to its target – Sharem El Sheikh, at the southern tip of Sinai Peninsula – by Day 5 of the war after an exhausting march from Eilat. A concentrated IAF air support effort was launched on November 2, 1956, to soften Ras Nazrani and Sharem El Sheikh prior to the planned Brigade 9 attack. By then the Anglo-French offensive had forced the Egyptians to abandon the air superiority battle over Sinai, so no enemy aircraft were expected to defend Sharem El Sheikh and the Hammers were ordered to fly their first daylight mission.

Reuben Narunsky signs 1623's book prior to mission to Sharem El Sheikh.

Air3 did not define to the Hammers which target to attack at Sharem El Sheikh, so 69 Squadron analyzed available intelligence data and came to the conclusion that there were three valid targets: the airfield, the barracks, and the port. Which of these to bomb was the subject of consultation with Wing 1 commander, and the "logical" decision was to bomb barracks and port; one wonders which targets would have been selected if the attacking force was the Israeli Navy? Airfield and barracks most probably!

Eventually Air3 notified 69 Squadron that the target was barracks, but by then the B-17s were already loaded with a mix of 250 kg and 50 kg bombs suited for barracks and port; there was no time to change to a whole load of 250 kg bombs. Take-off was at 12:30, as Jacob Ben-Haim with Reuben Narunsky and crew in 1623 flew lead to Nahum Efrat with Beni Yoskovic and crew in 1622.

Daylight identification of target was obviously easier than at night, but also improved the prospects of the defending anti-aircraft artillerymen. In order to confuse the local anti-aircraft artillery, the two bombers arrived simultaneously from different directions. But the Egyptian anti-aircraft artillerymen were not confused, and instead of splitting their attention between the two bombers as the Israelis expected, they concentrated fire against the lead B-17. The bombers were equipped with Mark 9 sights that required the crew to fly a steady bomb run at constant altitude and speed for at least 20 to 30 seconds. It was during this bomb run that 1623 got hit. Gideon Shenhav recalled:

"We were hit by anti-aircraft fire over Sharem El Sheikh and had a very tedious flight coming back home. At first it looked like smoke, but when I had a closer look from the ball turret I realized it was fuel leaking from the main tank. The pilot immediately feathered the prop and shut off this tank. One main fuel tank was severely damaged and we came back almost with no fuel to go around; at landing at the end of the runway the last engine cut out. Checking out the wing we observed a huge hole where the munitions went thru."

Mission 4: Sharem El Sheikh

Preserving its World War II reputation of robust construction and the return home of severely damaged bombers, B-17 1623 made it back to Ramat David all the way from Sharem El Sheikh. Shortly after its arrival another B-17 landed at Ramat David; it was 1621, which arrived from Bedek at 17:00. The bomber that was undergoing major refurbishment at the time of the emergency was hastily prepared for combat, major refurbishment work was stopped, and essential operational equipment was installed at Ramat David on Saturday, November 3, 1956.

Brigade 9 overtook Ras Nazrani on November 4, 1956, and pressed ahead towards nearby Sharem El Sheikh. Again IAF air support included a 69 Squadron mission to bomb Sharem El

The Hammers consumed 27 tons of bombs during the Operation Kadesh/ Sinai Campaign.

Sheikh. Originally the Hammers were tasked to bomb Ras Nazrani, but 15 minutes prior to take-off the target was changed to Sharem El Sheikh. First to depart Ramat David was Reuben Narunsky at 08:30, with Jacob Ben-Haim and Nahum Efrat in 1621 following to the air at 08:40. When Narunsky arrived over the target area he was notified by P-51 pilots and Mosquito crews that Sharem El Sheikh was deserted. Narunsky tried to call for orders from Central Control Unit 333 but was unable to make contact, so he orbited over Sharem El Sheikh until Ben-Haim and Efrat arrived. While orbiting Narunsky photographed the target area and noticed troops west of Sharem El Sheikh. The B-17 crew could not tell if the troops were Egyptian or Israeli, but they were sure that the troops were Israeli in line with pre-flight briefing. The Brigade 9 Air Liaison Officer could not be contacted to verify this issue. After Ben-Haim and Efrat arrived the two bombers did try to bomb Sharem El Sheikh as planned, but the bombs of 1621 did not fall away. Ben-Haim and Efrat tried another bombing run, and again the bombs did not release, so they flew a third run and jettisoned the bombs in emergency mode; the bombs were released but did not hit the target.

Only after the B-17s returned to Ramat David at 14:25 and after the photos that Narunsky took were processed and analyzed was it realized that the troops were Egyptian. This was proof that Sharem El Sheikh was not wholly deserted, so the photos were flown in a Piper from Ramat David to GHQ, but by the time the photos were accepted Brigade 9 was already engaging enemy troops at Sharem El Sheikh.

Campaign Summary and Lessons

69 Squadron flew four missions during the Sinai Campaign/ Operation Kadesh for a total of eight sorties and 32 flying hours. Gaza and Sharem El Sheikh were bombed, and total bomb load expended was 27 tons. The Hammers flew piston bombers in a war mostly fought by jet fighters; therefore, the B-17s initially operated under the cover of darkness. Once air superiority had been secured 69 Squadron switched to daylight operations.

Prewar preparations were effected by the low priority the IAF HQ and Wing attached to the B-17s, while lack of prewar training to the mostly reserve air crews degraded competence and efficiency. The optimum time frame for operation order from acceptance to take-off was defined as 3-4 hours for loading the B-17s and 2 hours for mission planning. Contrary to 69 Squadron operations during the 1948 to 1949 Israel War for Independence, which were mostly "strategic" bombings, the Hammers' missions during the Sinai Campaign/Operation Kadesh were actually close air support, yet no Ground Liaison Officer was attached to 69 Squadron and contact with Air Liaison Officers on the ground was nonexistent or troublesome.

69 Squadron Commander Jacob Ben-Haim concluded his postwar report that he signed on November 13, 1956:

> "The operational equipment of the aircraft is old and inadequate. The Mark 9 bomb sight should be replaced by Mark 14 bomb sight; oxygen system should be installed; electronic equipment should be complete; bombing system should be modified to drop illumination flares; incendiary rounds should be included in 0.5 ammunition magazines; shortage of safety and emergency equipment should be completed; bombing and gunnery cameras should be installed.
>
> It is essential to have a full crew for the third aircraft and to persist with fixed crews.[15] If any plans exist to operate this squadron in the future then it is essential to keep the squadron active during 'peacetime' with a nucleus of regular service persons."

Postwar Training

Postwar tension evaporated slowly, and as usual in such a situation the warring sides were worried about resumption of hostilities. The Hammers' reaction was four days of intensive training from November 6 to 9, 1956 – obviously training reserves after war rather than before war was not a new idea to the IDF and IAF, which repeated this peculiar procedure exactly 50 years later in the wake of the July-August 2006 Second Lebanon War!

69 Squadron Commander Jacob Ben-Haim planned classes covering navigation, bombing, gunnery, flight procedures, emergency procedures, and more. Bombing and navigation flights were planned over range and Sinai respectively. Requested armament allocation was 100 (100 kg) bombs and 5,000 rounds for 0.5 machine guns. Central Control Unit 333 was asked to coordinate interception exercises with fighters during the B-17s' navigation flights over Sinai.[16]

The Hammers moved from Ramat David to Hatzor on November 10, 1956, and continued to fly training sorties, mostly bombing practice and navigation over Sinai. Nahum Efrat flew six sorties from Hatzor: nighttime navigation over Sinai (1 hour 35 minutes with Yossi Toister in 1621 on November 12, 1956); bombing practice (2 hours 45 minutes with Yossi Toister in 1621 on November 14, 1956); nighttime bombing practice (1 hour 40 minutes with Yossi Toister in 1622 on November 14, 1956); nighttime navigation over Sinai (3 hours 45 minutes with Reuben Narunsky in 1621 on November 18, 1956); nighttime navigation practice and illumination flares training (2 hours 25 minutes with

B-17 1622 at IAI after the Sinai Campaign/Operation Kadesh, still adorned with campaign stripes. Another B-17 is parked behind 1622.

Beni Yoskovic in 1621 on November 21, 1956); and low level bombing and gunnery (2 hours with Yossi Toister in 1623 on November 22, 1956). As tension relaxed, the Hammers' reserves were released from active duty and the B-17s were returned to Bedek; Nahum Efrat ferried 1621 from Hatzor to Lod on November 26, 1956.

From Vautour to Oblivion

Israel progressively withdrew from Sinai until March 1957, and obviously the time frame of occupation was exploited to accumulate data, information, and knowledge of the frontier peninsula. B-17 1621 was therefore utilized to photograph Sinai during December 1956 and January 1957. The equipment on board 1621 was air tested in a 2 hour 30 minute flight on December 17, 1956. Two days later Nahum Efrat and Beni Yoskovic flew the first sortie in line with Air3 Operation Order K185. The navigator during the 3 hour 30 minute flight was Achikar Los (Eyal):

> "This was my last B-17 flight. I was assigned to this mission because of my experience on the B-17 and because of my experience as a photographer, though the latter I actually accumulated as a Mosquito navigator. We photographed the south of Sinai from high altitude, cruising at over 20,000 feet with a stream of cold air penetrating the fuselage through turret hatches and freezing me as I operated the camera."

Four more missions were flown: Operation Order L105 on December 26, 1956 (Efrat and Yoskovic in 2 hour 45 minute flight), L106 on December 27, 1956 (Efrat and Yoskovic in 5 hour flight), L107 on January 2, 1957 (Efrat and Emmanuel Giladi in 4 hour flight), and a repeat of L105 also on January 2, 1957 (Efrat and Giladi in 4 hour 15 minute flight).

The survey of Sinai was the final contribution of the B-17 to IAF operations. On January 4, 1957, IAF Material Department instructed Air Maintenance Unit 22 to stop flying 1621 except for special permission covering ferry from Tel Nof to Lod; and indeed Nahum Efrat and Beni Yoskovic ferried 1621 from Tel Nof to Lod on January 22, 1957, in a short 15 minute flight.

In preparation for the new Israeli Fiscal Year 1957 (from April 1, 1957), the paperwork covering the official retirement of the B-17 from IAF order of battle had to be attended, and Head of Air2 Nathan Eldar stated on March 5, 1957:

> "I officially inform that the B-17 aircraft were withdrawn from IAF order of battle. Therefore 69 Squadron regular and reserve is no longer active from March 1, 1957.
>
> "69 Squadron will be reactivated to operate the Vautour."

What should have been a Hammers' late 1950s scene! 110 Squadron Vautours at Ramat David in August 1958.

Sadly for the Hammers, IAF planning changed. Instead of 69 Squadron flying the Vautour as the natural successor to the B-17, the two engined jet bomber was eventually assigned to 110 Squadron as successor to the Mosquito. With no other appropriate B-17 successor available to the IAF, 69 Squadron was not reactivated and the colorful Hammers of Cairo bombing fame disappeared from IAF scenery until appropriate revival of "69" during the year of 1969!

Notes

[1] Back in 1954 69 Squadron handed over to 103 Squadron the three B-17s as 1601, 1602, and 1603. By then, however, the IAF ordered to paint on aircraft only the last two digits of the serial aircraft. 103 Squadron also flew C-47 1401, 1402, and 1403 during the same time frame, so to avoid confusion the B-17s were allocated new serial numbers: 1621 (ex 1601), 1622 (ex 1602), and 1623 (ex 1603).

[2] B-17 1621 suffered Category 3 damage in an accident on March 15, 1956, with pilot Misha Kener, co-pilot Emmanuel Giladi, and navigator Peter Tausig (Tadmor) on board.

[3] Estimated Time of Arrival.

[4] Forerunner of Israel Aircraft Industries that became Israel Aerospace Industries from 2006.

[5] Kadesh is, roughly, desert or dryness, but also the name of biblical cities.

[6] Yet all six air gunners listed in the official IAF list of 69 Squadron airmen in the Sinai Campaign/Operation Kadesh are Flying School Air Gunners Course Number 1 graduates.

[7] Air gunner Gideon Weiss (Shenhav) flew missions during the Sinai Campaign/Operation Kadesh, but he is not listed in the official IAF list of 69 Squadron airmen in the Sinai Campaign/Operation Kadesh.

[8] Reuben Narunsky was by then an El Al pilot, and the report to duty call caught up with him in London. He reported to 69 Squadron on October 28, 1956, and was re-checked as a B-17 pilot during a 35 minute refreshment flight with Nahum Efrat in 1622 on October 29, 1956 – D-Day for the Sinai Campaign/Operation Kadesh.

[9] Apparently Sokkie Kramer did not fly in 69 Squadron service during the Sinai Campaign/Operation Kadesh. In fact, 69 Squadron Commander Jacob Ben-Haim stated in his postwar report that one pilot was missing for the third crew to clearly indicate that the Hammers only had five pilots assigned.

[10] Most likely not assigned to two full crews.

[11] Shaul Kilion was actually Air Liaison Officer assigned to IDF Brigade 27 during the Sinai Campaign/Operation Kadesh.

[12] Zvi Freier (Avidror) served as liaison officer to the French deployment at Ramat David during the Sinai Campaign/Operation Kadesh.

[13] The Air3 Operation Order numbering system of the era was a Hebrew prefix letter denoting the month (the tenth letter in the alphabet for October), followed by numerical sequence that was started from fresh at "1" each month.

[14] IDF Brigade 27 actually requested air support for 04:00 on November 1, 1956; the Brigade 27 Commander plan was to assault Rafah immediately after IAF bombings, but the Brigade 27 request was delayed in the IAF air support network from 17:00 to 23:00 on October 31, 1956.

[15] On the same date but in a separate document 69 Squadron Commander Jacob Ben-Haim asked that the following service persons would be posted to the Hammers: pilots Reuben Narunsky and Yehuda Pritzker (Peri), navigators Shmuel Laron, Shaul Shaul, and Yosef Shimo (Shenar), navigator/bombardier David Yaeli, and one radio operator (Shlomo Brandes or Sinai or Sasson).

[16] Nahum Efrat, with Beni Yoskovic and crew, flew 1621 on a 3 hour 35 minute "navigation over Sinai" flight on November 8, 1956.

4

Hammering Tales
The Vital Link of Flying Fortresses and Phantoms

The stories described in this modest chapter are tales which happened between the years 1948-1952 in 69 Squadron. The writer, Zvi Avidror, regrets any inaccuracy in times, names, and places, as they are due to the passage of time and memory.

All Aboard!

In early 1949 69 Squadron was stationed at Ramat David, along with 101 Squadron, forming at that time the main fighting force of the IAF. The aircrew composition of the Squadrons at that time was mainly MAHAL,[1] and the inherent competition for superiority in importance as to single-seat fighters versus multi-engine heavy bombers was the rule of the day. Despite those differences they needed each other, as air warfare tactics depended on training fighters versus bombers. This resulted in many arguments as to who shot down whom. 101 Squadron had a clear advantage, as they had gun cameras and we had none. This went on when one day I took a picture of a Spit in a curve of pursuit clearly in my gun-sight. The Spit was flown by Ezer Weizman, then 101 Squadron Commander. He never owned up to it, claiming that the picture was shot out of range.

The rivalry ended as soon as time came for diversions. This mainly took the form of outings to the next major town, Haifa. This lovely town situated on the slopes of Mount Carmel offered many fun places as it behooves a naval town in the past, the RR port of the Royal Navy.

The Haifa outings always started with great revelry in the crowded confines of the squadrons' vans, which were mostly fit for the scrap yard. No transport officer at the base would have dreamt of scraping them, as no replacement would follow. On some of those outings we had a one way ticket — transport to Haifa and find your own way back. This took the form of hitching rides in milk trucks or army lories and trudging two miles to the main gate.

The three Forts in formation during 1949. 3-ship formations were quite a rarity, and were mostly flown during public highlights, such as Independence Day. The best known Hammers' 3-ship during 1949, and perhaps the only 3-ship flown during that year, was the Independence Day fly-past on May 4, 1949.

On one memorable night we gathered, not very sober but well content, in front of the "Piccadilly" Nightclub. The time was well past midnight and there were no vans or any other transport means in sight. A very busy day of training was scheduled for that morning.

This "looming" disaster was brilliantly solved by Ezer, the senior chap on the spot. He just announced to a score of weary aircrew, all dreaming of warm beds, "Just hang on – transport will show up in a jiffy."

He vanished down a side street, and a few minutes later we heard the unmistakable grindings of a bus. Around the corner a prewar REO bus hove into sight; it bore the sign of the Eshed Cooperative Bus Co. At the wheel was Ezer. The door crashed open and Ezer called "Hop aboard smartly before the night guard wakes up."

We all scrambled up and Ezer just drove away down the deserted streets of Mount Carmel, on the way to the Jezre'el Valley and Ramat David. Soon enough all were soundly asleep on the bus, and the amount of booze was soon heard in a chorus of snoring. Ezer, wisely so, avoided the base's main gate and instead drove to the rarely used Kfar Joshua gate. As soon all the chaps were at their billets the time was ripe to get rid of the bus. Then Ezer sounded off:

> "– Hershale,[2] were do we hide the bus?
> – Of course in pen number 5, behind a B-17"

> With dense camouflage netting in place the bus was invisible except at very close range.

During the following month both Squadrons enjoyed the luxury of a private bus service. During this time the MP searched high and low, but to no avail. Somehow somebody snitched, and we found the following note on the Squadrons notice board:

> "The missing bus will be parked at the Base Main Gate at 07:00 tomorrow morning or the base will be restricted to barracks and the MP will search for it."

> It was signed by Aharon Remez, IAF Commander.
> That was the sad end to both squadrons' private bus service.

Scarves at Three Paces

Life on the Base had the usual life cycle trying to adjust itself to peacetime routine. Lectures, some work on the aircraft, but very little flying. As soon as the gong went all those off duty headed to their respective billets, as all were trying to figure out what was in store as recreation for that evening. Ramat David was no different from other IAF bases. The choice was limited, but in one respect the air crews had one advantage — 101 had a terrific bar with unique decorations. The 101 bar committee was generous in invitations for 69 for their Friday night blowouts, which were known by all for the amount of good looking girls attending. The preliminaries usually started at around 21:00, but the real fun came later when the girls showed up.

One such night we were earnestly nursing our first drinks when Ezer called for attention, "We need something to enliven those evenings."

Various ideas were put forward when I chipped in with, "Let's have a duel between 101 and 69 aircrew, between Reds and Blacks."[3]

Ezer immediately agreed, but he wanted to know what sort of arms we were going to use. As initiator of the idea I had the right to name the arms, "Scarves at 3 paces." Everybody looked at me in consternation, "What scarves?"

I said "This scarf," and undid my parachute silk scarf. This 120cm scarf came from condemned parachutes and were in keen demand by air crews, especially Gunners. We knew how to toady up the parachute packing girls. I made a five turn knot in seamen's fashion as behooves an ex-Royal Navy PO. The result was a ball of silk, quite hard and as big as a grapefruit. I banged the scarf on the bar top and it gave back a solid sound. "What next?" called Ezer. "Now we form a ring," I said, and right there I drew a circle on the bar floor and declared "This is the ring," and went on with the rules:

> "One of each squadron will be chosen and will step into the ring. He will be holding the knotted scarf in one hand and his other hand behind his back. No hitting 'tender' parts. He can wallop the opponent for dear life, three one-minute rounds, the first man to step out of the ring loses."

Three of the four IAF squadrons were based at Ramat David for a short while from May 30, 1949: 69 Squadron (1601 on the left), 101 Squadron (Spitfires in the middle at the background), and 103 Squadron (C-47 on the right). These were known as Blacks (69), Reds (101), and Yellows (103) after the colors of their baseball caps.

The 69 club, with Milton Bottger, aka Butch Ben-Yok, standing (center) behind the bar.

All this was accompanied by wild cheers all round. Then the question arose "Who will be the first?" All as one shouted "Zvi for 69." Then some wag came in "Now as Ezer initiated this caper it is only right that he should represent 101."

That was it! The proponents were Ezer, 2m tall, thin as a reed, about 70kg, while I was 1.80m, solidly built at 80kg, and was active in five different sports at that time. Ezer, on the other hand, was not keen on sports. We took off our shirts and the fight started, accompanied by wild cheering from both sides. At the end of the first fight the score was declared a draw. But then the referee was a Red, so it was only the order of things. For weeks Ezer walked around with very sore ribs. The Scarf Duels lasted several months till a new pastime was invented.

Footprints in the Sky

In early 1949 a rumor spread on the base saying that the Reds were building a super club and a bar to rival the best in the RAF. Our spies confirmed the tale, as an unusual amount of carpentry, painting, and lugging furniture went on well past working hours. In short it was an all out effort.

All were full of expectation for the date of the grand opening, but the Reds were cagey and gave no sign of a date. One day Bill Katz got a call from Ezer, "Come along this Friday and practice some songs." This sounded mysterious, and the Sq. wags had a field day. We all knew that those miserable bastards expected us to sing for our drinks as the s.o.bs couldn't play their fancy piano anyway.

Come Friday we were all bunched up at the door of the new 101 Club. The doors were thrown open with a crash and we stood gaping at the sight. The newly furnished club had a lot of new furniture of dubious origin, not always matching. I spied a leather armchair I could have sworn was sitting two weeks before in the lobby of the Café Piltz in Tel Aviv, a favorite watering place of 101 pilots after ops.

The bar was enormous, and the wall behind it well stocked with the required liquids to ensure a spirited evening. What staggered the beholders was the ceiling: a series of black footprints marched on the wall from the baseboard towards the ceiling. We just stood there and gaped at this unlikely apparition. The Reds lining the bar, drinks in hand, just grinned. "Ain't it something?" one of them said, pointing at the unlikely footprints. "How the hell did you print them on the wall and when do you intend to finish it?" Was my question.

"We used natural printing blocks only, and we intend to finish the masterpiece tonight with your generous help" was Ezer's reply.

We looked at each other, failing to figure it out. Two Reds pushed a couple of tables together, placed a chair on top, and fetched a bucket of soot and a large brush, all handily laid out behind the bar.

One of the Reds took his shoes off, sat on the chair, pushed his feet against the wall and showed us how it was done. Ezer banged a glass on the bar and issued directives. "Now, of course The Hammers will be invited to our public functions in this place, but permanent membership will depend on individual signing in with original foot signatures." This drew forth the wildest cheering at Ramat David since VE Day. After a short consultation we decided that the aim was worth it, and we all got ready for the task. Each one of us was asked to sing a song after completing his chore.

When my turn came I asked if I needed to wash my feet first, but Ezer said "Never mind Hershele, we'll just mark the spot and warn all to keep away from it." I did my stint and sang The Hammers song – the Zulu War song, which was joined lustily by all the 69ers.

This fine club had a sad end, as both 101 and 69 were sent "south" and the club building was returned to Kibbutz Ramat David.

Flying Fortress 1601 undergoing maintenance out in the open at the Hammers' line, Tel Nof.

1602 under maintenance at Tel Nof; the IAF end of year report dated December 31, 1949, stated that only one of the three Forts was serviceable with 69 Squadron, while the other two were with Air Maintenance Unit 22 and unserviceable. The latter two included 1601 (500 hours inspection) and 1603 (repair after belly landing).

The Flying Piano

In autumn 1949 the IAF decided to reallocate 69 Squadron to Tel Nof[4] — not a very popular order with The Hammers. The move was akin to banishment, leaving the cozy warmth of a small but comfortable wing for the vastness of a major airbase where several squadrons were at home. It was a sad move. The only cheer in this sea of gloom was the fact that the central women's training base was next to the aircrew billets. This place was familiar to me from my FAA days when we used to land in the old Stringbag on the "milkruns," Alex-Ekron-Ramat David-Beyrouth-Akrotiry-Alex.

The billets were classy for those days, as they were prewar officer's lodgings with lawns between them. The only thing missing was the Sudanese batman I remembered from those bygone days. This move had another positive aspect. We got the Aircrew Club and Bar, which at that time were the best in the air force. Change of commanders and the lack of proper training schedules gave us the time needed to get organized, spruce up the club, and have the bar well stocked with the liquid refreshments needed by the large number of Mahalnicks in the Squadron. All this was done with uncommon zest and zeal until we were faced with the problem of the bar's ceiling. This whitewashed expanse was crisscrossed with cracks dating from the early part of the British Empire. When we asked for plaster from the Base Engineers we were met with unbelieving stares: "why don't you ask for flying elephants? I could probably get them for you sooner" was the curt reply, "come back next year."

Jerry Weinstein[5] was the live wire on the bar committee, and he decided, what we needed to cover the cracks, was wallpaper. Next day Jerry and I started to go the rounds of the meager Tel Aviv shops. All we saw was shoddy prewar stuff. Just when we were ready to call it a day we came across a wallpaper which had a deep blue background and sliver stars on it. It was startling, and Jerry said "this is just what we need" in an aside to me, "try to get a decent price." But haggling was not needed; when the merchant found out that we were from the IAF he practically gave us the stuff.

None of us Israelis had ever hung a foot of paper, but the Americans in the squadron gave us a demonstration on the finer points of paper hanging. With that the Club was ready for the grand opening. Next Friday was to be the day, but we couldn't get the Brass to let us invite the girls from next door, so it was an all male affair. We got the Yellows[6] and the boys from ATC to attend. Butch Ben-Yok[7] cranked up an old gramophone and got some old prewar sounds out of it. This got a lot of whistles and groans from the already well primed crowd.

A very vocal argument followed the cranky gramophone performance, and many proposals were presented as to how to improve our musical plight. Most were unlikely, including group sing-along or solo performances, and many shouted "God forbid." Finally Butch got up and said "Lets borrow the 101 piano." At this

69 Squadron Commander Trig Maseng (right) briefs Jacob Ben-Haim, aka "Black." Maseng commanded the Hammers from June 25, 1949 (though his assignment letter was dated July 25, 1949) until March 1, 1950, when Black took over as 69 Squadron Commander until March 1951.

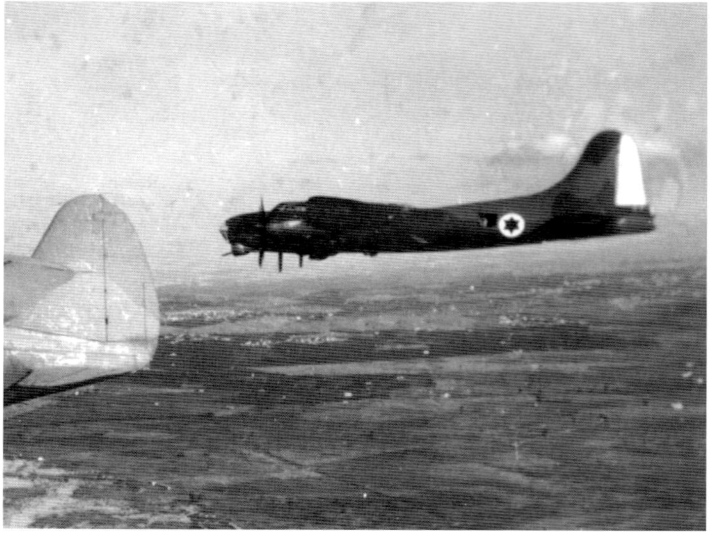

The repaired 1603 was returned to the Hammers more than a year after the August 1949 belly landing and was the first Fort to be equipped with a nose turret as illustrated.

all hell broke loose; everyone had his pet idea how to do it. The Yellows declined the honor to take part so the Dakotas were out. Someone said "Let's stick it in the bomb bay of 1602." Nahum Efrat consented, so preparation got under way. Equipped with stout ropes, the B-17 took of for Ramat David with a flight plan marked "Night navigational flight."

Well past midnight the Fort landed at Ramat David and parked at dispersal. The raiding party got hold of a bomb dolly from No 2 hangar and headed for 101's club rooms. Then the upright piano was tenderly placed on the dolly and the raiders rolled the valuable cargo to the waiting Fort. Bomb doors were readily opened, and the loading proceeded with remarkable ease.

We should have been suspicious. Nahum ordered all aboard, closed bomb doors, and started engines and took off. In less than an hour the Fort made an extra smooth landing at Tel Nof. Nahum opened the bomb doors and the crew got a cart ready to receive the "booty."

Incredibly the piano wouldn't get past the catwalk in the bomb bay. After a lot of sweat the wise offered a solution, "before we loaded the thing we had several drinks to smooth the way, so let's go to the bar and have a late nightcap." No other advice was offered so it was done. It was close to dawn.

The drink did the trick. When the crew got back to the B-17 and tried again the piano slid out effortlessly and was carted in triumph to The Hammers Club. It was then Friday, and of course the usual festivities were very special, and all who attended had a splendid evening, with Butch excelling at our purloined musical treasure. But dark clouds of doom were gathering up North, boding evil.

The T-Paper War

We had a splendid weekend with our new musical treasure, but Sunday we got a phone call from 101 ops, and in an unmistakable manner we were told "Return our piano within 24 hours or you will rue the day when you stole it!" Our joy with the piano was greater than the Reds' threat, so we ignored it.

A couple of days later we were at the lines when we heard the unmistakable snarl of a couple of Merlins[8] approaching from up North. We all stopped work and looked at a pair of Spits coming low, circling our lines. When they had our attention they came again, this time with open cockpits, and tossed a pair of round things. We ducked instinctively, but the round things started to unfold into long white streams of paper. The long rolls of toilet paper had red printing with the following massage, "The piano will be returned to its rightful place in 48 hours or the next time it's going to be real."

That evening we all gathered at the club and decided that the piano would have to go back. Some were against, while others agreed, but wanted the piano slightly damaged. Finally it was agreed to give it back, but the question was how? Nahum clearly indicated that a B-17 was out of the question. We then approached Danny Rosin, the 103 skipper. Being a sterling gentleman, Danny agreed to freight the piano back on the next Dakota flight to Ramat David.

The duty pilot on the next flight north was Claude Duval.[9] He was considered by experts on the C-47 as the best there was. Claude could do with a Dakota at naught feet tricks which had fighter jockeys stare open-mouthed. Claude's preflight preparations consisted of a hefty pull on his handy bottle of South African "Commando" Brandy. A most potent tipple guarantied to straighten overcooked spaghetti. With those preparations in hand Claude took off accompanied by one Hammer to witness the handover. He had this to report.

Claude made his usual smooth landing, and as soon as he put the breaks on the 101 truck drove up with three sour faced guys on it. They looked the piano over and even tried the keys to verify that we didn't temper with the wires.

Milton Bottger, aka Butch Ben-Yok, playing the Reds' piano at the Blacks' club.

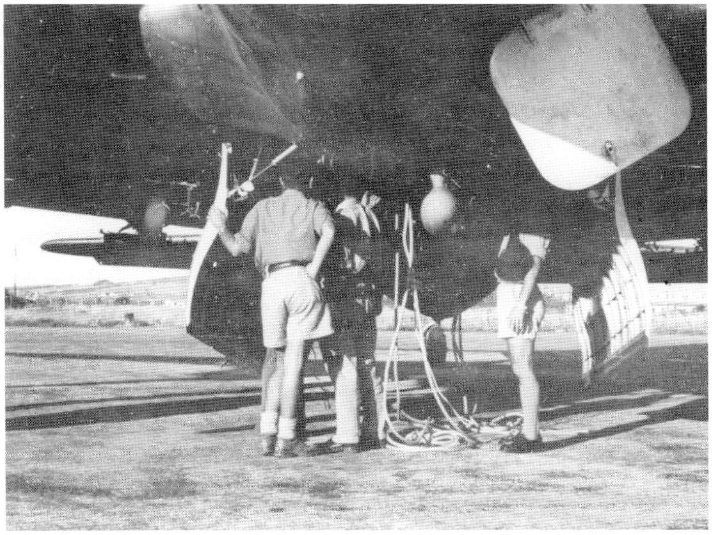

Blacks loading the reds' piano into the bomb bay of 1603 for the return trip from Tel Nof to Ramat David.

Navigator Stefan Falc, aka Shmuel Laron, in his station inside 1602. A World War II RAF navigator, Falc served with 301 Squadron. German Focke-Wulf fighters intercepted the Halifax he was navigating on the night of September 10 to 11, 1944. The Halifax was shot down and Falc was a Prisoner of War until May 1945.

Soon the piano was resting on the truck when Claude asked the guys if they had anything handy for a parched throat. "The bar is closed, but we have a can of glycol that could wet your throat." Claude let out a stream of choice African curses and took off. As he was on the take-off he spotted a row of new Indian type field tents with two long bamboo poles sticking out of them. They were about ten yard on the side of the runway. Claude chortled and said "I'll leave my visiting cards right here." With that he made a tight turn, got the Dakota down to nearly ten feet, and neatly toppled the bamboo poles over. He landed the plane 40 minutes later at Tel Nof and went to the bar for a much needed drink. The place was jammed with after work 69 and 103 crews. When asked how was the delivery Claude just said "Piece of cake."

The 1603 crew for the piano flight from Tel Nof to Ramat David included 69 Squadron Commander Nahum Efrat (first from left), radio operator Milton Bottger (fourth from left), and navigator Milosh Yalinek, aka David Yaeli (second from right).

Just then Bonny Boneh, our popular base commander, made one of his rare appearances at the bar and cornered Claude. "My dear chap, consider yourself confined to quarters and please present yourself in my office tomorrow at 09:00 precisely," all this in fine English as acquired in the RAF. Claude got two weeks confined to barracks.

Kaplan's Formula

At the end of 1949 the hard currency reserves of the fledgling Israeli government were rapidly approaching zero. The IAF did not escape the stringent cuts in expenditures imposed on the population by Mr. Kaplan, the energetic finance minister at that time. He was not to blame; the culprit was the defunct British Palestine Administration. When they left the country at the termination of the Mandate they simply took the foreign currency reserves with them. Only a year later did they hand it back. In the meantime 100 octane fuel could be had for cash only.

That's when Kaplan handed down his directive; 69 could fly only one B-17 at a time according to Mr. Kaplan's formula: one B-17 = 4 engines = four Spitfires. That put a stop on all close formation flying training

On top of this Mr. Kaplan asked his staff to investigate plans for the "gainful" employment of the B-17. One of his bright sparks found a brochure extolling the rain making possibilities of large aircraft. Right away they got the freshly minted Ministry of Agriculture interested in this revolutionary idea.

It's Raining Violets

Increasing rainfall by seeding was nothing new in the world in 1949. It was a new scientific rain making twist not yet used in Israel at that time. One fine day the squadron got a signal from AHQ indicating that we were to take part in a new "rain making" operation under the aegis of the newly formed Ministry of Agriculture. It was appropriately codenamed "Rain Clouds."

The rain bomber 1602 was equipped with an AN/APS-3 radar in a transparent Plexiglas housing from March 1952 until the end of that year, when the radar was removed and the nose turret refitted.

A few days later a couple of guys from the Agricultural Department of the Weizman Institute, along with the Base Met Officer, arrived at the squadron. We were informed that one of the B-17s was to be converted for rain making ops. It would also have to fly long-range flights over the Mediterranean Sea in search of suitable clouds. Due to experience to be gained during those long-range flights, only one crew would have to fly those ops. This piece of news resulted next morning in a rush to the base infirmary, where the squadron air crews presented the doctor with a long list of complaints, all of them attesting that the individual was not fit to fly.

I didn't take part in this rush, as I loved to fly, and it seemed to be something new and interesting. The crew was to be limited: pilot, co-pilot, navigator, radio operator, and gunner.

Next day our mecs, headed by line chief "Futy" Futerman, got busy installing in the bomb bay's cat walk of 1602 an enormous 200 liter steel tank. This monster was equipped with a pipe and a nozzle going through the bomb bay doors, and was to be operated by the gunner, me. The tank was to contain Iodine of silver to seed the appropriate cloud, and hopefully this should result in rain.

We started flying this op towards the end of August!

The instructions we received were to fly westwards about 100 miles, turn 180, and fly back towards the shore. We were to look for big fat stratocumulus clouds and start to seed them on the way, hopefully resulting in rain. The "farm boys" had an observer on the ground who was in radio contact with the plane. This guy from the Weizman Institute was a deep voiced water conservation expert named Yoav.

Having been briefed thoroughly on procedure we started flying the next day. The crews were on rotation: pilots Hugo (Agmon), Pini (Ben-Porat), and Blacky (Ben-Haim); navigators Johnny (Harris) and Stefan (Falc); and radio operators Butch (Milton Bottger) and Rafi (Goldman). The gunner was invariably the same, me. It was my choice and I had no regrets.

Day after day we took off armed with paper wrapped sandwiches and thermoses with strong coffee, an essential ingredient for long-

Hammers at work during major maintenance to 1603 at Hatzor, which started in October 1952 and was completed in January 1953.

As 1603 only emerged from major maintenance (in metal finish) during January 1953, 1601 (still camouflaged) and 1602 (already in metal finish) attended the 4 Wing command hand over parade on January 21, 1953.

range flights. This tedious enterprise went on for long weeks with scant results. As soon as we spotted a likely cloud we got on top of it and I squeezed the tit, dumping gallons of Iodine on the likely cloud. All we got for our pains was the invariable exchange with Yoga on the ground, "Yoav, does it rain? Noooo" was the long deep voice of Yoav.

We were well into September when we were told the next day would be the last flight on this operation. We took off at 10:00 and headed west. Blacky was at the wheel with Pini on the right side seat; Johnny was navigating and Rafi was on the horn. We flew for an hour and made a 180 degree turn towards the shore. About 30 mils out we spotted a real monster, a black and gray strato going up to15,000 feet, a mountain slowly sailing towards the shore; we all agreed, this is it. Blacky started flying circles, shepherding this monster towards Natanya. A few miles out I decided that in the best spirit of 69 not to come back from ops with munitions on board, I then and there dumped the remaining stuff in the tank. The cloud immediately started to boil like a pea soup. Rafi at this time kept calling Yoav on the ground:

"– Yoav, is it raining?
– Nooo!"

Came back Yoav's deep voice. This went on for quite a while, and Rafi got frantic, as the cloud was already over Natanya. Then finally Yoav's deep voice announced, "Yes it's raining, over in Jordan." We didn't know whether to cheer or cry. Natanya is only eight miles from the Jordanian border!

Next morning the Jordan Post had banner headlines, "The Zionists have a new secret weapon, floods in September." The oldest Arabs on the West Bank couldn't remember rains in September.

This put an end to Mr. Kaplan's plans to get a return on 100 Octane fuel expanded by the B-17. Many years later I read about rain making by experts, the Australians. Rain cannot be made, only augmented in the rainy season.

Don't Fence Me In

After a few weeks we got used to our new surroundings, especially the close location of our barracks to the women's units across the fence.

The standing orders on this base placed the girls' quarters out of bounds. This only led the keen knights of the air to sharpen their wits and find ways and means to surmount this drawback. In no time we found out that the fence separating the sexes was a joke. This supposed security fence was probably erected during

Hammers reserve air gunner Zvi Freier (Avidror) stands beside a belly turret (waist gun position was faired over) and poses inside a dorsal turret of a B-17 at Hatzor in the fall of 1953.

Superb views of immaculate 1601 and 1603 at Hatzor during a major IAF exercise, October 1953. The B-17s operated from Hatzor alongside the Mosquito equipped 109 Squadron and 110 Squadron; all three squadrons flew together from Ramat David from 1969 until 1986.

the early days of the British Empire and was a deterrent to donkeys only. We managed to surmount it with practiced ease.

On one of my nightly forays I got back over the fence at about 3 AM and headed towards my room at the barracks closest to the fence. I stepped on the porch when I suddenly spotted a white jellabiya-clad figure at the door of the last room. He had a gleaming knife in his right hand while his left was on the door handle.

The room was mine, and my room mate was Abe Nathan. I didn't hesitate for a moment, pulled my 9 mm FN, and fired two quick shots at the intruder. I hit him because he dropped the knife, rolled off the porch, and crawled in the dark towards the fence. When I got there there was no sign of him.

At this time the fence patrol, having heard the shots, arrived on the scene and raised the alarm. It was dawn when the base security officer started to sort out the situation. They found a blood stained jellabiya a few yards over the fence with tracks heading east. It was early 1950 and the first intrusion of an Arab terrorist.

Incredibly, during this racket neither Abe nor my next door neighbor, Reuben Narunsky, nor his roommate, Sokkie Kramer, woke up. When woken they flatly disbelieved the story and were convinced only after they saw the blood stained jellabiya.

A couple of days later the HQ brass and MP descended on the base and started taking a close look at the security situation. The conclusion was no surprise; the fence was to be replaced immediately. In the meantime guards and patrols were doubled.

In early 1950 cumbersome military contracts were in the future. At that time the Base Building section got the order to put up a new fence and got the suitable funding. I got wind of this from a friend I had in the section. Right away I saw the solution to the dire cash problems of the aircrew in the squadron. First I

Above and following: A November 16, 1953, activity covered all aspects of B-17 weaponry: loading bombs into the bomb bay, attaching bombs to the external racks, and servicing and zeroing the waist guns, tail guns, and all three turrets.

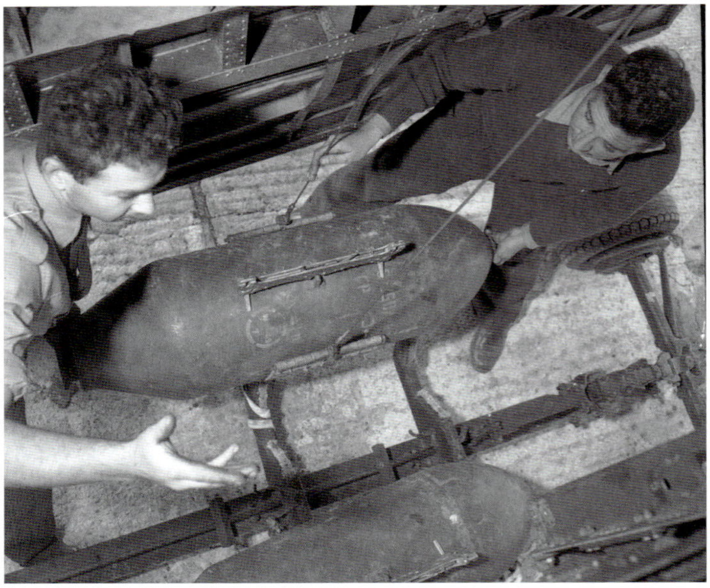

approached the chief of the Building Section and convinced him that we could put up the fence for much less than an approved contractor. The man was very skeptical as to the aircrew's ability in fence work. But he knew me from the time I made the first and only hand made wooden prop for a Piper Cub in the annals of Israeli aviation. I made it in his carpentry shop under the tutelage of Professor Piattely.

I told him we had several ex-kibutznicks in the squadron with vast experience in fence work. Then I made him an offer he couldn't refuse. Ten yards of fence free of charge, if he approved we get the work. We got the contract.

Israel ordered 50 Phantoms for delivery from autumn of 1969 until summer of 1970. IAF planning called for activation of two new squadrons, the first at Hatzor (201 Squadron activated from August 1969) and the second at Ramat David (69 Squadron activated from November 1969). The USAF assigned to the IAF five Phantom crew conversion training slots, but the IAF was short of navigators, so the team included six pilots and four navigators; pilot Isaac Peer attended the conversion course as navigator. The IAF Phantom team was in the USA from March until July 1969; their training included a visit to McDonnell Douglas at St Louis, where this photo was taken. Standing in fron of F-4E USAF 69-0417 (IAF Kurnass 122) from left to right: Ehud Henkin (69 Squadron Deputy A), Isaac Peer (201 Squadron Deputy B), Rami Harpaz (69 Weapon Systems Officer), Yoram Agmon (201 Deputy A), Menachem Eini (201 Lead Navigator), Shmuel Hetz (201 Commander), Avihu Ben-Nun (69 Commander), Shaul Levy (navigator, 69), Yair David (navigator, 201), and Achikar Eyal (69 Lead Navigator).

IAF commander Moti Hod and Hammers veteran Zvi Freier (Avidror) on stage during the 69 Squadron reunion on October 23, 1969.

The IAF Phantom conversion team flew with the 4452nd Tactical Fighter Training Squadron at George Air Force Base, California. Flying started in April 1969, and the course was completed in late July 1969. A reunion - of the USAF instructors (standing) and the survivors of the Israeli team - is planned for March 2010. Crouching from left to right: Ehud Henkin (killed in 1973), Shaul Levy (killed in 1973), Yair David (ejected in 1970), Rami Harpaz (Prisoner of War in Egypt from 1970 to 1973), Shmuel Hetz (killed 1970), Achikar Eyal (PoW in Egypt 1970 to 1971), Avihu Ben-Nun, Isaac Peer (PoW in Egypt 1970 to 1973), Menachem Eini (PoW in Egypt 1970 until 1973), and Yoram Agmon.

Next day we got down to work equipped with leather gauntlets, "kova tembel," water cans, wire cutters, and plenty of sun lotion. One of the Mahalniks turned up with a huge wooden mallet used to drive tenting pegs. Me and some other ex-kibutznicks rolled with laughter at this "tool." Then we showed the crew the real fence driving tool used in Israel, the "Halmania," a very heavy three inch pipe with a weight welded on top and two grips on the side.

We really got down to work, and in two weeks we got the fence up. The security blokes drove up and down the fence trying to find a weak spot, to no avail. The work was approved and we got paid. For many months 69 air crews were cash heavy and spent freely on our Tel Aviv forays. For many years the Tel Nof fence was a sound piece of work which I looked at with pride when years later I was doing reserve duty on the Base.

69 Flies Again

In 1968 the Israeli Ministry of Defense appointed my firm as the prime contractor for sealing a new series of hardened aircraft shelters. The ten shelters were constructed in various bases of the IAF. The work was done by several construction companies which kept me permanently on the road, as I had to keep an eye on the work in progress.

One day in early spring I was at Tel Nof, where three shelters were being worked on, when I heard some talking about a lot of new squadrons being commissioned. They sprung up like mushrooms after the rain. It suddenly struck me that amongst all those new squadron numbers one was obviously missing: 69.

It occurred to me then and there that 1968 marked the 20th anniversary of 69 Squadron, and I decided that this event should be commemorated in style, despite the fact that the squadron was decommissioned in 1957 and thus inactive for the best part of 12 years. To get this idea going I asked for a meeting with Moti Hod, IAF Commander, to see how he might react towards such an idea. Moti, being who he was, listened very carefully and asked me for my plans of organizing all by myself such a big ado.

Hammers veterans present the Flying Fortress era album to 69 Squadron Commander Avihu Ben-Nun (left) on October 23, 1969.

Bill Katz blowing his cigar during the Hammers reunion at Ramat David on the evening of October 23, 1969. Actor Danny Kaye is on the left.

Moti and I were old friends from bygone days when we played water polo. The meeting was very friendly, and my idea of a 69ers reunion was well received and approved.

I went over to the manpower division to get the names and addresses of the 69 crews. The young Lt on duty nearly laughed in my face, "You mean all those foreign guys from all over the world? We don't have anything on them." All they could give me was the aircrew list of 69 Squadron dated 1948. Had I known then of the task awaiting me I would have quit right then and there. But I didn't. With the able help of my wife Miriam I started a three continent, five country search to get the current addresses of the guys on the list. Things did not look very promising.

On my next report to Moti I told him about the problem. His advice was "Publish an ad in the papers but do not mention 69 Squadron, just say The B-17 Squadron." I did so, and had to pay for it out of my pocket, as this caper of mine didn't have any budget. The ad did wonders; I got enough names to start a world wide correspondence which lasted for six months. By that time it was already November 1968; 1968 was about to end, and a 20th anniversary party seemed to be unlikely.

While sitting in Moti's anteroom, awaiting my turn to present the final report, I overheard a clutch of Majors mentioning (once again) squadron numbers that I've never heard before. When my turn came to go in I presented Moti with the final report. "Zvi" Moti said "It's obvious that the 20th anniversary will turn out to be the 21st, so what now?"

An incredible idea came to my head, and I said "Moti, I've heard that you are commissioning a lot of new squadrons. How about bringing back to life a good one like 69?"

He replied "Zvika, that's not a bad idea at all, but say I agree. What do I equip The Heavy Bombardment Squadron with?" Right away I answered "Skyhawks, of course." Moti continued, "Have you ever seen a Skyhawk?" I said "No." "Well," Moti said, "It's a bitty and bitsy plane, not suitable for a heavy bombardment squadron like 69. But I'll tell you what, come back in a month's time and I might have some news for you. In the meantime keep the organizing going."

A month later I was again at AHQ, awaiting my turn to see Moti. He bade me to sit down, and without further ado placed a sheet of paper in front of me. The paper read:

> **Commissioning Order. I hereby commission the establishment of 69 Squadron as an active unit of the IAF. Equipment: Kurnass. Commanding Officer: Major Avihu Ben-Nun. To be based at Number 1 Wing.**

I was speechless, a most unusual state with me. "Moti," I said, "What's a Kurnass?" He said: "It's an F-4." I still looked at him uncomprehending, so he explained, "It's a Phantom." At that my jaw dropped. Moti said: "OK Zvika, you can close you mouth, and it better stay that way until I allow you to talk. If you open your mouth before that I'll jail you for a long time." It took me a few minutes to recover, as this was news far beyond my wildest dreams. Moti told me "Zvi, get yourself tomorrow morning at 10:00 to the Tel Nof Officers Club and meet Major Avihu Ben-Nun, the new CO of 69 Squadron. Tell him all there is to tell about 69 and plan with him future events."

Next morning I met Avihu for the first time. He was a charming, very good looking young man with elegant manners; quite the opposite of the cocky fighter pilot stereotype. In fact, he was a fighter pilot with kills to his credit. He was a very good listener, and for more than two hours I regaled him with "The Hammers" past. Avihu was very interested in my plan for a 20ies get together — in fact, he said "why don't you turn your plans into a commissioning party?"

This, of course, was a brilliant suggestion which I adopted on the spot. That was the moment that the birth of a permanent organization took place. No such group ever existed at that time in the IAF. I got hold of my phone book, and in no time "The

The active airman link between the Hammers' B-17 and F-4 eras was navigator Achikar Eyal, fourth from right on stage at the 69ers' reunion on October 23, 1969.

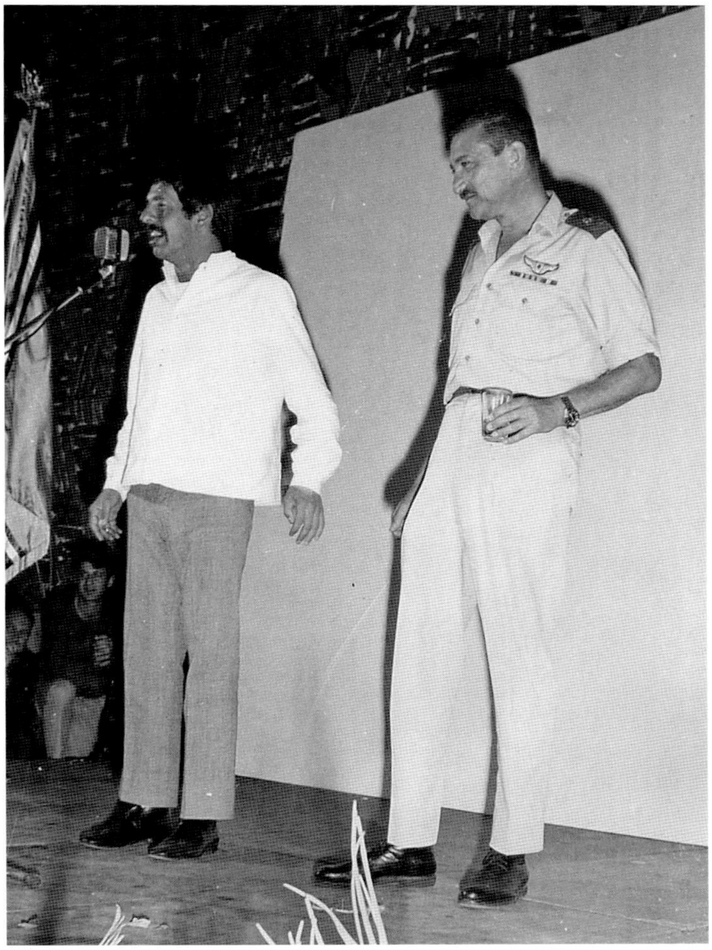

Old time friend of Hammers, Ezer Weizman (right) was IAF Commander from 1958 until 1966 and IDF Chief of the General Staff Branch at the time of 69 revival in 1969.

69 Squadron Veterans Club" was born. At the first meeting a committee was elected, composed of: Hayman Shamir Honorable Chairman, Bill Katz Chairman, Zvi Avidror secretary, Stefan Falc treasurer, David de Mayo architect, Lazar Hezekiah designer, and Amos Yarden.

I got to work right away, as we had only two months to get the party going. We decided to start the party with a ceremonial handing over of the 69 flag to the new boys. An exhibit in poster size pictures showing aircrew then and now was very ably planned by David and Lazar. It was lauded by all. Initially we planned on around 400 invites, but as the word got around I was suddenly inundated with calls from friends I never knew I had. That, coupled with the Brass getting themselves invited, snowballed the party to 1,700 "attending," choking the Number 2 hangar at Ramat David to the rafters. Luckily at that time no restrictions on donations existed, and I managed to "persuade" leading food companies to contribute freely to this event. It resulted in a very rich buffet, including spirits from all over the globe.

The show part was to match the event. The new Phantom boys put up a hilarious show followed by most of the luminaries of stage and screen at that time. But undoubtedly the show stopper was our star guest, Danny Kaye, who gave an unforgettable rendering of a furious Soviet Air Force General fulminating at the Egyptians for losing all his MiGs during the Six Day War.

It was well after midnight when the base crew started to clean up the mess. Today it is still considered the best party ever in the annals of the IAF.

Notes

[1] MAHAL was a Hebrew acronym for the "Overseas Volunteers" who had extensive wartime experiences in different air forces during WWII. They formed the backbone of the fledgling Israel Air Force and trained most of the air and ground crews.

[2] Hershale was Ezer Weizman's diminutive for Zvi Avidror.

[3] The Reds were 101 Squadron service persons who wore distinct red baseball caps; the Blacks were 69 Squadron crews who wore black baseball caps with two white stripes.

[4] Tel Nof was formerly RAF Aqir, aka Ekron.

[5] Lead bombardier, ex 8th USAAF.

[6] The Yellows were 103 Squadron service persons who wore black billed yellow baseball caps.

[7] South African radio operator Milton Bottger adopted the alias "Butch Ben-Yok" (loosely translated "Son of a B.....") while serving in the IAF.

[8] The Rolls Royce Merlin powered the 101 Squadron's Spitfires.

[9] Claude Duval was an ex-SAAF pilot, one of the most daring DC-3 pilots, who did incredible feats in flying the Dakota.

5

F-4 Kurnass
1969-1973: The Difficult We do Right Away, the Impossible Takes a While Longer

Ten years after 69 Squadron was inactivated as a B-17 unit, an event that eventually enabled the revival of the Hammers took place. The June 1967 Six Day War changed the way Israeli leaders and IDF commanders perceived the IAF. Until June 1967 the IAF promised air superiority to skeptic Israeli leaders and IDF commanders. From June 1967 Israeli leaders and IDF commanders took for granted IAF air superiority. As a result the IAF stake in the Israeli defense budgets soared, and the IAF was expanded to suit its new role as Israel's military cutting edge arm.

69 Squadron's new badge emphasized the Kurnass as central motif with implied linkage to the historical B-17 Hammer and a 1960s artistic style presentation of "69" (six in yellow on left side of shield and nine in yellow on right side of the shield). New badge designer was David de Mayo, once a B-17 air gunner and then an architect and designer. Along with the new badge came a new slogan: THE DIFFICULT WE DO RIGHT AWAY, THE IMPOSSIBLE TAKES A WHILE LONGER.

Also as a result of the Six Day War the IAF French era came to an end, and was replaced by an American age. U.S. commitment to secure the survival of Israel in the face of a hostile Soviet Block supported Arab World generated the supply of advanced weapons and combat aircraft. The latter replaced the heavy IAF Six Day War losses, as well as allowing for a major expansion of IAF order of battle in line with the new leading place of the IAF at the top of the Israeli defense tools. Two types of combat aircraft signaled the new Americanization process: A-4 Skyhawk deliveries started in late 1967, and F-4 Phantom II deliveries followed from the autumn of 1969.

Activation

Air1 issued Organization Order 69/54 on August 18, 1969, covering activation of the second IAF F-4 unit, 69 Squadron. Ramat David based 69 Squadron was to begin preparations for activation from November 1, 1969. The new unit was set to operate the F-4 Kurnass[1] for air defense and attack of surface targets on land and sea. Operational capability was to be achieved after acceptance of 12 aircraft, with initial operational capability prior to this milestone and full operational capability after delivery of the full complement of assigned aircraft.

Avihu Ben-Nun commanded the Hammers' Kurnass set up team. Ben-Nun's nomination was not obvious. IAF attitude was to assign experienced squadron commanders to oversee introduction of new jet fighters: Menahem Bar in command of the first Meteor unit back in 1953, Beni Peled in command of both first Ouragan and first Mystere squadrons in 1955 and 1956 respectively, Ezekiel Somech in command of the first Vautour squadron in 1958, Yak Nevo in command of the first Super Mystere squadron in 1958, Joe Alon in command of the first Mirage squadron in 1962, and Ohad Shadmi in command of the first A-4 Skyhawk squadron in 1967. All commanded first line combat aircraft squadrons prior to assignment to introduce new and mostly ground breaking equipment. The new Hammers leader did not command a fighter squadron prior to assignment as 69 Squadron Commander; he was a senior deputy commander[2] of a Mystere squadron during the Six

Most IAF Kurnass crews relied on Unit 180 computer reports to monitor their flights, but a few continued to write down their flights in old-fashioned logbooks that were occasionally stamped for authenticity and signed by the squadron commander, Avihu Ben-Nun.

Day War and Deputy A of a Mirage squadron from the summer of 1967. Avihu Ben-Nun recalled:

> "I was Squadron 119 Deputy Commander A until December 1968 when I was posted to an intermediate staff assignment. Moti[3] wanted deputy commanders with Six Day War experience, young and ready for a three year assignment as F-4 squadron commanders. I think that he made this decision against the opinion of some staff officers. From my own personal perspective, I was very happy with this decision. From a broader view perspective it might have been a risk, because the introduction of this new aircraft – something totally different, a quantum leap forward – had to be made in such a way that we would be able to train and qualify additional air crews – there were no plans to send more airmen for conversion in the USA – amidst war and casualties.
>
> "The decision to nominate Hetz[4] and myself was certainly "unconventional," but I think that it was the right decision to make. On the other side, I often thought that if I had the previous experience of a squadron commander then I might have done fewer errors in my command. Therefore, I cannot decide if it was good or not, but the fact is that the two commanders succeeded. For me it was the most difficult and most challenging period in my service career."

Airmen and Aircraft

The nucleus of the new Hammers included five airmen trained in the USA from January until August 1969: pilots Avihu Ben-Nun, Rami Harpaz, and Ehud Henkin; and navigators[5] Achikar Eyal and Shaul Levy. At the time the IAF only had a small number of navigators among its ranks; a few were Vautour navigators and the rest were transport navigators. In preparation to the introduction of the Kurnass the IAF Flying School stepped up navigator training,

First five Hammers airmen, from left to right: Ehud Henkin, Shaul Levy, Avihu Ben-Nun, Achikar Eyal, and Rami Harpaz.

69 Squadron Commander Avihu Ben-Nun, with 69 Squadron Lead Navigator Achikar Eyal in the back seat, arrive at Ramat David on November 15, 1969, to end the ferry flight from Hatzor in the lead of the first four Hammers jets. Ben-Nun and Eyal flew F-4E 68-0437, which became Kurnass 35 and later Kurnass 135.

F-4E Block 39 USAF 68-0434, 68-0435, 68-0436, and 68-0437 (Kurnass 26, 29, 32, and 35 respectively) were the third Peace Echo 4-ship delivery to Israel. The newcomers landed at Hatzor on November 14, 1969, and were ferried to Ramat David the next day still wearing their U.S. serial numbers. Visible in this photo is 68-0436 (initially Kurnass 32 and later Kurnass 132), which Ramat David Wing 1 Commander Jacob Agassi, with 69 Squadron pilot Aviem Sella in the back seat, ferried from Hatzor to Ramat David on November 15, 1969.

but in the meantime the first Kurnass navigators were former Vautour navigators, fighter pilots retrained as Kurnass back seat air crews, transport navigators converted to fast jets, transport radio operators retrained as fast jet navigators, and even veteran staff officers who initiated their careers as Mosquito navigators and rejuvenated their flying days in the Kurnass. Both Achikar Eyal and Shaul Levy were previously Vautour navigators, while Achikar Eyal was unique, as he was also the only air crew to set a bond between the old Hammers as a B-17 navigator and the new 69 Squadron as a Kurnass navigator. Rami Harpaz:

> "I was named Weapons System Officer for the new Ramat David Kurnass squadron. Prior to our USAF F-4 conversion course, IAF Commander Moti Hod briefed us that our mission was to prove that only a pilot can fly the Phantom on most missions. The example was the Vautour, an aircraft mostly flown by pilot with navigator joining mostly lead-ship in complicated missions. Right from the start of our F-4 flights we realized that this was not possible; the F-4 was a two seated fighter designed for teamwork that yielded special qualities unknown before in the IAF.
>
> "We began to plan changes and modifications during conversion in the USA. The F-4's air-to-air fixed ranges were 300 meters and 600 meters, but our standard was 200 meters. Henkin insisted to modify this feature; he argued that if pilots would be trained to open fire from 300 meters they would not close in during combat, so we made a compromise and changed the closer fixed range from 300 meters to 250 meters.
>
> "We flew 26 sorties during the USAF F-4 conversion course, barely enough to get to know how to fly the aircraft. Actual training was even less because of the rather long transit flights from air base to training areas. To learn more we had to explore technical manuals by ourselves."

Pending activation of their own unit at the beginning of IAF Year 1969 Term 3,[6] the 69 Squadron Kurnass qualified airmen flew training sorties and operational missions as 201 Squadron aircrew. Simultaneously, 201 Squadron ran the IAF Year 1969 Term 2 Kurnass conversion course.[7] Future Hammers aircrew attending the 201 Squadron IAF Year 1969 Term 2 Kurnass conversion course were pilots Gideon Magen, Aviem Sella, and Abraham Rodan, as well as navigators Shabtai Ben-Shoa, Pinchas Nachmani, and Reuben Fisher. Ramat David Wing 1 Commander Jacob Agassi – who would fly many 69 Squadron missions in the Kurnass – also attended that pioneering Kurnass conversion course.

The first four Kurnass airframes assigned to 69 Squadron were ferried from Hatzor to Ramat David on November 15, 1969. The Hammers initiated training flights with a cadre of airmen that included graduates of the USA conversion course and of the 201 Squadron IAF Year 1969 Term 2 Kurnass conversion course, as well as students of an IAF Year 1969 Term 3 Kurnass conversion course. Qualified air crews continued to fly operational missions from Hatzor as the Hammers frantically pressed ahead towards achievement of initial operational capability.

First Missions

Still a long way from the goal of 12 aircraft for the achievement of operational capability, the Hammers certainly achieved initial operational capability with five and a half "fully" qualified crews (six pilots and five navigators) and five jets (Kurnass 37 having joined the pioneering foursome). Avihu Ben-Nun and Achikar

IAF Chief Test Pilot Danny Shapira (left) flew the F-4 in the USA prior to deliveries to Israel. Shapira then flew his Kurnass "solo" with navigator Achikar Eyal (right) in Kurnass 37 on December 10, 1969.

Eyal flew in the lead of the first operational mission – air-to-air patrol – in Kurnass 35 on November 25, 1969. Launching operational missions with a cadre of inexperienced ground crews was a challenge. Avihu Ben-Nun recalled:

> "Most of our F-4 trained ground crews were still in the USA when we began flying, so we had to do with ground crews that were not trained on the F-4 and at most had A-4 experience. They were augmented by representatives of U.S. companies such as Litton that produced the navigation system, as well as representatives from manufacturers of engines, radar, etc. They were especially helpful when we decided to introduce operational modifications; an example was a sight camera that the F-4 lacked, so we took the Mirage camera and adapted it to the Phantom's sight within a time frame of two days. We wanted to insert a lot of logic into the fire control computer, such as switch from air-to-ground mode to air-to-air mode; brilliant technological minds such as Rami Harpaz used to show the engineers what we wanted."

It took a full night of hard work – with Ramat David Wing 1 Commander Jacob Agassi and 69 Squadron Commander Avihu Ben-Nun lending a hand alongside the ground crews – to properly load two Kurnass aircraft for the Hammers' first attack mission! At the time the IAF was battering the Egyptian air defense force west of the Suez Canal as part of an ongoing Attrition War air superiority battle. 69 Squadron's first air-to-ground mission was therefore an air superiority operation that targeted an Egyptian air defense force SA-2 battery at nearby Fayid. Avihu Ben-Nun with Shaul Levy and Rami Harpaz with Achikar Eyal flew two bombing passes to drop their load of 12 bombs each; 13 years after the old B-17s last bombed in anger Egyptian targets with equivalent bomb loads, the Hammers were back in business.

69 Squadron Lead Navigator Achikar Eyal participated in the Hammers' Kurnass air-to-air and air-to-ground operational debuts, flying Kurnass 35 (USAF 68-0437) and 29 (USAF 68-0435) on November 25 and 28, 1969, respectively; the first mission as leader with 69 Squadron Commander Avihu Ben-Nun and the second mission as wingman with Rami Harpaz. Attack configured Kurnass 35 – with 12 Mark 82 and six M-117 bombs - was photographed departing Ramat David in December 1969.

Aviem Sella flew his first Kurnass mission on December 25, 1969, when the IAF launched a massive suppression/destruction of enemy air defense offensive. Sella flew two missions that day: both in Kurnass 32, both with navigator Shabtai Ben-Shoa, and both targeted Fayid West. Kurnass 32 was photographed at Ramat David in December 1969.

Air Superiority

Israel's policy during the Attrition War was uncompromising, and aimed at forcing the Egyptians to abandon their static war concept and to deter Egyptian leadership from evaluation of the Suez Canal crossing option. The war was a series of escalating phases; the objective of each Israeli escalation was to de-escalate fighting to the point where Egypt would accept a ceasefire. By the time 69 Squadron joined hostilities the IAF was amidst an air superiority offensive. Gideon Magen:

> "I trained at Hatzor in the first IAF Kurnass conversion course. The squadron was activated at Ramat David in temporary housing – the squadron building that in the past was the home of 105 Squadron Mustang and 117 Squadron Meteor – pending construction of our own purpose built building.
>
> "I was Deputy Commander B, and my navigator was Pini Nachmani — we teamed up during conversion. Crews did not always fly together, but we made an effort to preserve regular crews, and most of my Kurnass flights at the time were with Pini — most, but not all.
>
> "Immediately after the squadron was activated we began to train in a Kurnass conversion course, lecturing to them and flying with them. All this was done while flying operational sorties during the Attrition War. For this reason we could not spare time and resources for our own training, so we trained on our way back from operational sorties, mostly air-to-air training and gunnery practice.
>
> "Most operations were over Egypt. Our shield was low altitude penetration; we did not know the real value of our countermeasure system, and eventually we learnt that these were not worth much. Anyway we penetrated low, pulled up abruptly to bomb, and returned at low altitude for as long as our remaining fuel capacity permitted.
>
> "At least on two occasions I remember looking out after the attack and seeing the whole desert firing at us with AAA and SA-7s. On another mission they launched seven SAMs against our Kurnass during pull-up!"

Egyptian SAM batteries west of the Suez Canal were all destroyed by early December 1969 and the IAF enjoyed total air superiority. The Hammers did not fly SEAD missions from December 7 to 24, 1969, and the lull was fully exploited to train more air crews; Ramat David Wing 1 Flying Squadron Commander Yalo Shavit flew his Kurnass "solo" on December 23, 1969, and Amos Zamir soloed the following day. Training and fighting simultaneously obviously produced conflicts that had to be smoothed out. An extreme example is 69 Squadron Commander's decision to integrate an operational order for night attack with a nighttime qualification examination flight. Avihu Ben-Nun:

> "We had to train airmen amidst war. In this case I flew in the back seat, and in the front seat was Amos Zamir, whom I had to qualify. He was an experienced pilot; most of our pilots were experienced, but he had to be qualified for night flying, so he flew two sorties with an instructor and then I had to qualify him. We armed the aircraft, flew to the Suez Canal, illuminated and bombed west of the canal. On our way back we practiced several interceptions using as target the aircraft incoming to replace us on the

The crew Ben-Nun/Eyal flew Kurnass 135 in the lead – call sign NELSON 1 – of a SEAD mission against an Egyptian SA-2 battery in the Jenifa sector on December 7, 1969. The successful IAF air superiority campaign of December 1969 paved the way to the Blossom series of attacks from January 1970. Kurnass 135 was photographed landing at Ramat David during October 1970 with a pair of neighboring Mirages awaiting their turn to take-off.

Aviem Sella with Shabtai Ben-Shoa flew Kurnass 26 during the Blossom 1 mission on January 7, 1970, when they dropped ten 400kg bombs on the Egyptian commando headquarters at Inchas. Kurnass 126 was photographed when 69 Squadron Commander Avihu Ben-Nun (pointing at the rear cockpit) took future IDF Chief of Staff Mota Gur (standing in G suit beside Ben-Nun) for a ride in the IAF's pride.

attack mission, flew three circuits, and landed to end an operational training qualification flight."

The same day that Amos Zamir flew his solo flight in the Kurnass, the Hammers returned to attack Egyptian SA-2 batteries west of the Suez Canal. Apparently the Egyptians were determined to challenge IAF air superiority, so they deployed a new air defense force network west of the Suez Canal that the Israelis first noted on December 24, 1969. That day's action was the prelude to a major air superiority battle on December 25, 1969, as the IAF launched some 100 SEAD sorties to repeatedly attack the eight newly deployed Egyptian SAM batteries until all were suppressed and/or destroyed so that IAF air superiority was restored.

Blossom

Prior to escalating the Attrition War against Egypt, Israel signaled Syria to stay out of the fight. The mission to demonstrate Israel's air power to Syria was entrusted in the hands of the Hammers, which launched a pair for a low level run over Damascus on January 6, 1970. Rami Harpaz with Shaul Levy and Gideon Magen with Pinchas Nachmani did their job well and smashed windows all over the Syrian capital.

This show of force may well have deterred Syria from opening a second front as the Kurnass force launched a new offensive over Egypt. Operation Blossom was the final Israeli escalating action during the Attrition War, and an operation that eventually resulted in the desirable ceasefire, but only after a painfully long and winding road of bitter hostilities.

IAF air superiority west of the Suez Canal was won during late 1969 and consolidated in the wake of the December 25, 1969, action. However, Egypt was not willing to cease fire, so Israel decided to escalate the conflict well away from the front and deep into Egypt. The Kurnass force made this action possible. Operation Blossom targeted headquarters, logistic centers, and training facilities all over Egypt. The message was again gradual escalation that would force Egypt to accept a ceasefire and to abandon the Attrition War policy.

Blossom 1 was launched on January 7, 1970, and set a pattern for Blossoms to follow: a pair of 201 Squadron and a pair of 69 Squadron simultaneously raided Egypt. The former bombed the SA-2 school at Dahashur; the latter – Avihu Ben-Nun with Achikar Eyal and Aviem Sella with Shabtai Ben-Shoa – attacked the commando headquarters at Inchas.

Echo

Blossom continued, Egypt refused to surrender, and Syria did not open a second front against Israel. A somewhat belated Syrian reprisal to the Hammers' boom over Damascus followed Blossom 5 on January 28, 1970. The next day a Syrian MiG-21, or MiG-21s, flew a supersonic boom mission over Haifa, and the Israeli counter action followed on the night of January 29 to 30, 1970. Operation Echo 5 was launched to attack five Syrian cities with supersonic booms. Avihu Ben-Nun recalled:

> "Following a Syrian teasing there was a decision to fly supersonic booms over the five principle cities of Syria regardless of air defenses: Damascus, Haleb, Hama, Homs, and Latakiya. We received the operational order in the afternoon, and three aircraft took off at 01:00 after midnight. There was a quarter or half moon that enabled us to fly low. I took Haleb and Latakiya, which were the most distant targets. Over Haleb we flew along the main road of the city that was at a heading of 240; we flew

Aviem Sella with Sabtai Ben-Shoa flew Kurnass 30 over Syria on the Operation Echo 5 mission to "boom" Latakiya and Homs on the night of January 29 to 30, 1970. Kurnass 130 was photographed at Ramat David slightly more than a year later in February 1971.

from the east and accelerated along the road. SAMs were launched but did not guide in a threatening manner as we flew supersonically at less than 1,000 feet. We repeated the feat over Latakiya, where we faced radar guided AAA as well as several launches of SAMs that were again inefficient.

"Years later, as a senior IAF officer, I gave a ride to a soldier hitchhiker and I started to question him. Who are you? Where are you from? And he answered in a noticeable Arab accent. He was born in Syria and his family sneaked in from Haleb to Turkey; from there they immigrated to Israel. When did you immigrate? 1972, I was 15 years old at the time. Do you remember anything abnormal or special that happened in Haleb when you were aged 13? I do not know what you mean he answered, but something happened then that triggered us to decide to immigrate. What was it? One winter night there was an awful boom, windows smashed, and the electricity stopped. We were five children and we all ran to our parents' bed. Then our father said this is a sign from God that we have to leave and immigrate to Israel. His decision was bolstered by the fact that the window of my father's shop did not smash; in fact, all windows of Jewish owned shops were not smashed!

"It took them some time to sell their possessions and arrange their journey but they made it to Israel. I was obviously satisfied, but also a little amused, so I asked him if he did not confuse his story with Passover? No, he answered confidently. I was completely surprised how come. Still later I checked this issue. I made contact with the Haleb immigrants' community and asked them if they knew this story. They did. I was still sure that it was a tale or a legend, but I questioned them in more detail. Perhaps there was something in this story. I dug more deeply and learnt that Jews were banned from having shops on the main road of the city; they could only have shops in the perpendicular streets. The pattern of our flight and the propagation of the supersonic shock wave had maximum effect on objects directly on its way but spared objects on the sides. The banning of Jews from having shops on the main road saved their businesses from looters that emptied shops with smashed windows, as well as saving them the expense of paying glaziers to repair the damage that we did!"

First Air-to-Air Kill

69 Squadron revisited the Egyptian commando headquarters at Inchas while 201 Squadron bombed an Egyptian logistics facility at Helwan during Blossom 8 on February 8, 1970. Avihu Ben-Nun with Achikar Eyal and Aviem Sella with Shabtai Ben-Shoa flew offensive combat air patrol over the northern sector of the Nile Delta. The strike has already ended when two MiG-21s sneaked in right behind the pair of Hammers. Luckily GCI was on alert and warned the Kurnass air crews in time. Aviem Sella recalled:

> "Circa 1968 I was planned for conversion to the Mirage, but I already realized that flying was not enough. I initiated academic studies in the Hebrew University, Jerusalem, immediately after the Six Day War. Two or three evenings per week I studied in Jerusalem; statistics and economy. The Mirage conversion course was at Ramat David, and the implication was that I would have had to discontinue my studies, so I turned down this offer. A fighter pilot turning down an offer for Mirage conversion was an unheard of event, and I was summoned by the IAF Commander. The general attitude at the time was that a pilot did not need to study any further than he did during his flying training. I insisted upon studying, renounced the opportunity to fly the Mirage, and for this reason I was later assigned to 69 Squadron.

Kurnass 126 was adorned with a kill marking – painted on the left hand side of the nose section just below the windshield – in honor of the Hammers' first ever air to air kill credited to Aviem Sella and Shabtai Ben-Shoa on February 8, 1970. Photographed in October 1970 during a presentation to the press of Israel's mighty war machine, the kill marking was ridiculously taped over.

"While I continued my studies the Kurnass was purchased and 69 Squadron was activated. In fact, I continued my studies during and after the Attrition War at the Haifa branch of the Hebrew University. Three or four times a week, as Deputy Commander B, I returned from missions over Egypt flying at low altitude over Haifa to inform my lecturers that I would soon attend their lessons, landed at Ramat David, and an hour later was sitting in the class at Haifa. After the Attrition War I finally got nine months of leave to finish my studies; I squeezed two academic years into this time frame and got my first degree in 1972. Then I returned to 69 Squadron as Deputy A, and I think that I was the first Deputy A in the history of the IAF with an academic degree.

"I attended the first Kurnass conversion course at Hatzor; in fact, I got married during conversion in September 1969. Five of us – pilots Gideon Magen, Abraham Rodan, and me; and navigators Shabtai Ben-Shoa and Reuben Fisher – were assigned to 69 Squadron, and we joined the set-up team of five air crews. I first flew the Kurnass on September 29, 1969, and flew my first Kurnass mission – attacking a SAM battery – on December 25, 1969; I only had slightly more than 30 flying hours in the Kurnass at the time.

"In February 1970 I shot down my first MiG. I am not sure if I practiced air-to-air gunnery prior to that air combat. I launched the first AAM — the wrong missile, as I confused the switches; instead of launching a heat seeking missile I launched a semi-active radar homing missile. I launched the second missile beyond effective range. I had only flown some 50 flying hours in the Kurnass until then and I hardly knew the cockpit, but luckily for me the Egyptian pilot had plenty of patience for me to do all possible errors until I shot him down. He flew slowly over the Nile Delta; I got into cannon range and managed to shoot him down during my seventh cannon burst! Effectively I completed my air-to-air training during this air combat, but I certainly made history; it was the first F-4 air-to-air cannon kill ever achieved, and it was also the first air-to-air kill in the history of 69 Squadron."[8]

Technical Modifications

Activating the squadron, introducing equipment, training airmen, and fighting enemies were all accomplished simultaneously. As though this was not enough, the Kurnass crews pushed for application of numerous technical modifications. Some of these were indeed innovative, others were not entirely helpful, and some were troublesome. Rami Harpaz:

Israeli fighter pilots considered the ergonomics of the Mirage stick (left) superior to the man-machine interface of the American F-4 stick. The Mirage stick protruded from the cockpit floor straight up, but the hand grip was inclined to the right; ideal for right-handed pilots and problematic for left-handed pilots. The Phantom stick (right) protruded from the cockpit floor straight up and was far from ideal for both right-hand and left-hand pilots.

"There were so many ideas that first thing to do was to filter proposals. Some proposals that passed initial filtering did not progress much. One of these was a proposition to replace the Kurnass stick with a Shahak stick. The former was not 'user friendly' and imposed physical stresses, but the latter connections were different and it had no aileron trimming option. Our Technical Officer Nathan Segall somehow got hold of a Mirage 5 stick that had aileron trimming and we began to examine this option, but eventually this idea was dropped and the Kurnass stick remained inconvenient forever.

"A modification that was applied but proved troublesome was MAMA, the Hebrew acronym for fast switch air-to-air. From our own experience we knew that switching from air-to-ground mode to air-to-air mode had to be accomplished quickly and easily, but the original switch was on the instruments panel, and therefore barely accessible under combat stresses. The USAF already realized this and extended the switch by 10cm or so, yet this was still not satisfactory. We modified the stick switches logic so that switching from air-to-ground mode to air-to-air mode was accomplished by a single switch on the stick. It was a field-level modification: problem was floated, solution was proposed, modification was made, test flights proved feasibility of fix, and Technical Officer approved. Interestingly, 201 Squadron devised a similar modification but in a different manner!

"The 69 Squadron modification was seemingly more convenient but it had a negative side effect. Apparently our modification disrupted air-to-ground bombing accuracy. We did not realize that the modification we introduced released vertical radar lock in air-to-ground bombing mode, so the radar did not feed accurate range to the bombing computer. All we knew was that we stopped bombing accurately!

"We did not know what happened, and for a while we preferred manual bombing, as we figured the bombing system was not good. Then one night I flew a bombing mission with Shaul Levy. The difference between daytime and nighttime attacks was that during nighttime the crew paid more attention to instruments reading. We dived to bomb when Levy said 'range increase!' This was an extraordinary phenomenon, since while diving range to target should decrease. I pulled up and repeated the bombing run. The strange phenomenon repeated. We bombed manually and discussed what happened on our way back. We came to the conclusion that somehow radar was not locked. We did not know why, but we figured that this was the trouble. After landing we conveyed our findings to Technical Officer Nathan Segall. The Technical Officer and his team dived into the bowels of the bombing system and discovered that our brilliant fast switch from air-to-ground to air-to-air modification was actually responsible for our inaccurate bombing trouble!"

Improvized Reconnaissance

Israel ordered six RF-4E Phantom II reconnaissance aircraft, but deliveries were only scheduled for early 1971. As a stop gap measure pending delivery of the dedicated reconnaissance birds the IAF decided to modify two Kurnass jets as interim reconnaissance platforms, and the Hammers were assigned to lead the introduction of reconnaissance qualification to the Kurnass community.

Kurnass 17 had its cannon removed and a camera inserted. Gideon Magen with Shabtai Ben-Shoa tested the reconnaissance

In a crush emergency project, the IAF Material Department designed a Kurnass reconnaissance modification and Air Maintenance Unit 22 at Tel Nof implemented the design in two Hammers aircraft; Kurnass 17 was the first to be so modified.

Gideon Magen was scheduled to lecture to IAF Year 1970 Term 1 Kurnass Conversion Course students upon his return from the April 2, 1970, mission over Syria, but the students were informed that his lecture was cancelled due to ejection. Standing from left to right: Amnon Gurion (pilot), Avraham Weiland (pilot), Menachem (WSO), Kurnass Conversion Course Commander Michael Dvir (pilot), Adi Benaya (pilot), Gad Samok (pilot), Kobi (WSO), Uri Ofer (WSO), and Dan (pilot). Sitting from left to right: Dani Shpitzer (pilot), Eitan (pilot), Gideon Sheffer (pilot), Yoram (WSO), Gidon Yahalom (pilot), and Amos Levitov (WSO). Kneeling from left to right: Paltiel (WSO), Isaac Katz (WSO), Ofer Zidon (WSO), Uzi (WSO), Lior (WSO), Meir Gur (WSO), Zeev Yogev (WSO), and Gil Haran (WSO).

converted Kurnass 17 on March 14, 1970; Magen flew seven such test flights until March 23, 1970. Aviem Sella with Pinchas Nachmani tested the new combination on March 21, 1970, while three days later Gideon Magen with Shabtai Ben-Shoa trailed a pair of 119 Squadron Mirage reconnaissance birds on a mission to photograph the new Egyptian air base at Kina. Another mission was flown two days later to capture images of a SA-3 battery reportedly under construction near Cairo West. The battery under construction was indeed photographed, but it was a SA-2 battery, and not a SA-3 as previously thought.

Air Combat Loss

Egypt was the main front during the Attrition War, but clashes along the Israeli-Syrian border erupted from time to time during the same time frame. A major clash on April 2, 1970, resulted in 69 Squadron's first ever air-to-air combat loss. The principle IAF air-to-air platform was the Mirage delta fighter, but Kurnass air crews were eager to prove their worth in that arena of warfare. Perhaps this eagerness was counterproductive, as the IAF had plenty of experienced razor-sharp Mirage MiG killers, while Kurnass air crews had to master both air-to-air and air-to-ground qualifications.

Four Mirage pilots and two Hammers air crews engaged MiG-21s over Syria on April 2, 1970. The former returned safely and were credited with three air-to-air kills. The latter lost a Kurnass. Deputy A Ehud Henkin with Shabtai Ben-Shoa and Deputy B Gideon Magen with Pinchas Nachmani were the Kurnass air crews. The pair separated with the wingman in pursuit of a Syrian MiG-21; they launched an AAM that missed, but immediately afterwards were hit by AAM and had to eject from Kurnass 36 over Syrian soil. Gideon Magen and Pinchas Nachmani were prisoners of war in Syria until June 1973; Aviem Sella took over as Deputy B.

Blossom 18: Engineless Landing

Two pairs (Ehud Henkin and Shabtai Ben-Shoa with Amos Zamir and Yossi Kamay; Rami Harpaz and Shaul Levy with Uri Gil and Daniel Wittmann) flew Operation Blossom 18 on Friday, April 3, 1970. The pairs were tasked to attack SA-2 batteries in the Mansura sector. In order to maximize bombing impact the four aircraft flew with a single external fuel tank under the fuselage. Rami Harpaz recalled:

> "We pulled up to bomb and saw MiG-21s. I bombed, jettisoned the external fuel tank, turned right, and pulled up. A MiG-21 pulled with me. Fuel reading was 4,000 pounds and I thought we were doomed. The MiG had a wingman and there were more MiGs behind them. Anyway, I zoomed upwards, the MiGs followed. I dived and accelerated. When we clocked 750 knots, at very low altitude, I switched off the afterburner. Very fast, very low; I was looking forward and Shaul scanned backwards. Each time a MiG launched an AAM[9] Shaul said launch

A day after Kurnass 36 was lost in air combat over Syria the Hammers almost lost Kurnass 38 over Egypt. Rami Harpaz with Shaul Levy engaged Egyptian MiG-21s, managed to disengage, but ran out of fuel and glided to a successful emergency landing at Refidim. Aviem Sella with Daniel Wittmann ferried Kurnass 38 from Refidim to Ramat David later the same day.

and I broke away. Four missile launches, four successful breaks, and the two MiGs disappeared. They had no more missiles and they had no guns.

"Fuel was down to 800 pounds. We were still west of the Suez Canal but I started to climb. We reached 20,000 feet over the Suez Canal when fuel starvation switched off both engines. No hydraulic pump apart from wind-milling, no radio, silence. I pointed our nose at Refidim Air Base and began to evaluate options and prospects. Engineless landing the F-4 was not considered safe because wind-milling could not supply adequate hydraulic pressure for elevator movements; an emergency system was only introduced from Block 54 onwards.

"I discussed this issue with Shaul and we decided to try landing but maintain high speed for as long as possible. I dived steeply for direct approach and avoided elevator movements as much as I could. Down to 350 knots I began to feel the elevator issue but it was still not a problem. My judgment was not optimal; the aircraft did not decelerate as fast as I thought it would so I was too fast. I deployed undercarriage circa 300 knots, deployed flaps, but these were only activated at 240 knots. The Kurnass was still too fast when we touched down. I released the braking chute but it was torn away; we were faster than the speed that the braking chute could sustain. I brutally pressed the brakes and the tires exploded. The Kurnass rolled on the rims, slowed down, drifted sideways, and finally stopped beside the runway, about two thirds down the length of the runway."

Making the Right Decision?

The wingman of Harpaz and Levy was the crew of Uri Gil and Daniel Wittmann, radio call sign OIL 2. Due to the echeloned attack pattern, OIL 2 trailed more than a mile after OIL 1 – and slightly to the left – when the pair completed bombing and headed for home. About that time Gil looked to his right and saw two MiG-21s flying parallel with his Phantom, right behind OIL 1. Gil warned his leader, but was worried that more MiG-21s were right behind him. To make sure he had to break and to look back. He could break left but, then he would expose his rear to the two MiG-21s that followed Harpaz. His call was therefore to break right.

Gil and Wittmann turned right into the pair of MiG-21s that trailed their leader. Their break assured them that no other MiG-21s were following them, while the two MiG-21s that followed OIL 1 also turned away. Now Gil and Wittmann were right behind two MiG-21s. They had no air-to-air missiles, but Gil figured that within a turn or two they would close the range down to cannon range, achieve an air-to-air kill, let go the other MiG and disengage because their fuel state was indeed worrying. After all, Uri Gil should have known, as he was already credited with a MiG kill as a Mirage pilot during the Six Day War.

While turning behind the pair of MiG-21s Gil noticed that they were over Mansura and saw four MiG-21s immediately after take-off and another 4-ship formation of MiG-21s. He could have completed the turn and shot down a MiG-21, but then they would have to face more than eight MiG-21s deep into Egypt with very little fuel to spare. It was time for decision making, and Gil decided to disengage. He knew that he could shoot down that MiG, but he was also sure that they would then be doomed.

OIL 2 turned east to fly back home, and it was then that Uri Gil made another critical decision. Gil decided that fuel was his enemy. He throttled back to economic cruise setting and scratched the surface over the Nile Delta. The analysis was cool simple: the MiG-21s had Atoll air-to-air missiles and cannon. The Atoll had plenty of difficulties locking on to such a low flying target, and Gil exacerbated the Atoll's troubles through cooling down the nozzles of his Phantom in economic cruise and without afterburners. For a cannon kill, the attacking aircraft had to fly lower than the attacked aircraft. Gil flew so low that nobody could fly lower within proper range to survive the Phantom's slipstream and shoot down OIL 2.

Thus, for a few very long minutes Gil flew very, very low and not very fast – in economic cruise settings – and did not look back. There may have been MiG-21s right behind him. They may have tried to launch their Atolls and they may have launched Atolls. They may have tried to achieve cannon firing solution and they may have opened fire. Gil did not look back and did not break to have a better look; he had already made his choice.

By then there was no turning back, literary. The decision was taken, and Gil could only point the attention of his navigator Wittmann to the wonderful scenery of the Nile Delta that flashed by them. Within minutes the Suez Canal was right in front of them. The MiG-21s were gone and they climbed for the Canal crossing. Friendly IDF troops opened fire at the lone aircraft that came from the west, but by then their ordeal was all over.

OIL 2 had plenty of fuel remaining for the flight back home to Ramat David. However, well aware of OIL 1's troubles, Gil decided to hang around and wait for his leader, who suddenly appeared on final to Refidim. Gil and Wittmann waited for OIL 1 to land and then they landed on the narrow parallel taxiway. Did they make the right decisions? Are there any right decisions in combat?

Encounter with the Soviets

Israel's mighty air power tipped the scales of the Attrition War. The air superiority campaign of late 1969 ensured Israeli air supremacy west of the Suez Canal and Operation Blossom – which started

The two 69 Squadron interim reconnaissance birds were Kurnass 17 and Kurnass 39; both appear in this January 1971 image along with Kurnass 102 and Kurnass 166.

from early 1970 – pushed war into the heartland of Egypt. Yet Egypt was not willing to admit defeat and asked for Soviet support. By the spring of 1970 a complete Soviet air defense division deployed to Egypt. At first the Soviet interceptors and missiles defended Egypt's rear (Cairo, Alexandria, and the Aswan Dam), while Israel continued Blossom in the hope that Egypt would blink first. Israel's policy was, however, shattered on April 18, 1970, when IAF combat aircraft encountered Soviet flown fighters for the first time. Avihu Ben-Nun recalled:

> "We flew to photograph an Egyptian exercise at a lake southwest of Cairo where they practiced the crossing of Lake Bitter. On our way in we photographed Kom Oshim and Bani Suef flying at 600 knots very low, so even if they would have scrambled their fighters there would be no way for them to catch us. There were about 3/8 of stratus clouds at about 2,500 feet and the terrain was a mountainous desert, Jabel Galalah. We saw interceptors taking off from Kom Oshim but we completed our mission as planned.
>
> "When we were already on our way back I noted that the leader slowed down. During the war I hardly had the opportunity to evaluate the leadership skills of the squadron's leaders, so as part of training during wartime I flew wingman to Rami Harpaz. He slowed down from the planned 600 knots to 480 knots, but we were under radio silence conditions, so I closed on him to have a look but I did not see any leaks or anything abnormal. I had a dilemma in between being squadron commander and wingman, while there was also the issue of personal example; a wingman was not supposed to question his leader all the time why he was acting as he did. A minute prior to crossing the coastline we had to climb, and on the other side was a combat air patrol to protect us, 117 Squadron Mirages that also flew at low altitude on the other side of the gulf and were to be vectored in only if the Egyptians would pursue us.
>
> "As we pulled up we began to hear total panic over the radio, 'MiGs are all around you, pay attention!' Harpaz accelerated to 600 knots as we climbed, and indeed there were MiGs exactly above us. Our exit pattern was, however, in line of planning to avoid Egyptian AAA along the coastline of the gulf, while as the Mirages were vectored towards the MiGs, the latter withdrew. Only then was it realized that these MiGs were Russian, and we did not yet have translators to understand their radio chatter. Why were we not warned earlier? The radar could not track us because we flew very low, so they had to calculate our position, and they used our pre-planned speed of 600 knots to do so, but we flew at 480 knots, so the MiGs were right above us while our command and control was sure that they lagged behind at a safe distance. They panicked from the moment they noticed that we did not climb along the planned timeline, but the MiGs never saw us; perhaps the Russian pilots were not accustomed to the glaring sun, maybe the clouds shielded us and our camouflage was very efficient and blended well with the terrain we were over flying; pure luck. If those eight MiGs had a glimpse of us, reconnaissance birds only armed with missiles, one can wonder what would have happened.
>
> "Rami Harpaz is a very well-thought out fellow. He figured that we completed our mission successfully without encountering any kind of threat. If we continued flying at 600 knots we had to land at Refidim to refuel, but slowing down to 480 knots enabled us to fly directly home to Ramat David. Apparently his calculation was that if we would fly nonstop to Ramat David he would arrive on time to kiss his child good night, a child who is now a fighter pilot and a wing commander!"

Array Ambush

The Attrition War turned static again. Blossom indeed escalated the conflict, but not to the point that the Egyptians would accept a ceasefire. Once the Blossom campaign was discontinued, the Soviet backed Egyptians seized the initiative and began to roll forward towards the Suez Canal their network of air defense assets. Until late June 1970 the IAF concentrated on a new campaign to bomb

Aviem Sella and Shabtai Ben-Shoa flew a two hour and 30 minute nighttime CAP in Kurnass 178 on June 16, 1970; Kurnass 178 was photographed landing at Ramat David in October 1970 still in Hammers colors, as it was later reassigned to 201 Squadron as Kurnass 678 and then to 119 Squadron, again as 178.

Rami Harpaz and Achikar Eyal ejected from Kurnass 38 on June 30, 1970; Kurnass 38 was photographed during Israel President Zalman Shazar's (in cockpit) visit to Ramat David with Wing Commander Jacob Agassi explaining Kurnass wonders to the President.

infrastructures west of the Suez Canal aimed at depriving Egypt the option of expanding air defense coverage towards the canal.

During June 1970 the Egyptians began to deploy forward at night SAM batteries to ambush the next day's IAF attack aircraft. Once the IAF realized the presence of such a battery a SEAD mission was called. On the night of June 29 to 30, 1970, the Egyptians changed their tactic. Instead of inserting a single battery or a small number of batteries for pinpoint ambush, they deployed forward an array of batteries overlapping in coverage for mutual defense.

IAF reaction was again an immediate SEAD mission, with each SAM battery attacked by a pair of Kurnass crews. The Hammers launched three pairs to attack three batteries, but soon after bombing the leader of the second pair reported troubles. Apparently Rami Harpaz with Achikar Eyal did not dive to low altitude after bombing as planned. A SAM nailed their Kurnass that was travelling at 10,000 feet, and the Hammers had no option but to eject over Egypt. Rami Harpaz:

Kurnass 183 was photographed at Ramat David in May 1970 loaded with a dozen bombs weighing 3.5 tons; the weight of bombs that the Hammers' B-17s lifted during the 1948 missions was approximately 2 tons or so.

Hammers airmen in July 1970 when the squadron cadre missed six prisoners of war, two in Syria (Magen and Nachmani) and four in Egypt (Harpaz and Eyal, Zamir, and Levitov).

"Our target was Kotamiya air base. There were two SAM batteries north of the air base and one SAM battery south of the air base. Three pairs, each pair bombing one battery. We flew low, climbed to 5,000 feet for Suez Canal crossing to avoid light AAA and back to low altitude. Two minutes prior to time over target we began to accelerate to 600 knots, and 45 seconds prior to time over target we pulled up to 20,000 feet. Two pairs turned right to the two northern batteries and I turned left with my wingman to attack the southern battery. Nose on target, bombing, rolling to look for results, and our bombs covered the whole target area.

"The two other pairs had to continue turning right for the outbound flight, but we flew south, so we had to turn 180 degrees and we trailed ten miles behind them. At this point we have a dispute. I remembered from briefing climb a minute after bombing. Avihu claimed that he briefed to fly low until one minute flight time prior to Suez Canal crossing. Anyway, I noted a SAM launch warning, a SAM that was obviously launched from another ambush SAM battery, exact location unknown but somewhere north of our target. The warning indicated launch from ten o'clock, so I said to Los (navigator Achikar Eyal) you watch backwards, I'll look forward. If the SAM was launched from long range then it would appear behind us, and if from short range then it would appear in front of us. The SAM came from seven o'clock. We broke away successfully but a second SAM followed. We were too slow, so I broke hard downside with full afterburners on, but the missile's proximity fuse activated and the explosion ripped off our tail section. The aircraft began to spin, and I was anxious to eject before a third SAM would show up. I ejected us, and later I learnt that Los also activated ejection. My ejection sequence worked as planned, and under the canopy of my parachute I saw Los parachuting nearby and our tail-less Kurnass spinning to the ground."

Amos Ejection

The new Egyptian tactic tipped the scales again in the Suez Canal air superiority battle. The IAF was experienced in knocking out SA-2 batteries, but was hapless against a massive network of SA-2 and SA-3 batteries overlapping in coverage and defended by AAA and SA-7 shoulder launched SAMs. The Kurnass force, which was the IAF's principle SEAD asset, suffered accordingly.

As the Kurnass squadrons continued their deadly duel with the Egyptian/Soviet air defense force the Hammers suffered – on July 5, 1970 – their second Kurnass loss in a SEAD mission over the west bank of the Suez Canal. The Hammers again launched three pairs; leaders were Aviem Sella, Ehud Henkin, and Avihu Ben-Nun. Once again bombing was accomplished, and once again

Aviem Sella and Yossi Kamay flew Kurnass 85 on a mission over Egypt on July 5, 1970, when Amos Zamir and Amos Levitov ejected from Kurnass 29.

Avihu Ben-Nun washing the tail section of Kurnass 132, the first Hammers jet to attack during Operation Challenge, the July 18, 1970, pod formation mission. Aviem Sella and Daniel Wittmann flew Kurnass 132 in the lead of the second Hammers pair. Since formation leader Ben-Nun was hit and aborted the mission, escorted by his wingman, which also jettisoned his bombs, the leader of the second pair attacked first.

a Kurnass crew reported damage after strike. Ben-Nun's wingman – Amos Zamir with Amos Levitov – ejected from Kurnass 29. Both Amos airmen landed safely to become prisoners of war in Egypt.

Pod Formation

Israel turned to the USA to seek aid. The American approach was "pod formation," an electronic warfare tactic based on massive utilization of the AN/ALQ-71 pod. AN/ALQ-71 pods were rushed to Israel, and SEAD missions were suspended pending assimilation of the supposedly revolutionary tactic.

The Kurnass force was ready by July 18, 1970, when an armada – including eight Hammers air crews – cruised in formation over the front line at an altitude of 18,000 feet to maximize the effect of the electronic warfare pods, and slightly above an extremely massive "carpet" of medium AAA explosions at an altitude of 15,000 to 16,000 feet. AAA explosions created an ugly cloud that covered the whole sky immediately below the Kurnass force. The "pod formation" tactic proved effective against SA-2 SAMs that failed to intercept the bombers. Also, the medium altitude approach enabled the Kurnass crews to verify which of the large number of SAM battery sites was indeed manned and active. The Egyptian/Soviet air defense tactic was to saturate the theatre of operations with SAM battery sites and to relocate actual batteries from site to site. Therefore, in the medium altitude approach the Kurnass crews could select to attack only the active sites; such perspective was not possible in the low altitude attack pattern. However, the pods were ineffective against the smaller and more maneuverable SA-3; this was a well known fact to the Kurnass crews, but they had no pre-mission indication that SA-3 batteries were deployed to the sector to be attacked.

Initially the attack progressed well. The Kurnass crews cruised above a layer of AAA explosions and the pods protected the attackers from the SA-2 missiles. Yet SA-3 missiles were indeed present, and two of these flashed by just before the force approached the target zone, the first missing the 201 Squadron mission leader, but the second exploding close to the big jet. Flying six miles behind, a similar episode repeated as two SAMs were launched against the 69 Squadron leader, Avihu Ben-Nun with Shaul Levy. The Kurnass crews were experienced in evasive action against the rather big SA-2 and the 69 Squadron Commander played his "usual" drill, but he was not aware that his opponent was the smaller SA-3. Ben-Nun's evasive action did not defeat the attack, but saved the Kurnass from total destruction. The first missile missed and the second exploded close to Kurnass 77.

The Kurnass flown by the 69 Squadron Commander suffered fire in the left engine, the fuel indicators signaled massive fuel leakage, and the intercom system ceased to function. Ben-Nun switched off the left engine and jettisoned all external stores. Two minutes later the right engine fire warning light also came ON and Ben-Nun thought that the time was right for ejection. Yet the Hammers Commander decided to ignore the right engine fire warning and pressed ahead towards the front line. Shortly after crossing the front line the right engine fire warning light changed to OFF and Ben-Nun decided to land at Refidim. The Kurnass rolled over if flown slower than 220 knots, so Ben-Nun landed that fast. The braking chute was released at 200 knots, but the expected cable arrest never came and the big fighter veered off the runway at 100 knots. Almost running over two horrified service persons, the

IAF engineers lift Kurnass 177 from where it came to a stop at Refidim air base in Sinai; what remained of the AIM-7 AAMs is still attached to the fuselage stations, but the secret ECM pod was removed.

Kurnass 177 was extensively damaged on the July 18, 1970, pod formation mission. The crew that returned Kurnass 177 back home was Avihu Ben-Nun and Shaul Levy. They were honored to first fly the repaired Kurnass 177 in February 1972 and were photographed upon completion of the flight, along with the technical team and former 69 Squadron Technical Officer Nathan Segall.

Kurnass luckily ran in between a huge pile of sand and a deep hole. Soon afterwards the nose landing gear collapsed and the useless war machine came to a halt after sliding roughly 100 meters. Ben-Nun and Levy jumped out of the cockpit and walked around to inspect the damage. The Kurnass was full of holes, as roughly 1,000 fragments peppered the jet, including one that entered the canopy, injured Avihu Ben-Nun's left arm, and exited to his right. Another fragment disabled the ejection system, so luckily for the crew they did not attempt to eject, not even when they should have as the Kurnass veered off runway and skidded along on the desert floor in what was perhaps the only five meters wide clear track in the whole Sinai. As this was not enough, Ben-Nun and Levy were surprised to see during their damage inspection walk around that the burning right engine was still melting down the explosive warhead of an AIM-7 AAM.

Meanwhile, the remaining Kurnass crews pressed ahead with the pod formation mission and claimed destruction of four SAM batteries. The pod formation mission was truly successful, as a significant segment of the Egyptian/Soviet SAM network was destroyed at the cost of a single attacking aircraft. In later years the IAF would define an acceptable ratio for a destruction/suppression of enemy air defense mission as one attack aircraft lost per one SAM battery destroyed. Judged against this later claim-to-loss ratio evaluation, the July 18, 1970, pod formation mission was indeed a success.

Getting Even

Israel abandoned the suppression/destruction of enemy air defense campaign but sought revenge to get even with the Soviets, who were – from Israeli point of view – responsible for the alarming

SEAMAN 1 – Avihu Ben-Nun and Shaul Levy – flew Kurnass 105 to engage USSR MiG-21 pilots on July 30, 1970.

Hammers welcome SEAMAN 2, Aviem Sella and Reuben Fisher, upon their return from the July 30, 1970, ambush of USSR MiG-21 pilots.

Ramat David Wing Commander Zorik Lev (left) and 69 Squadron Commander Avihu Ben-Nun (second from left) meet Aviem Sella (right) and Reuben Reshef (back to camera) after the latter two were "washed" by awaiting service persons and prior to the bus drive back to the squadron, where a formal reception was already prepared.

Hastily prepared reception for the USSR MiG-killers was in the best tradition of that era, a mix of Israeli modesty and American pomp.

Avihu Ben-Nun pours Champaign during the reception for the USSR MiG-killers on July 30, 1970. IAF Chief of Training Department Yak Nevo (left) was also a MiG-killer, having been credited with three kills from 1956 to 1958.

Kurnass 183 was photographed in August 1970 adorned with a kill marking dated July 30, 1970, when Aviem Sella and Reuben Fisher flew Kurnass 183 as SEAMAN 2 during the engagement between IAF fighters and USSR pilots over Egypt.

upheaval in the conduct of war. Fighting the Egyptian/Soviet air defense network promised little opportunity for such an event. Yet interceptors were an integral element of a Soviet air defense division. Along with the forward deployment of the terrestrial assets, Soviet flown MiG-21s fringed further east towards the front line to trigger an IAF plan for an aerial ambush of the Soviet interceptors.

Israel seemingly lost the air superiority battle to the Egyptian/Soviet air defenses, but still enjoyed a wide margin of absolute supremacy in the air-to-air arena. Operation Pomegranate was a series of such aerial ambushes that was launched in June 1969. The principle players of Pomegranate were Mirage pilots, but by the summer of 1970 the Egyptians mostly evaded air combats. Operation Pomegranate 20 was therefore aimed to draw into battle the Soviet flown MiG-21s.

As usual for a Pomegranate operation, the main force was delta fighters, but a 4-ship formation of 69 Squadron air crews was also included. The Israeli ruse worked well, and the Soviet MiG-21 interception pilots fell into the trap. Expecting to engage unarmed reconnaissance Mirages flying straight and level at high altitude, they faced four fully armed Mirages. The hunters became the hunted. The Mirages quickly shot down a MiG-21, its pilot ejected, and for unknown reason the parachute opened at high altitude instead of the usual drill: free fall to medium altitude where the parachute had to be deployed automatically. That MiG-21 pilot descended to earth under the canopy of his parachute throughout the engagement and became a "landmark" for the Israeli pilots. Whenever a pilot had to indicate his position during the combat he would report something like "five miles south of the parachutist."

The Soviets scrambled additional MiG-21 formations; it is generally accepted that 16 MiG-21s were scrambled to engage the Israeli "reconnaissance" mission, while IAF command and control vectored to engage the main force – including the 69 Squadron formation – that until then was flying combat air patrol at low altitude below coverage of the Egyptian/Soviet radars.

Avihu Ben-Nun with Shaul Levy chased a MiG-21 that flew west towards the Nile Valley at low altitude. The Hammers airmen launched an AIM-9 Sidewinder that harmlessly dropped behind the fast flying MiG-21. The longer range weapon on board the Kurnass was the AIM-7 semi-active radar homing missile, which was generally accepted to be totally ineffective at low altitude. Nevertheless, Ben-Nun and Levy had no other option, so Ben-Nun launched an AIM-7 immediately after Levy managed to lock radar onto the MiG-21. Unusually the AIM-7 guided in perfect manner and shot down the MiG-21; the pilot did not eject.

Aviem Sella with Reuben Fisher engaged another MiG-21 that also dived to the deck. The MiG-21 emerged seemingly intact from the explosive fireball of an AIM-9, so the Hammers air crew launched a second AIM-9. Just as the second missile ignited parts were seen to fall off the MiG-21 and the pilot ejected.

When Ben-Nun and Sella regrouped after disengagement, Sella noticed that Kurnass 105 had two AAMs missing, one AIM-7 and one AIM-9. The intrigued Sella asked Ben-Nun over the radio with which type of AAM did he shoot down the MiG-21? At that time the Sella family's pet was a dog named Sparrow, so Ben-Nun's answer was "with your dog."

RF Pair

Shooting down Soviet MiG-21s enabled Israel to agree to a USA mediated ceasefire agreement without losing face. The Attrition War thus ended on August 7, 1970, with mixed feelings on both sides of the Suez Canal. Egypt finally had an answer to Israel's air superiority, while Israel achieved its objective to deny Egypt a Suez Canal crossing option, at least for the time being. Obviously the respective drawbacks were the opposite: Egypt realized that it was still not ready for a large scale Suez Canal crossing offensive, and Israel lost air superiority over Egypt and the Suez Canal Zone.

Ceasefire did not end hostilities in the Middle East. The basic issues remained unsolved, and both sides were eager to prove their points: Arab nations that they would some time in the future

RF-4C Kurnass 151 taxis at Ramat David in February 1971; the RF-4C pair was tail numbered Kurnass 150 and Kurnass 151.

Ran Goren first flew the Kurnass in October 1970 and was 69 Squadron Deputy A until 1972. The IAF Year 1970 Term 2 Kurnass Conversion Course added to the Hammers' five pilots (Ran Goren, Levy Bar-Ziv, David Brisk, Aharon Sagi, and Yair El-Or) and five navigators.

eliminate the disgrace of the 1967 Six Day War defeat, while Israel was determined to preserve "status quo," or in other words, to deter Arab nations from launching actions to challenge Israel's military superiority. Thus, 69 Squadron emerged from the Attrition War somewhat confident and somewhat confused, but did not embark on an era of peace. The next round in the Arab-Israeli conflict was judged to be inevitable, and Israeli preparations covered new suppression of enemy air defense tactics and weapons, as well as monitoring the other side of the border.

The Hammers participated in both efforts. Reconnaissance, which was introduced with two modified stock F-4E aircraft, was bolstered during late August 1970. An element of ceasefire, the USA loaned to Israel two RF-4C aircraft pending delivery of Israel's own six RF-4E reconnaissance birds. Aimed to improve Israel's monitoring of the other side's ceasefire compliance, the two RF-4C aircraft were issued to 69 Squadron and became known as "RF."

Travel To Teheran

War weary 69 still suffered from temporary infrastructure and airmen shortages. Ceasefire was exploited to move the Hammers to their new purpose built squadron building and to draw pilots from attack squadrons that previously could not forgo experienced service persons to aid the new Kurnass squadrons' conversion effort. The Hammers undertook a massive Kurnass conversion course during IAF Year 1970 Term 2 (August to November). The conversion course was actually initiated in September 1970 after the winds of war finally calmed down. Five pilots and five navigators from this conversion course remained Hammers airmen from IAF Year 1970 Term 3 for further training, while the balance of converted airmen were assigned to other Kurnass squadrons. David Brisk recalled:

"I was a Vautour pilot from 1968 until 1970. Kurnass introduction was obviously a major blow to the prestige of the Vautour as a bomber and to Vautour airmen. We closely watched the Kurnass service introduction process amidst the Attrition War, and when hostilities ended I was inducted to the Kurnass conversion course in September 1970. We were obliged to commit to three years service from end of conversion, but Kibbutz members got a discount that Giora Furman arranged; one year full service, one year no pay leave during which we flew as Emergency Posting service persons, and one year of full service again.

"The squadron moved into the new squadron building just as we arrived. This was the 'reversed' building. The logic of IAF squadron buildings at the time was a U shape construction with official entrance via the inner side of the U, where the parking was situated and towards where the veranda faced, so you could see people arriving. Scrambled airmen ran to their aircraft from the back side of the squadron building, through the base side of the U shaped building. The 69 building was constructed opposite than normal practice; parking and entrance was

The Hammers' squadron building was patterned after the 119 Squadron building at Tel Nof Air Base, where Avihu Ben-Nun served as Senior Deputy Commander prior to his assignment to the Kurnass project. The Ramat David version was rotated to shield the balcony from rain, hence the generated image of a "reversed" building design.

on the base side and path to QRA[10] aircraft was via the open side of the U shaped building. Apparently designers and constructors got it wrong somehow. Right from the start the new building was too small to accommodate such a large squadron with dozens of airmen, mostly regulars. The balance was Emergency Posting; there were no reserve airmen in the Kurnass squadrons during this first phase of activity.

"The most impressive aspect in the squadron was Avihu Ben-Nun's dominance. Young, charismatic, and well connected, Avihu emphasized operational standards. The squadron was still in the shadow of the Attrition War when they activated the unit, introduced the Kurnass, trained service persons, implemented doctrines, waged war, and suffered casualties. Pilots and navigators were of mixed ages and disciplines. Shortage of navigators was especially noticeable; there were even radio operators retrained as navigators. So getting organized was difficult, but it was definitely felt that Avihu was in control.

"Once we flew in formation to bomb in range. First run and my bomb did not drop. Avihu asked why? I answered a switch, and Avihu's real-time verdict was go home. It was so beautiful. It was indeed a punishment, but what a great attitude. Other squadrons did not behave that way; in other squadrons such incidents were smoothed out. Avihu was sharp and to the point.

"The highlight of our conversion course was travel to Teheran for simulator training. In fact, we were the final delegation to attend F-4 simulator training in Iran. This was an interesting clash of cultures. There was no interaction between us and the Iranian pilots. We were accommodated in a hotel in Teheran and a military bus – we were all sure that the bus driver understood Hebrew and monitored us – drove us in the morning to base and returned us in the evening to the hotel. The simulator instructors were an IAF pilot and navigator who led our delegation. The Iranians handed over the simulator to the Israeli instructors and we trained all day long on our own. They knew who we were but we did not mingle, and the only time that there was some sort of interaction was during lunch break, when we used to eat in their luxury officers mess where a pianist was playing all the time!"

A Hammers Kurnass departs Ramat David loaded with two AGM-12 Bullpup ASMs. Aviem Sella and Shaul Levy tested Bullpup on board Kurnass 111 from October 1970.

Perfection and Expansion

Attrition War lessons were rapidly implemented, even though the plain truth was that technology available to suppression/destruction of enemy air defense operation was still immature. Nevertheless, the ceasefire bonus included a package of weapons tailored to the suppression/destruction of enemy air defense mission, including AGM-45 Shrike ARM[11] for suppression and the AGM-12 Bullpup ASM[12] radio control guided missile for destruction. 69 Squadron introduced the former and evaluated the latter.

From IAF perspective the Kurnass was principally a bomber, yet most Kurnass airmen preferred the much more glamorous air-to-air mission. Leading Edge Slats – LES – promised to improve

Kurnass 187 was the LES test vehicle; the flight test program was initiated on October 8, 1970.

The Kurnass 187 LES evaluation validated projected improvements and stimulated IAF adoption of LES for Kurnass.

Kurnass 195 and Kurnass 197 were the Hammers' RF-4E reconnaissance pair; the former was photographed at Hatzerim in December 1971.

the low speed maneuverability of the Kurnass, a domain of performance envelope section heavily utilized during close-in air engagements. 69 Squadron's Kurnass 187 was modified to have a set of fixed LES, and the evaluation indicated that the low speed gains were at the expense of high speed performance. With the former more appreciated by air-to-air proponents and the latter deemed more important for air-to-ground operations, the logical IAF decision would have been to relinquish LES. Yet the air-to-air biased community won and the IAF decided to equip the Kurnass third batch with LES from the outset, and to progressively modify previously delivered aircraft with LES.

Meanwhile, and also a ceasefire accomplishment, the USA agreed to supply Israel with a second batch of F-4s to enable activation of a third squadron. Airmen and engineers assigned to the new Squadron 119, which was slated for activation at Tel Nof air base in late October 1970, accumulated initial Kurnass experience at the already established first two Kurnass units. When the day of activation arrived, four second batch aircraft departed Ramat David bound for Tel Nof.

Reconnaissance Kurnass

Delivery of six RF-4E reconnaissance birds in early 1971 signaled the end of 69 Squadron's RF-4C operations. The pair of RF aircraft was returned to the USA while the Hammers introduced two RF-4E birds: Kurnass 195 and Kurnass 197. The balance of four reconnaissance Kurnass aircraft was issued to 119 Squadron at Tel Nof, with 119 specializing in high altitude photography and 69 in low altitude photography. Therefore, 69 Squadron got a slice of the prestige reconnaissance mission, but played second string to 119 Squadron.

Reconnaissance was especially important during "peacetime," so was called the low intensity conflict time frames between intensive violence in the Middle East wars. During "peacetime" most IAF combat aircraft occasionally experienced limited scale operational activity: combat air patrol here, attack mission there. The combat squadrons that flew operational missions on a regular basis were those qualified for air photography. For this reason the assignment of two reconnaissance Kurnass aircraft to the Hammers was so important, even if 69 Squadron was mainly in the shadow of the two principle IAF reconnaissance outfits: 101 Squadron with its reconnaissance Mirages and 119 Squadron flying the bulk of Israel's reconnaissance Kurnass fleet.

Accidents

1971 was a relatively uneventful year for the Hammers except for two accidents, one mission and a single event. The first accident was on May 3, 1971, when Kurnass 112 suffered Category 4 damage[13]; afterburner's fuel pump leaked and the jet caught fire but was eventually repaired. The second accident was fatal.

While preparing a QRA Kurnass loaded with four AIM-9D AAMs on September 13, 1971, an abnormal buzzing was noticed emerging from the right-hand pair of missiles. Electrical current was switched off and on again but the buzzing did not stop. A senior armorer approached the right-hand missile launcher installation and attempted to pull out a safety pin. As he did so the missile was launched due to short circuit. The missile killed the armorer as the weapon flashed and flew onwards across a taxiway until crashing into a hill without exploding.

Five days later the Hammers flew their first Fist missions. Israeli AAA fire downed an Egyptian Su-7 over Sinai on September 11, 1971, and the Egyptians responded with the shooting down of an Israeli LOROP[14] Stratocruiser on September 17, 1971, and Israel retaliated the next day when Kurnass crews launched AGM-45 Shrike missiles against the SA-2 batteries allegedly responsible

The Kurnass Conversion Course was opened three times a year at the beginning of every IAF Term. KCC injected fresh aircrew into the Kurnass force and was rotated between the F-4 squadrons. 69 ran the KCC during IAF Year 1971 Term 2 (August to November 1971). Standing from left to right: Avishai Knaan (pilot), Yigal Stavi (pilot, killed in action during Yom Kippur War), Micha Oren (WSO), Alex Harel (WSO, to 69 Squadron), Eli Tovel (WSO, to 69), Itamar (pilot), Ami Arnon (pilot, killed in accident), Amiram Shaked (pilot, killed in accident), Hanoch Patishi (pilot), Baruch Golan (WSO, KIA during YKW), and Eran Mor (WSO, to 69). In the middle: Yosi Yaari (WSO). Front row from left to right: Itzik Gat (pilot, to 69), Harel Gilutz (pilot), Avi Barber (pilot), Eilat Ziblat (pilot, to 69), Yehoar (WSO), Natan (WSO), and Hanoch (WSO).

Aviem Sella took along Zvi Freier (Avidror) in Kurnass 103 during an Independence Day fly-past rehearsal on April 27, 1971. Avidror was photographed prior to flight and afterwards in the ceremonial solo baptism "bath."

for the Stratocruiser's shoot down. The September 18, 1971, Operation Toaster was a pioneering event in the annals of Middle East SEAD ops but was not deemed successful.

The only significant event during 1971, other than accidents and missions, took place on December 10, 1971, when the Hammers loaned two aircraft – Kurnass 144 and Kurnass 159 – to the IAF's fourth Kurnass squadron. Each of the three established Kurnass squadrons loaned two jets so that the new Hatzerim based 107 Squadron would start flying pending delivery of its own Peace Echo IV aircraft.

Command Hand-Over

Avihu Ben-Nun handed over command of the Hammers to Amnon Arad on August 1, 1972.[15] Amnon Arad's term of office was relatively short, but certainly not uneventful. Clashes along and across the Israeli-Lebanese and Israeli-Syrian borders escalated. The Hammers bombed and intercepted. In the latter mission Avihu Ben-Nun and Zvi Kesler – flying Kurnass 183 and launching an AIM-9D AAM – were credited with a Syrian Su-7 air-to-air kill on September 9, 1972.

Meanwhile, Intelligence reported that the USSR delivered SA-6 mobile SAM batteries to Egypt and Syria, but the new threat was still mostly a mystery. Even proper photos of the SA-6 system were not at hand. In late April 1973, a 119 Squadron LOROP mission peeped deep into Syria and generated the first images of the SA-6. However, in order to extricate technical assessments a closer look was essential. 69's specialty in the realm of the photographic world was low altitude, so a unique team of two crews (Arad-Wittmann, Sella-Katz) began to practice a super

Avihu Ben-Nun taxiing Kurnass 159 at Hatzerim on December 10, 1971, after a ferry flight from Ramat David for loan to the IAF's fourth Kurnass squadron.

Hammers' jets prepare to take-off for a fly-past during Israel's silver jubilee Independence Day in May 1973. The package includes a 201 Squadron Kurnass 697, while 69's Kurnass 124 was later handed over to 119 Squadron; both were lost in action during the October 1973 Yom Kippur War.

secret mission that was finally launched on May 25, 1973. Aviem Sella recalled:

> "We trained for a month in preparation for that mission. The leader experienced a malfunctioning navigation system prior to take-off so the lead was handed over to me. We clocked 600 knots at 100 feet above ground level, and I think that we photographed that SA-6 battery south of Damascus from no more than 20 meters away. The leader's photographs were better as they overflew the battery; we flew 100, 200 meters sideways. The photographs were so good, and from such a short distance, that every nut and bolt was visible.

Command Crossover

Kurnass force next generation commanders' assignments were discussed during the summer of 1973. A crossover policy was adopted to fertilize squadrons from the experience accumulated among sister squadrons and to avoid isolationism or a trend in which each squadron had its own theory and tradition. Command crossover was to bond Kurnass crews as a force rather than four squadrons.

The problem was that most commanders were to hand over command during IAF year 1973 Term 3 (December to March). Obviously staggered hand over was more advisable, but with no clouds of war looming over the bright blue Middle East sky this plan was considered acceptable. All four named commanders were of a younger generation, and only one of them was fighter squadron commander at the time of the decision. The planned assignment was Yoram Agmon with 201 background to take over 69; Asher Snir with 119 background to 107; Ehud Henkin with 69 background to 119; and Ran Goren with 69 background to 201. For various reasons the 69 command hand over was brought forward to IAF Year 1973 Term 2 (July to November). Yoram Agmon recalled:

> "I was Squadron 109 Commander, a Skyhawk squadron based at Ramat David, so because of the urgency for 69 command hand over I was named to take over 69. However, I was a 'south' service person, I flew in the Hatzor squadrons, and my first choice was 119. I

Hammers flying in close formation to celebrate Israel's silver jubilee Independence Day in May 1973.

A Hammers' Kurnass blasts off the Ramat David runway.

wanted 119 primarily because of reconnaissance. 69 also flew reconnaissance, but the 119 Reconnaissance Flight was larger than 69's. I figured that I would command a Kurnass squadron during 'peacetime,' so 119 would be more of a challenge because of the reconnaissance issue; all other things were similar.

"I wanted to argue about this decision, and I understood that Ehud Henkin wanted 69, but I had to be sure, so I met Henkin and asked for his opinion. He wanted 69. I asked his permission to float the issue to the Ramat David base commander, Zorik Lev. He gave me his permission. I talked to Zorik and he was not happy with my suggestion; he wanted me as soon as possible to take over 69, but he gave the green light to meet IAF Commander Beni Peled. I said to Beni that I wanted 119 and Ehud wanted 69; I told him that I knew that 69 command hand over would be earlier than the 119 command hand over and I assured him that I did not mind waiting for 119."

However, the original plan was adhered to. The first phase was accomplished on September 10, 1973, when Amnon Arad handed over command to Yoram Agmon. The second phase of the command crossover plan was disrupted by later events.

Operation Don Juan 9

69 Squadron's pair was among the force that triggered a massive clash between Israel and Syria on September 13, 1973. Operation Don Juan 9 was planned to shoot down Syrian fighters. The bait was two pairs of Kurnass reconnaissance aircraft; one of these was a 69 Squadron pair. David Brisk recalled:

> "This was an odd flight. We flew all along Syria from south to north. The usual pattern was north to south, so that once detected we were already heading south. This time our egress point was 200 miles north of Israel, so when Syrian interceptors were scrambled we were far, far away from home. Ground control gradually changed our heading from 210, to 220, then 230, then 240. We were almost heading towards Cyprus when our fighters engaged their interceptors. We had a glimpse of the combat and headed for home."

The first round resulted in eight Syrian MiG-21s claimed shot down for the loss of a single 117 Squadron Mirage. The Mirage pilot ejected and was floating on the surface of the Mediterranean Sea in his dinghy. A rescue operation was launched with additional formations of IAF fighters scrambled to safeguard the pilot in distress. Among them were Hammers airmen, including Amnon Arad, who flew lead in the reconnaissance pair; he returned to Ramat David, switched aircraft, and took off.

The Syrians also scrambled fighters, and in a second round air combat the IAF claimed four more kills. Hammers crew Arad-Levy was credited with a single kill.

Villa and Pool

For the first time in IAF history a veterans association supported an active squadron. Compared to our constitutional era – perhaps too constitutional – that overshadows the many – probably too many – nonprofit associations in Israel, the early operation of the 69 Squadron Veterans Association was somewhat partisan and improvised.

Members of the 69 Squadron Veterans Association (from left to right: Zvi Avidror, Amos Yarden, and a donor) bid farewell to 69 Squadron Commander from August 1, 1972, until August 31, 1972, Amnon Arad (right).

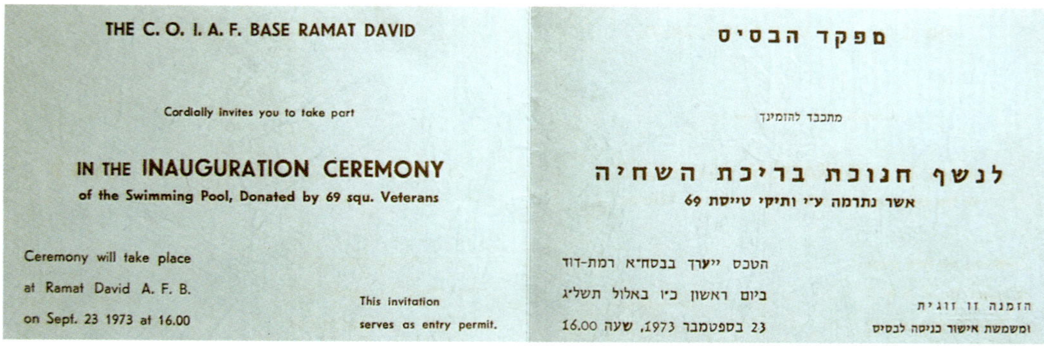

THE C. O. I. A. F. BASE RAMAT DAVID

Cordially invites you to take part

IN THE INAUGURATION CEREMONY

of the Swimming Pool, Donated by 69 squ. Veterans

Ceremony will take place
at Ramat David A. F. B.
on Sept. 23 1973 at 16.00

This invitation
serves as entry permit.

מפקד הבסיס

מתכבד להזמינך

לנשף חנוכת בריכת השחיה
אשר נתרמה ע״י ותיקי טייסת 69

הטכס ייערך בבסח״א רמת-דוד
ביום ראשון כ״ו באלול תשל״ג
23 בספטמבר 1973, שעה 16.00

הזמנה זו זוגית
ומשמשת אישור כניסה לבסיס

Invitation to inauguration of the Hammers' donated Ramat David swimming pool on September 23, 1973.

Chairman Bill Katz was in charge of donations and funding. The story – true or false discrimination is left to the imagination of the reader – was that El Al Israel National Airline Captain Bill Katz used to call for a list of passengers during the long range flights from New York to Tel Aviv and vice versus. Katz spread himself in the Captain's seat, lit up his eternal cigar, and started to survey the list with special emphasis on First Class passengers. Suddenly the name of a wealthy passenger popped up and Katz's drill was to invite the lucky man to the cockpit for a nice chat. While chatting in the warm atmosphere of an El Al airliner cruising high over the Atlantic, Katz would mention his 69 Squadron's B-17 days, the present revival of the Hammers, the veterans association, and its efforts to support Israel's air force heroes.

Nothing more was needed, in those glorious years of IAF public image, to secure immediate, on the spot donations. Most donations were quite "conventional" and were utilized for a host of small scale activities: furniture to the club, overalls to ground crew, etc. Yet there were two ostentatious exceptions.

The first was the villa. One of Bill's donors offered the free use of his Sea of Galilee villa as a Hammers private resort. The Lord Melchett Villa was on the shore of the lake and was extensively used for evening parties and daytime marine sports. Soon, however, the rumor that 69 "had" a villa spread all over the IAF. Envy threatened the villa, so 69 decided to share, and indeed IAF squadrons were invited to use the villa with proper reservation.

The second was the pool. Another of Bill's donors offered to fully finance a private pool for the Hammers right beside their squadron building. A private pool inside an IAF base was obviously one step too far, so it was decided that the pool would be constructed for the benefit of everyone serving at Ramat David. So it was, and the pool was inaugurated on September 23, 1973; less than a fortnight before a bitter war endangered the existence of Israel and changed the way Israelis perceived their nation and themselves. Thus ended an era of glory and arrogance, of villa and pool; an end that started on Saturday, October 6, 1973, during Yom Kippur, the Jewish Day of Atonement.

Notes

[1] From the 1960s the IAF began to assign Hebrew names to service items; the F-4 Phantom II Hebrew name was Kurnass (Sledgehammer).

[2] By then IAF fighter squadrons had two deputies: Deputy A was senior deputy commander and Deputy B was junior deputy commander. This followed the 1950s system of Flight A Commander and Flight B Commander.

[3] IAF Commander Moti Hod.

[4] Shmuel Hetz was – like Ben-Nun – a senior deputy commander during the Six Day War and was assigned to lead the first IAF F-4 unit – 201 Squadron, which was activated at Hatzor in September 1969 – without previously commanding a fighter squadron. Hetz was killed in action on July 18, 1970, in the cockpit of his Kurnass.

[5] The Israeli Air Force continued to label all F-4 back seat airmen "navigator," and did not adopt the more appropriate United States Air Force term Weapon System Officer.

[6] At the time the IAF Year overlapped the Israeli Fiscal Year from 1 April until the end of the following March. The IAF Year was divided into three terms: Term 1 from April to July, Term 2 from August to November, and Term 3 from December to March.

[7] Each term a fighter type conversion course was opened for reshuffled airmen. Since the IAF had no Operational Conversion Unit per every fighter type, the norm was that a fighter squadron from a similar community (meaning flying the same type of fighters) rotated the conversion course burden, so that each term one squadron would devote a large percentage of its resources for the welfare of the whole fighter type community. As this approach drained the resources of one squadron each term, an alternative scheme was for all squadrons to run smaller internal conversion courses only for assigned airmen.

[8] Hammers air crew Ehud Henkin with Achikar Eyal were credited with the first Kurnass air-to-air kill on November 11, 1969, while flying a 201 Squadron mission in a 201 Squadron aircraft, so this pioneering achievement was certainly a 201 Squadron kill, despite being credited to a 69 Squadron air crew. Aviem Sella with Shabtai Ben-Shoa were the first Hammers airmen to shoot down an enemy aircraft while flying a 69 Squadron mission in a 69 Squadron aircraft; therefore, the air-to-air kill credit to Sella and Ben-Shoa was definitely the first air-to-air kill in the history of 69 Squadron.

[9] Air-to-Air Missile.

[10] Quick Reaction Alert.

[11] Anti-Radiation Missile; IAF name Egrof (Fist). The tactic was to fly until radar emissions were detected and missile launched in similar fashion to combat air patrol missions; this suppression of enemy air defense action became known as Fist patrol.

[12] Air-to-Surface Missile; IAF name Sahar (Crescent). This optical tracking and manual guidance weapon proved unsatisfactory.

[13] Category 4 covered major damage but a still repairable airframe, while Category 5 covered "total loss" of aircraft — "write-off" in military parlance.

[14] Long-Range Oblique Photogrpahy.

[15] Avihu Ben-Nun is the only 69 Squadron Commander thus far to climb up the IAF command ladder, right to the top as IAF Commander from 1987 until 1992.

6

F-4 Kurnass
October 1973: The Yom Kippur War

Ambivalence surrounded the IAF in general and 69 Squadron in particular at the start of the Yom Kippur War. At the time 69 Squadron was an experienced unit well prepared for war, but IAF preparations for war mostly covered offensive scenarios. Hammers service persons were well trained, combat ready, and experienced, although their commander, Yoram Agmon, was a newcomer to the squadron and Deputy A Aviem Sella was abroad on an official IAF delegation to the USA. 69 Squadron was theoretically ready for war, yet the actual start of hostilities did surprise the Hammers, as it did all of the IAF units.

Yoram Agamon was an experienced fighter pilot and respected combat commander at the time of taking over as 69 Squadron Commander. Agmon was credited with the first IAF Mirage air-to-air kill back in 1966 and was a veteran of two wars, flying the Mirage during the 1967 Six Day War and fighting in the Phantom during the 1969-1970 Attrition War.

Preemptive Strike Preparations

Signs of imminent war began to gather during the second half of September 1973. Egypt and Syria deployed forces forward, towards the front. IAF readiness level was stepped higher, but still the general view was that if anything would happen, then this would be a limited scale clash with Syria following some kind of Syrian retaliation to the September 13, 1973, air combats. Yoram Agmon:

> "I took over command only weeks prior to war. I knew the Kurnass very well but not the squadron, so most of my time I devoted to getting acquainted with service persons. Everything was absolutely calm. Readiness was stepped up and we had four aircraft ready, but still this was a rather usual drill, nothing unusual.
>
> "On Friday's noon – October 5, 1973 – all base commanders and squadron commanders were summoned for a briefing at Dov Field. This was unusual. The briefing covered Operation Model 5, a fresh plan that was distributed to squadrons but was not yet briefed and exercised, as was the usual case. Model 5 was briefed, and IAF Chief of Intelligence presented a review of the situation. His summary was 'all signs of war emerge,' so someone asked 'OK, but will war break out or not?' and the Chief of Intelligence answered 'my evaluation is negative, war will not break out,' but when IAF

Commander Beni Peled summarized, he ended his words with the statement 'if there will be war then there will be casualties,' as he wanted to get us into the environment.

"The actual outcome of this meeting was another step up in readiness; we had to field eight aircraft rather than four. All other airmen were allowed to be at home during Yom Kippur,[1] which overlapped the weekend.

"Early next morning, prior to dawn, I was ordered to summon all airmen to the squadron. Nothing was clear, but guidelines were to gather all airmen, get into readiness, and refresh operational orders. Later that morning we were ordered to arm all aircraft for air base attack. Later I learnt that IAF Commander Beni Peled wanted to launch a preemptive strike against Syria, but he knew that the Government would only discuss this proposition at 11:00, so in order to be ready we prepared the aircraft and briefed the mission.

"Eventually, the Government rejected the preemptive strike idea. By then we were already in the aircraft waiting for signal to launch a preemptive strike. We were called back from the cockpits and ordered to reconfigure our aircraft: most aircraft in air-to-air configuration and the remaining aircraft in what we called 'supermarket' mixed configuration; a bit of general purpose bombs, a bit of CBU, a bit of AAM — ready for everything."

Siren Scramble

By then Israeli Intelligence was affirmative that war would break out at 17:00. If Israeli Intelligence was correct, then IAF service persons still had six hours to reconfigure combat aircraft and to prepare for defense. This belief was shattered at 14:00 when Egypt and Syria simultaneously attacked Israel.

Arab air superiority strategy was to pit the SAM against the IAF. Arab air power was only planned to play a secondary role and limited scale effort during the initial phase of war. In line with this strategy, the Arab war plan included an initial air strike that only targeted IDF installations in Sinai and the Golan Heights. The Arab war planners internalized that they did not possess suitable strike aircraft or properly trained airmen to penetrate deeper into Israel. This was not known to IAF command, so when hundreds of aircraft were noted taking off from Egyptian and Syrian air bases, assembling and setting course towards Israel, the obvious response was to scramble all air-to-air assets, including the Kurnass force. The IAF command and control could not predict that the Arab aerial armada would only attack right across the front line and turn back; nothing could reassure decision makers that Arab aircraft would not continue to fly towards Israel. Yoram Agmon:

> "When the siren scrambled us at 13:55 most of the air-to-air configured aircraft were ready, but some aircraft were still undergoing rearming. The siren was a surprise, and immediately afterwards we were ordered to 'run to the aircraft.' We organized pairs and took off pair after pair for air defense. Crews that took off in aircraft that were still loaded with bombs simply dumped bombs over the sea and joined the air-to-air mission.
>
> "I was vectored to Mount Hermon. Our mission was to intercept Syrian aircraft or helicopters over Mount Hermon. Weather was cloudy and visibility was poor, but we saw that there was war down there, guns flashing and typical dust. The aircraft or helicopters we were vectored to intercept were no longer there so we returned to Ramat David without doing anything, with no apparent contribution to the war effort."

Inside a Hammers' hardened aircraft shelter, reserve service persons prepare an air-to-air configured Phantom for a mission during the Yom Kippur War. The Hammers' Day 1 end of day report counted 37 sorties, of which all were air-to-air except for four attack sorties over the Egyptian front. Two Hammers' Phantoms suffered SA-7 damage over the Syrian front while flying low to look for enemy Mi-8 helicopters.

Kurnass 177 in a hardened aircraft shelter taxiway prior to a mission on the morning of October 7, 1973. This Phantom was lost that afternoon when flying an attack mission over the Egyptian front. The Kurnass crew was tasked to bomb an Egyptian bridge over the Suez Canal. A SAM shot down the Phantom; the crew – pilot Ami Alkalai and navigator Shuki Wolfson – ejected and became prisoners of war in Egypt.

Altogether a gap began to surface between AHQ and the squadrons. The former's decision to scramble all available air-to-air aircraft was logical in light of bleeps and tracks on GCI radar screens. The latter's frustration can be easily understood after launching so many aircraft in pursuit of nothing; the Arab attackers turned back long before the scrambled IAF interceptors arrived over Sinai and the Golan Heights. This gap evolved along the war's timeline into a mutual crisis of confidence; squadrons questioned details of AHQ operational orders prior to actual execution, and AHQ criticized squadrons for application of field-level adjustments to staff-level operational orders.

Challenge 4

In line with prewar planning and perception, the IAF ordered, during the night of October 6-7, 1973, the launch of Operation Challenge 4 for the morning of Day 2. Egypt was considered the most powerful opponent, so the actual front line situation was ignored and the operation to challenge air superiority over Egypt was prioritized. Challenge 4 covered four waves: the first to suppress Egyptian air bases and AAA positions, and the following three to destroy SAM batteries.

69's first wave principle mission was an air base attack mission to Gianclis, near Alexandria. Yoram Agmon was in the lead of the eight aircraft (actually only seven pressed ahead as one had to abort); most were loaded with five Mk 83 bombs and four Snakeye bombs, but the trailing pair had only three bombs and three external fuel tanks, as these rear guard Kurnass crews (Feldsho-Gur, Amizi-Israeli) had a double mission: attack Gianclis and protect the main force from hostile interceptors. Meir Gur:

> "Long flight, fine weather, pastoral scenery over the Nile Delta, but our warning systems began to chirp and in the distance we saw balloons over air bases. We began to sense that they were waiting for us, and indeed, as the pairs pulled up to bomb they began to report MiGs.
>
> "We pulled up, and I looked around and the sky was full of MiGs. Ignoring the MiGs we dived to bomb; I locked onto the runway, and once radar lock was stabilized I authorized Joel to release our bombs. Then I again looked outside and saw all those MiGs — MiGs were everywhere. The bombs dropped but Joel did not pull up. This lasted for a split second, and before I could ask Joel what was happening I heard our cannon firing a long burst. I was outraged. We bombed the runway; I saw that the others also bombed the runway, so why strafe the runway? We were the trailing pair, and our mission was to survive the MiGs and run for home; we needed our cannon ammunition for air-to-air so there was no point to strafe the runway. I yelled to Joel, 'what are you doing?'
>
> "He did not answer yet, but we pulled up and broke away. Then Joel said 'I strafed a MiG that took off.' Apparently as we bombed he noticed a MiG-21 taking off, so he followed bombing with strafing, but switching the sight from bombing to strafing was still not straightforward at the time and he missed that MiG. But it was a good show of spirit and determination.
>
> "The MiG that took off was now flying with undercarriage down; either the pilot panicked or experienced some kind of malfunction. By then we were two Kurnass crews and eight MiGs over Gianclis. Far away from home, with little fuel to spare, and we had already emptied the external fuel tanks, so we jettisoned the three empty tanks. But the MiG was flying slowly, gear down, maybe 200, 250 knots, possibly faster than normal gear down maximum speed. The last thing to do in air combat is to slow down, so we stitched; climbing, diving, and firing. Joel said, 'Guri, I am concentrating on this MiG, I am not looking anywhere else, everything except this MiG is your responsibility.' Meanwhile we all got into an Indian circle, turning behind the gear down MiG with another MiG turning behind us, Amizi turning behind that MiG, and another MiG trailing Amizi. Both MiGs opened fire but were ineffective; the turning angle could not produce an effective firing solution. We tried to slip back and open the distance for AAM launch but could not because the MiGs were quite aggressive.
>
> "Still turning with Joel firing short cannon bursts from time to time; twice I ordered Joel to break away as the MiG behind us launched AAM and then a second AAM. I saw that the MiG trailing Amizi maneuvered into good position and launched an AAM. While I was restraining myself to warn Amizi at the correct moment Amizi also launched an AAM. I yelled to Amizi over the radio 'break hard now'; Amizi broke away and the MiG-21's AAM passed by the Kurnass' tail, quite far actually. The next thing I saw was Amizi's AAM exploding onto the MiG that immediately afterwards dived 90 degrees from 2,000 feet or so and exploded on the ground.
>
> "The next time we headed north I yelled to Joel, 'disengage, we must go home, we do not have fuel!' Joel muttered a juicy curse but turned for home. The MiG pilots saw that we leveled our wings and dived to the deck; three or four of them launched a pursuit right behind us but we successfully disengaged.
>
> "Flying home bound, we were asked to report our results. We reported nothing and our wingman reported nothing. I asked Amizi:
>
> – 'Why aren't you reporting?'
>
> – 'What should I report?'
>
> – 'You shot down a MiG!'
>
> – 'I didn't see anything, if you saw something then report yourself.'
>
> "He launched the AAM and broke away so he did not see his kill. We were also credited with an air-to-air kill; IAF Intelligence reported that the gear down MiG crashed and concluded that this was our kill."

Many of the Hammers' Phantoms returned to Ramat David with battle damage from enemy aircraft AAA and SAMs. The LES evaluation airframe, Kurnass 187, was adorned with shark mouth nose art prior to the Yom Kippur War, when it suffered extensive battle damage. Kurnass 187 was transported to IAI, where it was photographed while being rebuilt.

Shooting down two MiG-21s was the better part of the Gianclis saga. This air base attack mission was not an overwhelming success, and IAF Intelligence concluded that Gianclis was closed for only 25 minutes. The runways at Ginaclis were indeed damaged, but operations from the Egyptian air base continued through utilization of the parallel taxiway for take-offs and landings.

Model 5

Preparations for Operation Challenge 4 were in full swing when Israel's leaders and IDF commanders correctly analyzed that the real immediate threat was up north, where Syrian armor was on the verge of sliding down the slopes of the Golan Heights towards Israeli cities, towns, and villages. Down south, the unpopulated Sinai Desert was a 300 km wide buffer zone that separated the Egyptian front from the heartland of Israel. Fixation to face Egypt first – as the more powerful opponent – had to be reviewed. Priority changed and new orders were issued, but Operation Challenge 4 was already underway.

Shifting the IAF principle effort from south to north, from Egypt to Syria, from Operation Challenge 4 to Operation Model 5, was a complicated and time consuming undertaking. Operation Model 5 was the IAF master plan for SEAD over Syria. Meticulous planning called for the four Kurnass squadrons to simultaneously attack the Syrian air defense network of SAM batteries east of the Golan Heights. In similar fashion to Challenge 4, Model 5 was a two phase operation. The first – preparatory – wave covered the attack of Syrian air bases and AAA positions, while the second – main – wave targeted SAM batteries. Among the principle support elements were electronic warfare screening and near real-time photographing. The latter was to precede the attack in order to pinpoint the location of SAM batteries. All opposing SAM batteries were mobile. The SA-6 was inherently mobile, and the SA-6 battery could relocate in a few hours, but the so-called static SA-2 and SA-3 batteries were also mobile and could be relocated in between several alternative pre-prepared locations, even though relocation of a "static" SA-2 or SA-3 battery took longer than relocation of a "mobile" SA-6 battery.

But on the morning of October 7, 1973, the Golan Heights was covered with clouds and reconnaissance was not an option. Not least disturbing was the deployment of the IAF electronic warfare units to Sinai in support of Challenge 4. There was no way to redeploy the electronic warfare units from south to north in time for Model 5. The IAF SEAD operation over Syria had to be launched with no up to date intelligence and without massive electronic warfare screening. These were not the only modifications to the master plan. The first preparatory wave was scrapped, and Model 5 was compacted into a single SEAD wave; the four Kurnass squadrons were ordered to discontinue Challenge 4 and to launch Model 5.

Time over Target for Model 5 was 11:20 for the loft bombers aimed at suppression of AAA, and 11:30 for the dive-toss main attack force tasked to destroy the SAM batteries. David Brisk:

"I changed status from regular to reserve only a couple of weeks prior to war. Friday, October 5, 1973. I was at the squadron but returned home to my kibbutz. Next morning fellow pilots woke me up. 'We were called to our squadrons, so you would be probably called too. Get organized and join us.' We drove to Ramat David and I went to the squadron. Confusion and disbelief greeted me. We did not know what to do, and we did not believe that we were going to war. Only Agassi preached again and again, 'this is war, get used to it.'

"In fact, I do not think that I realized we were in war until the end of the day. I perceived war in the lines of the Six Day War when we launched the attack. But compared to my perception reality was totally twisted.

"The squadron was in a peculiar status. A new squadron commander who did not know the airmen, not even their names. Deputy A Sella was abroad, along with Shadmi, who was an experienced leader, so senior leaders at the start were only Amnon Arad and Ehud Henkin.

"We flew Challenge 4 over Egypt, returned, and there was Itzik Gat, standing by the big board and organizing Model 5. I said to Gat, 'Itzik, do not lead.' He was fighting executive[2] all night long, but at the time the IAF did not comprehend the importance of rest and shifts during fighting, so he assigned himself to lead the operation.

"Preparations were hasty. Soon radio silence was broken. The leader of one of the formations had to switch to another aircraft. The plan was to initially fly very low in a train of formations so that leader, who finally took off, had to catch up flying higher than us to find his place in the train and to sink in. This was indeed accomplished, but after considerable discussion over radio.

"Navigation was planned in line with 540 knots at maximum dry thrust. This worked out fine in training, but fully loaded and flying uphill very low over land we soon realized that the Kurnass was unable to maintain 540 knots without afterburner. The trouble was that we were still consuming fuel from the under wing external fuel tanks. The afterburner's fuel consumption rate was so high that the fuel system had to stop pumping fuel from the external fuel tanks and had to pump in fuel from the fuselage tanks, so we did not empty first the external fuel tanks as planned.

"We managed to clock more than 500 knots, but this got us into the next trouble. We were too fast to follow earth when we crossed the ridge, so instead of flying downhill low over the surface we flew an arch beyond the ridge and were hanging in the air like sitting ducks with all of Syria right in front of us. We descended to low altitude again, but by then the whole surface shot at us; everybody just stood there and opened fire, from rifles to AAA.

"My navigator, Eli Tovel, kept telling me that we were off track, but there was nothing we could do, we followed our leader. We saw no target when we popped up. Our orders were to attack targets of opportunity in such a case, but not to look for our original target. We spotted some sort of ammunition dump on a hill and bombed it. All the aircraft in our formation got hit, but we returned safely to Ramat David."

Accidental Success

Most Kurnass pairs attacked empty Syrian SAM sites or didn't attack at all. Six Kurnass crews were shot down, including one Hammers crew. Postwar, IAF analysis concluded that only one Syrian SAM battery was destroyed during Operation Model 5, and that a second battery suffered extensive damage but wasn't destroyed. Dani Shpitzer:

"The whole operation was launched under the cover of electronic silence; radios and radars were switched off. There were two strict guidelines: do not fly alone and do not attack more than once. The plan was to fly north in pairs line astern, turn east over a certain Lebanese village, spread like a fan with each pair pointing towards its own target, attack all batteries at the same moment, and return west and turn south over Lebanon for the flight back home.

"While taxiing to take-off I saw my wingman with punctured wheels; I was all alone and I couldn't consult anybody what to do, electronic silence. I couldn't fly alone, so I decided to take-off and join a pair. I wouldn't know the target of that pair, but all SAM batteries had typical layout with launchers surrounding the control center, so I figured that upon pop-up we would be able to pinpoint the target. Our attack pattern was to pop up somewhere beside the target, a roll to watch over, pinpoint the target and attack.

"So I took off and joined a pair; the pair leader was Joel Feldsho. Trouble was that we turned east over one village too early. As a result, when the pair pulled up the SAM battery was right below them and they couldn't see the battery. We flew as Number 3, so we were a bit to the side. For this reason I was the only one to see the target. Number 1 dived but didn't attack, Number 2 followed, and then we bombed. The leader saw the explosion of our bombs, pinpointed the target, and returned to bomb with his wingman. That SAM battery was the only target to be damaged during Model 5. It wasn't out of action for long – the Syrians replaced damaged components and it was back in action the following day – but as a result of my decision to join a pair as Number 3, we were able to attack and damage that SAM battery.

First Loss Impact

Ehud Henkin and Shaul Levy were the first 69 casualties in the Yom Kippur War. As two of the most veteran IAF Kurnass crews – and the only ones of the original five Hammers from USAF F-4 conversion days to continue flying with 69 on regular basis[3] – their loss impacted the squadron severely. Yoram Agmon:

"We returned from Gianclis, and on our way back, after landing actually, I was notified to hurry to the

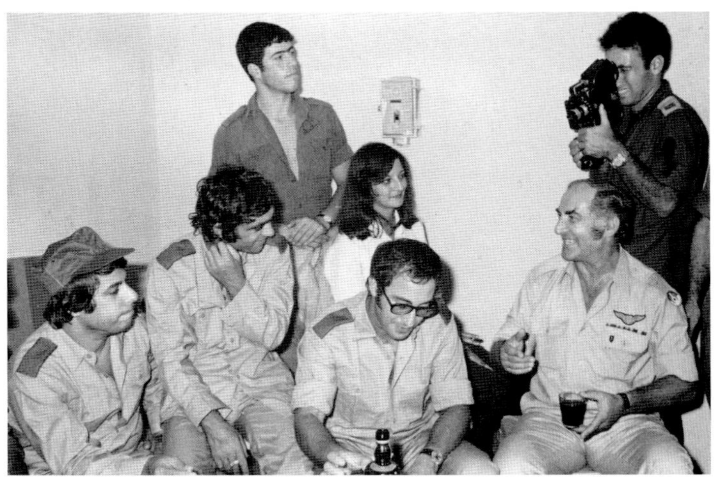

69 Squadron Yom Kippur War Administration Officer Zvi Avidror (sitting right) giving a Hammers treatment to Israel's leading artists of the era, the Gashash Hiver (Pale Tracker) threesome (sitting from left to right: *Shaike*, *Gavri*, and *Poli*) prior to performing in front of the squadron during the war.

squadron 'because there are changes,' so I ran to the squadron building. Going down the stairs an impressive figure surprised me.

– 'Yoram? Sir, I am at your command!'

"I looked at him, very well dressed, much older than us, wings on his chest — is he a pilot in my squadron? I did not know. I muttered 'OK' and rushed downstairs. Itzik Gat waited for me. He was holding his flying gear, ready to hand over the fighting executive position to me. Gat said 'planning was changed, we are executing Model 5.' I was amazed. Model 5 was not the kind of operation for a draw. 'This is manning,' he pointed at the board, 'I am leading and I already briefed the mission.' We only waited for several airmen to return from Egypt; one of them was Ehud Henkin, who flew sub-leader on our air base attack mission to Gianclis. I had my reservations, but that was his planning and he was ready to go.

"Before he disappeared I asked him, 'who was that man that I met on the stairway?' 'Zvi Avidror,' he answered, and went away.

"Zvi Avidror. I had heard that name before. The 69 airmen flew with us for a short while after we returned from the USAF F-4 conversion course. Then I heard that name. Avihu Ben-Nun told us about the Hammers veterans and mentioned that Zvi Avidror was the mainstay of the 69 Veterans' Association. I was relieved. I stopped worrying that he might jump into a Kurnass cockpit and fly away. Shortly afterwards I began to appreciate his tremendous contribution as administration officer.

"Then they took off to Model 5. From my personal squadron commander perspective I remember Model 5 on two accounts.

"The first was Feldsho. Young pilot, pair leader, who – in all that mess around him – analyzed the situation correctly. Flew a second bombing run and attacked. From that moment on I had an eye on him, and indeed, by the end of war I promoted him to 4-ship leader.

"The second was Henkin. Ehud Henkin was one of the most popular and well-liked pilots in the IAF in general, and in 69 in particular. He was a wonderful person and a great pilot. His personality and sense of humor were overpowering. One could not avoid liking him. Obviously if he was only a wonderful person, this was not enough for an air force in wartime. But he was also a great pilot, and this combination made him so unique. Yet Henkin – this wonderful person and great pilot that we all loved so much – was killed because of a pilot error. And this error resulted from over-determination. Enemy fire did not shoot him down. His bombing run was too steep, his recovery was too low, and he flew into the explosion of his own bombs.[4]

"Ehud Henkin's loss affected our airmen, especially the younger ones, more than any other loss. And I knew that it would, right from the start I knew. We airmen were built around the slogan 'This Will Not Happen To Me' (TWNHTM). Why TWNHTM? Because I am professional, because I am a good professional, and I always apply the correct action in the right time. For this reason TWNHTM. There was a negative aspect and a positive aspect in such attitude. The negative aspect was that it might have been a dangerous attitude. The positive aspect was that it kept us going even when times were rough. We flew into hell, we consciously entered hostile environments with AAA and SAM. In this hell each one of us figured that he would stay alive because he was good, because he would see all threats, and because he would react to all threats in time. That was the essence of TWNHTM. Yet this happened to our best pilot. Ehud was a symbol, and his loss shattered the TWNHTM belief of most airmen, and especially the younger ones. This happened to Henkin! What does it mean for me? Who am I compared to Henkin?

"The next morning, prior to general squadron briefing, Gat called me. 'We have to change manpower planning,' he said. I asked why? 'Three young airmen – a pilot and two navigators – are not fit to fly. They have flu and the doctor grounded them.' My decision was sharp as medical razor blade, 'do not change anything.' We entered the briefing room. I stepped to the podium and looked at the faces in front of me. I did not know most of them. But I knew that many of them did not internalize yet that we were in war, in a bitter tough war. I was absolutely sure that those three guys were truly ill and formally unfit to fly. But this was war. I opened my brief with a declaration. 'Gentlemen, we are in war! And in war one must do the best he can, no discounts. In war we fly even if we are sick. In this war, all of us will fly to the end of personal capacity.'

"They flew, and they continued flying till the end of war, but I am sure that this was one of the impacts of

The wrecked vertical stabilizer of Kurnass 123 – that Henkin and Levy flew on their final flight – on display in Syria sometime after the Yom Kippur War.

Agmon-Mor flew Kurnass 113 on a Day 2 afternoon mission against Egyptian assembly points and crossing bridges in the south sector of the Suez Canal.

Henkin's loss. Obviously this was also a symptom of fear, but we were all fearful during war yet we flew, we all flew until the war ended."

South Again

Operation Challenge 4 was discontinued and Operation Model 5 failed. Then the zig-zag from south to north continued. IDF Command South screamed for air support, so during the afternoon Agmon-Mor led three pairs to fly brief exposure dive-toss attacks against Egyptian bridges and assembly areas in the south sector of the Suez Canal. Eran Mor:

"Amos Mashiach and myself were to be Ehud Henkin's and Shaul Levy number 3 for Model 5, but our Kurnass 132 was not ready on time. I stayed at base ops when an operation order was accepted calling for three pairs to attack in southern Suez Canal.

"Yoram Agmon asked me to plan the mission. I did it while Model 5 was ongoing and heard on ops radio (00) distress calls from two 201 Squadron Kurnass crews who were making a crash landing on a Ramat David runway; one of them without the navigator. A third 201 crew ejected on final to a Ramat David runway. Our airplanes returned, and we realized that Ehud Henkin and Shaul Levy were missing. While some rumors were running I completed the planning of the mission. Then Yoram Agmon asked me to brief the mission and to fly it with him as leader.

"We flew high altitude to mid-Sinai and then went low altitude high speed and pulled at the southern bridge for fast and low exposure bomb run. The other pairs pulled minutes apart north of us. We found lots of vehicles at the parking area next to the bridge and released the bombs on them. I have seen good BDA for us and for our wingman, Gideon Yahalom.

"While flying back east the leader of the third pair, Joel Feldsho, reported that his wingman, Alkalai-Wolfson, was hit by Egyptian ground forces and ejected. Agmon asked Feldsho to stay behind and lead possible rescue while the two other pairs RTBed.

"That evening we returned to Sinai for loft bombing over bridges on the north sector of the Suez Canal. I flew with pilot Yair Elor. After take-off we flew into darkness; it was a moonless night and there were no lights on the ground, complete blackout. While crossing the Sinai line we saw the vehicle lights of IDF convoys driving west towards the front. We could follow the roads by the convoys' lights.

"Near Tassa we went into complete darkness again until we found the IP light set by IAF cadets positioned in the desert specifically for this mission. Over the IP we activated our Lofttoss bombing computer, a link between two analog computers which was working nice in training. Upon leaving the IP we received high chirp of SA-2 on our warning system. Reception was so high that it saturated the warning system and the chirp turned to a scream.

"We pressed ahead, flying at low altitude on full mil power until, on computer signal, we started to pull 4G for release. Unlike training, the aircraft was very heavy and we climbed over 10,000 feet before the bombs released. It was not a safe profile, especially not with steady SA-2 lock. Once the bombs were away we dove sharply, in complete darkness to very low altitude and flew high speed back east. At safe distance we were low in fuel but decided to RTB to Ramat David. The following night two Hammers crews were lost on the same mission."

Air Combat

Pure air-to-air missions were still assigned to the Kurnass squadrons. Air-ro-air missions mostly involved QRA or CAP. In QRA the pilots of the Mirage interceptors and the crews of the multi-role Phantoms sat for hours in the cramped cockpits, waiting for the scramble signal. Most QRA scrambles ended a long, nerve-racking, uncomfortable wait, but only rarely resulted in immediate engagement of the enemy. More often than not scrambled pilots or crews, after hours in the cockpit on the ground, were assigned to fly CAP. Flying racetrack patterns for up to an hour or so, the CAP mission was as tiring and boring as the QRA wait, but was obviously more demanding, for the aircraft was flying rather than safely parked.

Why the Kurnass squadrons assigned with these fatigue inducing air-to-air QRA and CAP missions and operating around the clock in a variety of air-to-ground missions, while Kurnass combat losses diminished the order of battle down to unacceptable levels and Kurnass crews were overloaded, and while plenty of dedicated Mirage interceptors were readily available, is a question that can only be asked after a war. Wartime actions are mostly way far from optimal, and in real time only a few actions can be still judged as optimal in post action analysis.

And so it was that after more than 24 hours of bitter fighting, after Kurnass combat losses already amounted to eight aircraft, after Challenge 4 was discontinued and after the Model 5 failure, the vital Kurnass bombers were still assigned to air-to-air QRA and were still flying air-to-air CAP missions. Zeev Raz:

> "I converted to the Kurnass in 119 Squadron at Tel Nof during 1971. Because I was from kibbutz Geva, in the Jezreel Valley near Ramat David, I asked for assignment to 69. Two years later I was the squadron's Weapon Systems Officer and I was qualified as 4-ship air-to-ground leader and air-to-air pair leader.
>
> "We were scrambled from air-to-air QRA and flew CAP until GCI vectored us to engage enemy aircraft over Mount Hermon. Immediately prior to engagement GCI lost contact, and our radar lock was also lost because we flew higher than they did. We turned and spotted them, a 4-ship of MiG-21s. Thus the initial engagement involved two Phantoms versus four MiG-21s. We separated, and each one of us engaged a pair of MiG-21s. My navigator Bobo kept reminding me to pay attention to altitude. The engagement was at an altitude of 9-10,000 feet above sea level, but we were quite low over ground level.
>
> "It was already past sunset — still some light, but I mostly followed the afterburners of the MiG-21s. I shot down a MiG-21 with a cannon burst, but more MiG-21s joined the combat and a gun burst damaged my wingman's Phantom. Two Mirages reinforced us but still we were outnumbered, fighting at least eight MiG-21s and perhaps as many as a dozen. The Syrians fought us the way they did, which was lucky for us because the MiG-21 was superior to the F-4 as an air combat aircraft. Still, we didn't emerge from this engagement as we hoped we would; I shot down a MiG-21, but my wingman was damaged and the Mirages' wingman was shot down."

Hammers airmen in their mess during the Yom Kippur War. Standing from left to right: reserve cook and administration officer Zvi Avidror. Sitting from left to right: navigator Uri Ofer, navigator Shabtai Ben-Shoa, and navigator Eran Mor. Sitting in the background: navigator Haim Shahar (aka Bobo).

Wartime Routine

Day 1 was characterized by confusion and surprise, and Day 2 yielded rushed and unsuccessful counterattacks. From Day 3 onwards the war was accepted as reality, and a war routine began to emerge. David Brisk:

> "Model 5's major blow on the squadron was the loss of Henkin-Levy. The next day Sella and Shadmi returned and the squadron began to get along much better. Administration functioned like clockwork. I weighed the same and wore the same size since I was 16. The only time frame in my life that I gained weight was during the Yom Kippur War. Our administration officer, Zvi Avidror, orchestrated four meals per day, a room downstairs for quiet and uninterrupted sleep, and a new set of underwear after each shower. This was really tip-top, and the only disturbance was that we flew tough missions…"

Missions were indeed tough. The squadron was well prepared for war, but the Yom Kippur War was a vicious conflict. IAF SEAD failed, and many other IAF prewar concepts did not materialize as planned. Arab opposition was tough; many aircraft and airmen were lost. Aviem Sella:

> "From my own personal perspective the Attrition War was tougher than the Yom Kippur War. The Attrition War was longer and we were less experienced; we did not know the aircraft very well, and the missions we flew were all a 'first' to us. We learnt while fighting and the workload was huge: learning to fly, teaching new airmen, managing a squadron, and fighting. The Yom Kippur War was a surprise, but we were prepared; we made errors and lost airmen but we were well prepared.
>
> "One aspect that came to light during the Yom Kippur War was the institute of base sociologist. Our sociologist was – prior to studying sociology – a naval commando fighter. Once he realized the magnitude of this war, he simply returned to fight as a naval commando and in reality abandoned us during wartime, when we most needed a sociologist. In this department I depended upon Gideon Magen. Gideon was a prisoner of war in Syria from April 1970 until June 1973; he was older than most of us, had a well balanced perspective, and did not fly a lot. He was my assistant for airmen issues, my right-

Backing Hammers' commanders during the Yom Kippur War was Gideon Magen, sitting behind 69 Squadron Commander Yoram Agmon in this wartime photo. Magen was prisoner of war in Syria from April 1970 until June 1973, yet he insisted upon return to combat flying and flew 14 sorties from October 16 to 23, 1973, including three missions — Fist patrols flown from October 20 to 22, 1973.

hand in manpower management. His observations and suggestions were priceless: give this airman a day to rest, send to sleep that airmen, team X with Y or fly with Z to renew his self confidence. This advice was very helpful for me."

In fact, Deputy A Sella summed up his lessons from wartime human resources on December 8, 1973:

"One of the major lessons that I learnt in this war is that treating people in wartime is not to be handled by amateurs. The issue is complicated and difficult, since the commander does not have any spare time for his men, he cannot monitor all of his subordinates (especially in Kurnass squadron), and moreover, the commander lacks theoretical knowledge to treat so many people under such ultimate stress – war.

"Luckily 69 Squadron had a mature and available man, Gideon Magen, who pointed Yoram and me towards people under stress or about to crumble. This assistance was priceless. I recall that Gideon pointed out to me several men with whom I had flown in formation, and I could not understand Gideon's view that they were in poor mental shape, in light of my perspective that they were in good spirit. Knowing and trusting Gideon, I followed his advice 100%. His help saved lives."

Day 3: Dmer

The main Day 3 morning effort was an air base attack mission to Dmer. Time on target was 07:20, and the operation involved three formations. The first was split into two pairs: the first pair (Zait-Katz, Ziblat-Mor) flew CBU loft attack against SAM batteries ahead of the main force. The second pair was tasked to fly local SEAD, attacking SAM batteries and radar stations in the vicinity of Dmer, while a 4-ship formation was tasked to bomb the runway with M-117 bombs and the third formation was armed with CBU and tasked to attack hardened aircraft shelter complexes. Aviem Sella:

"I finished my BA in economy and computers and returned to 69 as Deputy A in 1972. A couple of weeks prior to the outbreak of the Yom Kippur War I travelled to the USA to learn about simulators. War caught me in the USA, and this was the first of my three 'escapes' from the USA!

"I flew to Israel and arrived around midnight on the night of October 7-8, 1973. The squadron's administration

Hammering a Syrian squadron building at Dmer on the morning of October 8, 1973; the complex is surrounded by typical Syrian hardened aircraft shelters for two jets (left) and for single aircraft (right).

Battle Damage Assessment camera image of the CBU pattern during the October 8, 1973, morning attack air base mission to Dmer, Syria.

officer, Zvi Avidror, was waiting for me at the airport and drove me back to Ramat David. All the way back to Israel I was worried that war might end prior to me getting a chance to fly, so I was under the impression that I should hurry to get hold of operations. However I did not fly for about two months, as several weeks prior to departure to the USA I attended an escape exercise and got sick, relapsing fever, so I was grounded.

"I returned and immediately prepared to fly a mission, but because I did not fly for two months I decided to treat this mission as though it was a refreshment flight; therefore I did not lead but flew as sub-leader. Eventually I was the only one to score a direct hit on a hardened aircraft shelter."

The Day 3 air base attack mission to Dmer was an overall success. IAF Intelligence reported holed runways and hits on two hardened aircraft shelters plus a command post. Dmer was closed for operations for six and a half hours after the Hammers visit, but the Hammers also returned from Dmer with a scar, as the number 4 aircraft of the SEAD formation was lost to a Syrian MiG-21 interceptor. Pilot Yoram Shahar and navigator Gur Israeli ejected from Kurnass 130 to become prisoners of war in Syria.

Day 3 to Day 4: Canal Bridges

The Day 3 IDF Command South counterattack in Sinai failed. IDF GHQ was afraid that the Egyptians would exploit this success for another breakthrough east, deeper into Sinai. Therefore, the IAF was called for support and was tasked to bomb bridges across the Suez Canal to disrupt the flow of Egyptian logistics and reinforcements into Sinai.

Most Egyptian bridges were modular and narrow. There was only a slight chance to hit such bridges in loft profile attack at night. But there were indeed concentrations of motor traffic in the vicinity of the bridges, and the mission was primarily aimed at disturbing Egyptian deployment. The loft profile at night was extremely hazardous. Flying in singles, the Kurnass crews cruised to pre-set and lit-up points in Sinai, descended to low altitude over that marker, set course, and would fly as low as the crew dared until the pull-up point. Bomb and run away. Those who did not dare flying very, very low were tracked down by Egyptian radar systems well before pop-up and were immediately engaged. Others only faced SAM launches from the pull-up moment. The Hammers lost two aircraft on Suez Canal bridge loft attack missions that night. Pre-midnight SA-6 shot down Kurnass 247, and pilot Michael Dvir and navigator Shabtai Ben-Shoa ejected. They landed in no-man's land and a helicopter rescued them. Shortly after midnight a

Syrian MiG-21 shot down Kurnass 130 during the October 8, 1973, morning air base attack mission to Dmer. Pilot Yoram Shahar and navigator Gur Israeli were prisoners of war in Syria until June 1974.

Navigator Shabtai Ben-Shoa flew Kurnass 249, with pilot David Brisk, on an early evening loft mission to bomb an Egyptian bridge across the Suez Canal on October 8, 1973. Brisk went to sleep after their return to Ramat David while Ben-Shoa took-off in Kurnass 247 with pilot Michael Dvir for a second late evening loft attack that ended in ejection. Kurnass 249 was photographed landing at Ramat David on October 24, 1974.

second Kurnass was lost. A SAM shot down Kurnass 245, which crashed four kilometers east of the Suez Canal in the Egyptian Army 3 sector. Pilot Zvulun Amizi and navigator Zeev Yogev were killed. Yoram Agmon:

> "I was inside the squadron building when I was told that Amizi's father was outside. How he got there I just do not know. When I received this message we did not know what happened. We only knew that radio contact was lost, but was he retrieved? Killed? Captured? We did not know and his father was outside, waiting. This was pure coincidence, but it was not the kind of situation that a squadron commander should handle during wartime. I went outside, introduced myself, and told him what I knew, that contact was lost and that we were still waiting for additional information. I promised that I would report to him. He departed. Eventually Agassi and I went to inform him after we were reported to that they were killed."

Day 3 to Day 4: FROGS

Not directly a 69 Squadron affair, but one that did impact the Hammers in many ways, was the Syrian FROG attacks. Every IAF air base has its own small neighborhood where long term service persons live with their families. Wartime drill was to evacuate the neighborhood, as air bases were expected to be attacked. Also a wartime pattern was to base all airmen within the confines of squadron buildings where they lived and from where they departed to fly. This was a useful arrangement, but squadron buildings were not designed to accommodate so many service persons for so long. Several squadrons erected tents on the grass beside the squadron building to ease density, and all squadrons allowed airmen a few hours refreshment, or a night long rest, in the vacated air base neighborhood. Everything changed at Ramat David after the night of October 8-9, 1973. Yoram Agmon:

> "A nuisance that bothered us throughout the war, and for which we found no solution, was twisted evening

October 8, 1973, was the Hammers' worst combat losses per day during the Yom Kippur War. In between losing Kurnass 130 over Dmer in the morning and Kurnass 245 and Kurnass 247 over the Suez Canal during the evening, the Hammers lost Kurnass 155, which was in pursuit of Syrian MiG-21s attacking IDF forces over the north sector of the Golan Heights. Vectored above clouds, the Kurnass was hit by an SA-6. Pilot Gidon Yahalom and navigator Eran Mor ejected safely, were rescued by the tanks of Avigdor Kahalani's Battalion 77 (of Valley of Tears Battle fame), and were the first Hammers crew to eject and return to fly. Kurnass 155 (first from left) was photographed during an armoring drill exercise in January 1971.

Ramat David airmen examine the wreckage of Kurnass 155 in a postwar tour of the Golan Heights' battlefields.

'fighting clock.'[5] Every evening we were summoned to the base commander. We hastily collected data and reported to the base commander, who then had to fly to AHQ to attend a similar session of higher level hierarchy. We then returned to the squadrons for end of day briefings, but had to wait until base commander returned with guidelines for the next day.

"While attending the first evening base level session we heard the dull sound of a distant explosion. Zorik calmed us down and reassured us that this was the typical sound of his air conditioner, an old air conditioner that suffered from 'compressor stalls,' as he called it. Later we learnt that this was the sound of Syrian FROG rockets exploding in a nearby town. Exactly the same happened the following evening. We were sitting in Zorik's office, only this time the explosion was much closer. The FROG rockets exploded halfway from town to base. On the third evening they hit Ramat David. I slept in the neighborhood with my wife and children. The previous day my wife, as well as Zorik's, decided to ignore regulations and to visit me. A FROG landed on a house two houses away from mine. It was a house that was temporarily empty, so reserve pilots were housed there and one of them was killed. From then on we were only allowed to sleep in secured locations within the squadron building compound."

Agmon-Tovel in Kurnass 111 and Brisk-Lipshitz in Kurnass 102 were one of the pairs that attacked the Syrian SA-2 battery on October 9, 1973. Kurnass 102 was photographed inside the Ramat David Maintenance Squadron's Kurnass Workshop while being repaired after returning from a mission with battle damage.

Day 4: Wing Commander Agassi

Ramat David Wing Commander Zorik Lev did not return from a mission on the morning of Day 4; his Skyhawk dived into the sea over the Port Said sector and he was reported missing in action. Aviem Sella:

> "Jacob Agassi was wing commander during the 69 activation process. In July 1970 he handed over command to Zorik Lev and pursued a second career as an El Al airline pilot. Thus, from 1970 Agassi became a 69 reserve pilot and this was a peculiar situation. My former commander grew his hair long and was under my command!
>
> "I was with Agassi when IAF Commander Beni Peled called him on the phone and told him that he was the new wing commander. Agassi finished his phone call and said 'I was just notified that I am wing commander, what I shall do first?' 'Get a haircut,' I answered, 'and start commanding base,' and so it was. Thus he was my commander until July 1970, then I was his commander, and from October 9, 1973, he was again my commander!"

Hammers' end of Day 4 report counted 29 sorties. The main efforts were an extremely successful morning air base attack mission to Mansura, Egypt (12 aircraft that closed Mansura for six days), a successful afternoon SEAD mission against a Syrian SA-2 SAM battery in the Khan El Sheikh sector (four aircraft that

Brisk-Rubinstein flew Kurnass 126 during the Hammers' failed mission to the Syrian GHQ in Damascus on October 9, 1973. Mission abortion was a blessing to the 126 crew, as their jet suffered hydraulic malfunction, so they jettisoned their bomb load over the Mediterranean Sea and barely made it back home to Ramat David. Kurnass 126 was photographed in October 1970 during an arming drill demonstration.

reportedly destroyed the battery), and in between eight aircraft departed Ramat David on a mission that has generated considerable controversy ever since.

Day 4: Syria GHQ Damascus

In response to the Syrian FROG campaign and under the impression that strategic air raids can change the course of war, the Israeli Government authorized the IDF to wage a strategic air campaign that was pointed at key infrastructure targets all over Syria. Most targets were fuel storage dumps and electricity system elements, but one target was exceptional and actually launched the IAF strategic air campaign against Syria. The Syrian GHQ compound in the center of Damascus was the target selected to initiate the IAF strategic air campaign against Syria. Three Kurnass squadrons were tasked to attack, each committing to the mission eight aircraft flying in two four-aircraft formations one after the other. There was a 15 minute time interval between each attack with 119 Squadron tasked to bomb at 11:30, followed by 107 Squadron and 69 Squadron. David Brisk:

> "Amnon Arad flew in the lead of the first four aircraft formation and Itzik Gat was leading the trailing four aircraft formation. We flew out to the sea, crossed the Lebanese coastline, and were planned to fly over Lebanon and thence to Damascus. Hydraulic system warning light came on just as we crossed the coastline. I decided to ignore it and to press ahead with the mission. There were two hydraulic systems, and I still hoped that this was a false alarm. My logic was ABORT A MISSION TO THE SYRIAN GHQ? NO WAY! But I was flying a 'made in USA' machine, so there were hardly any false alarms. I was really in trouble.
>
> "The 107 Squadron formation leader ahead of us saved me. Maybe three minutes later he reported that he was turning back and aborting the mission. We also flew into clouds and saw nothing so we also turned back. A minute after turning back my hydraulic system failed. The 107 formation leader saved my life. I jettisoned my bombs over the Mediterranean Sea and barely made it to Ramat David while the other crews were diverted to bomb an alternative target."

Eventually the 119 Phantoms displayed outstanding maintenance of the aim. Regardless of extremely poor weather – low clouds and no visibility – the 119 leader pressed ahead and his Kurnass crews bombed the Syrian GHQ as planned. The 107 and 69 Phantoms turned back and were assigned to attack other targets.

Day 5: Quweisna

Yom Kippur War air base attack missions were generally divided into "suppression" and "destruction." Suppression were "normal" Six Day War style attacks with 4-ship formations attacking runways; the expected end product was neutralization for a short while. Destruction were "massive" air base attack missions that mostly involved three formations from a single squadron that

Rodan-Carmeli flew RF-4E Kurnass 191 during the October 10, 1973, air base attack mission to Quweisna, flying wingman to Gat-Primor in the lead of the CBU 4-ship formation. The trailing pair of the CBU 4-ship was Brisk-Tovel (in Kurnass 249) and Zait-Gavish in sister RF-4E Kurnass 195, which returned to Ramat David on one engine. Kurnass 191 was photographed in May 1973; it changed prefix to 4 after the Yom Kippur War as Kurnass 491.

Agmon-Wittmann flew Kurnass 105 in the lead of the noon air base attack mission to Damascus International on October 10, 1973. Kurnass 105 was photographed prewar when a mechanized tow-bar was tested to ease the challenge of pushing a loaded Kurnass back into the old "French" era hardened aircraft shelters. This mechanized tow-bar was not introduced into service, and the problem was solved with the introduction of the new "American" era hardened aircraft shelters, into which the Kurnass taxied on its own power.

targeted air base installations; IAF prewar practice called for two or three squadrons to attack one after the other so that the end product would be a non-operational air base for the following few days. Several "massive" air base attack missions were highly successful and left behind an air base in chaos that was unable to recover for up to six days, but wartime constraints dictated less than desired "massive" air base attack missions, and many of the flown missions were not full force efforts.

The Hammers' Day 5 morning air base attack mission to Quweisna, in the Nile Delta, was an "augmented suppression" mission that achieved the desired impact of a "destruction" air base attack mission. Itzik Gat flew lead in the first 4-ship that lofted CBUs at 08:05. The follow-up 4-ship bombed the runway. Quweisna – from where two Iraqi Hunter squadrons flew combat missions – was shattered. The CBU attack reportedly destroyed a Hunter, while the combined impact closed Quweisna for more than five days. Egyptian AAA damaged Kurnass 195 – flying as Number 4 in the CBU 4-ship – but Zait-Gavish returned safely to Ramat David on one engine.

A dozen minutes prior to time-on-target over Quweisna a QRA pair was scrambled to the Syrian front. Pair leaders Arad-Kesler were credited with a MiG-17 kill.

Day 5: Damascus International

The Hammers' Day 5 noon mission to Damascus International was a "semi massive" air base attack, as it only involved the three 69 4-ship formations; a following 4-ship formation from 201 Squadron was tasked to attack the nearby highway take-off and landing strip. Amnon Arad flew in the lead of the first formation armed with CBU and tasked to suppress AAA. Yoram Agmon and Aviem Sella were leading the follow-up formations tasked to bomb with general purpose bombs. Yoram Agmon:

> "We flew north, low over the sea, and preserved radio silence. When we approached our turning point east, GCI broke radio silence and asked if anyone of us was flying with an active IFF (Identification Friend or Foe) transponder. Then I suspected that we were being tracked down by the enemy, especially because this subject was mentioned during recent intelligence briefings.
>
> "We turned east, and shortly after flying over the coastline – while climbing to fly over the Lebanon Mountains ridge – the trailing formation reported MiGs. The MiGs were right behind them and within engagement range so they jettisoned external loads and turned to face the MiGs. However, their Number 4 was unable to jettison his external load and he had to break with all that mass.
>
> "I looked back and saw a worrying picture. The trailing 4-ship broke away and the MiGs had the upper hand; MiGs were right behind both wingmen – Number 2 and Number 4 in the formation – within firing range and in good deflection angle. My real-time evaluation was that my earlier suspicion of a Syrian GCI controlled interception had materialized. I was afraid that the MiGs would shoot down one of my crews, so I ordered my formation to dump bombs and to turn back towards the MiGs in order to change the balance of force to our favor. Obviously the leader of the first formation also had to consider turning back since there was no point to attack only with CBUs.
>
> "The bottom line was that we did not pursue our mission, and this decision bothers me to this day — was I right? In hindsight I don't think I did make the right decision. The Phantom proved many times that it could defend itself even against a supposedly superior enemy. The picture that I saw, with that bomb laden Number 4 under attack, and my personal fear, as squadron commander, of losing a crew over hostile territory overpowered cold blooded logic."

Both trailing 4-ship formations engaged the Syrian fighters; the leading 4-ship formation, indeed no longer having a reason to suppress AAA, turned back, but was unable to join combat. 69 did not attack Damascus International but did not lose a Kurnass and was credited with an air-to-air kill. Itzik Gat:

> "We flew 12 aircraft, and I was number 3 in the third four-ship formation. Just as we turned towards Damascus one of the navigators shouted 'MiGs.' A MiG attacked my wingman. I pushed the 'panic' button and maneuvered

right behind him. I was 200 meters behind him and I was just about to squeeze the trigger when he ejected."

Mashiach-Mor flew Kurnass 112 during an October 11, 1973, SEAD mission against a Syrian SAM battery in the Katanah sector. Kurnass 112 was photographed during the May 7, 1973, Israeli Independence War fly-past.

Day 5: Wartime Reconnaissance

Intelligence played a key role during the Yom Kippur War. Erroneous IDF Intelligence evaluation enabled Egypt and Syria to surprise Israel; lack of near real-time intelligence deprived IAF victory in the air superiority battle. Regardless of intelligence failure and shortcomings, IAF fighter force squadrons qualified for reconnaissance (69, 101, and 119) continued their heroic effort to collect vital imagery of the enemy amidst a horrible war. Daily reconnaissance flights surveyed the battlefields, and many of the Hammers missions were devoted to recce; a fine example is an October 10, 1973, noon mission over Lebanon with an escort of two 117 Squadron Mirages piloted by Herzle Bodinger and Uri Lis. Zeev Raz:

> "MiG-21s appeared to intercept us. They were very close and I was armed with air-to-air missiles, so I just wanted to turn into them, to engage them and to shoot them down. But I restrained myself — we call it tactical discipline. The brief was that if the MiGs appeared then the escorting Mirages would engage them while we would ignite our afterburners and run away to bring back home the vital photos that we took. Our mission was to photograph, not to shoot down MiGs.
>
> "This was the only recce mission during which I faced such a dilemma. Obviously the fact that we were in war had something to do with it, because during 'peacetime' recce missions such a thought did not occur to me at all. But it was war, and with all that mess around us we allowed ourselves more room for independent personal consideration. We were aware of all those odd operational orders so we exerted a lot of professional judgment. It was under such circumstances that I remember my hand on the stick and my will to break towards those MiGs, but still I restrained myself. The Mirages engaged the MiGs and I returned to Ramat David."

Day 6: Counterattack Syria

Syria suffered from Hammers' Day 6 attacks that supported IDF Command North's counteroffensive. Main missions targeted three air bases, SAM batteries, and a fuel storage complex.

The three air base attack missions targeted Dmer (4-ship), Nazariya (6-ship), and Damascus International (4-ship). All three missions successfully accomplished their objective to close the air base to operations for hours: two, seven, and six respectively.

Syrian SAM batteries were attacked in the morning and during the afternoon hours. In between these efforts a 4-ship formation was tasked to bomb a fuel storage complex. The mission was considered successful; IAF Intelligence reported destruction of 20 tanks containing 55,000 tons of fuel. Reportedly evading MiG-21 interceptors, the 4-ship leader had to eject from Kurnass 105 over Lebanon, where Arad-Primor were interned until November 1973.

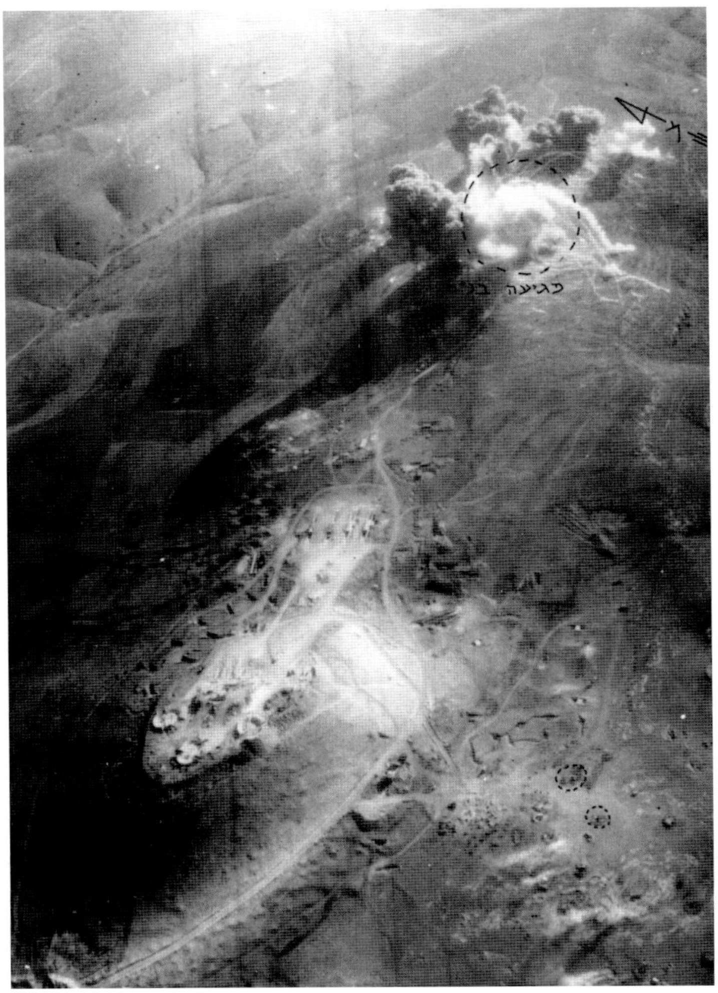

Syrian SAM battery under Hammers attack on October 11, 1973.

Agmon-Wittmann were credited with a MiG-17 kill while flying Kurnass 111 during a Day 7 air base attack mission to Dmer. Kurnass 111 was photographed in January 1971.

Day 7: Sal El Sachra

IDF Command North's counteroffensive gathered momentum and triggered an intensified Syrian effort to air strike IDF forces in the Golan Heights. Particularly active were the Elmaza-based MiG-17 squadrons. These MiG-17s took off from their well secured air base near Damascus, flew a few minutes to the front line only some 40 km away, turned to attack IDF troops, and completed the turn to fly back to Elmaza. Interception of these low flying short endurance MiG-17 missions was almost impossible, so IAF Kurnass formations were ordered to attack Elmaza in the hope that air raids would disrupt the MiG-17 attack missions over the front. Five air base attack sorties to Elmaza were flown on Day 6, and the effort intensified on October 12, 1973, but was initially ineffective, as three Day 7 early morning air base attack missions to Elmaza failed to close the enemy air base to operations. The MiG-17s continued to take-off, attack, and land.

The Elmaza air base attack mission was delegated to 69 during the late morning hours of Day 7. Four Kurnass aircraft were loaded with five M-117 and three Mk 83 bombs each, and the four crews were tasked to attack Elmaza from 10:50. David Brisk:

> "Elmaza was treated as a high value target, so a strong team, a senior staffed formation, was entrusted with the mission. We were flying the final run towards target when the leader suddenly pulled up. What happened? We were still short of Damascus! They pulled up to attack Sal El Sachra, a small general aviation airfield. The runway at Sal El Sachra was on a similar heading to the runway at Elmaza but was significantly less wide. They pulled and bombed the runway. I realized the error and remembered that an SA-3 battery was in position near the runway. I looked around and there it was, alive and well, so they bombed the runway and I bombed the SAM battery.
>
> "We returned to the squadron and they were all very happy; they were sure we attacked Elmaza and they knew that they bombed accurately. Sella was the fighting executive, and he was under pressure from IAF Operations. 'Did you accomplish the mission to Elmaza? Should we plan another mission to Elmaza?' I said 'sure, go ahead, plan, we attacked Sal El Sachra.' No one took me seriously until the BDA photos arrived 20 minutes later!"

The error was indeed realized and another mission was planned. Again four aircraft, this time loaded with eight M-117 bombs each.

MARGU call sign 4-ship formation attack Sal El Sachra; the three right-hand explosions indicate three Kurnass crews bombing the runways, while the left-hand, further away explosion is aimed at the local SAM battery.

Agmon-Wittmann were credited with a MiG-17 kill while flying Kurnass 209 on October 13, 1973. Kurnass 209 was photographed in May 1973 when still coded "109."

Toad Phantoms destined for 69 Squadron being hastily "localized" at the Ramat David Maintenance Squadron Kurnass Hangar during the Yom Kippur War.

Time over Target was 12:00 and Elmaza was attacked, but was not neutralized, not even for a short while. A third Hammers air base attack mission to Elmaza was launched for 16:05 time on target. Six Kurnass crews were dispatched, each aircraft armed with five M-117 and three Mk 83 bombs, but this mission was also not a success story. Only half the force actually attacked, as defending interceptors frustrated the attack of three Kurnass crews. One Kurnass was damaged and all six returned safely to Ramat David, but Elmaza was still an operational air base.

Day 8: Agmon-Wittmann Again

Hammers' end of day report for October 13, 1973, mentioned 34 sorties, including six to attack over the Syrian front and six for SEAD over the Egyptian front. 69 Squadron Commander Yoram Agmon and Lead Navigator Daniel Wittmann were again credited with an air-to-air kill. The crew Agmon-Wittmann was scrambled at 12:05 to intercept the notorious MiG-17s over the Syrian front. The two Kurnass crews intercepted four MiG-17s and Agmon-Wittmann, in Kurnass 209, launched an AIM-9D and shot down a MiG-17.

The following day – October 14, 1973 – the Hammers' main effort was SEAD over the Egyptian front. Fist and loft attacks were flown throughout the day; one crew – Zait-Tovel – ejected and two crews landed in damaged aircraft. That same evening the Hammers' inventory was reinforced when eight strange looking Phantoms landed at Ramat David.

Day 9: Toad

Two types of Kurnass aircraft were in 69's inventory at the start of war: F-4E Blocks 38 to 48 were BLC[6] aircraft, and F-4E Blocks 49 to 51 were LES[7] aircraft. The LES aircraft traded ground attack for air-to-air, as the LES improved slow speed maneuverability at the expense of high speed performance, as well as dispensing with several air-to-ground configurations due to the geometry of the LES. Not least important were the differing cockpit layouts.

Attrition replacement F-4E aircraft were delivered to Israel from October 14, 1973. These mostly included two groups, "old" airframes ordered in US FY 1966 or 1967 and newer airframes mostly from US FY 1972 vintage. The latter had a cutting-edge technological innovation, TISEO[8] – essentially a video camera bolted onto the leading edge of the right-hand wing.

All of these ex-USAF aircraft were flown to Israel in their darker USAF camouflage scheme and were rushed into IAF service without repainting, so they all became known as "Toad." The influx of the attrition replacement Toad aircraft triggered a reshuffle of airframes among the Kurnass force. The Hammers transferred their BLC aircraft to 201 Squadron and inducted the lions share of Toad airframes, so that by the end of the war most of the 69 aircraft were in the darker scheme.

Ramat David Wing Commander Jacob Agassi (right) greets Doodi Zait (left) and Eli Tovel (center) after being flown to Ramat David in a Bell 205 helicopter (seen in the background) from the crash site of their Kurnass. Zait-Tovel probably suffered "fiendly fire" damage and had to eject when flying the base leg of the Ramat David landing circuit pattern.

The combination Agmon-Wittmann in Kurnass 209 was again successful on October 16, 1973. This Kurnass 209 sight image was captured seconds before the AIM-9D intercepted the MiG-21 to claim a fifth kill for Yoram Agmon, the only pilot ever to achieve ace status in 69 Squadron service.

Day 10: Ace Agmon

The morning's main effort for October 15, 1973, was the attack of a Syrian fuel storage facility near Latakiya. IAF intelligence reported that the eight Hammers crews damaged nine tanks (total capacity 35,000 tons) out of the facility's 24 tanks (total capacity 85,000 tons).

Two pairs were tasked to fly air base attack missions to Mansura and Shubra Khit in Egypt during noon hours. The Mansura pair was called back over the Mediterranean Sea. The Shubra Khit pair sprayed the runways with CBUs; the lead Kurnass – Sella-Gur – added cannon strafing against a pair of MiG-21s that suddenly taxied out of a hardened aircraft shelter.

Hammering Syrian infrastructure targets continued the following day when 69 was tasked to bomb a major armored vehicle repair workshop. MiG-21s intercepted the bombers and escorts on their way back home and 69 crews (Agmon-Wittmann, Yahalom-Rubinstein) were credited with two kills during the ensuing air combat. Thus emerged the first and only pilot to achieve ace status in Hammers service; Agmon's three kills as 69 Squadron Commander were added to his previous two Mirage kills.

Day 11: If I Had Known

Operational sorties were obviously the lions share of 69's activity during the Yom Kippur War, but the squadron also flew non-operational sorties, mostly ferry flights and test flights. Gideon Magen:

> "I returned from Syria in June 1973. I flew a couple of flights to evaluate my options, if I could return to the cockpit. The first was with Amnon Arad, the second was with Sella. After we landed Sella said, 'what did you do

Gideon Magen test flew Kurnass 135 on the evening of October 16, 1973. Kurnass 135 was photographed in February 1972 while cutting the ribbon to inaugurate a new hardened aircraft shelter complex at Ramat David.

for three years? Did you fly all that time?' I was surprised how easy it was for me to return to flying.

"I initiated ground school, and I was surprised to learn that many of the modifications that we suggested in 1970 were still not implemented by 1973. Also, the squadron had Block 50 or so aircraft, newer and a bit different, so I learnt this, but my return to the cockpit was really smooth. Once that was ascertained I took a leave for a grand tour of North America and returned to Israel sometime in September; the plan was that I would start proper conversion course on October 7, 1973.

"War broke out a day before and what could I do? I was fighting executive, and during the first 48 hours I do not think that I slept or left my duty inside the squadron's operations cell. Morale was not high and we suffered casualties, so I asked Agassi — by then he was base commander — to return to fly. Agassi approved my request and I started flying non-operational sorties, ferrying and testing aircraft. One evening there was an aircraft that needed its bombing computer to be tested. We took off, dived 50 degrees, bombed the sea below and returned to base. After landing I told my navigator that this was my first night flight in more than three years. The navigator's reply was, 'if I had known this before take-off, I would not have flown with you!'"

Day 12: Syrian Bridges

Bombing bridges was also an element of the IAF campaign against Syrian infrastructure targets. Like power stations and fuel facilities, bridges were dual-purpose targets: disturbing flow of equipment to the front and signaling Syrian leaders that an ongoing war was a bad option for the future of their nation. The Hammers bombed Syrian bridges on October 17, 1973, to disrupt the flow of arms from Soviet ships that were unloaded at Latakia port, from where they were transported via rail and road to the Golan Heights front.

Day 13: SEAD Egypt

IDF Command South's counteroffensive gathered momentum and IAF SEAD operations were flown in support. The objective was to destroy local networks of SAM batteries, thus clearing the area for IAF air support. 69 Squadron Commander Yoram Agmon and his two deputies, Aviem Sella and Itzik Gat, flew in the lead of the initial three SEAD attacks.

IAF Commander Beni Peled facing Hammers in the 69's briefing room during the Yom Kippur War.

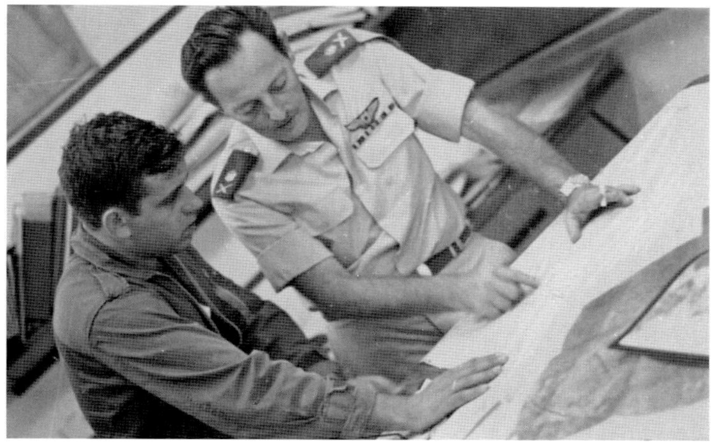

69 Squadron Commander Yoram Agmon (left) discusses the situation with IAF Commander Beni Peled (right) during the latter's visit to the Hammers amidst the Yom Kippur War.

Day 14: Fist Patrols

Main mission for October 19, 1973, was Fist patrols against Egyptian SAM batteries in the Ismailya sector. The Hammers maintained Fist patrols from dawn, flying in pairs and launching AGM-45 Shrike ARM each time an enemy SAM radar system was active. This effort accounted for 18 sorties out of 45 sorties flown until the end of day report.

Shrike launches did not generate specific "kill" reports. The only Day 14 credited kill to Hammers was achieved over the Syrian front when a pair flying noon patrol intercepted MiG-17s. Lead crew Gat-Katz was credited with an air-to-air kill, as Itzik Gat recalled:

> "Our mission was to escort U.S. airlift aircraft, but when we completed this mission we still had plenty of fuel left so we were assigned to a CAP. Suddenly GCI

Battle damaged Fist patrol Kurnass 139 photographed at Ramat David after a cable arrest landing during the Yom Kippur War.

David Brisk protects his ears from the roar of a passing by "toad" Kurnass 310. Brisk was a Hammers Phantom pilot from 1970 until 1994; he lost his wingman, Zait-Rubinstein, during the mission to Kotamiya on October 20, 1973.

> said 'a MiG-17 4-ship formation pops-up to attack.' I flew over there, it was not far away, and my navigator was the first to see them. They had just completed their attack, so I turned 270 degrees right behind them until they leveled their wings and flew east. I got organized, launched an AIM-9D, the AAM homed, a kill. It was already over Syrian territory and right in front of us there was an extraordinary AAA firewall, so we turned back."

Day 15: Kotamiya

The final IAF Yom Kippur War air base attack mission over Egypt targeted Kotamiya. This mission was actually flown twice: an abortive mission on October 19, 1973, and the real thing next day. The Hammers launched four pairs to Kotamiya: one pair tasked to bomb the runway and three pairs to attack surrounding SAM batteries. Time over target was 10:10. David Brisk:

> "Kotamiya was an operation that consumed many hours of planning, flying, and debriefing. We got as far as the final run but there was fog — the whole canyon over which we flew was covered with mist. We could see nothing and we turned back. The next day we flew the same mission over the same route. Obviously they expected us.
>
> "We split to attack when a SAM was launched. It headed straight onto my wingman, Zait-Rubinstein. Yoram (Agmon) ignored callsigns and said 'Doodi, this one is aimed at you!,' but a second SAM was launched and my wingman was hit. I escorted my wingman and we flew slowly at the rear. Bits and parts disintegrated and flew away, yet the Kurnass flew steadily and slowly climbed. We were only 5 to 10 km from the Red Sea coastline when suddenly I saw the canopies flying away; they ejected right beside me. Still under the canopy of his parachute, Doodi Zait reported that he was being shot at from the ground."

Pilot Doodi Zait and navigator Yoram Rubinstein ejected from Kurnass 231; they were prisoners of war in Egypt until November 1973. Their loss overshadowed this mission to Kotamiya, which was otherwise extremely successful. IAF Intelligence reported that the Hammers cratered runways, destroyed two MiGs, and damaged two MiGs. Kotamiya was closed for operations during the 24 hours that followed the Hammers' visit.

Day 16: Maritime Nighttime Encounter

Ophir Air Base, at the southern tip of the Sinai Peninsula, was the hub of IAF wartime activity in the Red Sea sector. No squadrons were permanently based at Ophir, but a pair of fighters was deployed and rotated; a pair of Super Mystere pilots was at Ophir during daylight and a pair of Kurnass crews took over during nighttime. Ophir operations mostly covered the special ops segment of the military portfolio: insertion of Egyptian commandos into Sinai, and Israeli Navy commando missions across the Gulf of Suez and down the Red Sea.

Egyptian vessels patrolled the Red Sea waters mostly during the night, and more than once the Kurnass crew on readiness at Ophir were scrambled during the night to attack Egyptian military vessels, mostly fast missile boats. The Kurnass crews attempted to engage the Egyptian ships with their AIM-7 Sparrow semi-active radar homing AAM but without success. David Brisk:

69 Squadron Commander Yoram Agmon (left) walks Yoram Rubinstein (right) back to the squadron on the evening of November 21, 1973, after his return from Egypt, where he was Prisoner of War since October 20, 1973. His pilot, Doodi Zait, returned to Israel the following day.

Latest available Hammers group photo prior to the Yom Kippur War is this image from IAF Year 1972 Term 3 (December 1972 to March 1973). Standing in the front row from left to right: Doodi Zait, Eran Mor, Uri Ofer, Idan Saar, Amos Mashiach, 69 Squadron Deputy Commander Aviem Sella, Avraham Rodan, Yosi (WSO), 69 Squadron Commander Amnon Arad, Alex Harel, Israel Primor, Eilat Ziblat, Eli Tovel, Moshe Lipshitz, and Amir Rafaeli. Second row from left to right: Yoram Rubinstein, Itzik Gat, Michael Dvir, unidentified, Isaac Katz, Daniel Lidai, Yair Elor, Meir Gur (aka Guri), Zvulun Amizi, Joel Feldsho, Haim Shahar (aka Bobo), Menahem Paz, Shaul Levy, Gur Israeli, unidentified, Yosi Bolles, Shlomo Granit, Avner Raz, and Levy Bar-Ziv. Standing elevated in the back: Beni Zinker, Gidon Yahalom, and Ben-Ami Peri.

"My finest Yom Kippur War mission ended in my usual lack of luck. The Ophir nighttime readiness mission was rotated, and the night of October 20-21, 1973, was our turn. By that time we flew in fixed crews, and my navigator was Eran Mor. It was already dark when we landed at Ophir and assumed readiness. Two hours later we were scrambled. The runway lights were switched on, we took off, the lights were switched off, and the night was pitch black — no moon, no lights, nothing.

"We were vectored to Gardaka, the Egyptians had two missile boats there. I knew that my best friend, also from my kibbutz Kfar Giladi, had already sunk one of these missile boats, as he was a naval commando frogman. After the war he was decorated for this action. Anyway, I was informed that the remaining missile boat was out to sea; my friend sunk one missile boat, so I was determined to sink the remaining missile boat. Flying in the dark was a demanding task; our radar was not so good, but nevertheless we achieved a firm lock on the missile boat. My plan was to launch a Sparrow and to follow this by strafing, if the Sparrow would hit and initiate some kind of fire that would enable us to see the missile boat.

"One second prior to squeezing the trigger the ground controller yelled, 'get the hell out of there!' For a moment I thought that we had locked onto an Israeli Navy ship and that for this reason the ground controller panicked. I turned away, but while turning I asked the ground controller what happened? 'You flew into a SAM defended zone,' he answered. 'Oh my god! What do you think? That this is training?' Anyway, we tried again to track down that missile boat but without success.

The first Hammers load of AGM-65 Maverick missiles armed "toad" Kurnass 311. Arming a Phantom with unfamiliar missiles was accomplished in a combined effort of U.S. team and IAF engineers orchestrated by 69 Administration Officer Zvi Avidror.

AGM-65 Maverick

Only four years old in Israeli service, the Kurnass was a major leap forward for IAF attack qualifications. However, the Yom Kippur War caught the Kurnass prior to introduction of a wider variety of attack qualifications that began to surface from the mid-1970s and flourished during the 1980s and 1990s. Apart from reconnaissance, except for regular cannon/AIM-9/AIM-7 air-to-air qualification and several air-to-ground delivery qualifications of unguided weapons (mostly general purpose bombs and a few CBU types), the then Kurnass PGM qualifications only included the AGM-45 Shrike ARM and the GBU-8 TV-guided glide. Three of the four Kurnass squadrons – including 69 – were AGM-45 qualified; one squadron – not 69 – was GBU-8 qualified.

For this reason multiple bomb loads and statistics reigned supreme in IAF prewar planning. Exercises, experiments, evaluations, tests, and studies were committed to the task of operations research. The end product was target, delivery pattern, type of weapons, numbers of bombs, and probability of hit. Obviously the stumbling point was technology. If the IAF had one PGM that could have ensured 100% confirmed kill rate then there was no point to drop many dumb bombs on a single target and hope that statistically the target would be destroyed.

Prewar the IAF – including 69 – evaluated PGM concepts, but technology was still immature or unavailable. The only Kurnass compatible PGM that the USA included in the emergency wartime aid to Israel was the AGM-65A Maverick.

Maverick was a TV-guided fire and forget missile optimized against small targets, such as tanks. The navigator locked the weapon onto a target, the pilot launched the missile, and from then on the procedure was very much like attacking with dumb bombs: the crew turned away, rolled to have a look if the weapon scored a hit, and exited the area.

Only TISEO equipped aircraft were AGM-65 compatible, so the Hammers were entrusted with AGM-65 service introduction. Weapon Systems Officer Zeev Raz was in charge, Zvi Avidror hosted the U.S. technical team that accompanied the missiles, and the first mission was flown against the Mount Hermon strongpoint, still in Syrian hands. This attack was a major success, as the first launched missile flew right into its target, the bunker's entrance! Aviem Sella:

> "There were no training flights. The first time I launched Maverick was in combat; we attacked Egyptian 3rd Army tanks in Sinai. The environment was almost sterile as by then we had achieved air superiority; there were no SAM threats and no enemy interceptors over there. For this reason practice in combat was not too difficult — we could make errors and still achieve good results. I remember launching at least six missiles and I think that four or five scored hits. Overall I think that we launched 40, 50 missiles."

DOG 2

Fighting over Mount Hermon intensified on October 21, 1973. Circa 15:40 a 201 Squadron pair engaged Syrian fighters over Mount Hermon. Air combat was tough, and the two Kurnass crews faced aggressive numerically superior Syrian pilots. But a 69 pair flying CAP nearby was not vectored to assist. Yoram Agmon:

> "This flight was never debriefed because I was so furious afterwards. We were scrambled from QRA to the

Earliest Hammers group photo available from after the Yom Kippur War is this image from April 1974. Standing from left to right: Squadron Commander Yoram Agmon, pilot Yair Elor, pilot Dani Shpitzer, navigator Moshe Carmeli, Deputy A Beni Zinker, pilot Avraham Weiland, navigator Yosef Bolles, navigator Rafi Melman, pilot Oded Bar-Ziv, pilot Iftach Shadmi, pilot Yosef Gonen, pilot Dani Sahaf, navigator Gil Ben-Betzalel, pilot Arik Ezuz, pilot Amnon Arad, navigator Eran Mor, navigator Avraham Baruch, navigator Alex Harel, and pilot Israel Parnes. Middle row from left to right: navigator Amos Levitov, navigator Meir Gur, navigator Uri Ofer, navigator Avner Raz, navigator Eli Gutterman, navigator Zvi Lipshitz, pilot Gidon Yahalom, and navigator Zvi Rotem. Front row from left to right: navigator Avihu Ikar, pilot Avri Hurin, pilot Aharon Moses, pilot Micha, pilot Zeev Raz, navigator Eli Tovel, and navigator Ofer Gavish.

north sector of the Golan Heights and flew CAP at 20,000 feet. I used to switch radio channels to learn what was going on in other sectors and suddenly I heard something. I switched back to my radio channel and asked my GCI what was going on. GCI's answer was, 'there is an air combat, not for you.'

"Nevertheless I began flying towards the air combat area. Still nothing unusual, but then I heard DOG 2 on the IAF combat search and rescue channel. He reported that he was OK, he was parachuting, but a MiG-17 was firing at him! I immediately set course, informed no one, and started looking for the mushroom for better resolution of the exact location. I saw the mushroom but did not see the parachute, so I headed towards the mushroom, got closer, and then I saw a parachute and a MiG-17. The parachute was descending and the MiG-17 was firing at the parachute!

"I had no doubts. I reported to my GCI 'going in' and aimed my nose at that MiG-17. Not for a kill but to scare him away. My top priority was to remove this threat from DOG 2 and to do it as soon as possible. Each seventh cannon shell was a tracer, and it was already afternoon, so I figured that the MiG-17 pilot would see my tracers. I dived and was at an angle off, but nevertheless I opened fire from long range and high G; I only wanted him to see my tracers so that he would stop firing at the parachute. I drew his attention with my tracers; he leveled his wing and escaped towards Damascus.

"The down side was that I opened fire while pulling a lot of G load, a classic situation for compressor stall. That is precisely what happened. I flew on one engine and the aircraft slowed down; we were already at 3,000 feet with AAA and SAM all around us. However, I remembered that our USAF F-4 conversion instructors always warned us not to restart an engine unless you were 100% positive that you were restarting the shut down engine. To restart you had to switch off the engine to be restarted, to pull back throttle. If you made an error and switched off the working engine then you were doomed.

"Remembering this warning, I did not restart immediately. I could not yet look inside the cockpit as I had to watch out and break away from SAM threats; so did my navigator, Daniel Wittmann. I decided to wait until I would be able to look inside the cockpit and be sure that I was restarting the correct engine and not switching off the other engine. We were already very low and very slow, down to 300 knots, when we had the opportunity to restart. We recovered and returned to Ramat David. Only there did I meet my wingman. Not only did he not follow me, but he also told everyone in the squadron that I was a madman!

"This flight wasn't debriefed at formation level. I assembled all airmen to the briefing room and briefly described the mission from my own perspective. It was not a textbook debrief. I then focused on one issue, personal commitment in wartime. I told my airmen that in wartime there are situations with no room for personal considerations. There are situations when one must act regardless of anything else. This was one such situation. When an enemy fighter is strafing a fellow pilot in distress, you simply have no room for decision making; you have to act regardless of all difficulties and threats. And I walked out of the briefing room."

Notes

[1] Jewish Day of Atonement.

[2] Fighting Executive is an IAF term for an aircrew on duty as Air Officer in Charge during wartime or on operations; the Fighting Executive shift is rotated between a small number of the most experienced commanders in the squadron. A Fighting Executive on duty does not fly during the shift and represents the highest hierarchy level in the squadron both up the command ladder or outside the squadron (IAF AHQ and Air Base or Wing) and down the ladder or inside the squadron (Flying Flight and Technical Flight).

[3] The first five Hammers airmen were Avihu Ben-Nun, Ehud Henkin, Rami Harpaz, Achikar Eyal, and Shaul Levy. Harpaz was still prisoner of war in Egypt, while Eyal had already returned from captivity in Egypt but did not return to fly fast jets. Avihu Ben-Nun was by then Head of Air3 Attack Section; this occupation prevented him from flying regularly with the Hammers, but nevertheless he managed to accumulate eight operational sorties during the Yom Kippur War, significantly less than the average number of sorties per regular, emergency posting, or reserve airmen that was circa 30 sorties.

[4] Obviously a pilot error is one of several possibilities to explain that combat loss; the true explanation may never surface.

[5] Fighting Clock is the IAF term for wartime routine; it is basically a timetable of events that enables commanders to improve their schedule management.

[6] Boundary Layer Control.

[7] Leading Edge Slats.

[8] Target Identification System Elctro-Optical.

7

F-4 Kurnass
October 1973-1982: From Multi-Role to SEAD Specialists

From 1973 until 1982, the IAF in general and the Kurnass force in particular implemented Yom Kippur War lessons. The principle issue was SEAD, and the Kurnass squadrons became pivotal in IAF efforts to field a viable answer to the Arab SAM challenge. From 1973 the Kurnass force, 69 included, transformed from bomb trucks to PGM platforms. If until 1973 the Kurnass force was considered multi-role as a compromise between pilots' wish to shoot down enemy aircraft and the IAF realization that the Kurnass was basically a bomber, then after 1973 the ambivalence was sorted out. Younger and better "teen" fighters – the F-15 and F-16 – entered IAF service, and AHQ could finally impose its will upon the field units, partially because the "fighter mafia" was reassigned from Kurnass squadrons to the F-15 and F-16. As these two processes progressed along the time line, the Kurnass cockpit's center of gravity shifted from front to back. This change was not sudden, nor smooth.

Hammers' mainstay after the Yom Kippur War were the "toad" Phantoms, emergency war aid aircraft delivered to Israel straight from USAF inventory. Darker camouflage scheme and tail numbers in the 300 range distinguished the "toad" Phantoms from "regular" IAF Phantoms. Kurnass fleet tail numbers were rationalized from the Yom Kippur War onwards into four groups: early BLC aircraft were in the 100 range, later LES aircraft were in the 200 range, the Yom Kippur War emergency aid batch was in the 300 range, and reconnaissance Phantoms were in the 400 range.

From 1973 until arrival of the F-15 (1976) and F-16 (1980), and effectively until 1982, the Kurnass community struggled to preserve pre-Yom Kippur War prestige, regardless of additional tasks and obvious plans. A few milestones signaled the way – first F-15 kill in 1979, first F-16 kill in 1981 – but still, Kurnass crews continued to implement and test techniques and tactics to fight the F-15 and F-16 pilots, an attitude that was sometimes counterproductive. Yet all ended in 1982 when the Kurnass force erased the Yom Kippur War's disgrace and scaled back the SAM threat from gigantic myth to manageable proportions.

Yom Kippur War Heritage

Hammers history from 1973 until 1982 was in line with Kurnass force developments. Air-to-ground was emphasized, especially SEAD, the navigators' impact became more and more profound, and crews – mostly pilots – struggled to preserve the multi-role nature of the IAF heavy attack tool. All of these processes were initiated and implemented as Yom Kippur War lessons.

The Hammers flew 789 sorties from October 6 to 24, 1973. Nine aircraft were lost for a sorties-to-loss ratio of 88-to-1; better than 201 Squadron's 54-to-1, and worse than 107's 188-to-1 and 119's 188-to-1. Two Hammers crews (Henkin-Levy, Amizi-Yogev) perished during the Yom Kippur War. Two crews (Alkalai-Wolfson, Zait-Rubinstein) were prisoners of war in Egypt until November 1973; one crew (Arad-Primor) was interned in Lebanon; and one crew (Shahar-Israeli) were prisoners of war in Syria until June 1974.

The three Yom Kippur War lessons that impacted the Hammers most were: lack of efficient PGM capability, vulnerability to enemy air defenses, and insufficient air combat superiority of the Phantom versus the MiG-21. The first two issues were interrelated. Lack of PGM capability enabled enemy SAM batteries to escape IAF attacks; active enemy SAM and AAA accounted for most IAF losses. 69's losses were attributed to SAMs (five), AAA (one), combat accident (one), enemy aircraft (one), and friendly fire (one).

Return to "peacetime" after the Yom Kippur War was gradual and involved many armed clashes. Reconnaissance was crucial to monitor enemy activity, and the Hammers' RF-4Es flew many missions until the situation was finally stabilized by mid-1974. Gideon Magen (with navigator Uri Ofer) escorted a reconnaissance mission over Egypt in Kurnass 264 on January 13, 1974; Kurnass 264 was photographed taxiing at Ramat David in June 1974. At the time most of the Hammers' fighter-bombers were 300 block "toad" aircraft, while the balance were late 200 block aircraft, including 264.

Therefore Yom Kippur War heritage influenced the Hammers for years. Introduction of stand-off PGM capability addressed kill probability and aircraft vulnerability issues, and the acquisition of F-15 and F-16 fighters widened the air combat gap and enabled the shift of the Kurnass from mult-role to air-to-ground. These two processes were not implemented at a stroke, but were accomplished over a time frame of nearly a decade, from 1973 to 1982.

Korean Kill

During the Yom Kippur War the IAF actually faced an Arab coalition, rather than the Egyptian Air Force in the south and the Syrian Air Force in the north. Fighter squadrons from Algeria, Iraq, Libya, and North Korea deployed to Egypt prior to October 1973. The North Korean MiG-21 squadron was based at Bir Arida to defend Egypt's south. The North Korean MiG-21 pilots did not engage Israeli aircraft until December 6, 1973.

That day two Kurnass pairs from two squadrons, 69 and 119, were scrambled to the Gulf of Suez sector. The pairs were teamed together, with the 69 pair (Shadmi-Gur, Shpitzer-Ofer) leading the 119 pair. Meir Gur:

> "We were fished out of a lecture and were briefly briefed: something was cooking down south, go there. No unusual preparations, no more details. We were part of a large-scale operation, and our mission was to patrol. We flew to the area at high altitude and flew a high altitude patrol. The sky was not clear; visibility was not good, cloudy and misty. We patrolled for a long time, and we were already low on fuel when we were vectored in and out, flying west into Egypt, turning northwest and exiting. We did not penetrate too deeply into Egypt but we did it a couple of times. Then we were told to look for targets; our radars did not function that well in a high-to-low search. We flew at 20,000 to 25,000 feet, but I managed to see a couple of blips down below, very difficult to lock. GCI vectored us to engage. We jettisoned external fuel tanks and flew a large racetrack pattern. Still seeing the blips but range did not decrease — they probably flew a similar pattern at low altitude. It was very difficult to track that blip against ground clutter, but we managed to do so and finally came within range for an AIM-7 launch; shoot down mode, not very good. Even more problematic was the mist that prevented us from seeing our wingman, so we had doubts. We decided not to launch.
>
> "Seconds later we saw them, two MiGs. Crossover and the two of us engaged them. One MiG disappeared; the other MiG remained for a 1-vs-2 air combat. The MiG pilot was extraordinarily good, flying wild and reacting in time. He was alone against the two of us and he attempted to draw us into a slow speed fight, but we insisted upon maintaining high speed. All that time the 119 pair was flying overhead, asking politely but firmly, 'would you step aside please?'
>
> "We did not step aside. We kept exhausting this Korean pilot; obviously at the time we did not know he was Korean. Anyway, we got into AAM launch position and launched an AIM-9D. A split second later another AIM-9D flashed by me not more than 200 meters away. Shpitzer was in similar AAM position but slightly behind us. Considering the poor weather this was an unpleasant situation, as he launched slightly behind a Kurnass flying with two afterburners. When I saw their AIM-9D flash by I panicked; we could have shot down each other since we were so eager.
>
> "Our AIM-9D homed perfectly. The AAM exploded, we pulled up, and the MiG emerged from the explosion flying seemingly intact. A second explosion followed, Shpitzer's AAM, and again the MiG emerged from the fireball and continued flying. We were already desperately low on fuel so we disengaged. As we turned east I looked back over my shoulder. The MiG turned west, descended to low altitude, and flew while trailing white smoke. I did not see him crash, but as we crossed the coastline something else grabbed my attention as I scanned the sky behind us. Suddenly I saw the characteristic trail of a SAM and then a huge explosion at roughly 20,000 feet. I monitored radio transmissions and I knew that all of our aircraft already disengaged, so I said to my pilot, 'they shot down one of their aircraft!' From my Yom Kippur War experience I figured that what I saw was a SAM exploding a fighter. I did not see the fighter because visibility was poor, but I clearly saw the missile's trail and the explosion.
>
> "By the time we landed we were notified that 'our' MiG crashed. We were awarded a shared kill, as the MiG was split between us and our wingman. I again reported what I saw on our way back, and shortly afterwards IAF

Ramat David Wing Commander Giora Furman (third from left) welcomes pilot Dani Shpitzer (first from left) and navigator Uri Ofer (second from left) immediately after their return from the December 6, 1973, air combat; Shpitzer is shaking hands with Ramat David Flying Squadron Commander Arik Ezuz.

The triumphant return from the hardened aircraft shelter to the squadron building after the December 6, 1973, engagement; from left to right: pilot Dani Shpitzer, 69 Squadron Commander Yoram Agmon, Ramat David Flying Squadron Commander Arik Ezuz, and navigator Uri Ofer.

Intelligence confirmed my story, the Egyptian Air Defense Force shot down a MiG-21."

Brotherhood of Arms

Air-to-air kill credit was the top aspiration of IAF fighter pilots. Once a year – during the traditional IAF aircrew ball on the eve of Independence Day – all air crews eligible for this top honor during the preceding year were invited to the stage, and the IAF Commander handed over a personal air-to-air kill credit certificate to each one of them as the assembled audience applauded endlessly for the heroes of the hour.

The kill credit certificate award was the end of an analysis process that started in kill claims. However, many air combats generated more kill claims than actual shoot downs. Rules had to be refined, but these tended to be somewhat flexible and actually evolved during the years. Initially the IAF didn't favor sharing of kills. When two pilots hit the same enemy aircraft, the rule was that the kill would be awarded to the one who delivered the coup de grace, the second pilot to hit the target. This rule was changed prior to the December 6, 1973, engagement. The new rule was that the first pilot to hit the target would be credited with the kill; the rationale was that the first pilot supposedly inflicted fatal damage, with the second pilot hitting a doomed target. Dani Shpitzer:

"The catalyst was a 69 recce mission that flew along the Nile River from south to north. We had a pair on QRA but I wasn't one of the readiness pilots. Then one of the pilots asked for replacement, so I took over as Iftach's wingman. Five minutes later we were scrambled!

"I suppose that we were scrambled because intelligence noted that they attempted to intercept our recce aircraft. We were teamed with a 119 Squadron pair and flew two pairs in line astern, looking for MiGs that GCI told us were somewhere over there. Then we saw a MiG above us. Iftach raised his nose and I followed. When Iftach pointed his nose at the MiG and was ready to launch an air-to-air missile I started to doubt that it was a MiG; from certain angles the MiG looked like a Kurnass. I looked back and didn't see the 119 guys, so I said to Iftach 'watch out, it might be one of ours!'

"Iftach had his finger ready to launch but he didn't. Then we flew past that aircraft and saw that it was a shining new MiG-21. The joke was that I knew it wasn't a Kurnass and only wanted him not to shoot him down so that I would have my chance too, but obviously this was only a fighter pilots' humor. Anyway it was really exemplary conduct: I expressed my doubt, we all looked for the 119 pair but didn't see them, so he didn't launch.

"We entered tight turning combat with that MiG and ended up with both of us right behind him. We both launched air-to-air missiles, and the 119 pair leader reported that Shadmi's missile hit first with our missile following. The MiG emerged from both explosions and flew away, but our intelligence reported that he didn't make it back to landing. The dilemma was who would be credited with the kill? The old rule credited the kill to us, but the new rule credited the kill to our leader. Ramat David Wing Commander Giora Furman told us that regardless of rules it would be our decision. Whatever we decide would be.

"Iftach and I were good friends, and I said to Iftach 'this is the role, the kill is yours.' An air-to-air kill was a wish of a lifetime; it was way more than anything else we could ever think of at the time. Still, Iftach insisted that the kill credit would be shared. He could have claimed the full kill, but he insisted that the kill would be shared and we received the kill certificates because of this unique spirit of friendship!"

Kurnass 320 was lost over Mount Hermon on April 8, 1974. Shadmi-Rafaeli ejected over Lebanon and was interned until June 6, 1974. Kurnass 320 was photographed at Hatzerim during the final days of the Yom Kippur War when it was still issued to 107 Squadron.

Mount Hermon

Two opposite processes took place in the Mount Hermon region during the spring of 1974: snow melted and fire resumed. The top summit of the high mountain ridge was the focus of hostilities. From early April 1974 IAF aircraft attacked Syrian engineering equipment struggling to pave a way to the summit. The stubborn Syrians pressed ahead with their plans and fighting intensified. Hammers' participation suffered a troublesome start as two pairs were scrambled, one after the other, to the Mount Hermon sector on April 8, 1974. They were tasked to search for Syrian helicopters. The sky was cloudy so the Kurnass crews had to fly low. No helicopters were observed and the first pair returned safely, but the second pair lost its leader. Shadmi-Rafaeli reported explosion and fire in the left-hand engine. The crew switched off the left-hand engine and headed for home, but fire erupted from the right-hand engine as well. They switched off the right-hand engine and attempted to restart the left-hand engine but had to eject from Kurnass 320 over Lebanon to become prisoners of war until June 8, 1974.

Deputy A Beni Zinker and navigator Meir Gur return from a Fist Patrol mission over Mount Hermon on April 8, 1974; "toad" Kurnass 319 is still armed with AGM-45 Shrike.

SA-7 probably shot down the crew Shadmi-Rafaeli. As fighting escalated and IAF pounding took its toll among Syrian troops, the Syrians attempted to improve their SAM coverage. First to face the new threat was a 69 pair (Zinker-Gur, Gonen-Ikar) tasked to fly loft mission on the morning of April 19, 1974. Meir Gur:

> "We were reassured that there were no SAM batteries in the Hermon sector. Our mission was loft across the ridge. Loft was a low altitude profile mission, but Mount Hermon was 9,000 feet high, so there was no way to hide from enemy radar detection. About half a minute prior to pull up – a long time in such a profile – our warning systems began to scream SA-6. SA-6? Over Mount Hermon? Yes, SA-6, and the warning pattern was definitely SA-6, unambiguous warning. The warning was a classic pattern, collision course — the SAM calculated the future point in space where aircraft and missile would collide.
>
> "A few seconds later we saw the launch. There was no doubt, that missile homed on us. What to do? We pressed ahead. Our wingman yelled a warning and we answered calmly, 'we see it, we are pressing ahead.' Our plan was that the loft pull up maneuver would be the break away from the missile. The missile got closer and closer. We waited for the last moment and pulled up, released the bombs, and as we were upside down over Mount Hermon the missile passed inside our turn radius and flew into the ground. We bombed as planned and escaped from that missile.
>
> "We returned and reported. All air strikes were stopped. A SEAD operation against that battery was planned and launched that same afternoon. A Kurnass formation from a sister squadron was planned to fly a dive-toss pattern while we race tracked high above and waited to finish off, striking from high altitude. It was a beautiful clear day, and from our grand view high above we saw them sneak in very low and pull up for the DT attack. The moment they pulled up the battery launched two missiles. One missile hit their number 4 during the pull up maneuver. The SEAD operation was called off and a rescue effort was launched.
>
> "We 'started' this affair when the SA-6 was launched at us in the morning, but we did not finish it off in the afternoon as planned."

Mount Hermon fighting ended in ceasefire agreement during May 1974, but prior to this the Hammers were involved in air combat and were credited with two kills. Agmon-Gur flew lead of four aircraft on CAP at noon April 29, 1974. The formation

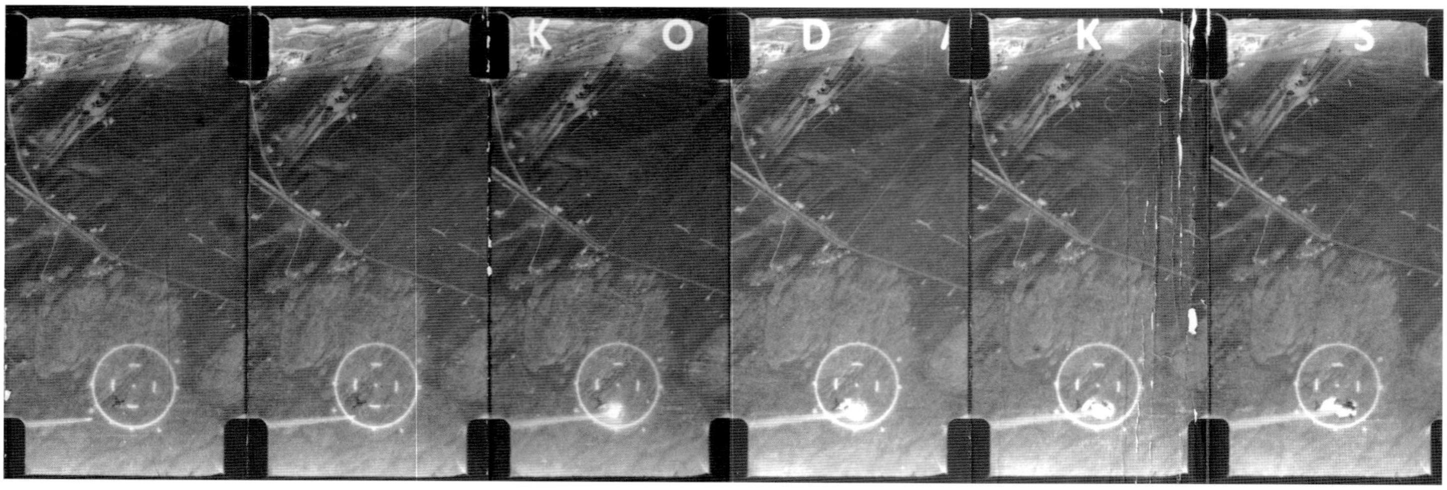

Hammers' Kurnass sight camera depicting an AAM kill of a Syrian MiG-21 on April 29, 1974.

was vectored north to engage Syrian MiG-21s over Lebanon, west of Mount Hermon. Agmon-Gur and their sub-leader Raz-Baruch were credited with one MiG-21 kill each, but the final moment of anxiety involved two Kurnass crews. Meir Gur:

> "In this combat I saw 'our' MiG-21 get hit and crash. We flew away, and I saw our number 4 flying straight onto our tail. I closed my eyes; I yelled to Agmon 'break, break, break,' and I shrunk my body in the cockpit, as though such an action would help. The next moment I sensed the typical shudder of an aircraft flying through the slipstream of another aircraft. We did not collide, I was alive."

SEAD Solution

Yom Kippur War lessons generated a requirement for a new SAM batteries attack concept. The complete IAF solution included real-time intelligence, efficient electronic warfare support, and stand-off PGM capability. The Hammers focused on introduction of the Rafael Tadmit (Image), an electro-optical guided bomb. Tadmit was released from high altitude with the Kurnass flying beyond effective range of the SAM battery under attack. Following release the pilot turned away while the navigator utilized a special stick to guide the glide bomb to its target via a data link. The up link transferred images from the bomb's TV camera to the bomber. The down link delivered the navigator's stick commands to the bomb.

In those years of pre-IAF Flight Test Center days, development projects and test flying were entrusted in the hands of squadron airmen. Tadmit development and testing was entrusted in the hands of the Hammers primarily because of the geographical proximity between Ramat David and the Rafael weapon systems development authority in the north of Israel. The Rafael glide bomb was revolutionary because it was not a "fire and forget" weapon, as were all other PGM already in IAF arsenal. 69 Squadron Weapon Systems Officer Dani Shpitzer was the Tadmit project officer, and his navigator during initial test flying was Eran Mor. Additional

Yoram Agmon (left, saluting Ramat David Wing Commander Giora Furman) handed over Hammers command to Menachem Sharon (right, beside Furman) on August 18, 1974. Menachem Sharon was 69 Squadron Commander until July 1, 1976, when Avsha Friedman took over.

RF-4E Kurnass 491 inaugurating the separate reconnaissance flight hardened aircraft shelter in April 1974.

Largest remaining part of Kurnass 305 after the December 29, 1977, accident was the tail section, which ever since forms a memorial to 69 Squadron Commander Avsha Friedman and reserve navigator Avihu Ikar.

pilots and navigators joined in along the project's testing time line, and among them were pilot Dani Sahaf and navigator Eli Tovel.

Tadmit was issued to 69 and 107 Squadrons; the latter was selected to demonstrate the new "wonder weapon" to Prime Minister Yitzhak Rabin and Minister of Defense Shimon Peres on October 23, 1975. The demonstration included two Tadmit bombers and two VIP Phantoms that followed the bomb from release to impact, with the Prime Minister and Minister of Defense closely watching from the back seats. 69's participation in this unique mission was limited to a single Kurnass (pilot Avihu Ben-Nun and navigator Alex Harel) that backed up the operation from the rear.

Reconnaissance Realignment

Another Yom Kippur War lesson was expansion of the IAF reconnaissance force. Six RF-4Es were added to the IAF order of battle, and three F-4Es were converted to RF-4E(S) standard. The Kurnass reconnaissance force was expanded from two small flights to three larger flights. The 69 flight's qualifications covered low altitude photography, 107 Squadron focused on synthetic aperture radar real-time collection, and 119 Squadron was entrusted with high altitude photography.

Actual expansion of the recce flight took place on November 5, 1976, when two ex-119 birds (tail numbers 488 and 489) arrived to augment 491, 495, and 497. The following year 69 and 119 swapped recce birds when 491 departed and 496 arrived. The reconnaissance highlight of this period was a mission over Jordan in December 19, 1977, during which Avsha Friedman took amazing photos from very close range of the famous Petra historical site.

Commander Collision

The IAF never assigned top priority to Kurnass air-to-air commitment. The F-4 entered Israeli service as "heavy attack aircraft" at a time when the IAF principle air-to-air platform was the Mirage. Yet the F-4 and the Mirage air-to-air performances were equivalent, so Kurnass crews aspired for higher stake in the air combat arena. Two parallel processes challenged the Kurnass air-to-air viability: introduction of SEAD stand-off PGM from 1975 and introduction of new generation interceptors from 1976. The former shifted focus from front-seat to back-seat; the latter dashed the self esteem of Kurnass crews with special impact on pilots because the PGM mission had already boosted the status of navigators.

Regardless of these two processes, Kurnass squadrons continued to invest a lot of effort in air-to-air training. The dream of every Kurnass pilot was to display a proper sight image of an F-15 during briefing. Obviously F-15 pilots had the upper hand in the vast majority of air combat training sessions versus Kurnass crews. The latter responded to the challenge with a variety of innovative tactics and dubious tricks but to no avail; the F-15 was the new master of the sky.

Transition lasted a decade, from 1976 when the F-15 joined IAF ranks until 1986 when the Kurnass relinquished air-to-air missions. A major characteristic of those years was air-to-air training accidents. The Hammers were impacted on December

The tail section of Kurnass 305 shortly after placement on a hill south of the Acre to Carmiel road – nearby the crash site – as a memorial to 69 Squadron Commander Avsha Friedman and reserve navigator Avihu Ikar.

Kurnass 310 was photographed taking off from Ramat David in October 1974, a year after arrival as Yom Kippur War emergency aid and three years prior to write-off in an accident. Pilot Rani Falk and navigator Peleg ejected from Kurnass 310 following a mid-air collision with Kurnass 305 on December 29, 1977.

Ramat David Wing Commander Rami Harpaz (left) and Ramat David Wing Maintenance Squadron Commander Nathan Segall (right) celebrate service introduction of the Rafael Python 3 air-to-air missile in March 1977 with Hammers Kurnass 315 serving as background; 69 Squadron was the first IAF unit to field the Python 3 AAM.

Kurnass 301 was lost in an accident on April 22, 1979; pilot Ami Alkalai and navigator Yaron Katz were killed. Alkalai was prisoner of war in Egypt from October to November 1973, but returned to fly and was Ramat David Wing Flying Squadron Commander at the time of the accident. Katz graduated IAF Flying School in March 1979 and was undergoing Kurnass conversion.

29, 1977, when Kurnass 305 collided with Kurnass 310 during a 3-versus-2 air combat training session between three Phantoms and two F-15s. The crew of Kurnass 310 ejected; the crew of Kurnass 305 – 69 Squadron Commander Avsha Friedman and reserve navigator Avihu Ikar – perished in the horrible accident.

Operation Litani

Zeev Raz took over as 69 Squadron Commander. Raz, a dedicated Hammer since 1971, recalled:

> "As Avsha's Deputy A, I was assigned to Topgun at Marine Corps Air Station Miramar outside San Diego; an extraordinary experience. A short while after I returned Avsha was killed and I was assigned as squadron commander.
>
> "Avsha had special personality; he always smiled, he was charismatic, nice, and warm, as well as an excellent pilot and extremely professional. We all adored him and we all respected him.
>
> "I entered office as a young Major with a strange feeling. My initial attitude was what would Avsha have done? I couldn't help myself avoiding seeing myself as Avsha's Deputy A. This phase lasted days or weeks until another accident hit us. I was sitting in my office when I heard a BOOM from Hardened Aircraft Shelter 15, and I immediately realized that something bad had just happened. Rushing to the spot I saw a ground crew lying down in a puddle of blood. Apparently he arrived at the Hardened Aircraft Shelter to enquire if a certain aircraft was ready, and the answer that he received was an air-to-air missile's nitrogen bottle that, luckily, flashed by the side of his head, so he was 'only' injured and not killed. This awful accident is, in my own personal memory, the point in time that started my own command of the squadron."

Shortly afterwards IAF activity over Lebanon intensified. The Hammers flew 28 support, 13 reconnaissance, and six CAP sorties during the March 1978 Operation Litani, when IDF units invaded south Lebanon to mop up Palestinian terror bases. The Operation Litani division of Hammers sorties emphasized the diminishing importance of the Kurnass as an air-to-air platform. Still, the Hammers air-to-air qualification was significantly boosted during 1978 when 69 Squadron became the first IAF fighter squadron to introduce into service the new Rafael Python 3 air-to-air missile. Zeev Raz:

> "I was privileged to participate in the Python 3 tests. It was an overwhelming experience to see that an air-to-air missile could maneuver as the Python 3 did. Previously we operated the AIM-9D Sidewinder, which was a good missile, but nothing like the Python 3."

A year after Operation Litani, the Hammers lost Kurnass 301 in an accident; pilot Ami Alkalai and navigator Yaron Katz were killed. Alkalai was Ramat David Wing Flying Squadron Commander; Katz was a Kurnass conversion course student, fresh from Flying School. It was a late winter rainy day, and squadron commander Zeev Raz banned flying of conversion course pilot students, but obviously allowed flying of experienced pilots. Ramat David Wing Commander Rami Harpaz informed the horrible news to Alkalai's family; Zeev Raz travelled to Katz's family and will

Long-Range Oblique Photography (LOROP) was added to the repertoire of the Hammers' Recce Flight from January 1980, when Kurnass 497 was transferred from 119 Squadron. As indicated, the latter's recce specialty was high altitude photography – over 50,000 feet – with space style pressure suit protection for the aircrew, while the Hammers specialized in low altitude photography. The arrival of the LOROP 497 enabled the Hammers to expand their recce portfolio, though without pressure suits the envelope expansion was up to medium altitude, mostly circa 40,000 feet. Kurnass 497 was also unique among Hammers jets for being painted gray; it was photographed in early 1984.

Fully armed Kurnass 207 in a "hot refuel" drill at Ramat David on May 29, 1980. An element of Operation Opera planning, "hot refuel" (refuel of powered aircraft) was aimed to top up, just before take-off, the fuel tanks of aircraft tasked to attack the Iraqi nuclear reactor.

never forget the feeling that grabbed him as he climbed up the stairs to the parents' apartment; it was as though every stair he climbed drained down more of his blood until he was virtually bloodless when he reached the apartment's door. Right on the spot he promised himself that he would do anything, anything to avoid such an experience, and indeed he didn't lose any more aircrew during the balance of his cadence as 69 Squadron Commander and during his future command assignments.

At the time the Hammers' commander was already well aware that his next assignment would be to command the first Israeli F-16 squadron. Zeev Raz:

> "I finished my command cadence and never flew an F-4 ever since. Then I converted to the F-16. I commanded the first F-16 squadron, I led the mission to attack the Iraqi nuclear reactor, and I shot down a Syrian MiG-23, but in my dreams I am not flying the F-16; in my dreams I am always flying the Phantom."

Iraqi Reactor and Foreign Interceptors

Eliezer Adar took over from Zeev Raz as 69 Squadron Commander on November 30, 1979. Adar was a reserve Mirage pilot when he was asked to return to regular service and take command of the Hammers. Eliezer Adar:

> "I was not a Kurnass pilot, and I was the first reserve pilot returning to regular service as squadron commander. No other squadron but 69 that was, in my opinion – and still is – the best IAF fighter squadron.
>
> "I rationalized the squadron's routine. Kurnass service persons were overloaded, and I tried to change habits so that the normal working day would end in the

Eliezer Adar and Alex Harel in Kurnass 304 (armed with four AIM-9 and two AIM-7 AAMs) leading the first four F-16s over Ramat David on July 2, 1980.

IAF fighter squadrons rotated to Eitham Air Base for the Panther Workshop — air-to-air training against the local Mirage squadron. The Hammers deployed to Eitham in December 1980, where this image was taken. Emphasis on air-to-air skills was so high during Eliezer Adar's term as 69 Squadron Commander that the Hammers returned from Eitham with flying colors.

afternoon and not late at night. Flying Flight schedule was commanders forum from 06:30, squadron daily brief from 07:30, and squadron debrief late at noon, so that by 16:00 or so most air persons ended their working day while officers in charge continued work as needed. Because of their endless working hours Technical Flight service perosns were known as 'slaves,' and they were proud to be called 'slaves.' To boost self esteem I appointed aircraft chiefs; their names were painted on their aircraft, and they were the only ones to hand over their aircraft to pilots prior to flights. This also generated positive competition: whose aircraft would be the best looking and whose aircraft would fly more hours than others.

"During my term of command I emphasized air combat maneuvering training and operational reconnaissance missions. My sole scale for evaluation of pilots was flying skills. I rearranged qualifications grading. Basic qualification was bombing, then air-to-air, reconnaissance, in-flight refueling, PGM, and leadership. The end product was that leaders were qualified for all missions."

A new 69 qualification, from January 1980, was high-altitude reconnaissance. This eventually led to Hammers participation in preparations for Operation Opera, an air raid on the Iraqi nuclear reactor Osirak. In fact, 69 was initially planned to raid Osirak. The Hammers practiced nighttime attack with Tadmit TV-guided bombs that were to be released from 40,000 feet some 40 miles away from the reactor. Concerns covered the Kurnass range and Tadmit penetration, so the Osirak attack mission was shifted to the F-16, which entered IAF service from July 1980.

As preparations gathered momentum a reconnaissance mission to Osirak was planned. Originally 69 and 119 were tasked to fly the mission. A unique model included demonstration of Kurnass in-flight refueling from a KC-130H Hercules flying low above ground level. 69 Squadron Commander Eliezer Adar (with IDF Chief of Staff Rafael Eitan in the back seat) and 119 Squadron Commander Zvi Kanor (with IAF commander David Ivry in the back seat) managed to connect to the Hercules, thus proving feasibility of such a demanding act. Shortly afterwards IAF AHQ decided that only one squadron would fly the mission, and 69 was selected for Operation Isabel 5.

Isabel 5 – flown on November 12, 1980 – was the longest IAF fighter force mission until then. The target was 600 miles away and mission planning included three in-flight refuelings. The second in-flight refueling took place over foreign land and was the low altitude fuel suction from the C-130. This took place over some 70 miles, and Kurnass crews noted that the Hercules was constantly deviating left from the planned route. Obviously they were unable to question the Hercules crew for reasons for this action. Apparently the Hercules crew knew that fighters were scrambled. This fact was unknown to the Kurnass crews, so when in-flight refueling was completed the two reconnaissance birds turned right. This route correction action placed them head-on and only six miles away

Kurnass 314 - photographed during 1980 still in "toad" scheme – was a faithful Hammer from IAF service introduction.

MiG-killer Kurnass 222 was lost in a collision with F-16A tail number 222 on January 20, 1981. The five kill markings on the nose of Kurnass 222 dated back to the Yom Kippur War when Kurnass 222 flew as 107 Squadron's Kurnass 122 and was credited with five kills: two Egyptian MiG-17s, two Egyptian MiG-21s, and one Syrian MiG-21.

from the foreign fighters. Vectored to intercept the Hercules, the foreign pilots were probably surprised to find themselves facing predators. Diving to the deck, one foreign interceptor crashed on the desert floor. The Kurnass crews ignored this fuss and pressed ahead to photograph Osirak as planned.

Triple Two Collision

IAF F-16 introduction from July 1980 impacted the Kurnass force in general and 69 in particular. The Phantom dropped from second tier to third tier, lagging behind the F-15 and F-16 and witnessing the IAF service's sunset of its counterpart, the Mirage. The Hammers suffered most because the first two F-16 squadrons were activated at Ramat David, and because Ramat David Wing Commander's policy was to prioritize newcomers at the expense of old timers. Within the Ramat David wing, manpower and material resources were redirected to the new F-16 squadrons, while neighboring fighter squadrons, especially 69, were drained of essential assets.

The Ramat David clash culminated in an amazing twist of fate when F-4 tail number 222 collided with F-16 tail number 222 during a 3-versus-2 air combat training session on January 20, 1981. Eliezer Adar:

> "Dani Weiss was a conversion student but did not graduate — he was not yet ready to fly the Kurnass. Weiss returned to his Skyhawk squadron, but several months later I phoned his squadron commander and requested his return to Kurnass conversion, second chance. This was unusual but my position was firm; I could ask for practically anything.
>
> "Why did I bend usual practice? I guess it was because of my own personal history. I was assigned to Mirage conversion when I was a young pilot, perhaps too young. Early in the conversion syllabus I flew a 'rat race' with Ramat David Wing Commander Jacob Agassi. The wing commander considered my style of flying as too 'hot' for such a young pilot and ordered the squadron commander to expel me from the Mirage conversion course. I was reassigned to a neighboring Skyhawk squadron. Several months later I was returned to the Mirage conversion course and was a successful MiG-killer Mirage pilot for nearly a decade.

"Weiss returned to 69. I accepted him under my wings and he flew many training sorties as my back seater.

"It was New Year of the Trees, a semi-holiday, and I was not planned to fly. The schedule that day called for relaxed flying in the morning and planting of trees around the squadron building during the afternoon. As a farmer I was in charge of preparations for the afternoon planting, so I only stopped by the briefing room prior to morning flying. Two 3-ship formations were planned for 3-versus-2 air combat training sessions against a neighboring F-16 squadron. Then I noticed that the concept was new and was never practiced before. The training session was planned to start with the F-16s approaching fast with AIM-9L lock on the F-4s. I resented this concept; I thought this concept was too risky for training, but everything was ready, so I decided to lead the first 3-ship. I changed into flying gear, entered my office, wrote down my reservations considering such an air-to-air training concept in a memo to the Ramat David Wing Commander, and went on to fly.

Regular Hammers cadre in December 1980 with Kurnass 225 as appropriate background. From left to right: Shuki Shkedy, Deputy B Gur Israeli, Paldi (WSO), Elizur (WSO), Nissim Yogev, Roni Shlomi (killed in F-16 accident on July 18, 1995), Oded Bar-Ziv (younger brother of former Hammer pilot Levy Bar-Ziv, who was killed in action during the Yom Kippur War as Deputy B of a Skyhawk squadron), Judah Weinstein, Avi (pilot), Shpitz, Iddo Zadok, Deputy A Avishai Knaan, Alex Harel, Yaron Kranz, Mosko, Dani Weiss, and 69 Squadron Commander Eliezer Adar.

Farwell Adar! Hammers aircraft and air persons assembled in a unique formation.

"As usual my back seater was Dani Weiss. The first session ended in a draw; I 'shot down' the F-16 leader while the F-16s 'shot down' one of us. We prepared for a second round, and I asked my Number 3 to swap positions, so he flew lead and I was Number 3, trailing two miles behind the pair. The F-16s turned towards up to start the second round, and by the time they completed their turn both of our leading F-4s were 'shot down.' I was supersonic and I climbed to avoid them when Weiss said 'watch out,' and I saw an F-16 flashing by. I could do nothing and we collided. Dani Weiss and the F-16 pilot were killed; somehow I managed to eject from whatever remained of my Kurnass."

Hammers! Slaves!

Amiram Eliasaf took over from Eliezer Adar as 69 Squadron Commander on July 6, 1981. Amiram Eliasaf:

"69 was loaded with heritage, and I had an image of 69 pilots and technicians as hard working serious people from the north. I faced three major challenges as I entered office.

"The second was Technical Flight, which was drained for the benefit of the F-16 squadrons. I demanded a new Technical Flight Commander and named an F-16 Technical Flight Commander as my candidate. The Ramat David Wing Commander opposed, and this was the only issue that I surfaced up to the IAF Commander, who ruled in my favor.

Three new distinctive symbolic features were added to the Hammers' Phantoms during Amiram Eliasaf's term of office as 69 Squadron Commander: black and yellow checkered rudders, blue circular background to the squadron badge, and a new kill marking for SAM-killer jets. All three can be seen applied to Kurnass 225, taxiing at Ramat David with Python 3 training AAM.

Close-up of SAM kill markings; this photo of Kurnass 317, credited with the destruction of two SAM batteries, was taken in June 1993.

TO at work; Shelly watches over as Kurnass 306 taxis from the "last chance" inspection point to take-off. Eliezer Adar (with WSO Bobo) flew 306 during a nighttime recon along the Syrian and Lebanese coasts on June 17, 1981.

"The third was morale. 69 was a glorious squadron and suddenly the F-16 squadrons appeared. Previously I flew the F-15, so I knew that there was no competition in the air-to-air arena. I therefore asked to discontinue air-to-air QRA. Our specialty was air-to-ground. So it was attack expertise for Flying Flight and hard work for Technical Flight. I realized that we were on the right track one evening during a wing gathering. Our Technical Flight guys arrived a little late. They entered the hall and shouted 'HAMMERS,' so that everyone would notice their entrance. The already assembled crowd answered 'SLAVES,' but 69ers were not a bit offended; they treated the nickname 'slaves' as a compliment. As this was not enough they immediately responded with a unified shout 'LEGO,' which was their term of abuse to the F-16 guys: kids playing with toys compared to the Hammers' blue collar working men."

The TO View

IAF fighter squadrons are divided into a Flying Flight and a Technical Flight. More often than not the aircrew perspective represents a squadron's heritage, and this fact is simple and true, because aircrew are the warriors of the squadron and because aircrew actually fly the squadron's missions. The mission of the Technical Flight is to support Flying Flight; the less Technical Flight is noticed, the better Flying Flight can function and the squadron as a whole will have better prospect of achieving its missions.

The key figure for smooth running of a squadron is therefore the Technical Flight Commander, mostly referred to as Technical Officer, or TO. 69 Squadron TO from December 1981 until July 1984 Guy Shalev – known to all as Shelly – recalled:

"I completed a successful cadence as F-16 squadron TO, a squadron that was credited with the first F-16 MiG air-to-air kill and a squadron that took part in the mission to destroy the Iraqi nuclear reactor. Upon completion of this cadence I was planned to attend engineering studies in university. Then I was summoned to the Ramat David Wing Commander and was 'offered' to give up studies and take over as 69 Squadron TO. I was stunned. I was informed that the IAF Commander backed this 'proposition,' and I realized that I had no option but to agree.

"I prepared a furious speech for my first meeting with the service persons of the Technical Flight. In my speech I described the squadron's poor shape, placed guilt upon the shoulders of all present, and threatened those who would not cooperate with me to improve the situation. That was my plan until I walked towards the assembled service persons on the lawn behind the squadron building. I looked at them, put the paper in my pocket, and talked from the bottom of my heart.

"I told them that 69 is the most important squadron; that it is the best squadron; that they are doing a great job in an almost impossible situation with all of the spotlights placed upon the new F-16 squadrons. As a former F-16 TO I was entitled to tell them that maintaining the F-16 was like a Lego game for kids, but that maintenance of the Kurnass was a true challenge. I promised them hard work, harder than anyone could imagine, and I offered them the option to leave. I said that I only looked for total commitment, the kind of commitment that would return 69 to the top. I looked around and total silence surrounded me, but I sensed the click and fell in love."

Lebanese Mud

F-16 action in April 1981 almost triggered a Kurnass versus Syrian SAM battery confrontation. The F-16s shot down Syrian helicopters over Lebanon and the Syrians responded with deployment of three SAM brigades to the Lebanon Valley. Kurnass squadrons were ordered to prepare for a SEAD operation against Syrian SAM batteries in the Lebanon Valley. However, the Israeli Government rejected simultaneous action over two fronts and assigned higher priority to the Osirak mission, which was eventually flown on

69 Squadron Commander Eliezer Adar flew Kurnass 313 in the lead of two 4-ship formations that bombed a Libyan SA-9 SAM battery in the Damur sector of Lebanon on May 28, 1981, during Operation Mole 9. Kurnass 313 was photographed on March 25, 1980, during a Hammers Open Day when fast cycle was demonstrated to visitors.

June 7, 1981. Prior to this, the Kurnass force was authorized to fly a limited SEAD action against Libyan SA-9 batteries deployed south of Beirut to protect PLO bases. Eight Hammers crews took part in Operation Mole 9 on May 29, 1981.

Once Osirak was destroyed Kurnass attack of Syrian SAM batteries was only a matter of time. Kurnass crews practiced PGM delivery patterns on the real thing and prepared for war. Amiram Eliasaf:

> "I was a 201 Squadron graduate, a pilot during the Yom Kippur War. 201 was not ready for war at the start of the Yom Kippur War. My lesson was that 69 should be ready for war. I initiated a lot of planning exercises and a lot of armament exercises; not very popular, but eventually this investment paid for itself.
>
> "I emphasized air-to-ground and praised SEAD. I stressed to 69ers that destruction of a SAM battery was equivalent to three air-to-air kills. An SA-6 model was placed in the aircrew's mess and was promised to the first crew that would destroy an SA-6 battery. A special SAM kill marking was designed for painting on SAM-killer aircraft, and I stated that SAM-killer crews were entitled for a 'buzz' over the squadron building."

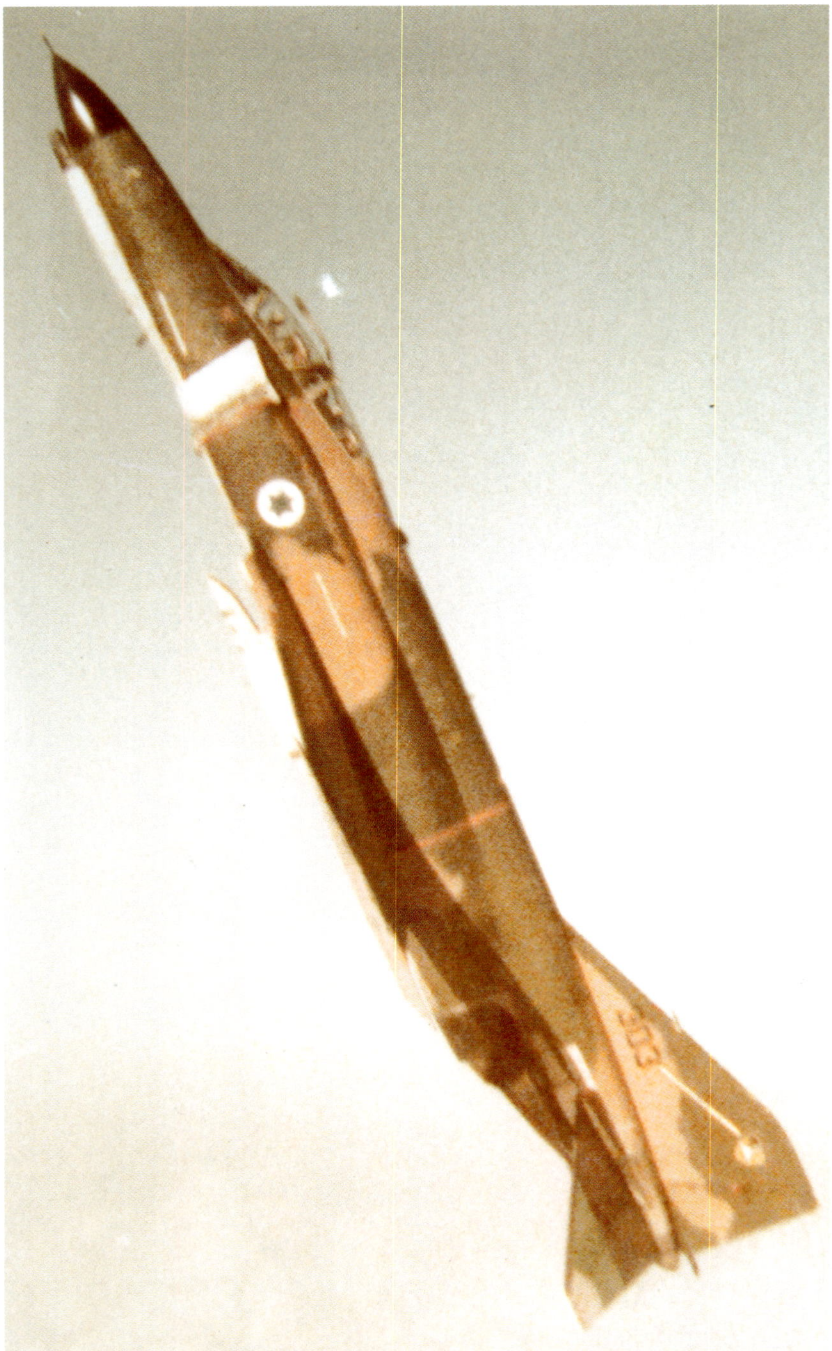

Almost a decade after delivery, the Hammers still flew many Yom Kippur War emergency aid Phantoms still in their original "toad" scheme. Reserve pilot Gideon Magen flew Kurnass 303 in a simulated Tadmit SEAD mission on September 22, 1981.

8

F-4 Kurnass
1982-1994: Peace for Galilee, Move to Negev

Osiraq attack "fallout" vanished by the spring of 1982, but the Syrian SAM deployment in the Lebanon Valley was still intact. The opportunity to confront the Syrian SAM deployment to the Lebanon Valley finally surfaced in June 1982 when Israel launch Operation Peace for Galilee.

PINE Preparatory Phase

IDF code for the invasion of Lebanon was PINE. Preparations for PINE were ordered on Friday, June 4, 1982, and the actual invasion started on Sunday, June 6, 1982. Emergency Posting and reserve airmen were called to the squadron; a total of 30 pilots (plus Ramat David Wing Commander Herzle Bodinger) and 36 navigators took part in the Hammers' Lebanon War effort. 27 sorties were flown during the preparatory phase from Friday afternoon until Sunday morning: 15 offenive air support, two illumination air support, eight reconnaissance, and two air-to-air patrol.

First mission TOT was at 16:00. A 4-ship formation bombed the Beirut stadium that the PLO used as a weapons storage facility. Facing no real opposition, except for sporadic AAA, the Hammers split into pairs, flew a medium altitude circuit pattern, and bombed pair after pair. The first circuit was utilized for visual identification of the target. The following two circuits included two bombing runs per crew, with one pair bombing from "final" and one pair watching over from "downwind."

The 18 sorties flown on Saturday included three attack missions. The first of these involved a 4-ship call-sign SHOE tasked to bomb

Battle Damage Assessment image of the Beirut stadium after IAF attack on June 4, 1982. The Hammers' aim point was the west side grandstand, which was heavily damaged.

Damage to Kurnass 225 as a result of an AIM-9D missile inadvertently release during the SHOE mission on the morning of June 5, 1982. SHOE 4 (Weinstein-Bobo) returned safely to Ramat David.

AAA damage Kurnass 314 sustained during an air support mission over Nabatiya on the morning of June 6, 1982. Battle damage included holed rear canopy and left-hand air intake, but the crew returned for a safe single engine landing at Ramat David.

bunkers in the Sarafand sector at 11:20. COMB attacked in the Nabatiya sector at 15:20 and WATERMEION attacked at 18:00. The only exceptions were damage to SHOE 4 from an AIM-9D missile that broke loose and a bombing computer malfunction in WATERMEION 2, which nevertheless pressed ahead and bombed in "direct" mode.

Morning Malfunctions

Offensive air support intensified from the morning of June 6, 1982, as IDF troops invaded Lebanon to uproot the PLO. 69 launched nine sorties from 06:05 to 06:18, but three Phantoms were damaged. AAA damaged a Kurnass during an air support mission in the Nabatiya sector, and the crew returned for a single engine landing. Two other crews experienced landing accidents. Braking malfunction forced Keidar-Tal into the runway's arresting net. More seriously, Tamir-Bobo lost their right-hand wheel during take-off. Unaware, they completed their CAP mission and returned to Ramat David. ATC noticed the missing wheel so a "normal" landing changed to emergency landing. The runway's arresting cable failed to stop Kurnass 186, which veered off the runway and was heavily damaged.

Fourteen sorties followed from 06:50 until 19:58. The fog of war was thick and proper PLO targets were in short supply; only six crews actually attacked. PLO AAA and SA-7 missiles were a nuisance rather than real opposition. It was expected that the IDF advance north would eventually lead to some sort of clash with the Syrian SAM deployment to the Lebanon Valley; the first signal for Hammers was in the Brisk-Moskovic debrief. They reported that SA-6 batteries from the Lebanon Valley locked on their Phantom during an 11:40 TOT reconnaissance mission.

Day 2 Air Support Issues

IDF units entangled with the PLO called for air support, but CAS was hampered by the absence of a clear forward line of troops, communication malfunctions, poor weather, and a shortage of targets. The PLO enemy lacked regular army features, and on many occasions "bazooka boys," Palestinian youth armed with RPGs, were the source of fire that harassed IDF troops. IAF

Left and following: Kurnass 186 suffered Category 4 damage (one level below Category 5 total loss) when landing without a right-hand wheel on the morning of June 6, 1982. Fully armed with Python 3 missiles for a CAP mission, the Phantom was not yet painted with the distinctive Hammers black and yellow checkered rudder, a symbol that was introduced after the June 1982 Lebanon War.

airmen, Hammers included, were unable to track down such small resolution engagements. For these reasons only nine of the 20 Day 2 Hammers air support sorties actually attacked.

One crew in a 3-ship with 05:20 TOT did not bomb after running out of fuel by the time attack was authorized. A pair with TOT at 12:40 did not attack because of communication and weather. A 14:35 TOT 4-ship aborted air support due to target ambiguity and an undefined forward line of troops. Communication prevented a 4-ship from air supporting IDF troops in the Damur sector.

Overall Hammers activity on June 7, 1982, covered 20 air support sorties (of which 11 were ineffective), four reconnaissance sorties, and two CAP sorties.

Navigator Ron Arad with fellow Hammers in the 69 Squadron briefing room during the June 1982 Lebanon War. Arad flew four sorties from June 6 to 10, 1982; all were air support missions. From left to right: navigator Meir Shamir, navigator Doron, navigator Ron Arad, pilot Shpitz, and pilot Amos Zamir.

Day 3 Preparations for SEAD

Activity slowed down on June 8, 1982, when Hammers flew only 16 sorties, including four air support sorties, four reconnaissance sorties, and two CAP sorties.

Air-to-air was the domain of F-15 and F-16 squadrons, while air support was the principle mission of A-4 and Kfir pilots. Kurnass crews' expertise was in heavy attack and SEAD, but both missions were simply nonexistent in the type of warfare fought over Lebanon from June 4 to 8, 1982. A change surfaced on June 8, 1982, when the balance of Hammers sorties included four SEAD training sorties and two SEAD sorties.

The SEAD training sorties covered an early noon 4-ship that flew Tadmit delivery profiles. This was the first unmistakably clear signal to Hammers that a clash with the Syrian SAM deployment to the Lebanon Valley was imminent. Additional evidence followed at 17:55 when a pair bombed a Syrian electronic warfare facility on top of Jabel Baruch, west of the Lebanon Valley.

69 Squadron Commander Amiram Eliasaf was photographed in the Hammers' building "veranda" prior to a Lebanon War mission; one of the nine sorties he flew from June 4 to 10, 1982. Eliasaf graduated the IAF Flying School in 1970 and flew the Kurnass during the October 1973 Yom Kippur War. After commanding the Hammers, Eliasaf went on to command an F-15 squadron, a fighter wing, and an air base; the latter assignment of Hatzerim Air Base Commander from 1992 actually renewed his connection with the Hammers. A regular fighter pilot from 1970 until 1993, Eliasaf accumulated 650 operational sorties.

Day 4 Operation Mole Cricket 19

Hammers flying slowed down further on the morning of June 9, 1982, when only six sorties were flown: four air support and two recce. The 06:30 TOT air support 4-ship reported SA-6 launches from the Lebanon Valley. No more attack sorties were flown until noon, when the IAF launched Operation Mole Cricket 19, a SEAD offensive against the Syrian SAM deployment in the Lebanon Valley.

69 was tasked to launch 13 Tadmit bombers to attack from 14:00 and four follow-up "iron" bombers with TOT from 15:43. Tadmit bombers operated individually; each was armed with two bombs. Primary targets for Tadmit attack were the SAM batteries' fire control centers and radars. Hammers lead crew (Gonen-Kesler) was the first Israeli Phantom to attack a Syrian SAM battery during Operation Mole Cricket 19. The right-hand Tadmit malfunctioned so the crew quickly switched to the left-hand bomb, which was released from 38,000 feet and 18 miles away from the targeted SA-6 battery. Reporting ALPHA (IAF code for direct hit), the lead crew was followed by another 11 Tadmit bombers that engaged a total of seven SAM batteries. Ten ALPHA were reported against five batteries. Yaron Kranz:

> "Prior to war we actually trained on the real thing, so we were intimately acquainted with most targets. However, our assigned target was, obviously, the only battery that we didn't know at all. I flew with navigator

A Hammers Tadmit bomber in full operational configuration as flown during Operation Mole Cricket 9 on June 9, 1982. The Phantom is armed with two Tadmit bombs plus data-link pod, as well as loaded with ESM pod for self-protection and two external fuel tanks in an asymmetric configuration.

Spot the SAM! Where is the SAM battery? Illustrating the challenge faced by Kurnass crews during Operation Mole Cricket 9 - to discriminate from far away the high-value fire control unit, to hit precisely a small target blended into the local terrain – is this image of the first SA-6 battery to be attacked and destroyed. The lead Hammers crew (Gonen-Kesler) placed their Tadmit bombs right into the fire control radar of the battery, with another Hammers crew (Shlomi-Ovadya) repeating this feat some 30 minutes later to confirm destruction of the SA-6 battery.

Pilot Gidon Yahalom flew Hammers Phantoms from March 1970 until March 1994. Yahalom flew nine sorties from June 4 to 11, 1982: four recce missions, three support missions, and two SEAD missions. The latter included an Operation Mole Cricket 19 first wave Tadmit mission with navigator Gotti that resulted in two ALPHA reports. The wooden "suitcase" that Gidon Yahalom holds in this photo contained a 16mm camera that the pilots placed in the cockpit prior to flight and returned from the cockpit after the flight ended.

Hammers crew Magen-Cohen flew Kurnass 315 during the PGM wave of Operation Mole Cricket 9. They released two Tadmit bombs against the fire control unit of a SA-6 battery and reported two ALPHA. Kurnass 315 was photographed in August 1982 still in "toad" camouflage and already adorned with the new SAM kill markings.

Post-strike image of the headquarters of the Syrian Forces in Lebanon after the Hammers' dusk "visit" on June 9, 1982. The four bombers dropped 36 Mark 83 bombs that devastated the high-value target.

Moshe, and we orbited for quite a while until we figured out where it was. We flew towards our target and we were all alone, so from the moment GCI said 'watch out, MiGs,' I looked out of the cockpit while Moshe guided the bomb. I asked Moshe to notify me five seconds to impact so that I too would look inside the cockpit and watch the hit on the screen.

"Moshe said 'five seconds.' I looked at the screen and saw the SA-6 fire control unit disappearing to the left of the screen and we hit a launcher. By then we were quite far away and low on fuel. At the same time missile warnings were shouted over the radio, but these related to the SA-6 launcher that we destroyed; the three missiles were launched but were not aimed at anything.

"We already knew our target well so, ignoring our low fuel state, we turned back. I pointed the nose at the explosion of our first bomb and we dropped the second bomb. At that time we were down to 2,000 pounds of fuel; a quantity that is normal for downwind during the landing circuit pattern. So instead of turning back I set course to Ramat David and throttled back to idle. Moshe therefore guided the bomb to a direct hit at the fire control unit while we were gliding back home."

One more Tadmit bomber was tasked to attack the headquarters of a SAM brigade and reported ALPHA against a command and control post. Finally, two pairs of iron bombers were planned to follow the PGM wave with a conventional general purpose bombs attack pattern. Only one of these actually attacked. Target of the first pair was a SAM battery that had already suffered two Hammers' ALPHA. The wingman was below minimum fuel by the time the pair was authorized to attack, so only the leader (Eliasaf-Rafaeli) bombed in the face of massive AAA. The second pair was not authorized to attack simply because the PGM wave was an overwhelming success, with 14 SAM batteries (out of 19 attacked) claimed destroyed. TO Shelly recalled:

> "That Wednesday was one of the climaxes in my 30 year long IAF career. We prepared 14 aircraft armed with Tadmit and ready to attack the SAM batteries. Jeano was the first to line up on the runway. This was an exciting moment for me. I was well aware of the huge effort that the IAF had invested in SEAD development, I knew that many air crews had their own personal memories from past engagements with the SA-6, and I just could not hold myself from shedding tears as the aircraft lined up and took off one after the other.
>
> "Time passed slowly until the first Phantom returned for a low altitude victory roll over the squadron. Then a second appeared and a third, and I just couldn't believe it; I felt I was dreaming and I just couldn't wait any longer. I jumped on my service Vespa scooter and rushed to escort the first aircraft to land from the runway back to the hardened aircraft shelter. Riding my Vespa alongside the Kurnass, I looked at Jeano in the cockpit and his 'answer' was a 'bullseye' signal. The feeling of pride that filled me was even greater than that I felt as TO of the F-16s that returned from the nuclear reactor destruction mission to Iraq back in June 1981."

The 1982 Lebanon War Operation Mole Cricket 19 was the amendment of the 1973 Yom Kippur War Operation Model 5. Almost a decade of preparations and training enabled the Kurnass

Ramat David Wing Commander Herzle Bodinger (center) awarded the first SAM kill trophy to Hammers crew Gonen-Kesler, flanked by F-16 Squadron Commander Zeev Raz (left) and Ramat David Flying Squadron Commander Eli Tovel (right). Bodinger commanded Ramat David from January 1982 until August 1984 and flew an air support mission in a Hammers Kurnass on June 7, 1982. Raz was 69 Squadron Commander from December 1977 until November 1979 and F-16 squadron commander during the Lebanon War. Tovel was a veteran Hammers navigator; he flew an air support mission in a Hammers Kurnass on June 5, 1982.

force to defeat an extensive SAM deployment. Moreover, this definite victory was achieved without a single loss. The disgrace of the unsuccessful Yom Kippur War SEAD campaign was finally erased and IAF air superiority was again an unquestionable fact.

Two hours after Mole Cricket 19's H-Hour the Syrian SAM deployment in Lebanon was effectively destroyed. IAF's exploit of this success included a Hammers 4-ship mission (TOT at 18:27) to bomb the headquarters of the Syrian Forces in Lebanon near Shtura in a formerly out of bounds SAM defended zone.

Day 5 IAF Commander Citation

Action peaked on June 9, 1982; the 29 sorties flown covered 17 SEAD sorties, eight air support sorties, and four recce sorties. Phantom force activity significantly declined after air superiority was achieved. This was natural for a limited war scenario like the Lebanon War; the IAF order of battle was in excess to actual battlefield demands, both from an enemy size and target availability perspective. Therefore only 12 sorties were flown on June 10, 1982: six SEAD, four support, and two recce. The first of the two air support pairs was tasked to fly interdiction east of Beirut. Uri Bacal:

> "We were armed with six AGM-65 Maverick missiles, a weapon that was rarely used those days. Our mission was to patrol at 6,000ft over the Lebanon Valley and wait for orders. It was rather peculiar to fly that low over a sector that once was out of bounds. Thus two Phantoms flew low, there and back over the Lebanon Valley.
>
> "A while later we were ordered to attack Syrian armor along the Beirut-Damascus highway, east of the Lebanon Valley towards the Lebanese-Syrian border. We flew over there, and indeed we saw Syrian tanks running for shelter. Our first attack was from south to north, probably because of lighting considerations, since achievement of proper lock in the then Maverick depended upon good contrast.
>
> "We launched our first Maverick that evidently missed, as the seeker head switched to cloud halfway to target. Anyway, it was a two-way reality, as we fired at them and they fired at us. While finishing the first attack run we felt a major kick.
>
> "Flying quite low, maybe 3,000-4,000ft, and relatively fast, we pressed 'panic' and turned west towards the Mediterranean Sea. With our wingman escorting us we climbed slowly, switched off the damaged right engine as we cleared the 'danger zone' of Syrian controlled territory, and returned for a single engine landing at Ramat David."

Small scale SEAD remained the primary mission of the Kurnass force until the end of war. Syrian efforts to insert fresh SAM batteries into Lebanon presented additional targets to the SEAD warriors. 69's six Day 5 SEAD sorties included four individual Tadmit hunters and two iron bombers. The Tadmit hunters were tasked to engage four SAM batteries. The morning hunters reported two ALPHA; the afternoon hunters did not attack.

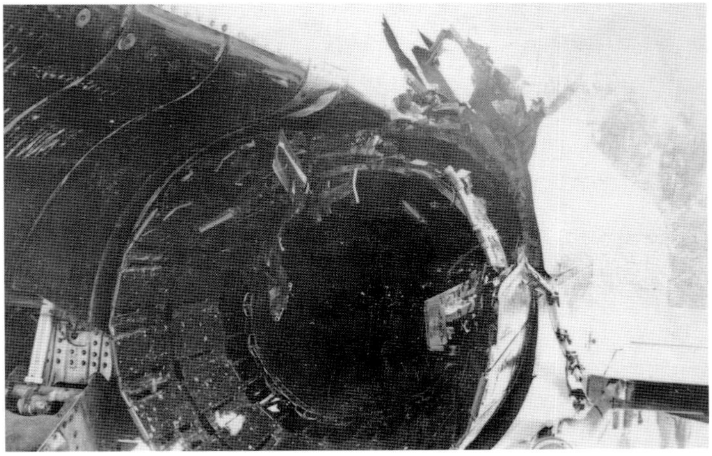

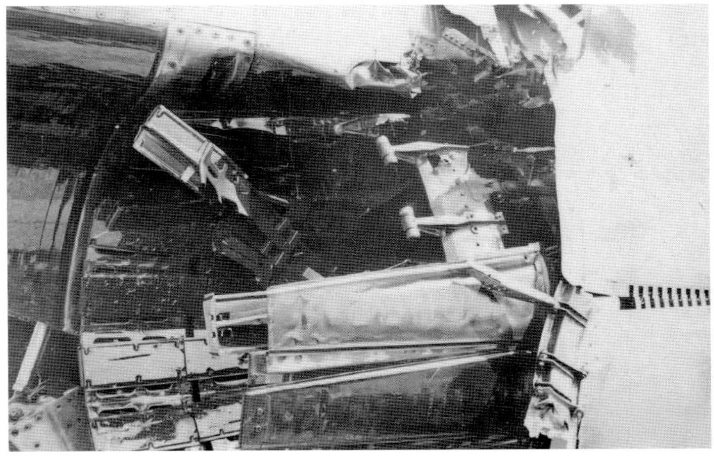

An SA-7 shoulder launched missile damaged Kurnass 319 during an air support mission east of Beirut on June 10, 1982. The crew (Bacal-Rafaeli) returned safely to Ramat David.

In between a 4-ship planned to fly air support was re-tasked to SEAD prior to take-off. Two Phantoms malfunctioned between re-tasking and take-off so only a pair took off to attack a SA-6 battery spotted on the move from Syria to Lebanon. Amiram Eliasaf:

> "We received the general location of the SAM battery prior to take-off and were told to work with UAV for exact location. However, contact with UAV operators was not established. I therefore notified ground control of my intention to attack from high altitude; I figured that such a profile would enable us to pinpoint the location of the battery.
>
> "Ground control did not approve high altitude approach and insisted upon a dive-toss profile attack. I turned back, contacted the squadron's operations, and asked for hasty planning of a dive-toss attack. While holding we received planning, but I considered this plan inadequate and asked for alternative planning from a different approach. This was quickly achieved and we flew to our new initial point.
>
> "We flew low altitude and pulled up. While pulling up I saw a lot of vehicles and mistakenly identified a vehicle concentration as our SA-6 battery. The moment we released our bombs I realized my error and saw the convoy of the SA-6 battery. I reported to my wingman to switch to the real target but their bombs did not release. We flew three circuits and returned to bomb three more times, but the bombs would not release; a technical malfunction. Meanwhile AAA intensified and our fuel state got low. A brief discussion inside the cockpit and we decided to strafe. We flew a long strafing pass along the SA-6 convoy. I expended all of the cannon ammunition in

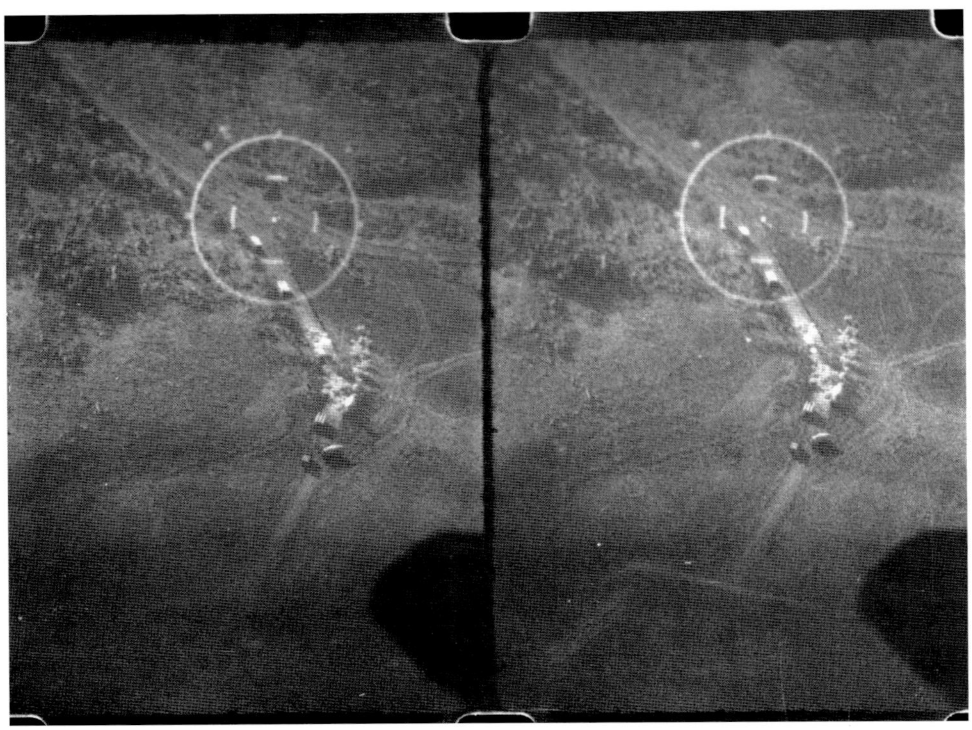

At least three Syrian SA-6 vehicles are clearly visible in these two frames taken from the Eliasaf-Sadan sight camera during a strafing pass on June 10, 1982. The Kurnass crew's unorthodox action earned them well-deserved citations.

The Ramat David Wing mix of fighter types was representative of the IAF fighter force mix: the F-16 represented the air-to-air segment, the Phantoms were the IAF heavy attack force, and the Kfir represented the light attack aircraft section. These images were taken in a wing level exercise shortly after the end of the June 1982 Lebanon War.

IAF operations over Lebanon continued past the June 11, 1982, ceasefire and were still hazardous, regardless of destruction of the Syrian air defense deployment. A shoulder launched SA-7 missile damaged Amiram Eliasaf's Kurnass 255 while attacking targets near the Beirut-Damascus highway. A fire warning light in the cockpit and his wingman's report that an engine was on fire forced Eliasaf to shut down the left-hand engine. Flying all the way back to Ramat David on one engine, the runway's cable safely stopped Kurnass 255 after a perfect single engine landing.

this single strafing pass. Battle damage launched missiles all around us and three launchers definitely exploded."

This action demonstrated flexibility, maintenance of the aim, initiative, improvisation, and professionalism; five of the most highly praised IDF values. In recognition of "initiative and professionalism" the lead crew (Eliasaf-Sadan) was awarded with the IAF Commander Citation.

Day 6 Ceasefire

IDF activity intensified as time ran out towards ceasefire, and Hammers flew 19 sorties on June 11, 1982: six SEAD, four support, four recce, four CAP, and one illumination. The final day SEAD was not a smashing success (no SAM kill claims). The highlight of the day was a support mission with TOT at 11:25 when a pair claimed destruction of four vehicles in the Lebanon Valley.

Overall the Hammers flew 152 sorties from June 4 to 11, 1982: 71 air support sorties, 35 SEAD sorties, 31 recce sorties, 12 CAP sorties, and three illumination sorties. The average of 19 sorties per day was evidence to the limited scale of the June 1982 Lebanon War. Prior to war the IAF fighter force's main missions were air-to-air (F-15 and F-16), air support (Skyhawk and Kfir), and SEAD (Phantom). IAF policy was to divide the limited number of missions between all qualified squadrons. This policy added to the Phantom squadrons' air-to-air and air support sorties that were not within the core expertise of Kurnass crews (heavy bombing, recce, and SEAD). Yet it was SEAD – THE Phantom core mission – that generated success, boosted morale, and stamped the seal on the already well known, if somewhat repressed, fact that the Kurnass was no longer a multi-role combat aircraft but a PGM platform.

SEAD SA-8

Israeli victory over the Syrian SAM deployment to Lebanon was overwhelming. Still, Syrian SAM batteries continued to challenge IAF air superiority over Lebanon. A new mobile SAM system, the SA-8, was first noted in Lebanon during July 1982. Operation Scraping 2 was launched on July 24, 1982, to hunt down the four launchers of one SA-8 battery. Yaron Kranz:

> "At the time I was a student, so it was convenient for me to schedule my reserve service to weekends. That Saturday we were scrambled to hunt down the SA-8. Aviem Sella was in command of the operation; he saw the UAV images in his command post and radioed the target

The Rafael Tadmit TV guided glide bomb was the Hammers' principle SEAD weapon from 1975 until 1986 and beyond. Reportedly credited with more than 50% of IAF SAM kill claims during the Lebanon War, the Israeli weapon was also credited with two SA-8 kills on July 24, 1982. These images of 69 Phantoms preparing for a Tadmit mission were taken in August 1984.

Hammers ground crew welcome pilot Yaron Kranz (fourth from left) and navigator Jacob Ovadya (fourth from right) after their return from the SA-8 hunt mission on July 24, 1982. Still in their flying gear, Kranz holds a bag containing his personal helmet with Ovadya – still holding a pack of maps and photos – smoking the traditional "after cigarette."

location to us in the air. We hung around for quite a while until we finally received a target. Our leader attacked, so we switched bomb data channels to his channel in order to see his attack. The aim point was a tree, and the SA-8 was supposed to be near that tree, but we didn't see it and the bomb hit the tree. Apparently it was impossible to see the SA-8 from our point of view, but the UAV picture clearly revealed that the SA-8 was right behind that tree and it was destroyed.

"The second SA-8 ran for cover in a wood. This time the aiming point was approximate, somewhere in the middle of that wood. Our leader attacked and hit that point, but the SA-8 was not there. However, the bomb was quite massive and the explosion literally blew the leaves from all trees in the wood and the SA-8 was suddenly exposed.

"Our leader had expended his two bombs so it was our turn. We aimed at that exposed SA-8 in the middle of the wood and we dropped our first bomb. Shortly afterwards the picture started to roll as the bomb entered some sort of a spin. We turned back, dropped the second bomb, and hit the SA-8."

Phantoms from four squadrons were launched to the hunt. Eventually the IAF claimed destruction of all four launchers, though contemporary reports only claimed three launchers destroyed. The two 69 Tadmit crews reported three ALPHA against two launchers; therefore Hammers were credited with destruction of 50% of the SA-8 targets.

Hummus in Beirut

Lebanon was in turmoil in the summer of 1982 when three regular armies (Israel, Lebanon, and Syria), several task forces (including American and French), UN Interim Force In Lebanon (UNIFIL), and numerous militias (including Christian, Shia, and Palestinian) were present in the tiny nation that once was a resort for wealthy tourists from all over the Middle East. Uri Bacal:

"One morning I flew to Ramat David in the liaison Cessna for a day of reserve service, a usual drill. Only this time I was asked, upon entering the squadron building, if I had a pistol! I did not even put on my flying gear. Still dressed as a reservist in short pants, T-shirt, and sandals, I was told that I was due to join a leader's recon in Lebanon.

"A helicopter flew us from Ramat David to Beirut. The recon schedule was tight and included briefings, meetings, and observations. But most bizarre of all – even more than an IDF officer touring Beirut in T-shirt, short

From 1980 until 1991, the Ramat David F-16 squadrons overshadowed the Hammers' Phantoms as the north wing's cutting edge. This image – of Hammers Kurnass 225 leading a pair of Ramat David F-16s – was taken after the June 1982 Lebanon War, when 69's Phantoms were already adorned with black and yellow checkered rudders.

Ramat David Wing Commander Herzle Bodinger (right) inspects a lead pair Kurnass prior to the mission on January 4, 1984.

Trailing attack pair for the January 4, 1984, mission was armed with four 2,000lb Mk 84 bombs.

pants, and sandals – was that the recon schedule included lunch in a local restaurant. Middle East reality is indeed beyond imagination, so much that one hot summer day I found myself eating hummus in a restaurant somewhere in Beirut."

Suicide Bombers

Meir took over from Eliasaf as 69 Squadron Commander on April 6, 1983. Israel expelled the PLO from Lebanon, but the year that followed the Lebanon War was not without events. Iranian sponsored Shia organizations began to fill in the vacuum. Shia suicide bombers started to attack French, Israeli, and USA targets in Lebanon from October 1983.

Israeli reprisal came on January 4, 1984, when the IAF launched a major strike against Shia bases in the Baalbek sector, Lebanon Valley. Hammers' contribution was a 4-ship formation with mixed armament. The lead pair lifted eight 1,000lb bombs (and QRC massive chaffe pods); the trailing pair was loaded with four 2,000lb bombs each. En route the lead 69 Phantom malfunctioned and turned back, but the three other crews pressed ahead and bombed as planned. IAF attack impact was overwhelming; contemporary media reports stated that the bases were devastated and that the number of casualties exceeded 500, including more than 100 dead. The strike signaled the start of an anti-terror IAF campaign aimed against spreading Shia organizations and returning PLO groups as IDF troops started to withdraw from Lebanon. Each bombing was massive, but the overall Israeli anti-terror air campaign over Lebanon consumed only a fraction of IAF assets. Air strikes were rotated between all IAF attack squadrons, so 69 only attacked once every several months.

Third Fatal Collision

Air combat maneuvering training took its toll on September 12, 1984. Quite rarely, all eight participating airmen were reservists, though this was obviously not the reason why Kurnass 255 and Kurnass 307 collided. A pilot and two navigators ejected safely; pilot Yuval Shemi was killed.

Kurnass 175 was put on display during U.S. Chairman of the Joint Chiefs of Staff General Vessey's visit to Ramat David in January 1984. Formerly a 107 Squadron aircraft, Kurnass 175 was a Hammers machine during the 1980s prior to assignment to Kurnass 2000 upgrade, from which it emerged as Kurnass 575. Loaded with 500 pound Mark 82 bombs and 360 kg IMI bombs (often confused with US M-117 750 pounds), the Kurnass is also armed with AIM-9 Sidewinder and Python 3 AAMs for self defense.

Lost in an accident on September 12, 1984, Kurnass 255 was photographed on August 16, 1984, armed with two Tadmit TV-guided bombs.

Kurnass 307 was lost on September 12, 1984, in the Hammers' third fatal mid-air collision; it was photographed landing at Ramat David on October 27, 1974, still in "toad" scheme, though it was repainted by the time of its demise.

The four Phantoms that flew Operation Cattle Head 4 line up on the "last chance" apron at Ramat David on September 4, 1985. Kurnass 303 flew lead with Kurnass 210 as wingman; Kurnass 308 flew sub-leader with Kurnass 209 as wingman. Each was armed with one Python 3 and one Sidewinder AAM for self protection. A fifth Phantom, Kurnass 306, was prepared as spare.

Cattle Head 4

69's next turn to attack terror bases in Lebanon was on September 4, 1985. Operation Cattle Head 4 targeted bases in the Kab Elias sector, east of Beirut and well within coverage of the reinstated Syrian SAM deployment to the Lebanon Valley.

Four Hammers crews led the mission with a midland Phantom squadron follow up. SA-6 locks were defeated, SA-7 missiles were outrun, AAA fire was evaded, and the designated targets were reportedly destroyed.

Popeye

Rafael Tadmit TV guided glide bomb had been the principle PGM in 69's arsenal since 1975. Tadmit was a very successful weapon system, credited with more than half of all Israeli SAM kill claims during the Lebanon campaign. As is often the case with military weapons development processes, a vastly more advanced Rafael PGM was already in the design phase when Tadmit entered IAF service. The new Rafael PGM was the Popeye, a TV guided missile.

With both Rafael and 69 residents of Israel's northern region, the Galilee, it was only natural that the Hammers would be involved with development, and entrusted with introduction, of the Popeye. Initial Operational Capability was achieved during IAF Year 1985 Term 3 (December 1985 to March 1986) when Popeye joined Tadmit in the Hammers' PGM inventory. An operational test launch was successfully accomplished on January 28, 1986. Full Popeye operational capability was officially announced on July 24, 1986, and for nearly a decade 69 was the only IAF squadron to field Popeye.

Ron Arad

Uri Bacal took over from Meir as 69 Squadron Commander on August 20, 1986. Originally, in October 1985, Rani Falk was named as the next 69 Squadron Commander, but sad circumstances led to a change in plans. F-16 squadron commander Yosef Eliel was killed in an accident on July 3, 1986, and Falk replaced Eliel. A Kfir squadron commander until May 5, 1986, Bacal was asked to take over 69.

Hammers' Kurnass 315 "modeling" the Popeye at Ramat David for the benefit of a Rafael marketing image. Actually, the association of Hammers and Popeye continues to the present day.

Unfortunate Number 5! Kurnass 306 was "number 5" during the September 4, 1985, and October 16, 1986, missions. In the first it did not participate, as then "number 5" was a spare and none of the first four Phantoms aborted the mission. In the second it was lost in action. These fine views were taken when 306 was still in "toad" camouflage, and later on in standard IAF scheme on September 4, 1985.

Bacal was seemingly fortunate to have the then rare annual attack mission over Lebanon early in his command cadence. Operation Father House 12 was activated on October 16, 1986, with 69 tasked to bomb PLO targets in the Sidon sector of Lebanon. Four crews were planned to attack at 16:30; two more crews were at Ramat David ready to take-off and follow up the attack with eventual TOT at 16:40. All six aircraft were armed with ten 360kg bombs each. Uri Bacal:

> "That day the majority of air crews were at Hatzor to attend an IAF sports day. There, I was notified that an operational order was activated. We returned to Ramat David in time for final preparations. The operational order specified a 4-ship formation, plus a pair back at Ramat David in 'start and wait' position, ready for scramble to follow up our bombing.
>
> "I flew lead in the 4-ship and we bombed as planned. The pair was scrambled when we were already on our way back. I was told that 'something happened' when I arrived at the squadron building, so I rushed downstairs to the operations cell still wearing my full flying gear. The message was that an aircraft was hit, that the crew ejected, and that two parachutes were observed. Along the time line of this event we started to realize that pilot Aviram was OK. There was no contact with navigator Ron Arad."

Apparently a rare combination of less than optimum bomb release and technical malfunction sealed the fate of Kurnass 306; a bomb exploded underneath the Phantom immediately after release, possibly due to a mid-air collision of two released bombs and premature activation of a detonator. Sometime after sunset an AH-1 Cobra attack helicopter rescued reserve pilot Aviram from a terrain compartment full of unfriendly armed people. Navigator Ron Arad landed a few hundred meters away but did not make contact with IAF search and rescue teams. Eventually,

Reconstruction of how a Cobra attack helicopter rescued 69 pilot Aviram on October 16, 1986. Aviram clinged to the Cobra's skid when the attack helicopter flew away from a hot danger zone. En route to Israel, the Cobra landed in a deserted spot near the Lebanese coast of the Mediterranean Sea, where Aviram changed his position from hanging on the skid to sitting on the skid. After crossing the Israeli border the Cobra landed again and Aviram's transport was changed for the better in the shape of a Bell 212 helicopter that flew the rescued pilot to hospital for post ejection medical care.

Final participation of navigator Ron Arad in 69's Term regular group cadre photo (standing third from left) was the IAF Year 1985 Term 1 (April to July) group photo taken on March 28, 1985. Arad graduated IAF Flying School Class 87 during November 1978 and was a regular Hammers navigator, except for two periods of emergency posting status during staff assignment and chemical engineering studies from October 1985.

the Lebanese Shia organization Amal admitted capture of the Israeli navigator and mediators negotiated exchange of prisoners. Obviously negotiation was not concluded fast enough. Reportedly last seen alive on the night of May 4 to 5, 1988, Ron Arad vanished without a trace and his fate is still unknown.

"Iron Eagle II"

Ramat David transformed into a Hollywood filming site for a few weeks, from December 1987 until January 18, 1988. "Iron Eagle II" was the largest aviation film produced in Israel. The plot was a bit far fetched from reality at the time, but startlingly realistic

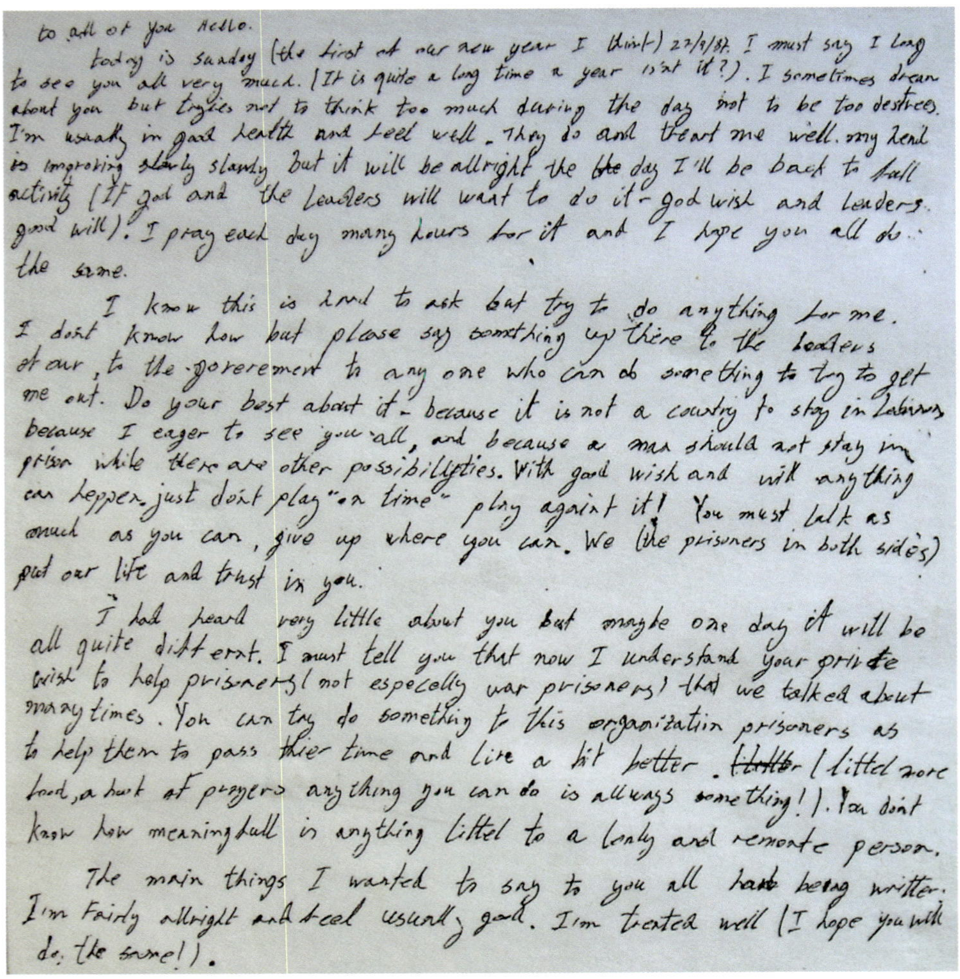

to all of you hello.

today is sunday (the first of our new year I think) 27/9/87. I must say I long to see you all very much. (It is quite a long time a year isn't it?). I sometimes dream about you but trying not to think too much during the day not to be too destress. I'm usually in good health and feel well. They do and treat me well. my hand is improving slowly slowly but it will be allright the ~~the~~ day I'll be back to full activity (If god and the leaders will want to do it - god wish and leaders good will). I pray each day many hours for it and I hope you all do the same.

I know this is hard to ask but try to do anything for me. I don't know how but please say something up there to the leaders of our, to the goverement to any one who can do something to try to get me out. Do your best about it - because it is not a country to stay in Labinon because I eager to see you all, and because a man should not stay in prison while there are other possibilyties. With good wish and will anything can happen just don't play "on time" play againt it! You must talk as much as you can, give up where you can. We (the prisoners in both sides) put our life and trust in you.

I had heard very little about you but maybe one day it will be all quite differnt. I must tell you that now I understand your private wish to help prisoners (not especelly war prisoners) that we talked about many times. You can try do something to this organization prisoners as to help them to pass thier time and live a bit better. ~~littler~~ (littel more food, a book of prayers anything you can do is allways something!). You don't know how meaningfull is anything littel to a lonly and remonte person.

The main things I wanted to say to you all ~~have~~ being written. I'm Fairly allright and feel usually good. I'm treated well (I hope you will do the same!).

Ron Arad's letter dated September 27, 1987, was the last sign of life received in Israel. Negotiations between the Israeli Government and Lebanese Amal Shia organization dragged along without positive results. It is believed that Arad was definitely alive until the night of May 4 to 5, 1988 (incidentally it was his 30th birthday); from then on Israel lost track of Ron Arad and his fate is unknown to this day.

In full "Iron Eagle II" USSR MiG-29 custom, Hammers Kurnass 207 was photographed over typical Arabah terrain during filming of the Hollywood movie.

Reserve pilot Yaron Kranz (left) stands in front of Kurnass 225, acting as a USSR MiG-29 during filming of "Iron Eagle II."

nowadays. The USA and the USSR joined forces to attack an imaginative Islamic nation that threatened the world with nuclear weapons.

The assembled aerial task force included selected individuals from the USA and from the USSR armed services grouped together for the classified mission at Ramat David, a secret air base somewhere in the Middle East. A U.S. General – previously commander of an air force museum! – was assigned to lead the air task force that included U.S. F-16s (played by the IAF Ramat David based F-16 squadrons) and USSR MiG-29s (mimicked by 69 Squadron's Phantoms). Obviously the secondary plot involves a love story between a U.S. F-16 male pilot and a USSR MiG-29 female pilot that developed as the former museum commander forged the unique task force for its fateful mission.

Mission filming of the air action took place over the Arabah with IAI Kfir fighters playing the interceptors of the imaginative Islamic nation. Naturally, the combined force of U.S. F-16s and USSR "MiG-29s" defeated the Kfirs, with the U.S. F-16 male pilot saving the life of the USSR MiG-29 female pilot in a classic "sandwich" scenario: the "MiG-29" leading, the "Islamic" Kfir trailing the "MiG-29," and the "savior" F-16 following the Kfir; all air action was filmed from two locations: a mountain near Masada and a Learjet business jet especially fitted for filming movies. Eventually the combined task force overcomes the differences, accomplishes the mission, and saves the world for a true happy end.

Iron Eagle II filming – through pure coincidence – overlapped an IAF Phantom force reshuffle of airframes. This suited filming quite well, since several former 105 Squadron Phantoms were reassigned to the Hammers and these were still adorned with 105's distinctive red flash painted on both sides of the fuselage, perfectly fitting in the plot as "USSR MiG-29s" for filming ground scenes. Other Phantoms – original Hammers airframes with their own distinctive black and yellow checkered rudders – received fake "USSR" badges that replaced the IAF David Shield for participation in the filming of the air scenes.

Mountains Miracle

The Hammers did not bomb terror targets in Lebanon during 1987; their 1988 first foray was Operation Mountains Miracle 4

Popeye introduction highlights involved operational test launches and demonstration flights to IDF and USAF "top brass." Two Popeye operational tests were conducted on March 12, 1987, and January 4, 1988; both were successful. The operational tests simulated a surprise operational order with a special code denoting training. Only the squadron commander was a "secret ring member" of the impending test. Obviously a squadron commander had to know all about his unit and was trusted not to tip service persons under his command. Uri Bacal not only avoided the temptation to tip, but once forgot all about the planned Popeye test and agreed to another mission scheduled for the same date. The Hammers easily accomplished both missions. Popeye demo flights were also successful; Uri Bacal flew with IDF Chief of Staff (flown on August 2, 1987) and two USAF generals (flown on January 28, 1987, and March 21, 1988) in the back seat. Eventually the USAF purchased Popeye to arm B-52 bombers.

69 Squadron Kurnass 304 first flew as the Kurnass 2000 upgrade prototype on July 15, 1987. The objective of the Kurnass 2000 project was to rejuvenate the veteran warriors. The upgrade did not involve the whole fleet and triggered a comprehensive Kurnass force realignment program that also impacted the Hammers. Kurnass 304 was photographed at Ramat David on February 10, 1983, after a landing accident. Hydraulic malfunction prevented proper braking, so pilot Eliezer Adar raced Kurnass 304 into the runway's arresting net, which was powerful enough to stop the big and heavy Phantom.

on February 10, 1988. However, the 69 bombers were called off prior to pull up; someone up the ladder of command decided to abort the mission.

By then, IAF air strike missions over Lebanon intensified as a result of the First Intifada, the Palestinian uprising against Israeli rule that lasted from 1987 to 1993. The Israeli-Lebanese border heated up, especially in the wake of the "ultralight night" on November 25, 1987. That evening a PLO ultralight flew across the Israeli-Lebanese border and landed near an IDF encampment of tents. The PLO pilot attacked and killed six IDF soldiers before return fire silenced him for good. From then on 69 was the IAF's frontline illumination support. The nighttime illumination QRA crew was scrambled each time IDF troops suspected an attempt to cross the Israeli-Lebanese border. Naturally nighttime illumination was not considered a demanding task. However, winter weather at Ramat David added risks of heavy showers, poor visibility, and wet runways. Mixing hasty transition from sleep to combat, demanding weather conditions, and routine flying of operational missions was obviously a recipe for troubles. Luckily for 69 the nighttime illumination QRA did not lead to accidents, but several ground incidents were a constant reminder of possible hazards. The highlight was when a young crew was scrambled. Sleeping in the bachelor's dormitories on the other side of base, the usual practice was to drive the QRA jeep along the perimeter fence road. Those youngsters were so keen to take-off as soon as possible that they decided to take a shortcut along the runway that stretched straight from their doorstep to the QRA aircraft shelter. Obviously they were aware that such over-enthusiastic behavior would not be acclaimed by their commanders, so they switched off the lights of the jeep while dashing along a dark, misty, and wet runway!

Time frame between strike missions over Lebanon per squadron narrowed down from roughly a year to an average of once every few months. It was 69's turn again when Operation Mountains Miracle 11 targeted PLO targets in Lebanon on March 23, 1988. Symbolically, the first Hammers bombing over Lebanon since October 16, 1986, was also in the Sidon sector. A pair of 69

Reportedly the IAF's final Phantom in "toad" scheme, Kurnass 316 participated in Israel's 40th Independence Day fly-past on April 21, 1988. The 69 crews trailed a Boeing 707 tanker during the fly-past to demonstrate a new in-flight refueling capability that considerably extended the reach of the IAF heavy attack force.

Eliezer Adar flew Kurnass 303 during operation Restless 15 on November 1, 1988, and Kurnass 316 during Operation Restless 36 on June 15, 1989; two of his 700 operational sorties! Kurnass 316 was photographed at Ramat David after its repainting from "toad" scheme to standard IAF camouflage.

crews took part in the operation that involved a total of 14 bombers from three squadrons. However, Hammers bombing results were considered inadequate, so four Phantoms flew a repeat mission the following day.

Restless and House Circle

The next series of IAF air strikes over Lebanon were Restless and then House Circle. The Hammers flew Operation Restless 15 on November 1, 1988, when four Phantoms attacked in the Damur sector and Operation Restless 36 on June 16, 1989, when a 4-ship was tasked to attack a PLO target in the Tyre sector with AGM-65 Maverick missiles. As already noted Maverick was a problematic weapon. That day lighting conditions over Tyre prevented proper lock, so no Mavericks were launched and the attack was called off.

In between the two Restless attacks 69 supported IDF Operation Blue Brown, a major assault against caves in PLO use in the Damur sector on the night of December 8 to 9, 1988. The PLO utilized natural caves as shelter against IDF commando attacks and IAF air strikes that previously harassed PLO bases in the open. The two House Circle missions that the Hammers flew also targeted caves in PLO usage: Operation House Circle 10 on September 20, 1989 (caves in the Damur sector), and Operation House Circle 14 on November 23, 1989 (caves in the Soltan Yacoub sector).

A pause of almost 20 months followed before 69 again flew an attack mission over Lebanon, only by then the black and yellow checkered Phantoms did not depart from their beloved Ramat David Wing in the heart of the green and fertile Galilee region, but from detested Hatzerim Air Base in the middle of the yellow and dry Negev Desert.

Gulf War

Prior to the Hammers' forced change of environment, Iraq invaded Kuwait in August 1990; the same month that Avi took over as 69 Squadron Commander.

Hammers preparation for war mostly involved long range air strike profiles, utilizing in-flight refueling from Boeing 707 tankers to achieve long range and Popeye for precision attack. Innovative Popeye profile attack missions were practiced during countdown to war from August 1990 to January 1991.

The UN ultimatum to Iraq to withdraw from Kuwait ended on January 15, 1991, so by then the Hammers were fully ready to strike with all reserve and emergency posting service persons present at Ramat David to back up the regular cadre. Eventually, the USA led coalition launched the offensive to free Kuwait during the night of January 16 to 17, 1991. As was expected, Iraq launched surface-to-surface missile attacks against Israel from January 19,

At a time when Phantom force sister squadrons utilized Laser Guided Bombs as their main weapon for air strikes over Lebanon, the Hammers lacked LGB qualification and had no proper PGM fit for limited conflict scenarios. 69's PGM arsenal included AGM-65 Maverick, Tadmit, and Popeye. The Maverick, in Hammers service since 1973, was considered the most suitable to limited conflict operations over Lebanon. Compared to LGB Maverick was less accurate (lock on necessitated sharp contrast). Short ranged and armed with a relatively small warhead, the AGM-65 was certainly not a weapon of choice for the type of IAF operations over Lebanon. The Kurnass squadrons that lacked LGB qualification but had AGM-65 capability (69 and 107) attempted to utilize Maverick as an alternative to LGB, but combat experience was a disappointment. Normal Phantom Maverick combat load was six missiles, but for training purposes a single missile was an adequate load.

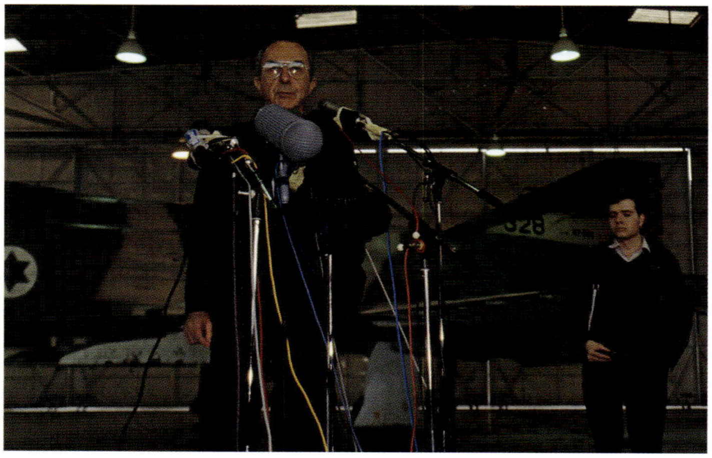

The first phase of the IAF Kurnass force realignment program was redistribution of airframes. Older Phantoms, not assigned for Kurnass 2000 upgrade, joined 69 from January 1988. An early such arrival was Kurnass 328, which was photographed in a Ramat David Maintenance Squadron hangar as background to Israeli Minister of Defense Moshe Ahrens during a January 1991 Gulf War briefing to the media. The IAF, 69 inclusive, was ready to attack Iraq, but diplomacy suppressed Israeli plans for reprisal raids following Iraqi SSM attacks against Israel.

In flight refueling from Boeing 707 tankers was essential for effective Phantom operations over Iraq. The IAF inducted into service IAI modified Boeing 707 tankers from 1984 following U.S. reluctance to furnish its Middle East ally with KC-135 tankers. By 1991 the Hammers were fully qualified in the art of mid-air fueling from "airborne gas stations."

An amazing view of downtown Tyre, Lebanon, for a fast low flying Hammers Kurnass on April 29, 1991, shortly after the end of the Gulf War. Of special note is the poor field of view from the Phantom's rear cockpit and the flare (visible in front of the left high story building) that the leader released to deceive the potential threat of heat seeking shoulder launched missiles.

The Popeye air-to-ground missile would have played a key role in 69's contribution to IAF offensive operations against Iraq, had Israel launched the planned reprisal strike operation and missile hunt missions. Loaded with Popeye, Kurnass 209 is adorned with four air-to-air kill markings, including two credited to Yoram Agmon and Daniel Wittmann during the Yom Kippur War.

Reconnaissance Kurnass 489 landing at Ramat David in January 1991 during the Gulf War crisis. Kurnass 489 (previously 499) was reassigned from 119 Squadron to 69 Squadron during November 1976 and was a Hammers jet until 1994.

Line up at Ramat David on June 4, 1991, prior to take-off of a fighter-bomber ferry flight to Hatzerim; the Reconnaissance Flight was left behind at Ramat David, as it was gearing for service introduction of the Ophir real-time digital recce pod.

Eliezer Adar – 69 Squadron Commander from 1979 until 1981 and Hammers reserve pilot until 1994 – and Israel Primor – Hammers navigator from September 1970 until April 1993 - flew Kurnass 149 from Ramat David to Hatzerim during the mass fly-past that signaled relocation from north to south on June 4, 1991.

1991. Obviously the Iraqis hoped that these missile attacks would draw Israel into the war and would prompt a falling apart of the UN coalition assembled to free Kuwait, as Arab nations would be reluctant to attack an Arab nation fighting Israel. Therefore diplomacy stopped the planned Israeli reprisal that the IAF spearheaded with an armada of combat aircraft already briefed and ready to go. Likewise, no IAF missile hunt missions were flown over Iraq, so Hammers' readiness was gradually relaxed along the conflict's time line as the intensity of Iraqi missile attacks decayed and Gulf War fire effectively ceased on February 28, 1991, after Kuwait was liberated and Iraq was defeated.

Moving South

Avihu Ben-Nun entered office as IAF Commander on September 22, 1987, and launched a series of Plan Flower force realignment redeployment schemes. The Plan Flower phase that caught up with the Hammers called for Kurnass force redeployment. The Kurnass squadrons that operated for years from four air bases were to be concentrated at two bases. 69 Squadron was slated for redeployment from Ramat David, in the green rural north, to Hatzerim, in the yellow desert south, from where 107 Squadron had been flying the Kurnass since 1971.

Grouping 69 and 107 together made sense not only from a logistics point, but also on operational grounds; the two sister

Hammers heritage often compares the move from Ramat David to Hatzerim to banishment from Eden. These two images of Kurnass 158 – taken during the flight from Ramat David to Hatzerim on June 4, 1991 – unveil the origins of comparison, with the Phantom flying from the cultivated Jezreel Valley in the north of Israel to the arid Negev Desert in the south of Israel.

Oasis in the desert. The Hammers' squadron building at Hatzerim was photographed in June 1992; previously the home of a Skyhawk squadron, this building was returned to its "rightful owner" in 1994.

The very first Israeli F-4 – IAF Kurnass 101 - was issued to 69 at the twilight of its distinguished service career. The historic aircraft was photographed prior to the Hammers' first operational mission from Hatzerim, an air strike of PLO targets in Lebanon on July 17, 1991. The Phantom was loaded with 10 360kg bombs (two under the left wing on Triple Ejector Rack, five under the fuselage attached to Multiple Ejector Rack, and three on TER under the right wing), a Python 3 AAM for self defense attached to the left-hand TER, and a balance pod loaded onto the forward left under-fuselage AIM-7 station to compensate for the weight difference between the Python 3 and a 360kg bomb.

squadrons shared several key unique operational qualifications, including Maverick and Tadmit. However, many Hammers air crews resented the idea of moving out of Ramat David. The northern air base was viewed as the Hammers' birth place and home base, even though the absolute accuracy of both statements can be argued. Adding insult to injury was the fact that leading the relocation plan was IAF Commander Avihu Ben-Nun, the Hammers' own beloved Avihu, their first Kurnass age commander. But the truth was that Avihu presented two options to his Hammers friends: remain at Ramat David or move to Hatzerim.

Remaining at Ramat David depended upon re-equipment as an F-16D squadron. Re-equipment could have secured the Hammers' future for many years and bonded the squadron to Ramat David; the F-16D squadron that was activated at Ramat David in 1991 is still there, still occupying the old Hammers' "reversed" squadron building. The downside of the "remain at Ramat David" scheme was that many of the Kurnass veterans were not expected to convert to the F-16D. Most Hammers service persons were planned to move to Hatzerim along with their black and yellow checkered Phantoms.

At this stage the Hammers' aircrew arranged a meeting to discuss ways and means to avoid what most considered as **banishment to the desert**. This meeting concluded with a decision to delegate a representative to Avihu in an effort to dissuade him from this move. All agreed that the representative should be an inactive aircrew in good relations with Avihu. The choice fell on Zvi Avidror of the 69 Veterans Association, who was in amicable relations with Avihu. Avidror's meeting with IAF Commander Avihu Ben-Nun lasted well beyond its allocated time but ended with a clear message from Avihu to the Hammers air crews: **69 will move to Hatzerim in good order or it will have to be decommissioned within a few months**. Next day Zvi got back to the squadron and passed on Avihu's final words on the issue.

Relocation to Hatzerim was an option that chopped off the bond with Ramat David but preserved the squadron "as is." This alternative evidently risked the future of the squadron but still was the preferred Hammers option. Avihu honored the Hammers' choice, and 69 Squadron moved from Ramat David to Hatzerim on June 4, 1991.

Song Poison

A Hezbollah planted Improvised Explosive Devise killed five IDF soldiers in south Lebanon on October 26, 1992, and triggered two days of massive IAF air strikes against Hezbollah targets in Lebanon and slightly beyond. The Hammers flew two missions

With empty bomb racks, Kurnass 153 was photographed while flying back from the Operation Song Poison 9 target at Jabel Safi, Lebanon, to Hatzerim on October 26, 1992.

69 Squadron Commander flew Kurnass 323 in the lead of Operation Song Poison 10 on October 26, 1992; the jet was photographed loaded with bombs en route to target near the River Atzi.

Snow in the desert! The Israeli winter of 1992 was the rainiest ever since survey of climate had started in the region. Snow covered the Negev Desert from February 23, 1992 – including the Hammers building and aircraft at Hatzerim – while amidst the snow storm the Hammers flew a unique extreme weather training mission over the snow covered Golan Heights.

during this offensive that – "as usual" – escalated, as Hezbollah responded to Israeli air strikes with rockets attacks, but – also "as usual" – abruptly ended before the situation completely deteriorated out of control.

The Hammers flew Operation Song Poison 9 on October 26, 1992, when the usual 4-ship formation bombed Hezbollah targets at Jabel Safi, south Lebanon.

Vastly more unique was Operation Song Poison 10, which the Hammers flew on October 27, 1992. The target was a Hezbollah training camp near River El Atzi, nearby the north segment of the Lebanese-Syrian border and actually on the Syrian side of the border, though this fact was concealed at the time. The Hammers' 4-ship penetrated Lebanon north of Beirut and flew east inside a canyon that led them to the Lebanon Valley. There the Hammers turned north and flew low all along the Lebanon Valley – well within the engagement envelope of the Syrian Air Defense deployment – towards their target just across the Syrian border.

Having completed their mission as planned, the Hammers later learnt from Israeli Intelligence reports that the Hezbollah training camp was actually evacuated prior to the attack. Apart from this fact, the Song Poison 10 mission was extremely successful and was an exemplary demonstration of Hammers skills under the leadership of a new commander that took over from Avi on March 30, 1992.

The Hammers Attack the Knights

Getting accustomed to the yellow desert surroundings of Hatzerim was a painful process for Hammers' service persons. A series of events was implemented to ease adaptation, and these included an open day to Hammers' families on April 1, 1993. Dating the event on April First was probably an error, as on that date 69 Squadron attacked 107 Squadron, and this was not a joke!

A fire power demonstration was planned to impress service persons and their visiting families. The targets were a group of old vehicles south of Hatzerim's north runway; a legitimate bombing range for demonstrations with water bombs. Officially,

Reconnaissance Flight operations from Ramat David continued throughout 69's association with Hatzerim as a Kurnass outfit. The Ophir digital real-time recce pod was introduced in December 25, 1992, with service introduction test flights following from April 1993. All of the Hammers' RF-4E recce birds were in standard IAF camouflage scheme except for Kurnass 497, which was painted in air superiority gray. Kurnass 497 was photographed at Ramat David prior to the mission with a standard camouflaged RF-4E and escorting F-16Ds; the latter were from the squadron that had occupied the Hammers' former squadron building since 1991.

only Hammers and their families gathered for the firepower demonstration. Unofficially, many Hatzerim service persons took a break and stepped outside to see the show, and among them were many 107 Squadron Technical Flight service persons.

Low cloud base welcomed viewers as they emerged from offices and workshops. Everybody was puzzled what would happen, would 69 scrap the firepower demonstration? No, they did not. Bombing was impossible so strafing was ordered.

Unfortunately, cannon rounds sprayed the 107 Hardened Aircraft Shelter complexes. Two 107 Orange Tail Knights NCOs were injured.

Hammers or Knights

69 and 107 were bonded together since 1971, when the Hammers loaned two Phantoms to enable the Orange Tail Knights to initiate their Kurnass flying days. The bond was strengthened in the post-Yom Kippur War PGM introduction era when 69 and 107 were the only Kurnass squadrons to share Maverick and Tadmit qualifications. A decade later, both squadrons were not included in the Kurnass 2000 program that upgraded the inventory of the other IAF Phantom squadrons. Thus, it was only natural to base together

Kurnass 102 blasts from Hatzerim's north runway during IAF Day's rehearsal fly-past on June 16, 1992. The photographer's location is opposite to the range that was the venue of the April 1, 1993, incident.

The Ron Arad Missing Man Fly-past is flown on 16 October with a group of aircraft flying in perfect formation except for one empty slot, waiting for the return of the missing Hammers navigator. The Hammers handed over responsibility for the Ron Arad Missing Man Fly-past to the Knights from 1994 to 1997 before taking over again from 1998. These images were taken during the October 16, 1992, Ron Arad Missing Man Fly-past.

Hammers Kurnass 321 was honored as background to IAF "top brass" gathering with President Haim Herzog (sitting eighth from left) and IDF Chief of Staff Ehud Barak (sitting seventh from left) during their visit to Hatzerim on January 5, 1993. Among them: IAF Commander Herzle Bodinger (sitting ninth from left), IAF Deputy Commander Eitan Ben-Eliyahu (sitting 10th from left), and Hatzerim Air Base Commander Amiram Eliasaf (sitting 11th from left).

69 contributed four crews to the IAF fly-past during Israel's 45th Independence Day on April 26, 1994; one of the crews flew Kurnass 153. A veteran IAF Phantom, 153 served 119 Squadron from 1970 until 119 converted to the Kurnass 2000 from 1992. Not selected to Kurnass 2000 upgrade, 153 was re-issued to 69 and served the Hammers until 1994, when it was passed on to 107. Many veteran Hammers crews – mostly reservists not expected to undergo conversion to more advanced combat aircraft – continued their Kurnass flying days with the Orange Tail Knights, just "across the road" at Hatzerim.

69 Squadron's farewell from veterans on March 1, 1994, included this 4-ship air-to-air photography mission.

69 Squadron Deputy Commander B Amikam – Tel Nof Air Base Commander since 2009 – flying Kurnass 323 over the Dead Sea, in the lead of his 4-ship VETO section, during the Hammers' farewell from veterans fly-past on March 1, 1994.

Hatzerim Air Base Commander Avi Barber (left) and 69 Squadron Commander Elisha (wearing the traditional Hammers black cup) watch from the stage as the Hammers' flag is handed over to IAF Commander Herzle Bodinger (marching towards the flag) during the farewell from veterans on March 1, 1994.

Kurnass crews taxi in to the farewell from veterans line at Hatzerim on March 1, 1994. Eight formations took part in the fly-past. Pilot Gidon Yahalom flew lead in the AGREEMENT section; pilot David Brisk was HARRIS leader; past commander Eliezer Adar was ARGUMENT leader; and navigator Meir Gur flew lead in the CURTAIN section.

the two sister squadrons, armed with unique weapons and flying the legacy Phantom.

Deliveries of the Kurnass 2000 were completed during 1992. IAF experts started to evaluate acquisition options of a "future Phantom" – of which there will be more in the final chapter of our odyssey. Dark clouds of uncertainty gathered over the squadron buildings of the two Hatzerim Kurnass squadrons. Training and operations were obviously not compromised, and it was during this time frame that 69 and 107 participated in Operation Accountability; an Israeli attack against Hezbollah targets in south Lebanon from July 25 to 31, 1993. The Hammers flew 74 sorties, including many "boom" sorties; low level supersonic dashes aimed to frighten population, whose objective was to trigger escape so that IDF artillery fire and air strikes would not harm civilians. An estimated 300,000 civilians were thus displaced north, towards Beirut, from south Lebanon.

Initial "future Phantom" operational requirements called for re-equipment of 69 and 107 with modern combat aircraft. However IAF plans changed, and by early 1994 it was clear that only one of the two sister squadrons would be re-equipped. IAF Commander Herzle Bodinger – a firm believer in heritage and tradition – favoured re-equipment of 69, which was the older unit among the two and also had a significant heavy bomber past. A strong lobby of Hatzerim leaders and Knights veterans promoted priority of 107 as the southern base "home unit" over the newcomers from the north.

Thus, IAF Commander Herzle Bodinger's rule that 69 would re-equip signaled to then Hammers a present blow rather than a future hope.

9

From Phantom to Thunder 1994-1998: Flight of the Septuagenarians

Bill Katz – of July 1948 Cairo raid fame and Chairman of the 69 Squadron Veterans Association – passed away in September 1994. Avihu Ben-Nun – 69 Squadron Commander from 1969 until 1972 and IAF Commander from 1987 until 1992 – took over as Chairman of the 69 Squadron Veterans Association. Avihu succeeded Bill Katz in sad circumstances, but transition from B-17 old-timers to F-4 veterans was an inevitable process.

Meir Gur – Hammers navigator from 1970 until 1994, known to all as Guri – started transition with Zvi Avidror as the driving force behind the 69 Veterans Association. David Brisk – still an active Kurnass pilot after all those years – was the caretaker of Hammers heritage.

Hammers veterans during an April 5, 1995, reunion, from left to right: pilot Reuben Narunsky, bombardier-navigator Jules Cuburnek, navigator John Harris, gunner Lazar Heskia, navigator Stefan Falc, radio operator Lou Maserow, gunner Amos Yarden, pilot Maurice Segal, and gunner Zvi Avidror. Five of the present - Avidror, Cuburnek, Harris, Heskia, and Narunsky - were planned to participate in the Flight of the Septuagenarians project.

Avihu Ben-Nun – 69 Squadron Commander 1969-1972; IAF commander 1987-1992 – has been Chairman of the 69 Veterans Association since 1994. Avihu was photographed on stage during the "Hammers Evening" at Hatzerim on August 25, 1994, with the old slogan "69 IS MORE THAN A NUMBER" painted on the background board.

Zvi Avidror (right) hands over a Hammers gift to IAF Commander Herzle Bodinger during the "Hammers Evening" at Hatzerim on August 25, 1994.

Ezer Weizman flew "his" Black Spitfire from 1955 – when he was Ramat David Wing Commander – until he entered office as Israel Minister of Defense during 1977. The Black Spitfire was the cornerstone of IAF heritage preservation pioneers – Weizman, Zorik, and Terner – that led to the current IAF Museum at Hatzerim, where the Black Spitfire is still airworthy as the centerpiece of the collection. Weizman was photographed taxiing the Black Spitfire at Ramat David in June 1970.

Zorik Lev graduated Flying School Class 10 in April 1953 and was a Mosquito pilot until conversion to jet fighters during 1956. Zorik flew the Meteor, Ouragan, Mystere, and Super Mystere, and commanded an Ouragan squadron (113) from 1961 until 1962, a Super Mystere squadron (105) from 1962 until 1963, and a Mirage squadron (101) from 1963 until 1965. A farmer and fighter, Zorik realized the reach for the sky should be firmly based on mother earth as the past feeds the future. Therefore Zorik created a unique collection of historic IAF aircraft, all airworthy. His work ended abruptly on the morning of October 9, 1973, when the Skyhawk he flew during a Yom Kippur War attack mission over the Egyptian front disappeared in the waters of the Mediterranean Sea. Zorik was photographed in October 1970 after the ceremonial "baptism" that IAF engineers celebrated after each solo flight; all solo pilots – regardless of rank and status – were similarly bathed in a mixture of water and oily fluids. The ceremony bonded together IAF air and ground crews, and for a short while waved barriers between "white collar" pilots and "blue collar" engineers.

Most prominent Hammers heritage piece during the Phantom era was this "last extinct turret of a B-17 in the world" (exact translation from 69's historical records) that the 69 Veterans Associations tracked down in Spain. The turret – obviously not of a B-17 – was on display at the Hammers squadron building from 1969 until 1994. During inactivation the historical artifact was transferred to the IAF Museum, where it is on display. The placard states: *This machine gun turret was part of a British "Avro Lancaster" bomber from the WWII period. The turret is the closest thing we have to a "souvenir" from one of the original Boeing B-17Gs ("Flying Fortresses") which served on the "Patishim" Squadron in 1948. It was located by the "Patishim" Squadron Veterans' Association.*

Terner's Museum

Ezer Weizman was Ramat David Wing Commander from 1953 until 1956. When the Spitfire was due for retirement, Weizman ordered to paint one Spitfire in pitch black as his own personal airplane. The Black Spitfire – also known as "Ezer's Spit" – was maintained by a group of dedicated engineers and flown exclusively by Weizman (IAF Commander from 1958 until 1966) as a symbol of IAF heritage preservation.

Zorik Lev accepted responsibility for Ezer's Spit upon entering office as Ramat David Wing Commander from 1970. Zorik started to build up a collection of airworthy historical aircraft with the Black Spitfire as the centerpiece. A Meteor, an Ouragan, a Mystere, and a Vautour were added to what became known in IAF circles as Zorik's collection. Sadly, Zorik Lev was declared missing in action during a Yom Kippur War mission on October 9, 1973.

Jacob Terner entered office as Hatzerim Air Base Commander during 1977. Terner was 107 Squadron Commander from 1966 until 1967, Flying School Commander from 1972 until 1974, a staunch supporter of the Orange Tail Knights and a firm believer in IAF heritage preservation. During 1978 Terner managed to move Zorik's collection from Ramat David to Hatzerim as the core of a future IAF Museum. Many old aircraft – serving as "gate guardians" at IAF bases, educating young children to the love of flying in kibbutz kindergartens, and elsewhere – were tracked down, transported to Hatzerim, repaired, repainted, and placed on display to bolster Terner's museum. However, these included none of the 69 historic icons; the B-17 Flying Fortress bombers were scrapped and the PBY Catalina amphibians were sold abroad.

Years went by and the IAF Museum idea turned into reality. Terner accepted a reserve assignment of IAF Museum Commander from 1985, and the Museum was officially opened on June 20, 1991. Five years later the Museum was growing from strength to strength, but 69 Squadron was inactive. Veteran Hammers promoted 69's revival in line with then current plans while Knights supporters challenged the original plan and called for 107's re-equipment. At the same time, a veteran Hammer (Zvi Avidror) joined the effort with a dedicated Knight (Jacob Terner) to add a B-17 to the IAF Museum collection.

Old Gentleman Idea

Al Schwimmer purchased the B-17s for the Hammers back in 1948, but the highlight of his many enterprises was Bedek Aviation; forerunner of Israel Aircraft Industries (IAI), now Israel Aerospace Industries (IAI). Schwimmer was Chief Executive Officer of the Israeli Government owned corporation from its founding in 1953 until forced retirement in 1977. By 1995 Schwimmer was again in the B-17 purchase business, but this time the idea was to add a B-17 to the IAF Museum collection.

Zvi Avidror – former Fleet Air Arm (FAA) Telegrapher Air Gunner (TAG), former Hammers B-17 gunner, and founder of the 69 Squadron Veterans Association – joined Schwimmer in September 1995 in a daring enterprise. Schwimmer was 78; Avidror was 70 years old. They initially aimed at acquisition of a B-17 and located a B-17E under restoration to flying condition in Fort Lauderdale, Florida. By then an airworthy B-17 was valued at millions of U.S. dollars, but raising funds proved more of a challenge than back in 1948. The money was never found and the B-17E was sold to an American museum.

The breakthrough idea was to "pay" for the B-17 with surplus IAF aircraft. Since the value of a batch of IAF surplus aircraft was higher than the value of a single B-17, an ambitious scheme was launched to include in the still notional transaction five historic aircraft missing from the collection of the IAF Museum: a B-17 Flying Fortress, a PBY Catalina, a C-46 Commando, a Beaufighter, and a Mosquito. Schwimmer purchased for Israel its B-17s, C-46s, and PBYs, and was involved in the acquisition of Mosquitoes in Canada, and if a Mosquito then why not a Beaufighter? So on the surface it all seemed plain logic.

Scanning options, it soon became evident that the purchase of an airworthy C-46 and PBY was easy, and that acquisition of a flyable B-17 was possible, but that the Beaufighter and Mosquito were nearly extinct species. The objective was changed to an airworthy B-17, C-46, and PBY, plus display replicas of the Mosquito and the Beaufighter. Negotiations and red tape were exhausting; Schwimmer retired in January 1998 and Avidror

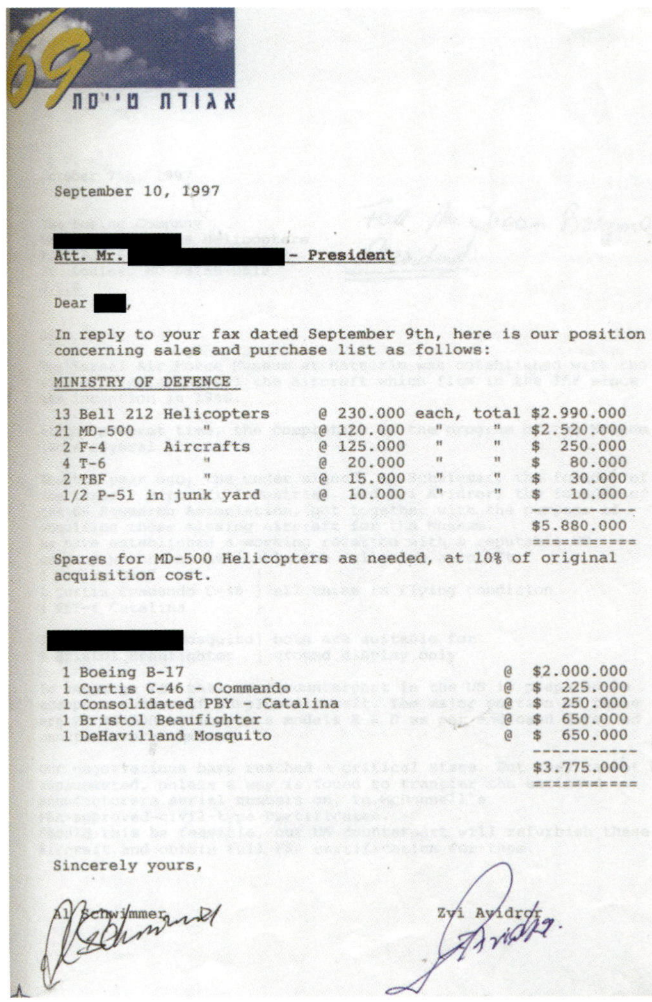

אגודת טייסת

September 10, 1997

Att. Mr. [redacted] - President

Dear [redacted],

In reply to your fax dated September 9th, here is our position concerning sales and purchase list as follows:

MINISTRY OF DEFENCE

13 Bell 212 Helicopters	@ 230.000 each, total		$2.990.000
21 MD-500 "	@ 120.000 "	"	$2.520.000
2 F-4 Aircrafts	@ 125.000 "	"	$ 250.000
4 T-6 "	@ 20.000 "	"	$ 80.000
2 TBF "	@ 15.000 "	"	$ 30.000
1/2 P-51 in junk yard	@ 10.000 "	"	$ 10.000
			$5.880.000

Spares for MD-500 Helicopters as needed, at 10% of original acquisition cost.

1 Boeing B-17	@ $2.000.000
1 Curtis C-46 - Commando	@ $ 225.000
1 Consolidated PBY - Catalina	@ $ 250.000
1 Bristol Beaufighter	@ $ 650.000
1 DeHavilland Mosquito	@ $ 650.000
	$3.775.000

Sincerely yours,

Al Schwimmer Zvi Avidror

A September 10, 1997, letter from Schwimmer and Avidror outlining the science fiction trade proposal of Israeli Ministry of Defense surplus equipment for historic aircraft to the IAF Museum.

Photographed inside a hangar at North Weald, United Kingdom, the Catalina that Boeing purchased for the IAF Museum was named SPIRIT OF ZVI AVIDROR and numbered "190425" to signal Avidror's birthday: April 19, 1925.

The Catalina at Beauvais, France, on June 29, 2004, a month after the emergency landing on May 28, 2004.

realized that it was "now or never"; Israel would celebrate its 50th Independence Day in April, and the Hammers would commemorate their golden anniversary in September. Obtaining and delivering all five historical aircraft to Israel during the golden anniversary year was obviously unrealistic. Still, there was hope to deliver a B-17 to Israel within the time span of 69 Squadron's own jubilee.

Reconstructing an Epic Flight

Avidror involved Boeing, which manufactured all of the Hammers' aircraft: from the B-17 Flying Fortress, via the PBY Catalina and F-4 Phantom, to the future F-15I Thunder. Boeing accepted the challenge and took over control of the project from early 1998. Following this breakthrough, an incredible vision was planned for the Hammers' golden anniversary celebration on September 14, 1998. Three historical aircraft would fly into Hatzerim one after the other. First would land the C-46, then a PBY, and finally the B-17. All three would taxi to a line up along with perfect replicas of a Beaufighter and a Mosquito. If this was not science fiction enough, the men to emerge from the B-17 were to be veterans of the Hammers squadron who had just completed a reconstruction of the June-July 1948 epic flight of the original Hammers' B-17s from the USA to Israel.

The Flight of the Septuagenarians was planned to follow the original route of the three B-17s. Ages of the crew members ranged from 64 to 80. They were to be pilots Reuben Narunsky and Yossi Toister, navigator John Harris, bombardier Jules Cuburnek, and air gunners Zvi Avidror, Lazar Heskia, David de Mayo, and Bill Wadman. A documentary film was schemed to follow the flight; named director was Yaron Ben-Nun, son of Avihu and former IAF fighter pilot.

IAF Museum Dakota 042 donated an engine to the Catalina and an IAI team replaced engines; this image was taken at Beauvais, France, on August 1, 2005.

The Catalina's arrival at the IAF Museum on June 12, 2008.

From Five to Thunder

The plan was ambitious, perhaps too ambitious. None of the three historical aircraft landed at Hatzerim when the Hammers' jubilee was celebrated on September 14, 1998. The replicas were never constructed, and the aircraft did not fly to Israel — at least not ALL the way to Israel.

Following the foundering of the grand scheme, Boeing still owned – through an intermediate agent – a PBY Catalina. Stored in England, the Catalina in question was a former fire fighting water-bomber that last flew in 1996. Boeing donated the Catalina to the IAF Museum – through the ceaseless endeavor of Zvi Avidror – and after protracted preparations the old amphibian departed England on May 28, 2004. An arrival ceremony was planned for May 31, 2004; the plan called for President of Boeing Israel David Ivry, Eliezer Adar, and Zvi Avidror to board the Catalina in Cyprus for the final leg of the journey.

However, a connecting rod of the left-hand engine broke loose and the Catalina had to be landed at Beauvais, France. The first ferry flight to Israel attempt was thus terminated. A storm damaged the Catalina during the following winter, but a second attempt to fly the Catalina to Israel was made in the summer of 2005. The ruined engine was replaced and storm damage repaired, but the Israeli team was unable to bring the "old lady" back to safe flying condition, and the ferry flight idea was abandoned prior to take-off.

Avidror handed over the project to the Israeli Air Force Association, which arranged maritime transportation. The Catalina finally completed its journey on October 30, 2008, when it was

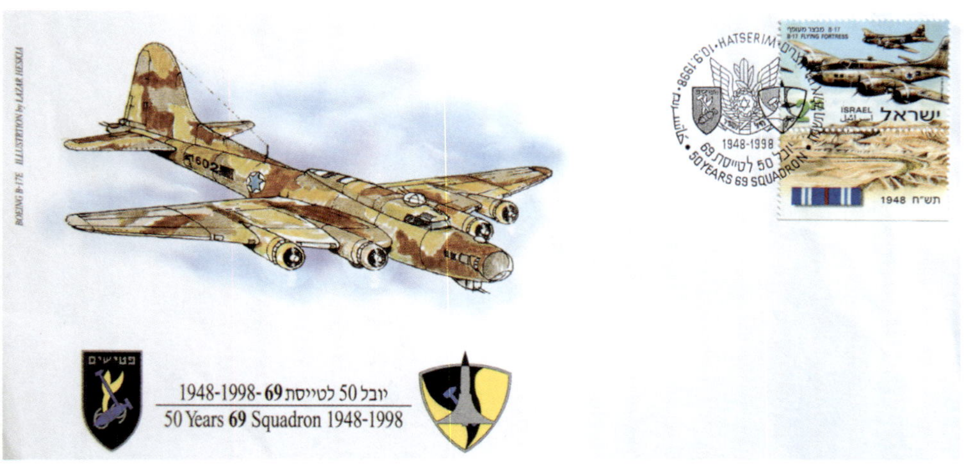

Lazar Heskia – former 69 Squadron B-17 air gunner – painted 1602 for a special jubilee envelope that Zvi Avidror produced; the envelope was stamped September 10, 1998, while the Hammers celebrated their golden anniversary at Hatzerim on the evening of September 14, 1998.

Assembly of the Catalina's wing center section at the IAF Museum on August 14, 2008.

Completion of the Catalina's re-assembly at the IAF Museum with outer wing sections in place, September 1, 2008.

handed over to the IAF Museum. Previously the Catalina was revealed to Hammers during the 60th anniversary evening on September 18, 2008. Old and new flanked the stage. Representing past glory, the Catalina was placed west of the stage. The east side was occupied by an appropriate successor to the B-17, PBY, and F-4, a successor that the Hammers had been flying since 1998 — the Boeing F-15I Thunder.

End of en effort! The Catalina hand over ceremony at the IAF Museum on October 30, 2008; from left to right: Vice President Boeing Israel Avi Barber, Hammers Squadron veteran Zvi Avidror, and IAF Museum Commander Jacob Terner.

10

F-15I Thunder
1998-2009: Power Projection

Routine renewal of the IAF fighter fleet triggered an acquisition project every half a decade or so. The time gap from issue of operational requirement through contract signature to service introduction steadily grew. The early 1990s fighter acquisition program was expected to bolster the IAF order of battle towards the end of the millennium.

Circles Concept

Previous IAF fighter purchase project covered 60 F-16C/D multi-role combat aircraft. These were selected in 1987, ordered in 1989, and delivered to Israel from 1991 until 1993. Evaluation of the next fighter lot options started prior to completion of F-16C/D deliveries. Core operational requirement was all-weather long-range combat aircraft. Obvious options were the F-16D and F-18D.

What had changed in five years – from 1987 to 1992 – was the end of Iran-Iraq war in 1988 and nocturnal Iraqi missile attacks against Israel during the 1991 Gulf War; hence the all-weather long-range requirement. From peace treaty signature with Egypt in 1979 – and even more so after defeat of the Syrian SAM deployment to Lebanon during 1982 – Israeli military thinking started to evolve the engagement circles concept. The first circle included Arab nations sharing a border with Israel. The second engagement circle covered Arab nations that did not share a border with Israel and had one buffer nation in between. The third engagement circle included hostile nations that had two buffer nations in between their territory and Israel.

The threat to Israel from first engagement circle nations diminished during the 1980s. SSM technology enabled a second circle nation (Iraq) to attack Israel. Third circle nations (such as Iran) were expected to acquire even longer range SSM capability. IAF sustained all-weather long-range operations was the Israeli answer to second and third circle threats. Long-range was the new hot buzzword.

Clinton's Commitment

Right from the start it was plain and simple that both jets – F-16D and F-18D – easily met the nighttime attack requirement. This capability was demonstrated to IAF Commander Herzle Bodinger

Frontrunner of the 1993 evaluation of new combat aircraft was the McDonnell Douglas F-18D Hornet. The F-18D was evaluated in Israel from March 15 until April 2, 1993, when this image was taken over the historically significant site of Masada, beside the Dead Sea. Sandwiched in between the two visiting F-18Ds is a resident IAF General Dynamics F-16D Fighting Falcon from a batch of a previous IAF combat aircraft acquisition project. An advanced F-16D was evaluated in Israel from May 4, 1993, and both – the F-16D and the F-18D – competed one against the other until emergence of the F-15E option.

IAF Commander Herzle Bodinger sitting in the front cockpit of a USAF 334th Fighter Squadron F-15E at Langley, Virginia. Bodinger flew an F-15E demonstration flight from Langley on March 18, 1994: "weather was awful, 40 knot wind gusts, and I thought that the flight would be delayed, but we took-off as planned; in fact, we were the only aircraft to take-off. Our target was a tank in the swamps. Weather was so bad that we could not see that tank but still we bombed that tank – with unguided bomb – and scored a direct hit!"

during a visit to the USA in February 1993. Bodinger flew a terrain following radar demo flight in the F-16D on February 22, 1993, and a nighttime sortie in the F-18D on February 23, 1993. Both fighters were then demonstrated in Israel – the F-18D from March 15, 1993, and the F-16D from May 4, 1993 – with special emphasis on compatibility with Israeli weapons and evaluation of long-range capability.

Both fighters lacked in both departments. The F-16D and F-18D could not meet the IAF long-range requirement, while their extreme range mission profile weapon load was abysmally disappointing. After all that trouble to fly that far, the punch of both contenders was simply too weak to matter.

At this point a third option – previously out of bounds to Israel – started to surface. In the wake of the Oslo Accords, U.S. President Bill Clinton promised Israeli Prime Minister Yitzhak Rabin, in March 1993, to maintain the military qualitative edge of Israel, an incentive for Israeli willingness to proceed with the diplomatic process as well as weakening Israeli objections against the planned sale of the F-15S to Saudi Arabia.

Father of Thunder

Herzle Bodinger should have been a 69er. As already mentioned at the end of chapter 3, IAF planning – back in 1957 – called for preservation of the Hammers' long range heavy bombing heritage through re-equipment as a Vautour squadron. Somehow planning was not adhered to, and the IAF Vautour squadron took over the tradition and number of 110 Squadron, previously a Mosquito fighter-bomber unit. So 69 Squadron went into a decade of oblivion while 110 Squadron was the IAF Vautour heavy bomber arm.

Bodinger was a 110 Squadron Vautour pilot from 1963 until 1970. Therefore IAF Commander Herzle Bodinger was personally acquainted with heavy bombing long range operations from within a unique, elite squadron spirit. In the wake of Clinton's commitment Bodinger aimed at a modern Vautour for the IAF: the F-15E Strike Eagle. Herzle Bodinger:

> "I was IAF Commander from January 1992 until July 1996. My expectations from the next fighter acquisition program were preservation of air combat superiority and introduction of all-weather long-range strike. The F-16D and F-18D were very good air combat platforms, and by then both had acquired all-weather strike capability. The two were excellent combat aircraft but suffered from one deficiency: lack of range. The manufacturers offered solutions. McDonnell Douglas suggested larger external fuel tanks for the F-18D. General Dynamics proposed Conformal Fuel Tanks for the F-16D. Both propositions would have required considerable development effort.
>
> "Meanwhile, President Clinton's commitment to the qualitative edge of Israel was repeated several times. I prepared a map with range circles of the F-16D with Conformal Fuel Tanks, of the F-18D with large external tanks, and an 'off the shelf' F-15E. As this was not enough, I added the actual offensive load of each aircraft at the presented range. I presented this map in a meeting with Minister of Defense Yitzhak Rabin, Ministery of Defense General Manager David Ivry, and IDF Chief of Staff Ehud Barak. Obviously everyone present was well aware that the F-15E was not on offer for export. Yet I argued that if the USA was committed to Israel's qualitative edge than this – the F-15E – was the true meaning of such a statement. This was in January 1993, only a short while prior to the routine annual visit of the IAF Commander to the USA. Therefore I suggested that I would mention the F-15E issue during my visit to the USA. All present agreed.
>
> "As usual I forwarded issues on the agenda prior to my visit so no surprises were expected. As can be expected, the U.S. Navy promoted the F-18D and the USAF backed the F-16D for Israeli acquisition. I presented to USAF Chief of Staff General Tony McPeak our evaluation of the F-16D and F-18D, emphasized their inadequate range, and concluded that there was another aircraft that could fully fulfill our operational requirement, the F-15E. I ended my presentation with a question, 'should we ask for acquisition of the F-15E?' USAF Chief of Staff's answer was 'it will be a very wise decision'; so was the answer of the U.S. Under Secretary of the Air Force.
>
> "I returned to Israel, reported, and suggested to ask for acquisition of the F-15E. A month later, March 1993, Minister of Defense Rabin visited the USA. One evening

during this visit I had to attend a Ministry of Defense evening reception at the Hilton Tel Aviv. It was noon in Washington, and a media conference was expected on the lawn of the White House. I waited in my car at the parking lot of the Hilton and listened to the evening news on the radio. President Clinton and Prime Minister Rabin reported positive talks, but from my perspective the most important thing was that President Clinton repeated his commitment to the qualitative edge of Israel. Then I knew that our F-15E request was accepted and so it was."

Thunder's First Fight

McDonnell Douglas – Boeing from 1996 – was obviously pleased. Their F-18D was rejected in favor of their own F-15E. General Dynamics – which sold the F-16 program to Lockheed in March 1993 – was less happy. Other opponents of the F-15E highlighted the prohibitive unit cost. The IAF's allocated budget was originally sufficient for re-equipment of two fighter squadrons with modern F-16D or F-18D combat aircraft. The same budget supported acquisition of only a single squadron of the more capable – as well as more expensive – F-15E.

An Australian F-111 in the background of an impressive array of weapons; the under wing stores emphasize the Australian F-111's Israeli link: a pair of Rafael Popeye missiles, the Popeye data-link pod, and an Elta electronic warfare pod.

The old-fashioned 1960s vintage complexity of the F-111's swing-wing configuration is evident in this image of an Australian F-111 during Popeye integration tests in April 2005; by then the Israeli F-15I Popeye combination was already fully operational for several years.

The solution to the numbers game was the purchase of a single squadron of new F-15E fighters and acceptance of two squadrons of used F-16A/B fighters, Cold War surplus equipment offered free of charge from USAF stocks to America's ally. At this stage Lockheed offered to reverse the acquisition plan: purchase two squadrons of new F-16C/D fighters and accept a single squadron of used F-111G attack aircraft!

If Israel needed range, then the F-111G had plenty of range. Thus Lockheed offered Israel to join Australia, which announced acquisition of USAF surplus F-111G attack aircraft on October 15, 1992. The downside of Lockheed's offer was that the F-111 was an old aircraft. In fact, the F-15E was the successor of the F-111. The Australian acquisition of the F-111G was not as a new customer, but simply an opportunity to augment their fleet of F-111s, in service since 1973. Still, Lockheed's proposition stirred considerable public debate in Israel. Herzle Bodinger:

> "Lockheed presented the F-111 to the Minister of Defense. The F-111 was designed for all-weather strike with adequate range, seemingly fulfilling our requirement. Therefore the Minister of Defense asked the IAF for a professional evaluation of the F-111. IAF evaluation was that the all-weather long-range F-111 was outdated and had no air combat capability. Moreover, the USAF wing that flew the F-111 during the 1991 Gulf War was based in RAF Lakenheath, UK, and had just converted to the F-15E. It would have been logical to ask for their opinion about the two aircraft. So I travelled to RAF Lakenheath together with one of our F-15 squadron commanders. My flight in the F-15E was over mountainous Scotland on a typical bad winter weather day. I was deeply impressed with the ease of mission accomplishment under such weather conditions.
>
> "Both pilots and maintenance officers told us that they loved the F-111, but it was an old aircraft with outdated technologies and many maintenance issues. Their bottom line advice was to avoid acquisition of the F-111. Obviously all of this was not new to us, but then we had an independent F-111 versus F-15E report to present to the Minister of Defense.
>
> "With F-15E acquisition assured, Hatzerim was our base of choice for such a unique strategic long-range combat aircraft. Then it was time for squadron selection. I am a firm believer in flags, symbols, and esprit de corps. One of the Phantom squadrons had to temporarily close prior to future re-equipment. My opinion was that 69 Squadron – already based at Hatzerim and with long-range heavy bombing heritage – should be the squadron. Obviously 69ers resented inactivation and delegated representatives to present their objections to me as IAF Commander. I answered that this short-term delay is for the benefit of long-term prosperity. I did not add anything

The first four Hammers team undergoing F-15E conversion training in the USA during 1997; 69 Squadron Commander Dror Ben-David is first from right.

beyond that, but my intention was that 69 Squadron would be reactivated to fly the F-15E."

I for Israel

A letter of offer and acceptance for 72 F-15S – S for Saudi Arabia – was signed on May 10, 1993. The F-15S was an F-15E tailored to Saudi specifications. Thus, the F-15E for Israel became the F-15I Thunder; a letter of acceptance dated May 12, 1994, covered acquisition of 21 Thunders and four were added in a December 22, 1995, contract.

Over the same time frame a heated debate developed within IAF ranks; the subject was the identity of the new Thunder squadron. IAF Commander Herzle Bodinger gave the Hammers a head start, but Orange Tail Knights protagonists claimed that 107 was Hatzerim's premier fighter squadron from 1971, and as such entitled to re-equipment prior to 69, which was only briefly a

The first F-15I flying for the first time on September 12, 1997. This combat capable Thunder is specially instrumented for test flying and assigned to the IAF Flight Test Center.

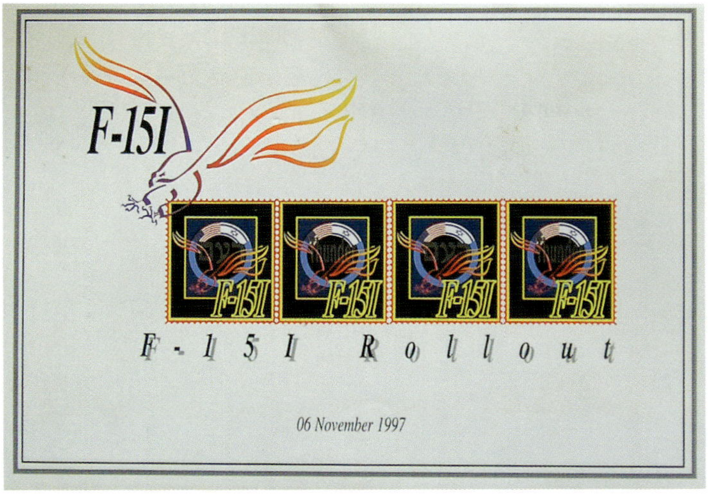

Boeing's invitation to Thunder's rollout on November 6, 1997.

ISRAELI F-15I ROLLOUT

SALAD
Ceasar Salad with Sourdough Croutons and Red Pepper Garnish
Semolina Rolls and Butter

WINE
Hess Select Chardonnay (1996)

ENTREE
Grilled Beef Tenderloin Filet
and
Swordfish Steak with Nicoise Sauce
Vichyssoise Torte
Melange of Roasted Winter Vegetables

WINE
Freemark Abbey Merlot (1994)

DESSERT
Dessert and Coffee Buffet
To Be Served in the Grigg Gallery

Menu of the Thunder's rollout reception.

resident at Hatzerim from 1991. The contest gathered momentum when planning called for basing of the new Thunder squadron inside the Knights' squadron building and hardened aircraft shelters. Bodinger backed his initial heritage hunch and the matter was closed on May 9, 1996.

The same year Dror Ben-David was named as the future 69 Squadron Commander. Ben-David was F-16C squadron commander from July 1994 until August 1996. Previously Ben-David was Head of Long-Range Attack Sub-Section of Air Headquarters Operations Department, and for this reason he was Bodinger's preference for the job to lead the introduction of Israel's new long-range heavy bomber.

Also during 1996 Major Harel was assigned as Thunder Project Officer. Major Harel's assignment actually emphasized naming of Hammers as the Thunder squadron and was surely not a coincidence, for Major Harel was a Hammers navigator from 1988 until 1994. An enthusiastic Hammer, Major Harel was the human heritage link between the Hammers' Phantom glory and Thunder promise; exactly following in the foot steps of another IAF legendary navigator figure Achikar Eyal, who was the human heritage link between the B-17 and F-4 ages of the Hammers.

Boeing Bond

The F-15I's first flight was accomplished on September 12, 1997, and Boeing's statement summed up the event:

> "The aircraft took off at 9:42 AM CDT from Lambert International Airport in St. Louis with Boeing test pilot Joe Felock and weapons system operator Major Rick Junkin of the U.S. Air Force at the controls. Normal flight assessments were conducted, as well as a comprehensive check of the aircraft's new flight control software. Flight time was one hour and thirteen minutes.
>
> "The pilot reported that the flight was smooth and that the aircraft performed flawlessly. 'This plane carries on the F-15's tradition of excellence,' Felock said. 'During

Obviously attending the Thunder's rollout was 69 Squadron Commander Dror Ben-David (center), flanked by two former Hammers B-17 air gunners: Zvi Avidror (left) and Lazar Heskia (right).

the course of the flight we achieved an altitude of 40,000 feet, reached Mach 2, and pulled some 9 G turns. It was a great flight,' he said.

"The two seat F-15I, known as the Thunder in Israel, incorporates new and unique weapons, avionics, electronic warfare, and communications capabilities that make it one of the most advanced F-15s ever. Israel selected the F-15I in January 1994 after evaluating a variety of aircraft to meet its defense needs. The F-15I, like the U.S. Air Force's F-15E Strike Eagle, is a dual-role fighter that combines long-range interdiction with the Eagle's awe-inspiring air superiority capabilities."

The bond between Boeing and 69 was emphasized during the rollout ceremony that followed on November 6, 1997; all of the Hammers aircraft from 1948 were part of the Boeing stable by 1998: the B-17 Flying Fortress (an original Boeing design), the PBY Catalina (a Consolidated design, but Consolidated was sold to McDonnell Douglas in 1994), the F-4 Phantom (a McDonnell design, and McDonnell and Douglas merged in 1967), and the F-15I Thunder (a McDonnell Douglas design; McDonnell Douglas was merged with Boeing during 1997).

Two Thunders landed at Hatzerim on January 19, 1998, and delivery of the 24 issued to 69 were completed by June 1999 (the 25th – actually the first Thunder – is an instrumented airframe delivered to the IAF Flight Test Center during September 1999).

Inside the I

The Thunder is Israel's heaviest bomber since the B-17. Effective range and offensive load of the Thunder were double the range and load of all other contemporary IAF attack aircraft. B-17's keyword was statistics: the Hammers' first bomber dropped a stick of bombs that exploded along a track under the bomber's flight path in the hope that some bombs and/or fragments would damage something. Thunder's buzzword is precision: the Hammers' current bomber can unleash an equivalent number of bombs over a similar sized target with each bomb precisely destroying its own pre-designated sub-target.

The F-15I differs from the F-15E in Israeli systems (electronic warfare self protection suit, communication sets, helmet mounted display and data transfer equipment) and weapons (Popeye and Python). Low Altitude Navigation and Targeting Infra Red for Night (LANTIRN) is the cornerstone of Thunder's nighttime attack capability. The navigation pod's Terrain Following Radar

A Boeing photo of the first Hammers' Thunder – actually the second production example – flying in the USA prior to delivery to Israel.

A "conventional" IAF F-15 – gray colored – leads the first two Thunders for 69 as they near the Israeli coastline to end a long delivery flight from the USA to Israel on January 19, 1998. The two trailing F-4 Phantoms were added to represent the Hammers upon opening a new chapter in the unit's history.

Hammers service persons (in blue overalls) and officers (in red outfit) welcome their new mounts during an arrival parade of the first two Thunders at Hatzerim on January 19, 1998.

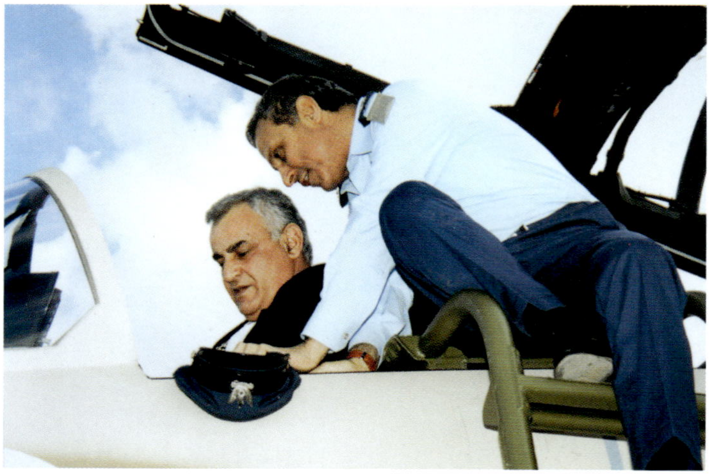

IAF commander (1996-2000) Eitan Ben-Eliyahu (right) introduces the Thunder's front "office" to Israeli Minister of Defense Isaac Mordechai at the end of the Thunder arrival parade on January 19, 1998.

Assembling in front of a Thunder during the Hammers' official open parade on February 11, 1998 (from left to right): B-17 pilot Reuben Narunsky, B-17 air gunner Zvi Avidror, first Thunder era commander Dror Ben-David, B-17 pilot Nahum Efrat, and B-17 navigator Smoky Simon.

(TFR) system is linked to the automatic pilot of the F-15I, while the pod's Forward Looking Infra Red (FLIR) image is projected on the pilot's Head-Up Display (HUD). LANTIRN can fly the F-15I down to 30 meters above ground level. Control law inputs from the pod are relative to altitude; the lower the pod flies the aircraft, the more gentle the turns would be.

In nocturnal operations aircrew use night vision goggles attached to their lighter nighttime helmets. Israeli F-15I air crews have two tailor-made helmets; there are no sizes for helmets in the IAF. The daytime helmet is compatible with the helmet mounted display system; the nighttime helmet is night vision goggles compatible. To minimize light returns that might deteriorate aircrew`s vision during night vision goggles operations the complete interior of the F-15I is painted black.

First Fire

Initial operational capability was achieved on January 1, 1999, when 69's inventory included 16 Thunders. The first F-15I operational sortie was flown on January 11, 1999; at the time IAF operations over Lebanon intensified towards Israeli withdrawal from south Lebanon in May 2000.

Hammers' highlight for this time frame was during the early evening hours of June 24, 1999; only seven days after arrival of the 23rd and 24th Thunders to top-up 69's order of battle. Dror Ben-David:

> "The scenario was IAF reprisal strikes after Hezbollah rocket attacks. Apparently, prior to our mission, circles of the Prime Minister criticized that time frame from

69 Squadron Commander Dror Ben-David taxis the Hammers' first Thunder – tail number 205 – out of its hardened aircraft shelter for the first time on January 26, 1998, prior to the Hammers' first Thunder flight ever.

Moment of impact of a laser guided bomb smashing into a Lebanese bridge on the evening of June 24, 1999.

operational order to actual attack bypassed the eight o'clock evening news broadcast. So the IAF prepared an operational order in advance to suit such a scenario.

"That day I was at air headquarters when rocket attacks were reported. I returned to the squadron and asked for the air executive officer on duty and for status of aircraft on readiness. The former was jogging somewhere on the base; the latter were still lacking a couple of ingredients for immediate scramble. I took over as executive officer in charge and ordered to prepare the readiness aircraft for immediate scramble when IAF Commander phoned in. 'Scramble the jets,' he said. I asked for targets, and his answer was that targets would be handed over during flight. All of our high-tech operation order systems were simply shortened to a single phone call from IAF Commander to 69 Squadron Commander.

"The standing order for such a case covered dozens of bridges in Lebanon. I handed over data of all optional targets to the two readiness crews and told them to take-off. They took off, and a couple of minutes later another phone call came from IAF Commander: 'can you scramble more planes?' 'There is nobody here,' I answered — only me on executive officer in charge duty and a navigator that was not yet combat ready. 'Do what you can,' he summed up the conversation.

"I told the unqualified navigator to come along with me and left behind a squadron empty of aircrew. We took off and trailed some 100 miles behind the readiness pair. Then the pair received a target, and it was indeed one of those bridges. They attacked a bridge over the Litani River and I orbited over the sea, alone in the dark. I realized from radio chatter that IAF Commander was in command, so I contacted him directly and asked to attack another bridge, the largest bridge in Lebanon. 'OK, he said, go ahead,' and we bombed the coast highway bridge across the Awali River."

The two bridges collapsed under Hammers' attack in a mission that demonstrated the Thunder's all-weather accurate heavy punch. For many years destruction of a bridge was the ultimate challenge for a bomber force. A bridge is a slender, massive structure usually located within a confined area and mostly well defended. In the B-17 era – during World War II – hundreds of bombers dropped thousands of bombs to strike at a bridge that in most cases survived the attack. Three Thunders – each armed with four 900kg laser guided bombs – collapsed two massive bridges while flying in cloudy dark nighttime skies and evading massive anti-aircraft fire. Only a single drawback overcasted a perfect mission: time over target was 22:00, well after broadcast of the evening news....

Far, Far Away

Early operations over Lebanon demonstrated the Thunder's all-weather attack accuracy. This was the initial operational requirement that led to F-15I acquisition. However, the ultimate requirement – and the one that tipped the scales in the F-15I's favor – was for an all-weather long-range heavy-weight attacker, with no "fair self-defense" capability or need for escorting fighters, but with absolute air combat superiority over all potential adversaries. All of these ingredients were refined in a series of overseas deployments that tested Thunder in a variety of ultimate scenarios against some of the best friendly training "opponents" on earth.

A Thunder flying off the coast of Haifa.

Thunders in Turkey, August 1999.

Even before achievement of initial operational status, 69 made history as the first IAF squadron to participate in the prestigious U.S. Air Force Red Flag exercise. Red Flag is the world's premier air combat exercise, a simulation of combat situations involving a "blue" force versus a "red" force flying over Nevada. Previously IAF aircrew participated in Red Flag as individuals, but a new era dawned in October 1998. Dror Ben-David:

> "We were the first Israeli squadron to take part in Red Flag. The squadron was still young, few people, little experience. We arrived at Nellis in a Boeing 707 and our three Thunders were flown to Nellis fresh from the factory, aircraft that flew only two test flights. Each Red Flag mission involved some 70 versus 70 aircraft, wild flying beyond anything allowed in Israel, including 4 versus 4 air combats, low altitude gun engagements, and low level supersonic dashes; an absolutely amazing experience very early along the squadron's build-up process.
>
> "Hundreds of participating aircrew attended every brief and debrief; the end product of each formation was presented to them all during debrief. All targets were fully filmed, so range replays backed aircrew's presentations, and if my memory serves me correctly on most days we were the only ones to report and score direct hits on all of our designated targets."

Hammers B-17 air gunner Zvi Avidror in front of younger Hammers and their modern day long-range heavy bomber, the Thunder, at RAF Waddington on June 30, 2001.

Prior to participation in the RAF Waddington Air Show, Thunder 267 was adorned with an experimental version of the current Hammers tail art.

Star performer of the air show over RAF Waddington was Thunder 269, which flew a spirited display while loaded with a dozen red bomb dummies to remind spectators that regardless of the calm environment over Yorkshire, the F-15I was really a mean war machine.

High Profile Heavy Bomber

Overseas deployments were viewed as essential to hone the Thunder's long-range skills, but also exposed Hammers to worldwide media. First Hammers deployments – to Turkey in August 1999 and to Italy in September 1999 – were quite close and still secretive. Full public exposure was first achieved over the weekend of June 30 to July 1, 2001, when three Thunders attended the RAF Waddington International Air Show in the United Kingdom.

The Hammers were stars of Waddington. One Thunder took part in the fly-past loaded with a dozen dummy red bombs to emphasize that the F-15I was not an innocent air show performer but a mean war machine. Flares were released during the Thursday rehearsal but were not allowed over the public weekend. A contemporary British press report stated:

> "Unfortunately, it was decided that on safety grounds flares could not be used for the two air show demonstrations on Sunday, the Israelis not flying on Saturday due to it being the Sabbath."

A second Thunder – adorned with "prototype" tail art – headed the long line of static exhibits, further attracting attention from thousands of visitors. British aviation magazine Air Pictorial reported:

> "The undoubted stars of the show were the Israeli Air Force contingent of three Boeing F-15Is, named *Ra'am (Thunder)* in Israeli service, from 69 Sqn, and a Hercules. Not only was one of the fighters placed on static, but a solo 'role demonstration' was performed carrying 12 orange practice bombs. Speaking to *Air Pictorial*, Major (res.) Mizrahi, head of IAF Media Desk, said the reason for the visit was due to the respect the Israeli Air Force (IAF) had for the RAF, which the Major described as the air force's 'father,' with much of their tradition emanating from the RAF. The F-15Is were chosen to appear as they are the most capable fighters the IAF currently fields."

Opposite: The Thunder's public performance routine that RAF Waddington spectators did not see was the release of flares in all sorts of flying attitudes, including during vertical climb and tight turning.

Hammers service persons – female and male – inspect a Thunder at the "last chance" position prior to a training sortie.

A Day in the Squadron

Previously the IAF ruled against acquisition of additional Thunders, emphasizing quantity over quality with purchase of 102 F-16I Storm long-range combat aircraft from 1999. A younger, smaller "brother" of the F-15I, the F-16I also employs conformal fuel tanks to achieve adequate range for sustained "third circle" operations, but still cannot match the heavy lift capability of the Thunder.

Four years after Thunder introduction and two years prior to initiation of F-16I deliveries, 69 Squadron Commander (since May 23, 2001) Hagai Topolansky was confident that his pilots and navigators would not be tempted to ask for a reassignment to the F-16I, except perhaps for a few aircrew who would find the new combat aircraft service introduction phase a professional challenge. Topolansky admitted that the F-16I closed the range gap between the F-15 and the F-16, but expressed his view that the F-15I would remain superior by virtue of its larger physical dimensions that enabled the F-15I to deliver a heavier punch than the F-16I over a similar mission profile.

By 2002 the Hammers were firmly based at Hatzerim in a unit compound located around the old Knights' squadron building. The

Hammers commanders 54 years apart! 69 Squadron Commander from 2003 until August 25, 2005 (right), introduces the Thunder's front "office" to 69 Squadron Commander from January 1949 until June 25, 1949, Sam Feldman, during a veterans visit in October 2003.

Hagi Topolansky (left) was a Hammers F-15I Set Up Team member from June 1997 as Deputy A and commanded the Hammers from May 23, 2001 until 2003. From June 2008 until May 16, 2010 - this photo was taken in October 2009 - Topolansky was Hatzerim Air Base Commander and from May 27, 2010 Topolansky is Chief of Air Group.

latter is home of Flying Flight, which encompasses all aircrew as well as related specialists working in the navigation, intelligence, and operations cells. The Technical Flight is responsible for the preparation and maintenance of the aircraft, while a small Adjutants Section backs the squadron in the administration department.

The squadron`s missions are defined as interception and attack during daylight and nighttime. A typical day in the squadron`s life commences with a general squadron briefing attended by all the aircrew. The briefing is general in its nature, and among the subjects covered are weather conditions and training areas allocation. Aircrew then divide to air-to-air and air-to-ground mission briefings. Next comes the formation briefing; the typical formation is either a pair or a four ship formation, and the briefing officer can be either the lead pilot or the lead navigator. The IAF still classify the Guy In the Back seat (GIB) as a navigator, though the U.S. term Weapon System Operator (WSO) is much more appropriate. Finally, the aircrew leave the squadron complex and head to the aircraft about 45 minutes prior to take-off.

Training missions usually last for about an hour. The cost of a single flying hour was quoted during 2002 as 15,000 U.S. dollars, half of which covered the fuel. The F-15I maximum fuel load is

Hammers dynasty; the son of a Hammers veteran briefing a Popeye training mission during 2004.

Two Thunders prepare for a Rafael Popeye training session at the "last chance" ramp in October 2004. The Hammers continuously preserved their Popeye qualification since 1987, except for several years from 1994 when Popeye qualification was handed over to the neighboring Knights.

Missing in Action navigator Ron Arad is still listed in the Hammers' aircrew roster. This "missing formation" was flown over Tel Aviv on October 15, 2004, to remind the Israeli public of Ron Arad.

35,000lb and the maximum war load is 15,400lb. Most multi-role combat aircraft must trade a lot of fuel to carry a significant war load, but the F-15I can still carry a respectable 8,800lb war load with full fuel load. Range is theoretically unlimited (thanks to In-Flight Refueling), and the F-15I even has an onboard oxygen generating system rather than time-limited oxygen bottles.

A formation level debriefing to evaluate results and to learn lessons is performed at the end of each and every training mission. Debriefing is aided by a video tape recorder that simultaneously records four of the multi-function displays. There are no less than sixteen computers and nine computer screens in the F-15I: four in the front cockpit and five in the back "office." Each of the seven lower screens has 27 display options; the most "popular" screens are the radar picture, the moving map display – on which locked-on targets are superimposed – and the electronic warfare screen.

A regular flying training day is closed with a squadron level debriefing, but one day each week is a no-flying day devoted to office time, as each of the air crews in the squadron has an assignment: Intelligence Officer, Navigation Officer, and Operations Officer, to name but a few. Night training missions are flown once a week, while in each IAF Term (the IAF divides the calendar year into two six months terms) the squadron operates two "upside down" weekly nighttime training sessions. During such a week the squadron flies at night and sleeps during the day, with every working "day" starting at noon and ending at dawn.

The Hammers welcomed the Knights - on July 5, 2006 - in typical fashion. First to arrive was a truck trailing blue balloons and winding its way right behind the stage during the speech of the Orange Tail Knights Commander. A huge placard attached to the truck conveyed the message THUNDER IS ALWAYS AHEAD OF STORM. In the spirit of this message a Thunder followed the Hammers' lead truck.

A pack of Thunders prepare to depart Hatzerim.

The heat is ON! The Thunder's pair of engines produces nearly 30 tons of thrust.

A Thunder releasing flares during a demonstration over Hatzerim.

Second Lebanon War

The second Intifada prompted IAF bombing of Palestinian Authority targets, and the Hammers returned to attack targets within the Gaza Strip; the same targets that the B-17 Flying Fortresses bombed during the Israeli War for Independence from 1948 until 1949 and during the 1956 Suez War. Offensive operations over Lebanon were resumed on November 21, 2005, when Thunders bombed Hezbollah targets. A prelude of summer 2006 operations across the Israeli-Lebanese border followed on May 28, 2006, when Hezbollah launched rocket attacks against Israel, who responded with massive air strikes; the Hammers bombed Hezbollah outposts north of the border.

Israel attacked Lebanon again from July 12 until August 14, 2006. A reprisal to Hezbollah attack on an Israeli border patrol, the 2006 Lebanon War started as an ultra-modern air campaign and ended with an old fashioned invasion. 69 flew 1,400 sorties that totaled 2,300 flying hours; significantly more than any other IAF combat aircraft squadron. Thunders lifted 7,000 bombs and dropped 3,500. Flying around the clock in true all-weather fashion, the Hammers thus averaged 40 sorties per day and 2.5 bombs dropped per sortie out of five bombs lifted. Targets attacked included Lebanese infrastructure (fuel storage facilities, airports, bridges, etc.), Hezbollah bases (headquarters, depots, fortifications, training camps, etc.), interdiction against arms transports from Syria to Lebanon, isolation of south Lebanon from mainland Lebanon, hunting of rocket launchers (the Hezbollah launched 3,906 rockets against Israel during the conflict), and close air support.

End of mission. A Thunder generates smoke upon impact with the runway as it lands at Hatzerim. The F-15I has a perfect safety record; none of the Thunders has been lost since service introduction in 1998.

Paradoxically – because the F-15I originated as a long-range heavy bomber – the Thunder excelled in the close-range close air support mission. Lifting more bombs and fuel than the F-16 – the IAF standard close air support combat aircraft – a pair of Hammers crews could remain on station for a longer time frame and attack more targets than a pair of F-16s. Moreover, less aircraft with longer endurance eased control and improved the already complicated communication between aircrew and warfighters through forward air control mediation. The same applied to safety and vulnerability with less aircraft flying over danger zones. Soon the IAF forward air controllers pleaded "send in the Thunders"; arguing to their superiors that one pair of Thunders was equivalent to three pairs of F-16s.

Thunders flew all sorts of IAF offensive operations, often swinging missions mid-air. A fine example is call sign BARRElL, a pair that took off one morning for a rocket hunt mission. En route to their rocket kill box patrol, BARREl was ordered to switch to the forward air control channel in support of a hard-pressed IDF force. Surrounded and under fire, the IDF force in distress had already suffered casualties and was unable to return fire or to retreat. Distance between friendly forces and the enemy was a mere 180 meters. Five sources of enemy fire were identified, and the two Thunders attacked in turns: one bombing while the other was watching. Real-time battle damage discussion followed after each attack. If the source of fire was not silenced a second bomb was dropped on the same target. Additionally, the two Thunders even utilized the old "carpet bombing" tactic to separate between friendly troops and the enemy. Ten minutes after initiating their attack the BARREl Thunders had dropped a total of 18 bombs that completely silenced the enemy fire.

I for Illusive

Lieutenant Colonel Z took over as Squadron Commander from May 31, 2007. Blue eyes Z is a prototype Hammers air person; seemingly shy and reticent, Z is actually determined and decisive. Having graduated from the IAF Flying School July 19, 1990, as top student of his class, Z commanded a "normal" F-15 squadron from 2005 until 2007 and switched to the Thunder in the wake of the Second Lebanon War, but only a short while prior to an alleged mission that again rocked the Middle East.

A formidable Israeli long range heavy bomber, the Thunder is also a lively and deadly air-to-air platform. The depicted pair is in air-to-air configuration armed with cannon and three types of air-to-air missiles, a configuration that enables Thunder to engage enemy aircraft within ranges of a few hundred meters to dozens of miles.

The importance ofThunder as Israel's long range heavy bomber is emphasized again and again, as in this August 2009 presentation to Israeli Prime Minister Benjamin Netanyahu; IDF Chief of Staff Lieutenant General Gabi Ashkenazi, Minister of Defense Ehud Barak, and IAF Commander Iddo Nehushtan (from left to right) accompanied the Prime Minister (in the cockpit).

Syria stated on September 6, 2007, that Israeli combat aircraft penetrated deep into Syrian territory on the night of September 5 to 6, 2007. Later on – still September 6, 2007 – reports from Turkey indicated that external fuel tanks were found on the ground not far away from the Syrian border. These external fuel tanks were identified by the foreign press as belonging to F-15 aircraft, so worldwide media reports immediately linked this Turkish finding and the Syrian statement.

The incident was shrouded in secrecy. Israel officially ignored the whole issue, but foreign media reports soon revealed that the target of the alleged attack was an installation near the city of Dir A-Zur, in eastern Syria. Satellite images began to appear on newspaper pages, TV screens, and internet sites. Reporters and analysts came to the conclusion that the site was some kind of nuclear installation, possibly erected with North Korean support. Comparison of pre-September 5, 2007, and post September 6, 2007, satellite images yielded that the site was "flattened" after the attack, leading reporters and analysts to conclude that Syria destroyed evidence.

Ignoring the Syria strike mission – of which not a single small operational detail has emerged ever since – there is no doubt that the IAF has the capability to fly precise nighttime missions far, far away from Israel. Obviously the centerpiece of IAF long-range all-weather precision strike force is the Hammers' F-15I Thunder.

Therefore, one can truly imagine the determined and decisive blue eyed Lieutenant Colonel Z, sitting at night in the black painted cockpit of a Thunder, flashing low over unfriendly terrain, far away from Hatzerim, leading his fellow Hammers on yet another historically significant mission, following in the footsteps of Kurtz and Katz, Ben-Nun and Agmon, Adar and Eliasaf, Ben-David and Topolansky, and all Hammers service persons ever that flew their B-17s, Catalinas, F-4s, and Thunders over land and sea, during wartime and during peacetime, fighting the enemy and overcoming their own internal fears in defense of their Hammers homeland, the State of Israel.

Appendix A:
69 Squadron Air-to-Air Kills

DATE	CREW	SECTOR	KILL	NOTES
Nov 11, 1969	Henkin/Eyal	Egypt	MiG-21	69 crew in 201 Kurnass flying a 201 mission
Feb 8, 1970	Sella/Ben-Shoah	Egypt	MiG-21	first genuine 69 kill
Apr 2, 1970	Magen/Nachmani	Syria	MiG-21	shared kill credit
Jul 30, 1970	Ben-Nun/Levy	Egypt	MiG-21	USSR pilot in USSR aircraft
Jul 30, 1970	Sella/Fisher	Egypt	MiG-21	USSR pilot in USSR aircraft
Sep 9, 1972	Ben-Nun/Kesler	Syria	Su-7	
Sep 13, 1973	Arad/Levy	Syria	MiG-21	
Oct 7, 1973	Feldsho/Guri	Egypt	MiG-21	
Oct 7, 1973	Amizi/Israeli	Egypt	MiG-21	
Oct 7, 1973	Raz/Bobo	Syria	MiG-21	
Oct 10, 1973	Arad/Kesler	Syria	MiG-17	
Oct 10, 1973	Gat/Kesler	Syria	MiG-21	No Weapon Squadron Kill
Oct 12, 1973	Agmon/Wittmann	Syria	MiG-17	
Oct 13, 1973	Agmon/Wittmann	Syria	MiG-17	
Oct 16, 1973	Agmon/Wittmann	Syria	MiG-21	
Oct 16, 1973	Yahalom/Rubinstein	Syria	MiG-21	
Oct 19, 1973	Gat/Katz	Syria	MiG-17	
Dec 6, 1973	Shadmi/Guri	Egypt	MiG-21	North Korean, shared kill credit
Dec 6, 1973	Shpitzer/Ofer	Egypt	MiG-21	North Korean, shared kill credit
Apr 29, 1974	Agmon/Guri	Lebanon	MiG-21	Syrian
Apr 29, 1974	Raz/Baruch	Lebanon	MiG-21	Syrian

Appendix B:
69 Squadron Aircraft Losses

DATE	CREW	AIRCRAFT	SECTOR	NOTES
Apr 2, 1970	Magen/Nachmani PoW	Kurnass 136	Syria	combat loss to MiG-21
Jun 30, 1970	Harpaz/Eyal PoW	Kurnass 138	Egypt	combat loss to SAM
Jul 5, 1970	Zamir/Levitov PoW	Kurnass 129	Egypt	combat loss to SAM
Sep 6, 1973	Ron/Ben-Betzalel ejected	Kurnass 243	Israel	accident
Oct 7, 1973	Henkin/Levy killed	Kurnass 123	Syria	combat loss
Oct 7, 1973	Alkalai/Wolfson PoW	Kurnass 177	Egypt	combat loss to SAM
Oct 8, 1973	Shahar/Israeli PoW	Kurnass 130	Syria	combat loss to MiG-21
Oct 8, 1973	Yahalom/Mor ejected	Kurnass 255	Syria	combat loss to SAM
Oct 8, 1973	Dvir/Ben-Shoah ejected	Kurnass 247	Egypt	combat loss to SAM
Oct 8, 1973	Amizi/Yogev killed	Kurnass 245	Egypt	combat loss
Oct 11, 1973	Arad/Primor PoW in Lebanon	Kurnass 105	Syria	combat loss
Oct 14, 1973	Zait/Tovel ejected	Kurnass	Egypt	combat loss
Oct 20, 1973	Zait/Rubinstein PoW	Kurnass 231	Egypt	combat loss to SAM
Apr 8, 1974	Shadmi/Rafaeli PoW in Lebanon	Kurnass 320	Syria	combat loss
Dec 29, 1977	Avsha/Ikar killed	Kurnass 305	Israel	accident
Dec 29, 1977	Falk/Peleg ejected	Kurnass 310	Israel	accident
Apr 22, 1979	Alkalai/Katz killed	Kurnass 301	Israel	accident
Jan 20, 1981	Adar ejected/Weiss killed	Kurnass 222	Israel	accident
Sep 12, 1984	Shemi killed/navigator ejected	Kurnass 307	Israel	accident
Sep 12, 1984	crew ejected	Kurnass 255	Israel	accident
Oct 16, 1986	Aviram ejected/Arad PoW	Kurnass 306	Lebanon	combat loss